Y0-BCV-907

Documents of the American Revolution

Volume III

Transcripts
1771

DOCUMENTS
OF THE
AMERICAN REVOLUTION

1770–1783

(Colonial Office Series)

Volume III

TRANSCRIPTS

1771

Edited by

K. G. DAVIES

The Library
Colby College-New Hampshire
New London, New Hampshire

IRISH UNIVERSITY PRESS
Shannon Ireland

FERNALD LIBRARY
COLBY-SAWYER COLLEGE
NEW LONDON, N.H. 0325

E
173
D 33
vol. 3

65207

Documents © Crown copyright 1973

Introduction, Index and other editorial matter
© Irish University Press 1973

Printed by permission of the Controller of Her Majesty's
Stationery Office.

ISBN 0 7165 2085 0 Set
ISBN 0 7165 2088 5 Volume III

Irish University Press Shannon Ireland

T. M. MacGlinchey Publisher

PRINTED IN THE REPUBLIC OF IRELAND

CONTENTS

ACKNOWLEDGEMENTS

The typing of this volume was done by Miss Teresa Hall of the Irish University Press and by Mrs Elaine Porter. The copy-editor was Miss Clare Craven, also of the Irish University Press.

INTRODUCTION

The Transcripts

This volume consists of 138 documents drawn from the Colonial Office records of the year 1771. Nearly all have been described in calendar form in Volume I of this series. A small number, mainly of the closing months of the year, are preserved in the Public Record Office in the form of enclosures to covering documents dated 1772: these will be found in calendar form in Volume IV of the series, now in preparation. Thus, John Thomas's letter to John Stuart of 12 December 1771 (below, No. CXXXIII) is one of a file of thirty-one papers on the subject of Thomas's strange behaviour on the Mississippi, which Stuart sent to the Earl of Hillsborough on 12 June 1772. The whole file will appear in calendar form under the covering letter of that date.

The principles of selection of documents to be included in the *Transcripts* and the conventions of transcription are the same as those set out in the Introduction to Volume II. And for 1771, as for 1770, a brief statement of the principal themes of the documents has been appended.

The Seaboard Colonies

News reaching Whitehall in the later part of 1770 gave grounds for a slightly more hopeful view of American affairs than had been possible for many months. The improvement can be dated from New York's decision (taken on 9 July 1770 and received in Whitehall on 17 August) to resume importing from Great Britain, and it continued with good news from Massachusetts. There was, to begin with, the trial of Captain Preston on a charge of murder arising from the Boston Massacre and his acquittal on 30 October: this was officially known in London on 8 December. Six of the soldiers facing similar charges in Boston were acquitted on 29 November, two others being found guilty only of manslaughter. And on 12 December Manwaring, a Customs officer, and three others were found not guilty of firing into the Boston crowd on 5 March from the balcony and windows of the Customs-house. These events appeared to clear the air. If the official correspondence of Governor Hutchinson of Massachusetts continued to be restrained, his private letter of 22 January 1771 to the Secretary of State for the American Department sounded a rare note of optimism.[1] The change in the colony, which he dated from the occupation of Castle William by the King's troops, had come about 'sooner and to a greater degree than anybody could expect'. If any alteration was to be made in the

---

1 Below, No. IX.

1

constitution (that is, the replacement of an elected Council by an appointed one) Massachusetts was now as ripe for it as she was ever likely to be. The detachment of Maine and the country east thereof could be used, Hutchinson advised, either as a way of punishing the province or as a threat to guarantee good behaviour. Above all, the present moment called for frequent assertions of Parliamentary authority. 'Every Act of Parliament carried into execution in the colonies tends to strengthen government there'; and Hutchinson cited the Act of 1770 enabling New York to issue bills of credit as a model of what should be done to familiarize America with the omnipotence of Parliament.

This mood cannot have lasted long, but there are traces of it in Hutchinson's official letters in the first half of 1771. In April he praised the Council's conduct as 'unexceptionable'.[2] In May, having issued writs for electing a new House of Representatives, he dared to hope for a majority in favour of government.[3] Even on 4 June, after meeting the new Assembly, he was 'not wholly disappointed in my expectation of a better temper'.[4] Only after the House's protest of 20 June against the Assembly's sitting at Cambridge instead of Boston[5] and a deadlock over tax-bills, was he forced to admit that the denial of Parliamentary authority was gaining strength in 'this and other colonies'.[6] The General Court was prorogued soon afterwards, and Hutchinson's correspondence for the remainder of the year was given over to smuggling,[7] the state of the Eastern Country,[8] the mode of pardoning murderers,[9] and the functioning of the Council as a court.[10]

This slight improvement in Anglo-American relations may have been helped by the war-scare at the end of 1770 and beginning of 1771. Hillsborough's circular of 28 September 1770 had alerted governors of colonies to the dispute with Spain over an incident in the Falkland Islands.[11] Apprehensions of war were heightened by a second circular of 15 November,[12] and were not allayed until the dispatch of a third, on 22 January 1771, which announced that an accommodation had been reached.[13] The first of these messages arrived in the seaboard colonies in late November and early December, the second in early January and the third in early May. Allowing for the fact that unofficial news generally travelled faster than official advices, the duration of the alert in North America was between three and four months. It is not possible, from the Colonial Office records, to gauge the effects of the crisis on American opinion. War with Spain, though not to be compared to former wars with New France, would have put East and West

2　No. XXXVII.
3　No. XLII.
4　No. LIX.
5　No. LXVII.
6　Below, No. LXXVI. Compare No. LXXXVIII.
7　Vol. I, No. 1631. Below, Nos. XCIII, XCVIII.
8　Vol. I, Nos. 1508, 1580. Below, No. CV.
9　Vol. I, No. 1508.
10　Vol. I, No. 1594.
11　Vol. I, No. 621.
12　Vol. I, No. 729.
13　Vol. I, No. 935.

Florida into some danger,[14] and by making the Caribbean unsafe for merchant-shipping would have affected the commerce of most colonies. The remoter possibility of some kind of French *revanche* could not be ignored, though Lieut.-Governor Cramahé assured Hillsborough that the French in Quebec were quiet at the prospect of war with Spain.[15] Best of all, war would have found non-controversial employment for the British regiments in America and made the Royal Navy appear as the protector rather than the oppressor of American trade.

In London the crisis was at its height in the first three weeks of January 1771. Hillsborough's letter of 2 January to Lieut.-General Gage, with which this volume opens, told him to expect war and to assemble land-forces for an attack on New Orleans, which he was to lead in person.[16] The packet carrying this letter was ten weeks in passage from Falmouth to New York, so that Gage did not get it until 21 March. He at once put in hand the preparations described in his dispatch of 2 April.[17] Six regiments, totalling about 2000 men, were to be concentrated at New York and proceed by sea to New Orleans. The Navy, on both the North Atlantic and the Jamaica stations, was to co-operate, and it was Gage's expectation that frigates would ascend the Mississippi. At the time this letter was written in New York, all danger of war in Europe had been over for more than two months. Unfortunately, Hillsborough's circular of 22 January to Gage and all governors, for which special conveyance by warship had been commanded,[18] took even longer than his letter of 2 January, not reaching New York until the beginning of May.[19] This was much slower than the usual time for a merchant-ship. The expedition to New Orleans was of course immediately countermanded, but not before the 64th and 65th regiments had been transported from Halifax to Boston where there was nothing to do with them but send them back again.[20]

The Falkland Islands crisis came and went too quickly to have any effect in rallying American support for the British connection in either South Carolina or Georgia, two colonies in which governors were at odds with assemblies. Relations between Lieut.-Governor Bull and the Commons House of South Carolina were entirely dominated in 1771 by the House's determination never to accept the royal instruction of April 1770 respecting the issue of money from the province's Treasury.[21] Bull found 'their prejudices too deep to be removed by reasoning';[22] and the arrival of Governor Lord Charles Montagu in the colony on 16 September 1771 served only to make a bad situation worse. Georgia's problems were discussed by Governor James Wright in letters of 28 February and 30 April. He dissolved the Assembly at the beginning of March, following a wrangle over representation and the

14   Below, No. XXIV.
15   No. XL.
16   No. I.
17   No. XXXII.
18   Vol. I, No. 937.
19   Vol. I, Nos. 1200–1201.
20   Vol. I, No. 1217.
21   Vol. II, No. XXXV.
22   Below, No. XXIII.

Lower House's claim to possess independent powers 'which in every respect they suppose to be equal to those of the House of Commons in Great Britain'.[23] When the new Assembly met on 24 April, however, a fresh quarrel immediately began over the right of the Crown to reject the choice of Speaker, and on the following day they were once more dissolved.[24] Wright went home on leave on 10 July, leaving the President of Council, James Habersham, in charge. It was to Habersham that Hillsborough issued his impolitic order of 4 December to negative the Lower House's next choice of Speaker, whoever it might be.[25]

In the three colonies so far mentioned, Massachusetts, South Carolina and Georgia, the matters on which opposition developed in 1771 were of a domestic character, though all naturally raised the greater issues of the ultimate authority of King and Parliament. What appeared to be lacking, for the moment, was a common political issue that could be contested in a practical way without raising too many matters of abstract principle. Non-importation had been such an issue, but in 1771 it slipped from the prominence it had formerly occupied in the correspondence of royal governors and the Secretary of State. Smuggling, on the other hand, as an administrative problem came to the fore, partly as the result of an initiative by the British Treasury. On 13 July John Robinson, Secretary of the Treasury, sent the American Department thirteen papers going back as far as 1768 on smuggling and kindred matters in Rhode Island, Pennsylvania, Massachusetts and New Jersey.[26] One of these papers, dated 20 December 1770, was included in the *Transcripts* for that year;[27] another, the case of the *Polly* at Newport, R.I., is printed in the present volume.[28] Three papers related to smuggling and mob violence in Philadelphia in April and October 1769 which had not previously been officially reported to the American Department: Hillsborough wrote at once to the Proprietors of Pennsylvania for an explanation.[29] The Penns' bland reply, dated 24 December 1771, is notable only for having taken five months to compose,[30] another instance of the carelessness with which the American Department was treated by the proprietary colonies.

An effect of the Treasury's initiative was to bring up the question of the present status of the Naval Officer in Rhode Island. Hillsborough's first concern was to establish whether the Crown or the Governor had the right to appoint this officer: the question was put to the Attorney and Solicitor-General on 19 July,[31] and a rather unsatisfactory reply received.[32] Later in the same year Governor Wentworth of New Hampshire raised the matter of Naval Officers in a much more general way.[33] His anxiety was at the effect of the establish-

23 No. XXII. Compare claims of New York, No. XXVI; and New Jersey, No. LXXXI.
24 No. XXXIX.
25 No. CXXVI.
26 Vol. I, No. 1393i-xiii.
27 Vol. II, No. CXL.
28 Below, No. XXXV.
29 No. LXXX.
30 No. CXXXV.
31 No. LXXIX.
32 Vol. I, No. 1425.
33 Below, No. CI.

ment of the Commissioners of Customs in America on the powers and functions of Naval Officers and the consequent 'decay of the governors' power in matters of trade'. Governors were required on appointment to make oath to see that the Acts of Trade were observed, but appeared no longer to possess the authority to perform their oath. Wentworth's complaint was material: it may also be reckoned an example of the suspicions entertained by some royal governors of the American Commissioners of Customs.

Smuggling also preoccupied Governor Hutchinson in 1771. His private letters of August and September evinced little hope of stopping the illicit import of tea into Massachusetts by means of land-based Customs officers.[34] Cruisers, with an increased share of the prize-money for the captain, were his proposed solution: 'We have not virtue enough to become obnoxious to the people merely from a sense of duty.'[35] The second of these letters contains interesting estimates of the consumption of tea in America, the effect of which was that a 3d. duty ought to yield at least £76,000 a year.[36] Hutchinson's lack of confidence in land-officers was probably confirmed for him by the case of the Comptroller of Customs at Falmouth, Mass., which came before the Governor and Council in November.[37] Arthur Savage was the victim of an assault by 'disguised persons' who entered his house at night, hauled him off to the river bank, and with threats extracted the name of an informer.[38] Savage, like other Customs officers roughed up by the mob, complained of lack of support from the magistrates and fled to Boston. In New Hampshire, on the other hand, a riot of 14 November, which also arose from informing, was nipped in the bud by smart action on the part of the authorities.[39]

The Frontiers

The back parts of North Carolina, the lands west of Connecticut River and the Eastern Country of Massachusetts, the three frontier territories which had given trouble or apprehensions of trouble in 1770, did so again in 1771. In North Carolina the long-smouldering conflict between the Regulators and the colony's government erupted into war. The Regulators were smallholders or squatters whose purposes were to obtain security of tenure of their lands, to pay as little as possible in taxes, and to put a stop to the extortions of eastern office-holders and lawyers. Their quarrel was only remotely with George III or Whitehall, far more with what they saw as eastern tyranny and corruption. The outcome in 1771 was a brief civil war between the frontiersmen and the settled inhabitants of North Carolina. No regular British troops were involved: all the governor asked for and got from General Gage was two light field-pieces and a train of ammunition.

Though the Regulator movement itself was older, this particular

34 Nos. XCIII, XCVIII.
35 No. XCVIII.
36 *Ibid.*
37 Vol. I, No. 1631i-vii.
38 Below, No. CXVII.
39 No. CXV.

manifestation may be dated from the riot at Hillsborough, N.C., on 22 September 1770.[40] The province's Assembly met on 5 December following and proceeded to take two decisive and provocative steps. First, it expelled the elected representative of Orange County, Hermon (or Harmon) Husbands, a Regulator leader. He was promptly arrested for libel and denied bail. Brought to trial on 8 February in the excited atmosphere of an expected attempt at rescue, he was acquitted by grand jury, to the disgust of Governor Tryon.[41] The Assembly's second move was to pass a Riot Act under which it was intended to indict the Hillsborough rioters and to declare outlaws those who declined to take their trial.[42] More than a year later this law came, in a routine way, into the hands of Richard Jackson, the Board of Trade's legal adviser. His opinion, reported on 14 January 1772, was that 'the clause (fo: 7) permitting anyone to kill with impunity a person outlawed in the manner therein described (although the circumstances of the province may excuse the inserting such clause in this Act) is yet altogether unfit for any part of the British Empire.'[43] A Regulator opinion, given in March 1771, said much the same in more colourful language: "A Riotous Act! there never was any such Act in the laws of England or any other country but France, they brought it from France, and they'll bring the Inquisition next.'[44]

Governor Tryon's decision to call out the militia and march against the 'insurgents' was accepted by the Council of North Carolina on 18 March.[45] By this time his attitude was quite uncompromising. An attempt at a negotiated settlement by John Frohock and Alexander Martin he stigmatized on 5 April as 'unconstitutional, dishonourable to government and introductive of a practice the most dangerous to the peace and happiness of society';[46] and he remained equally set against treating with the Regulators when the two armies met in battle.[47] The campaign proper began on 24 April with the Craven and Carteret militia-troops marching out of Newbern with Tryon, an old soldier, in command. They were joined by more troops in Johnstone County and marched thence to Hillsborough. For these movements, the governor's letter-book sent to Whitehall from New York on 2 August, is a major source: several extracts are given in the present volume.[48] Tryon mustered about 1100 men with eight pieces of artillery including Gage's two which arrived in the nick of time. The plan was to rendezvous with General Hugh Waddell, who had 400 men near Salisbury. This was frustrated when the Regulators surrounded Waddell, destroyed his ammunition train and drove him into Salisbury. Tryon, however, made a forced march to the Alamance River and there, on 16 May, met about 2000 insurgents. Samuel Cornell's private account

40   Vol. II, Nos. XCIV, XCVII.
41   Below, No. XXXVI.
42   No. X.
43   Public Record Office, C.O.5/302, fo. 90d.
44   Below, No. XXV.
45   No. XXIX.
46   Nos. XXXIV, XXVIII.
47   Nos. XLIX, L.
48   Nos. XVII, XIX, XXIX, XLI, XLVIII.

of the battle, testifying to the boldness of the enemy and the value of the artillery, is a useful complement to the governor's official dispatch.[49] Casualties in the militia were 9 killed and 61 wounded,[50] and 'upwards of 300' amongst the Regulators.[51] Many rebels surrendered after the battle and many more in the course of mopping-up: altogether 6409 took the oath of allegiance.[52] At least one, Few, was hanged in camp as an outlaw, presumably under the Riot Act;[53] twelve were sentenced to death at a special court of oyer and terminer at Hillsborough on 19 June, of whom six were hanged and six reprieved.[54]

Tryon left Waddell the job of dealing with the remains of resistance and quitted the colony on 30 June to take up his new appointment as governor of New York. Here he received not only the thanks of the King[55] but also the applause in prose and verse of the students of King's College, New York.[56] This document is perhaps the only expression of student views to be preserved in the Colonial Office records: whether its sickening adulation of the conqueror of American peasants is typical of undergraduate opinion in general cannot, from these sources, be established. Back in North Carolina the new governor, Josiah Martin, spent the rest of 1771 trying to think of ways of paying for Tryon's campaign without infringing the Act of Parliament restricting issues of paper currency, a task which vexed him sorely.[57]

The dispute between New York and New Hampshire concerning the lands to the west of Connecticut River acquired three documentary landmarks in 1771. First came the Earl of Dunmore's letter from New York, dated 9 March and enclosing a vast amount of evidence of riot and lawlessness and some evidence of improper encouragement thereof by the government of New Hampshire.[58] Next was the long-awaited report of the Board of Trade.[59] The delay, from 5 July 1770 to 6 June 1771, appears to have been caused by the announcement in a letter of Governor Wentworth's that the Council of New Hampshire proposed to submit a report of its own.[60] This was possibly a delaying tactic: the Board of Trade eventually became impatient and decided to wait no longer for the New Hampshire case. It reported on 6 June, having considered merely the rights of individuals on lands assumed to be within New York's jurisdiction and how to reconcile claims of grantees under the two governments where these were found to conflict with one another. Priority was proposed, first, to a small number of ancient New York grantees; secondly, to grantees under New Hampshire who had made actual settlement and improvement; and thirdly,

49 Nos. LI (official dispatch), LXIV (Cornell). Cornell gives the number of Regulators at Alamance as 'near or quite 3000'.
50 Vol. I, No. 1434.
51 Below, No. LXIV.
52 No. CXXXVI.
53 No. LXXXV.
54 *Ibid.*
55 Vol. I, No. 1435.
56 Below, No. XCII.
57 Nos. CXXV, CXXXII, CXXXVI.
58 Dunmore's letter, below, No. XXVI. Enclosures, Vol. I, No. 1047i-lviii; see also Vol. II, Nos. LXXX–LXXXI; and below, Nos. XX–XXI.
59 Below, No. LXIII.
60 Vol. I, No. 135.

to the reduced officers and soldiers whose petition[61] had brought the matter into official view in 1770. Grants under New Hampshire which had not been improved were deemed of 'little weight', though holders of such titles were to be allowed to apply to New York for up to 500 acres free of purchase-money. Two further recommendations are of more than local interest. The Board proposed that what was left of these lands after prior claims had been met should be surveyed for timber for naval purposes, and then disposed of at economical prices and rents. There was, the Board thought, 'no reason why His Majesty may not in this case at least reasonably expect the same advantages which the proprietors of the provinces of Maryland and Pennsylvania derive from the grants of their waste and uncultivated lands'. Finally, governors of colonies were criticized in strong if general terms for 'irregularities and abuses' in land-grants and for charging 'exorbitant and unreasonable fees'. New York was not specially pointed at, but was clearly one of the provinces in view.

Meanwhile the Council of New Hampshire were still working on their report. They submitted it to Governor Wentworth on 16 August,[62] he forwarding it to Whitehall with an explanatory letter of 20 August,[63] which did not reach the American Department until 26 December. After so long a period of gestation, the Council's case turned out to be of no great force. Both they and Governor Wentworth appear to have convinced themselves that there was a real possibility of moving the Crown to alter the decision of 1764 whereby the lands in question had been assigned to New York. Instead of concentrating on making the best case they could for individuals claiming under New Hampshire grants, the Council argued at length for re-annexing the lost territory to New Hampshire. As Hillsborough made clear in a letter to Tryon on 4 December,[64] this point was not negotiable in 1771; it had not been in the Board of Trade's brief; and it was not mentioned in their report of 6 June. The New Hampshire case, though six months too late to be considered by the Board, was in time to be put before the Privy Council where the matter once again stuck; in 1772 it was back with the Board which produced a longer and more comprehensive report on 3 December which will be included in the volume of *Transcripts* for that year. Meanwhile, in America, the situation on the ground was unchanged.[65]

Massachusetts' 'Eastern Country', to the Earl of Hillsborough, was another example of the imprudence of 'a colony so remote from the seat of government'.[66] It figured largely in the correspondence of 1771, partly because the anarchy there affronted his and Hutchinson's notions of good order and government, and partly because of the region's importance in the supply of masts and timber. As for the anarchy, thirty-two inhabitants of the Fifth Township, commonly called Pleasant River, gave Hutchinson a perfect definition: 'everyone doing

61   Vol. I, No. 455i.
62   Below, No. LXXXIX.
63   No. XCI.
64   No. CXXIV.
65   Nos. C, CVI–CVII.
66   No. XXXI.

what's right in his own eyes and a great spirit of mobbing and rioting prevails, cursing, swearing, fighting, threatening, stealing, pulling down houses and the like as we can't sleep a' nights.'[67] Hutchinson more than once brought the matter to the notice of the General Court but could get no satisfaction beyond the appointment of a committee of the Council of Massachusetts to tour and inspect the region. This committee reported in September that very little damage was being done to the King's timber, that the inhabitants were mostly genuine settlers not loggers, and that all that was needed was the provision of a gaol and the appointment of ministers.[68] Predictably, Hutchinson thought the report a whitewash job 'evidently calculated to excuse or justify the two Houses in their refusal or neglect to take any measures to remove intruders.'[69]

As for timber, two opinions by Richard Jackson in May and June 1771 provide a useful summary of the laws relating to the preservation of pine timber in America.[70] His own opinion was even more interesting: while the law protected trees on private property 'it deprives them at the same time of another protection (the vigilance and care of the owner) that might perhaps have been more efficacious, as experience has shown it to be in most other cases.'[71] Both the sentiment and the language could have been Adam Smith's. These opinions were sent to Surveyor-General Wentworth who replied with a long discourse on the practical problems of preserving and felling mast timber.[72] In one district 102 out of 106 healthy-looking trees cut in 1771 had proved rotten. Others were damaged in falling. Add to this the cost of prosecutions, the difficulty of obtaining judgements against despoilers, and the even greater difficulty of executing those judgements, and Jackson's preference for private enterprise becomes a matter of common sense. Nothing, however, was done. With the Treasury surveyor preparing a report on 'the country eastward of Sagadahoc' Hillsborough thought the business 'certainly not yet ripe for consideration'.[73]

The West

Hillsborough's hopes of holding up or at least deterring westward expansion and settlement suffered no formal setback this year. The 'Western question', as it appears in the Colonial Office records of 1771, has four components, by no means unrelated to one another but which it is convenient to mention separately. They were: the pressure to sell the lands on the Ohio ceded to the Crown by the Six Nations at the Treaty of Fort Stanwix (1768) to a group headed by Thomas Walpole; the Illinois country and the future of the British military presence at Fort Chartres; the settlement of the Lower Mississippi Valley; and relations with the Indians.

67   No. XI.
68   No. XCIX.
69   No. CV.
70   Nos. LII, LXII.
71   No. LXII.
72   No. CXXX.
73   No. CXXIII.

A.R.—2

So far as the American Department was concerned, the question of the proposed new colony on the Ohio was virtually at a standstill throughout the year. Hillsborough promised President Nelson that proper attention would be given to Virginia's claims in that quarter,[74] which Nelson gratefully acknowledged.[75] Dunmore, who arrived in September to take over the government of that colony, did not bring up the matter during the remainder of the year. Indeed the only document in the present volume of *Transcripts* which can be said to have much bearing on the subject is Governor Wright's submission to the Board of Trade of 27 December.[76] This paper was connected with a case Wright was trying to put to the American Department for extending Georgia's frontiers by a purchase of land from the Cherokees and Creeks (see below). He was arguing, not surprisingly, for a gradual westward extension of the seaboard provinces and against large grants of land in the remote interior. The Ohio scheme was not mentioned but Wright's memorial was palpably directed against it. It is indeed possible that the paper was put in at the Board's (or Hillsborough's) invitation as ammunition to be fired at the scheme: certainly it was used for that purpose when the Board reported on the Ohio application on 29 April 1772.[77]

Hillsborough had long ago been convinced that the advantages of keeping up Fort Chartres in the Illinois were outweighed by the cost in money and lives. His distaste for this outpost did not extend to what were collectively referred to as 'the posts on the Lakes', vizt. Michilimackinac, Detroit and Niagara. In the secret orders to Gage of 2 January to assemble a force to attack New Orleans and in Hillsborough's separate letter of the same date,[78] the commander-in-chief was explicitly required not to leave these forts in a state of insecurity. The days of Fort Chartres, however, were numbered. Late in September 1771 Ensign Hutchins of the 60th regiment arrived in New York from the Illinois and reported to Gage that it would need 'constant expense' to defend the fort from the encroachments of the river.[79] Gage's letter to Hillsborough of 1 October bearing this latest information reached Whitehall on 8 November, perhaps in time (if more evidence were wanted) to influence the decisions contained in the Secretary of State's important dispatch of 4 December.[80] This ordered the abandonment of Fort Chartres, though leaving to Gage's discretion when it was to be done and what if anything was to be put in its place. Hillsborough wanted all troops out of the Illinois but offered the possibility of a reduced temporary establishment at Kaskaskia, a few miles from Fort Chartres. He also wanted Fort Pitt, of no use except as a stage between the established colonies and the Illinois, abandoned and demolished 'unless you shall be of the opinion that it is absolutely necessary to be kept up'.

74   Vol. I, No. 988.
75   Below, No. LIII.
76   No. CXXXVII.
77   Vol. V, No. XXXVI.
78   Below, Nos. I–II.
79   No. CIII.
80   No. CXXII.

There remained the less tractable problem of the inhabitants of the Illinois. In this connection Hutchins's report, forwarded and recommended by Gage, is of some interest.[81] Largely factual, with estimates of population, trade and distances, it nevertheless contains some comments on the people, both Indian and white, including the villagers of St Louis, 'some of them very genteel and well-educated'. What to do with them was Hillsborough's worry: 'the thing most to be wished for' was to shift them to Quebec or some other established colony, but this appeared impracticable. A 'permanent plan' was wanted and Gage's views were solicited on what it ought to be.[82]

In the Lower Mississippi Valley Hillsborough appears to have been less hostile to settlement; on the other hand, he was not willing to involve the Crown in expenditure beyond the already burdensome cost of fortifying the West Florida coast and holding congresses with the Indians. Consequently, while Governor Chester's dreams of promoting settlement took clearer shape in his own mind in the course of 1771, they did so nowhere else.[83] Durnford, lieut.-governor and surveyor of West Florida, returned in June from a trip up the river and reported enthusiastically on the prospects, though cautiously on the proposed canal joining the Iberville to the Mississippi.[84] This, he later estimated, would cost £9150[85]; which caused Chester in his long and informative dispatch of 28 September to decide that it might be better to spend the money—as if money was already in view—on transporting settlers from Europe and the Northern Colonies.[86] Chester clearly thought that he was making some impression on the American Department and went on thinking so until he received the estimates for 1771–1772. Finding nothing had been voted to encourage settlement, he wrote reproachfully (13 August 1772) of the disappointment of his 'sanguine expectations that a considerable sum of money would have been granted for the effectual settlement of the lands in this province';[87] to which the Secretary of State (by then Dartmouth) briskly replied that if the lands were as good as represented they ought to answer the expense of settlement without burdening the public.[88] Hillsborough himself wrote only four letters to Chester in 1771, only one being of much length or substance,[89] and none holding out hopes of a subsidy.

Indians

These different aspects of the Western problems were clamped together by the repercussions which any move by Whitehall, or even no move, was certain to have on Indian relations. These, anyway as seen from Whitehall, were in some confusion in 1771. The basic

81   No. CIV.
82   No. CXXII.
83   Nos. LXVIII, CII.
84   No. LXIX.
85   Vol. I, No. 1535i.
86   Below, No. CII.
87   Vol. V, No. LXXXI.
88   Vol. IV, No. 811.
89   Below, No. LXXIV.

grievances of the Indians—encroaching settlers, white hunters on Indian lands, fraudulent traders and vendors of rum, and the powerlessness of the colonial authorities to stop any of these abuses—were plain enough and were expressed in numerous documents contained in this volume.[90] What was unclear was what, if anything, the Indians were going to do next. One can understand Gage's puzzlement: 'I continue to receive advices of councils, meetings, machinations and intrigues amongst the savages, though no certainty of any consequences likely to arise from them.'[91] His own opinion was that the Indians would start a war soon because they had nothing to do but hunt and fight, though whether it would be war amongst themselves or against the whites he was unable to say. Hillsborough continued to hold that the 'natural enmities and jealousies' amongst them were a sufficient security against their causing real trouble.[92] All that was needed was consistent non-intervention in Indian politics. Sir William Johnson, Superintendant in the Northern District, took a more serious view of the current situation. In his submission the Indians had 'gradually become more and more alarmed for themselves'; though they respected the English more than in French times, they still believed themselves capable of stemming the tide of settlement. 'Many will talk, some will think, and a lesser number will act otherwise, but this is nevertheless the true political state of their sentiments in general at present'[93] was Johnson's lapidary verdict. Unfortunately he wrote only two letters to Hillsborough in 1771: both, with Hillsborough's replies are printed below.[94] His main concern this year was to scotch a rumour that the loyalty of the Six Nations to the English was in doubt. This, it appeared, had arisen from the conduct of a detached tribe of Senecas living on the Ohio, who in negotiation with Western Indians had pretended to speak, or been represented as speaking, for the Six Nations as a whole. Johnson called 350 chiefs to a congress at Johnson Hall and obtained all necessary reassurances.

In the Southern District, Western 'machinations' were more fully reported. Against Johnson's two, Superintendant John Stuart wrote nine letters to Hillsborough in 1771 and enclosed no fewer than thirty-six supporting documents. Amongst enclosures included in the present volume are parts of Stuart's correspondence with his deputy, Alexander Cameron,[95] with Ouconnastotah[96] and Emistisiguo,[97] with Governor Chester of West Florida,[98] and with John Thomas, newly appointed deputy on the Mississippi.[99] In the early part of 1771 Stuart was at Charleston, still mainly concerned with countering the diplomatic initiative of the Western Indians. Cameron, on the frontier,

90 For example, Nos. XXX, CXII, CXXVII, CXXIX.
91 Below, No. LVII.
92 No. XLV.
93 No. XVI.
94 Nos. XVI, XLV, LXXXVII, CXXVII.
95 Nos. XIII, XVIII, XXX.
96 No. XV.
97 No. LXXVII.
98 Nos. XCIV, XCVII.
99 Nos. XC, CVIII, CXXXIII.

picked up the notion that it was Indians from the North who were urging the Cherokees to strike at the whites,[100] but Stuart did not believe it. Cameron was told to 'be careful to distinguish between the Northern and Western Indians': it was the latter who were to be feared.[101] No one was sure how the Cherokees, Chickasaws and Creeks were reacting to Western approaches, the task of guessing being made harder by the inability of the whites to construe the wampum belts the Indians used for messages.[102] Just how complex Indian affairs in the Southern District had become is suggested by Stuart's involuted order to Cameron: 'You will conceive it our interest to unite the Cherokees to the Northern confederacy if you find their views to be such as we imagine, and if you succeed in accommodating matters between them and the Chickasaws I doubt not but the latter would be brought to join the Northern confederacy in which event the Creeks would be awed, especially as the war between them and the Choctaws still continues.'[103]

Stuart left Charleston at the end of April to settle the Indian affairs of West Florida, directed there by Hillsborough's letter of 3 October 1770.[104] After concerting the agenda with Governor Chester,[105] he met the Upper Creeks in congress at Pensacola on 29 October. The full proceedings of the meeting are printed below.[106] Stuart was almost obsessively concerned to establish that the Creeks had not been promised a congress by him in 1765, as the Council of West Florida had alleged.[107] On this point he was satisfied, but in other respects the outcome was by no means satisfactory. On the second day, with the Creeks asking for boats to take them home, the congress was on the point of breaking down. Things were patched up but the hoped-for cessions of land were not granted, and the Indians on their side produced a convincing catalogue of white abuses and misdoings. The congress over, Stuart continued to hope that the Creeks would come round and cede land on the Scambia River, but his disappointment was barely concealed. This, and apprehensions of what the Creeks might do next, occasioned David Taitt's mission early in the following year.[108] Meanwhile, on the last day of 1771, Stuart met 1500 Choctaws and Chickasaws in congress at Mobile. No land was sought; Indian complaints were heard; and arrangements made for running boundary lines.[109]

Stuart's sojourn in West Florida coincided with the beginning of the farcical adventures of John Thomas on the Mississippi.[110] This lieutenant of artillery had been foisted on the Superintendent by Hillsborough,[111] and given the job of deputy to the 'small tribes' of

100 No. XIII.
101 No. XVIII.
102 E.g. No. XXX.
103 No. XVIII.
104 Vol. I, No. 637.
105 Below, Nos. XCIV, XCVII.
106 No. CXII.
107 Vol. II, No. LXVI.
108 Vol. V, No. IV and Appendix.
109 Vol. I, No. 1700.
110 Instructions to Thomas, below, No. XC.
111 Vol. I, No. 272.

Indians on the Mississippi. Thomas's letters, of which there are more
to come in 1772, reveal a man of exaggerated self-importance, distinctly
short on common sense.[112] The 'small tribes' to which he was accredited
really were small, not enough to satisfy his ego. During his few months
up the river he interfered with Indians on the west bank, upset the
Spaniards, quarrelled with the traders and finished by killing one of
them, reporting all (except the last event) to Stuart in a style compound-
ed of such bombast and slyness as led Charles Stuart to doubt his
sanity.[113]

Thomas was a problem because of Hillsborough's patronage, but
the Superintendant's difficulty in 1771 was not how to deal with
this *farceur* but how to go on negotiating with Indians whose grievances
he could not redress and how to stop governors of provinces from
taking an independent line in Indian affairs. This last point is aptly
illustrated by the documents concerning the traders to the Cherokee
and Creek nations. Stuart first reported on 27 April that the Cherokees
proposed to settle the debts they owed to their traders by a cession of
land on Broad and Oconee Rivers.[114] A form of conveyance had actually
been completed on 22 February without the consent or knowledge
of the Superintendant.[115] Hillsborough replied that it was 'a transaction
that ought to be discountenanced as much as possible'.[116] Meanwhile,
the traders had sought an ally in Governor Wright, who saw in the
transaction an opportunity to strengthen Georgia's western frontier.[117]
Wright realized that the unauthorized cession would have to be set
aside, if only because the Creeks laid claim to the lands in question,
also owed money to their traders which they could not pay, and also
hoped to clear their obligations by conveying the same land. Returning
to London, he presented Hillsborough on 12 December with an
elaborate plan for annexing the land, selling it in small lots to immigrants, using part of the proceeds to pay off both Creek and Cherokee
traders, and devoting the balance to raising two troops of rangers to
police Georgia's back-country.[118] Although a breach in Hillsborough's
policy of containment and initiated without prior consultation with
Stuart, this scheme won Board of Trade approval on 9 November
1772.[119]

Miscellaneous

Amongst many other subjects raised or discussed in the *Transcripts*
for 1771 (to which the index to this volume is intended to supply a
guide), three deserve special mention. There is, first, a long and largely
self-explanatory complaint against the Superior Court of Rhode Island
for disregarding the King's order in a private suit.[120] This was deemed

112 Below, Nos. CVIII, CXXXIII.
113 Vol. IV, No. 1011v.
114 Below, No. XXXVIII.
115 Vol. I, No. 1157ix.
116 Below, No. LXXV.
117 No. CXXXIV.
118 *Ibid.*
119 Vol. V, No. CXIV.
120 Below, No. LXXXII.

of enough importance by the American Department to be sent to the
Privy Council,[121] where it can hardly have done that colony's reputation any good. Secondly, attempts were in progress to survey the
boundary line between New York and Quebec and to establish the
status of French land grants on Lake Champlain.[122] And, finally, there
is sufficient evidence in this volume to indicate that a renewed campaign
was in progress for the appointment of a Church of England bishop in
America. Twice in 1771 the clergy of Connecticut appealed to Hillsborough.[123] The clergy of New York and New Jersey added their
voices.[124] And the Bishop of London's commissary in Virginia—'in
compliance with the pressing instances of some episcopal clergy in
the northern provinces'—summoned a meeting of that province's
clergy to discuss the same topic.[125] Whatever other obstacles there
may have been in the way of such an establishment, the Bishop of
London himself was not disposed to hinder it. On the contrary, he
declared in favour of any solution approved by government which
would relieve him of the 'pain and anxiety' he felt in having responsibility without power.[126]

121   Vol. I, No. 1623.
122   Below, Nos. CVI, CXXI, CXXXI.
123   Nos. LIV, CXVIII.
124   No. CIX.
125   No. LIII.
126   No. V.

LIST OF DOCUMENTS

17

TRANSCRIPTS 1771

I

Earl of Hillsborough to Lieut.-General Thomas Gage (Most Secret)

2 January, Whitehall

Sir, nothing has happened since my last letter to you [Vol. I, No. 811] to strengthen our hopes that the public peace might be preserved; on the contrary there is but too much reason to apprehend that the matter in negotiation with the Court of Spain will have its issue in a speedy war, the success of which will depend upon the most vigorous exertion of every strength this kingdom is able to put forth.

In this situation it has become necessary to give full scope to the consideration not only of those measures which it may be proper to pursue for the defence and security of His Majesty's possessions but also in what places the enemy may be annoyed and attacked with the greatest advantage and best hope of success, and also what steps may be advisable preparatory to any enterprise that may be undertaken.

The result of this deliberation, so far as it regards offensive operations in America has been the adopting a proposition to begin those operations by an attack upon New Orleans.

The advantages that would attend the entire possession of the Mississippi, both in point of commerce and of security to the rest of the King's possessions in North America, have been fully expatiated upon and explained in the course of our correspondence, and those advantages combined with the general intelligence of the small number of troops left in Louisiana by General O'Reilly, the indisposition or rather aversion of the French inhabitants to the Spanish government, the great extent and weakness of the defences of the town of New Orleans, and the supposed practicability of approaching it either on the side of West Florida or by the rivers Ohio and Mississippi, have been the grounds on which this proposition has been adopted. The practicability however of such an undertaking, as well as the quantum of force to be employed and the manner in which the attack is to be made, must entirely depend on your own judgement, forming that judgement on a variety of facts and circumstances that cannot be known here; and therefore it is the King's pleasure that you do give the fullest consideration to this proposition, and if you see no reasonable objections to it that you do take such preparatory steps as shall be necessary for carrying it into immediate execution so soon as you shall receive the King's orders to commence hostilities, in case His Majesty should be driven to that necessity, an event that will probably be decided upon in a few days.

It is the King's present intention from the reliance His Majesty has upon your ability and zeal for the honour of his arms that you should command upon this expedition in person; and as the assistance of a

21

naval force may be necessary on the side of the Gulf of Mexico to prevent any succours being thrown in either before or after the operations are commenced, the commander-in-chief of the squadron at Jamaica will be ordered to cooperate with you in this important service and to afford every aid the nature of his command will admit of.

The King's servants having submitted to His Majesty their opinion that, as well for carrying into execution the proposed attack upon New Orleans as for answering any other purposes which government may have in view in the prosecution of a war, it may be advisable that a large body of troops should be collected together in one convenient spot; I am therefore commanded to recommend this measure for your consideration, but at the same time I must not omit to mention to you that it is by no means the idea that the force in the province of Quebec should be diminished nor any reduction made of that in Newfoundland or in West Florida, nor that the posts upon the Lakes should be left in a state of insecurity.

An estimate having been laid before and agreed to by Parliament for beginning and carrying into execution such parts of the fortifications intended to be made for the security of the harbour of St. John's in Newfoundland as are thought more immediately necessary, I enclose to you for your information copies of the letters which have passed between myself and the Board of Ordnance on that subject.

The speedy recruiting the regiments in America upon the present plan of augmentation being of very great importance, I enclose to you for your information copy of a circular letter from Sir Jeffrey Amherst to the several North American governors in the year 1762, wrote in consequence of orders given at that time for recruiting the King's forces in America by levies in the colonies, which letters may possibly contain some hints that may be useful to you on the present occasion. *Draft.* [C.O.5/89, fo. 1]

II

Earl of Hillsborough to Lieut.-General Thomas Gage (No. 39, separate)

2 January, Whitehall

Sir, I have received and laid before the King your despatches Nos. 51 and 52 [Vol. II, Nos. CXVII-CXVIII].

Your letter No. 51 in answer to mine on the subject of the posts in the interior country and on the Mississippi is very full and satisfactory, and I entirely concur with you in the reason you adduce to refute the arguments in support of the utility of those posts so far as regards the influence they are supposed to have upon the commercial and political connections between the King's subjects and the savages; but I must at the same time confess to you that such of those posts as by their situation on the passes between the great waters of communication give security to the dominion of the country do appear to me to be of very great importance and especially in the present conjuncture.

The posts I mean to refer to are those upon the Lakes; and as the possession of them at this time may be of very great consequence it has been thought fit as you will see by my secret letter of this day's date [Vol. III, No. 1] that they should not be left in a state of insecurity.

The commotions among the savages as related in your letter No. 52 are alarming but without farther information of the issue of the intrigues stated to be carrying on among them, I am not able to say more than that it is of great importance that we should avoid as much as possible intermeddling in the disputes and quarrels between one confederacy and another; for if it be true that those quarrels and disputes are the effect of the intrigues of French emissaries, their object must be to entangle us, and therefore we should by becoming parties fall into the snare they have laid.

Captain Preston's acquittal has given universal satisfaction, and I shall not fail (as you desire) of recommending his case to our royal master's consideration.

Governor Hutchinson informs me that he has appointed two officers to reside at Castle William, one to take care of the stores, the other to report the arrivals of ships; and His Majesty having been pleased to approve these appointments, it is His Majesty's pleasure that you should make such allowances to those officers out of the military chest as you and Governor Hutchinson shall think just and reasonable. *Draft*. [C.O.5/89, fo. 5]

III

Earl of Hillsborough to Governor Thomas Hutchinson (No. 3)

2 January, Whitehall

Sir, I have received and laid before the King your dispatches, Nos. 29 [Vol. II, No. CXXII], 30 and 31 [Vol. I, Nos. 759, 774].

The different motions made in the House of Representatives antecedent to the prorogation seem to have been calculated merely to save the credit of party by measures of opposition in which they hoped to have that support and concurrence from the country which had been refused to their more violent propositions, but I hope their drift if I am not mistaken in the object of their motions will be discovered and their expectations disappointed.

Your refusal to concur in the votes for the payments intended to be made to Mr Bollan and Mr De Berdt was consistent with your duty to the King and at the same evinced your regard for the real interests of the province, which never can be either properly or effectually served by agents whose authority from the irregularity of their appointments is liable at least to be questioned here on every occasion.

The enclosed extract of my letter [Vol. III, No. II] of this day's date to General Gage will inform you of the directions I have given in respect to the two officers you have placed in Castle William, and I have the satisfaction to acquaint you that His Majesty approves of those appointments.

There is no doubt that if the legislature of the Massachusetts Bay persists in refusing to provide adequate remedies to the disorders in the Eastern Country, so loudly complained of by the magistrates and inhabitants in the petitions [Vol. I, No. 759i-ii] enclosed in your letter No. 30, those disorders will soon get to such a head as may be productive of very dangerous consequences. You will therefore, I presume, think it fit to repeat your recommendations both to the Council and House of Representatives on the subject of those disturbances and again point out to them what must be the consequence if effectual measures are not taken to prevent enormities that tend to the dissolution of society.

The result of the prosecution of the soldiers has answered the just wishes and expectations of all who are friends to truth and justice and gives good ground to hope that the colony is approaching fast to that state of order and tranquillity for which it stood so eminently distinguished before the late unhappy prejudices took place. *Draft*. [C.O.5/760, fo. 1]

IV

Earl of Hillsborough to Governor William Franklin (No. 29)

2 January, Whitehall
Sir, I have received your letter of the 5th of November, No. 24 [Vol. II, No. CXVI], and have laid it before the King.

Nothing would have been more unbecoming than the Assembly's refusal to provide for the King's troops from resentment for the repeal of the Paper Currency Act, a measure to which (however erroneous in its principle) the King would not have withheld his royal concurrence if it could have been given without violating the law and the constitution, and therefore it gave me great pleasure to find they had receded from so indecent a resolution. *Draft*. [C.O.5/991, fo 1]

V

Bishop of London to Earl of Hillsborough

11 January, London House
My Lord, I have in obedience to your lordship's commands considered the several papers which I had the honour of receiving from your lordship relative to the exercise of ecclesiastical jurisdiction over the clergy of Virginia.

As I have had no complaints of the behaviour of the clergy of that province from the two last governors with whom I had the honour of frequent correspondence, and as Mr Nelson has taken the occasion of raising the difficulty with regard to the article of the governor's instructions without pointing to any particular case which calls for an immediate remedy, I am rather at a loss to understand the reason of the present application, especially as I have not had the least intimation of it from the person who bears the character of my commissary and who thinks it his duty, though he exercises no jurisdiction, to correspond with me upon all matters relative to the clergy.

I am very sensible that for want of a proper ecclesiastical jurisdiction in the colonies doubts will arise in whom the power is lodged of taking cognizance of the clergy and punishing them for neglect of duty, immorality etc. It was I am persuaded intended when the colonies were first settled and the clergy were few in number, to be in the hands of the Bishop of London: Bishop Compton and Bishop Robinson exercised it whilst they lived, and Bishop Gibson likewise for some time, without any commission from the Crown, merely upon the footing of usage and custom. They appointed commissaries within each government with power to exercise jurisdiction according to the method of the ecclesiastical courts in England. Many disputes arose betwixt the governors and commissaries which prevented the latter from proceeding judicially and their authority became merely nominal. These and other circumstances induced Bishop Gibson in the year 1724 to apply for a commission from the Crown. It was granted with a power to appoint commissaries who were to correct the manners of the clergy by ecclesiastical censures after due process in a judicial way, as is practised in the Church of England. This for some time and in some places seemed to produce more regularity but still the jealousy of governors, who thought the commissaries interfered with their authority, and the misbehaviour of the commissaries themselves who too far removed from any control were imprudent in the exercise of their power, rendered the plan of employing commissaries ineffectual to the purposes intended. Bishop Sherlock, therefore, when he succeeded to the see of London, examined the commission which had been granted personally to his predecessor, and not choosing to accept one of the same kind which he thought could do little or no service, nor venturing to exercise a jurisdiction as Bishops Compton and Robinson had done without a commission and which the Law Officers of the Crown had declared to be illegal, he confined himself entirely to the offices of ordaining and licensing ministers for the Plantations without pretending to any jurisdiction himself and of course without attempting to delegate it to a commissary.

In this manner have the three succeeding bishops proceeded without any great inconvenience except in one or two instances, and unless it shall be thought advisable to establish one or more bishops to reside in the colonies I know of no other method *sufficient* to answer the purpose of preserving in all cases good order amongst the clergy with proper authority which will not be liable to objections as encroaching upon the Supremacy of the Crown or giving powers unknown to the constitution of the Church of England.

The method which Mr Nelson refers to in one of the Acts of Assembly is quite new to me. If there is any clause of that kind giving to the General Assembly a *power and jurisdiction to hear and determine all cases, matters and things whatsoever relating to or concerning any person or persons ecclesiastical,* His Majesty's Law Officers best know how far such a power is consistent with that jurisdiction which is inherent in the Crown as part of its Supremacy and which I apprehend has not been delegated by commission to the General Assembly. I would only observe that it makes no provision for the exercise of the jurisdiction of the Bishop of London or of any other bishop who may be honoured with a commission from the Crown, though it is an instruction to all governors *to give all countenance and encouragement in the exercise of the same.* It does not even place any part of the jurisdiction in the hands of the governor who is the representative of the King in whom all ecclesiastical jurisdiction is inherent as part of the Supremacy, as is the case in the Leeward Islands where the governor may suspend an incumbent, *giving notice thereof to the Bishop of London that he may give such direction as to him shall seem meet.* Nor does it appoint any of the clergy to be the assessors in the hearing and judging of the cause who may be supposed in some instances to be the best judges how far the conduct of any clergyman deserves censure and punishment. It seems upon the whole to transfer the King's Supremacy and the bishop's jurisdiction to a General Assembly, which is rather a plan formed upon the model of a Presbyterian Independent government than on that of the Church of England.

For my own part there is nothing I have more at heart than that some plan might be formed which, however it may not answer all we could wish, may be productive of some good. In the present extensive state of the colonies, a Bishop of London who undertakes to exercise a jurisdiction either by himself or his commissaries will find the office not very consistent with the care and superintendency of a large and important diocese at home. He will find it at the same time a difficult matter to prevent disputes betwixt the governors and the commissaries, to regulate the behaviour even of the commissaries themselves, and to act in every case as he would wish to do with justice and impartiality to all parties. This can only be done in a regular effectual manner by a bishop resident in America. In the meantime, till a more favourable season for adopting that measure offers itself, I would submit to your lordship whether an instruction may not be given to the several governors explanatory of the general one, to this purpose.

Whereas doubts have arisen or may arise what may be the proper means intended by the 67th instruction for the removal of any minister who shall appear to give scandal either by his doctrine or manners, you are to understand our intention to be that if neither the Bishop of London nor any other bishop is authorised by a commission under the Great Seal to exercise ecclesiastical jurisdiction over the clergy in the Plantations nor any commissary acts by his appointment under his hand and seal, you proceed by your authority (calling to your assistance two of the Council and two clergymen licenced by the Bishop of London, of whom in the province of Virginia the person who corresponds with the Bishop of London as his commissary shall be one) to cite the person against whom the complaint is made as well as the witnesses to prove the charge, and upon full and sufficient evidence laid before you suspend him from the exercise of his function till you have transmitted the evidence and the whole proceedings upon the charge to His Majesty in Council and wait his royal pleasure either to remove or continue the suspension or to pass any other censure upon him which the nature of the offence may require.

If an instruction of this kind is not liable to any particular objection it would I think be a more eligible method than to leave the cognizance of such matters to a General Assembly, which I never understood had any pretence to a jurisdiction relative to ecclesiastical persons till I saw the extract your lordship sent me from the Act of the General Assembly, 27 Geo. 2d.

With regard to your lordship's answer to Mr Nelson I would take the liberty only to observe that the predecessors of Bishop Gibson exercised episcopal authority in the colonies, considering it as belonging to them from usage and custom, but that his successors have declined the exercise of it in any matter of jurisdiction, confining their care of the Plantations to the ordaining and licencing ministers who take the oath of canonical obedience to the Bishop of London and to the corresponding with them upon any occasions which call for their advice and assistance.

In this method I am willing to proceed. At the same time, if any other shall be thought more eligible, I am very ready to part with the little authority I have, the loss of which would be amply compensated by more ease and satisfaction to myself as well as by a relief from the pain and anxiety I feel in having the shadow of a power which I cannot discharge with any effect to those good purposes which I have sincerely at heart. *Signed*, Ric. London. [C.O.5/1349, fo. 13]

VI

Governor William Franklin to Earl of Hillsborough (No. 25)

14 January, Burlington

My Lord, I was yesterday honoured with the duplicate of your lordship's circular letter of the 28th of September and another of November 15 relative to the prospect of a war with Spain [Vol. I, Nos. 621, 729]. The original of the first letter never came to hand, which I much wonder at as I observe by the contents that Lord Dunmore must have received the one directed to him before the 11th of December last when he made his speech to the Assembly of New York. Let the event be what it may, His Majesty may have the firmest reliance on my attention to the security of the colony under my government and that I shall use my utmost endeavours in case matters should proceed to extremities to prevail on the Assembly to do what may be in their power towards putting the province into a better state of defence. This, I doubt not, they will be the more encouraged to do from His Majesty's most gracious assurances that the security of the possessions in America will be a principal object of his care and attention.

I am likewise honoured with your lordship's two dispatches of November 15 [Vol. I, No. 722, Vol. II, No. CXX]. The one respecting Indian affairs is the first I have ever received on the subject either from His Majesty's ministers or the neighbouring governments, so that this colony must stand excused for not having complied with His Majesty's expectations in that respect. I shall not fail, however, to take the first opportunity to represent this matter to the Council and Assembly and urge their concurrence with the other colonies in such regulations of the Indian commerce as may be thought requisite on their part to answer the valuable end His Majesty has in view. However, I think it my duty to inform your lordship that though some such regulations as are proposed would not only be highly advantageous to the commercial interests of Great Britain and her colonies but contribute greatly to the security of the latter from Indian depredations, yet in all probability the very colonies which are largely interested in the commerce with the Indians and whose frontiers are immediately exposed to their incursions will never be able to agree among themselves on any effectual measures for this desirable purpose. And as New Jersey has no inhabitants anyways concerned in the Indian trade, her frontier surrounded by the colonies of New York and Pennsylvania, and every Indian claim on the province settled to the satisfaction of the Indians, it is not at all improbable but that the Assembly here may decline engaging in any expense on that account. Every colony, I am apprehensive, will consider only its own immediate interest and grant in proportion to what they conceive that to be, a circumstance in which hardly any two colonies will concur in opinion. But this is not the only instance by many which evinces the absolute necessity there is (for the sake of the colonists themselves) of a general superintending power over all the British dominions in America.

I send your lordship by this opportunity copies of the Minutes and Proceedings of the Council and Assembly, and of all the Acts passed during the late sessions. There are only three of the latter which contain anything of a new or particular nature and those have clauses suspending their taking effect till they receive His Majesty's approbation. Their titles are as follow vizt. 1st. An Act for establishing the Boundary or Partition Line between the Colonies of New York and Nova Caesarea or New Jersey and for confirming the Titles and Possessions of certain lands adjacent to or near the said line; 2d. A Supplementary Act to an Act entitled An Act for the better enabling of Creditors to recover their just Debts from Persons who abscond themselves; 3d. An Act to enable Persons who are His Majesty's Liege Subjects either by Birth or Naturalization to inherit and hold Real Estates notwithstanding the Purchase, Grant or Devise were made before Naturalization within this Colony.

The Hon. John Ladd Esq. departed this life on the 20th of December last, which has occasioned a vacancy in His Majesty's Council for this province. He resided in the western division of this colony, which circumstance I mention as I find it is generally understood here that it was one of the terms on which the government was surrendered to the Crown that there should always be an equal number of Councillors as well as Assemblymen in each division. This matter, however, has not been so strictly attended to of late years as formerly, there being now only three Councillors in West Jersey to eight in East Jersey, which is not only too great an inequality but as they mostly reside from 50 to 80 miles from the present seat of government, which is in the capital of the former division, it often occasions considerable delay and detriment to His Majesty's service and the public business. It is indeed but seldom that I can collect a sufficient number of them to form a Council on sudden emergencies, and those who reside at a distance expect that I will never require their attendance (which is always attended with expense and trouble to them) but at the time of a sessions of General Assembly unless upon very extraordinary occasions. On this account I think it particularly necessary that the vacancy occasioned by Mr Ladd's death should be supplied by some gentleman residing in the western division, and I therefore take the liberty to nominate and recommend (for His Majesty's choice) two gentlemen who are in every respect the best qualified to serve His Majesty in that capacity of any I am at liberty to mention. One is Daniel Coxe Esq. of Trenton (about ten miles from hence) and the other John Lawrence Esq. who lives in this town. The first was lately in England and had I hear the honour of being personally known to your lordship. The latter was lately a member of Assembly, has a good estate, and is a lawyer by profession. Both of them are members of the Church of England. *Signed.* [C.O.5/991, fo. 4]

VII

Lieut.-General Thomas Gage to Earl of Hillsborough (No. 55)

16 January, New York

My Lord, as the contents of your lordship's letter No. 37 [Vol. I, No. 714] require no particular answer, I have only to acknowledge the receipt of it and have little to trouble your lordship with by this opportunity but shall proceed to lay before your lordship such intelligence as I have received since my last letters.

The chiefs of many Indian nations have assembled at Fort Pitt where the deputies of the Northern and Western leagues have had a conference in presence of the commanding officer, and mutually desired peace. The Northern deputies then proceeded with their belts on their journey to Siota where they are to deliver their messages. And from the peaceable disposition shown by both parties it is now apprehended they may all join in one general union. Sir William Johnson hopes still that the sentiments with which the Indians returned from the last treaty will dwell on their minds for some time and prevent any union with the Southern nations that may be prejudicial to us.

A Shawnee chief gave information at Fort Pitt on the 2nd of December that a few days before he left home some of his nation returned from the Chikesaw country who said they saw in the Mississippi below the mouth of Ohio about forty large boats full of Spanish soldiers and several French officers whom they knew in the late war, proceeding towards Fort Chartres.

Indians are never distinct in their accounts of numbers, and though their intelligence is not much to be relied upon yet it has often some foundation. And I apprehend if any boats were seen that they might have belonged to the trade from New Orleans, which usually sets out for the Ilinois in the months of March and August. The autumn traders might have got above the Chikesaw country in the month of October and the news of their proceeding get to Fort Pitt the beginning of December.

Mr Stuart will have given your lordship every information about his treaty with the Cherokees for fixing the boundary of Virginia and the impediments thrown in his way by the land-jobbers. There has been of late frequent complaints from the people of Georgia and the Creek Indians of insults committed on each other; two white men have been killed and satisfaction is demanded of the Creek nation but the quarrel is not yet accommodated. The Western Indians continue to make incursions in the Cherokee country and there is no great likelihood of the peace between the Creeks and Choctaws being of long duration. The Creek nation does not seem unanimous in the desire of peace, for which some tribes are strongly soliciting our good offices to bring the Choctaws to conclude a peace, others take every favourable opportunity to attack them.

Mr Stuart acquaints me of his intention to set out for West Florida time enough to meet the Indians at their return from hunting; that his going there will render a congress unavoidable, which has long been demanded by the Choctaws; and as it is the sense of government there should be a congress, he would prepare to execute it with as much economy as possible and send me an estimate of the expense. He does not however explain whether the expense of this congress is to be defrayed out of his annual fund or whether an extraordinary sum is to be allowed for that particular service.

This province is in general so desirous of striking money that the Assembly will be obliged to pass the bill for emitting a paper currency in the manner they are permitted to do it; and I have hopes from thence that the arrears due by the province for providing the King's troops with quarters, fire and candle will be paid.

Captain Preston will have laid before your lordship the particulars of the trials of the soldiers at Boston as well as of his own trial, all which have ended very much to the satisfaction of most people of character in all the provinces.

I have the honour to transmit your lordship a plan of Castle William and the additional works lately made by Captain Montresor [Vol. I, No. 923i-ii], engineer, with his report of the same and a list of the ordnance and stores found in the fort and in the island [Vol. I, No. 923iii-iv]. *Signed.* [C.O.5/89, fo. 33]

VIII

Governor Thomas Hutchinson to Earl of Hillsborough (No. 34)

17 January, Boston

My Lord, I have the honour of your lordship's letters of the 15 November [Vol. II, No. CXXI, Vol. I, No. 729] by the packet, also the original of the 28th of September [Vol. I, No. 621] by the *Mercury,* duplicate of which I had before received. The several letters to the governors of the other colonies I had immediate opportunities of forwarding direct except that to Mr Grant of East Florida, which I enclosed to Mr Bull, lieut.-governor of South Carolina, and that to Mr Patterson of St John which waits for a vessel, there being none at present near sailing for that island.

It gives me the greatest pleasure when my conduct meets with His Majesty's approbation. I knew that not only the enemies to government here but the Opposition in England would take the advantage of any unguarded step in the affair of the Castle, which made me more cautious and explicit with respect to retaining the command than I should have thought necessary at any other time. I hope soon to receive further orders relative to the Castle in answer to letters which your lordship had not received. I have ever since the change of the garrison kept two officers there for whom the Assembly refused to make any establishment. As I have no views in it but His Majesty's service, and they are most evidently necessary, I flatter myself that provision will be made for them.

Your lordship will receive under this cover [Vol. I, No. 925i] the printed trial of the soldiers and of the persons charged with firing out of the Custom-house. An attempt is making by a seditious writer again to poison the minds of the people but I hope an antidote will be found, a very judicious person who has an exceeding good pen having undertaken the defence of the court and jury and I think will lay open to view of the public the artifices which have been employed to deceive and abuse them.

I have further prorogued the General Court and will keep off a session until the spring when I hope to meet them in a better temper than I have ever done before. In the meantime I shall give constant attention to the improvement of every incident for increasing the disposition which at present appears in so great a part of the people to promote order and a submission to government.

I am sorry that I gave your lordship any trouble about the copies of letters sent from England. I have since discovered that they are the letters which were laid before the House of Commons the last session. I have made only one of mine certain, a letter I wrote to Mr Hood in October 1769, copy of which he sent to Mr Stephens, Secretary of the Admiralty. The Speaker acknowledged to me that they were sent to him by a person who had no pretence to write to him as Speaker, and therefore he did not think himself obliged to lay them before the House or make them public. I rather think the true reason was that they fell short of their expectations and contained nothing to make the writers obnoxious. *Signed*. [C.O.5/760, fo. 13]

IX

Governor Thomas Hutchinson to Earl of Hillsborough (Private)

22 January, Boston
My Lord, the disorders in the colonies do not seem to have been caused by the defects in the forms or constitutions of government. They have not prevailed in the several colonies in proportion as one colony has been under a more popular form of government than another. They must be attributed to a cause which is common to all the colonies, a loose, false and absurd notion of the nature of government which has been spread by designing artful men, setting bounds to the supreme authority and admitting parts of the community and even individuals to judge when those bounds are exceeded, and to obey or disobey accordingly.

Whilst this principle universally prevails in any community, be the form of government what it may, or rather let it have what name it will for it must be a name only, there can be no interior force exerted and disorder and confusion must be the effect.

When this principle prevails through any distinct parts of a community and there is no apprehension of force from the supreme authority of the whole or from any power exterior to such parts, the effect is the same in those distinct parts as it is in the whole community when the principle universally prevails there.

Measures for reforming the constitution of any people under such circumstances will probably be ineffectual and tend to increase their disorders.

The colonies were under these circumstances when I wrote my first private letter to your lordship. There was a general opinion prevailing that they had it in their power to distress the kingdom by withdrawing their commerce from it and that there was not the least danger of any compulsory measures to cause obedience to any Acts or Orders respecting them. In this colony there was room to hope for a change of circumstances but it was uncertain and probably at a distance.

They had just felt the shock of that most fortunate stroke which freed the Castle from any dependence upon the people and kept the harbour and town of Boston under the command of the King's ships, but the effects did not appear. I was striving for a just decision in the case of the soldiers and not without hopes, but far from being certain, of success. There was a prospect of the dissolution of the confederacies against importation though several of the colonies appeared to be more resolute and confirmed. There was also an expectation of a rupture between Great Britain and France or Spain or both, which would tend to show the people their dependence upon the kingdom and the reasonableness of their submission to the supreme authority of it.

I was not insensible of the peculiar defects in the constitution of this province and I have complained of the Council as being under undue influence and casting their weight into that scale which had much too great proportion before; but I was doubtful myself, and I found some judicious persons in whom I could confide to be doubtful also, whether while the body of the people continued in the state they were then in such Councillors as should be appointed by the Crown would dare to undertake the trust, or if they should do it whether the people in general would not refuse to submit to their authority, and I feared the consequences of either would more than countervail the advantages which would arise merely from an alteration in the constitution if accomplished.   '

To this state of our affairs and a mind influenced by it, I beg your lordship to attribute that want of determination which appeared in my private letters and not to any degree of unwillingness to trust with your lordship my real sentiments upon any occasion whatsoever.

The change in the temper of the people has been brought about sooner and to a greater degree than anybody could expect, and we seem now to be as well-prepared either to receive such a change in the constitution as we probably shall be at any time hereafter, or if it shall be thought more eligible to defer it we may probably remain in tolerable good order until such time as shall be judged more convenient, provided something is done in the meantime which shall discover the resentment of the kingdom against our avowed principles and the practices consequent upon them, and which shall give us cause to imagine that farther measures are to be taken with us. Such resentment has been everywhere expected; if omitted, we shall go back to our former disorders.

That wise step of changing the garrison at the Castle began our cure. In the heighth of our confusion a citadel upon Fort Hill seemed also to be necessary. I now think the same end is answered without it as would have been with it. It may however not be improper for the King to have the actual possession of that spot, either by erecting at a small expense a warehouse or magazine for stores or by making some kind of enclosure to restrain from encroachments, and yet not prevent the inhabitants from using the place to walk and air themselves in as they now frequently do. There is a vote of the town for selling it. I will watch their motions, and if anything farther is attempted will take public notice of it. If no farther advances are made for securing the good behaviour of the town there certainly will be no receding. To depart suddenly from what has been done at the Castle etc. would be very dangerous.

Every Act of Parliament carried into execution in the colonies tends to strengthen government there. A firm persuasion that Parliament is determined at all events to maintain its supreme authority is all we want: few or none are now so weak as to question their power to do it. If Acts were passed more or less to control us every session we should soon be familiarized to them and our erroneous opinions would die away and peace and order would revive.

An Act to enable the King to alter the bounds of the province by his commission, the charter notwithstanding, by making the province of Main and country east of it a distinct and separate province, and to annex or not annex as His Majesty may think fit New Hampshire to the Massachusetts, or to separate the country east of Penobscot and annex it to Nova Scotia, might either be kept as a rod over us and a security for our good behaviour until the King's pleasure should be determined; or if it should be executed immediately it would show a just resentment against the province for countenancing the intrusions in the eastern country whereby the King's timber is exposed to waste and havoc, and it would be a striking instance of the power and authority of Parliament.

The Act would be executed, for nobody would risk their property or be concerned in any judicial proceedings relative to it under a jurisdiction assumed contrary to an Act of Parliament, seeing such proceedings sooner or later will be deemed a nullity.

If no exception be taken to the vesting such a discretionary power in the Crown, perhaps it may be thought expedient whenever the charter and case of the province comes under consideration, instead of expressly declaring that the power of electing Councillors by the Assembly shall determine and cease, to enable His Majesty by his royal Order or declaration to determine it and to appoint a Council instead thereof as he may think proper.

The late Act permitting the issuing bills of credit at New York was extremely well-adapted to maintaining the authority of Parliament,

65207

The Library
Colby College-New Hampshire
New London, New Hampshire

and others of the like nature might be mentioned as convenient to be passed here.

I hope to receive your lordship's directions concerning the two officers at the Castle which I thought necessary for His Majesty's service to continue in pay, and which is all the expense I have occasioned since the withdraw of the garrison.

I took the liberty to mention to your lordship the case of Capt. Phillips, the late commanding officer at the Castle. He is without support for himself and family and is by far the greatest sufferer of any belonging to the late garrison, his place being worth between two and three hundred pounds sterling a year.

I hope the rest of the garrison being scattered abroad will never occasion any charge to the Crown. He presses me very hard and though his removal was absolutely necessary and I did my duty, yet as I was the immediate instrument his case affects me more sensibly, and this is all which moves me to apply in his behalf, having no sort of connexion with him. I could not refuse his request to transmit to your lordship his petition [not found] to the King but I let him know it must be presented or suppressed just as your lordship should think fit. As it respected his military post I was in doubt of the propriety of his address to His Majesty in Council, but if those words are necessary I have authority from him to pray they may be added.

I am taking every measure in my power consistent with the honour of government to reconcile civil and military, Whigs and Tories, and we begin to be sensible that it must be a very bad constitution indeed which is not preferable to the savage state we have been in for some years past. *Entry* [C.O.5/246, p. 2]

X

Governor William Tryon to Earl of Hillsborough (No. 60)

31 January, Newbern

My lord, since my letter of the 20 of October last [Vol. II, No. CVIII] I have been discouraged from communicating the occurrences of this government so frequently as your lordship probably might expect, occasioned by the vast uncertainty of the issue of events depending from the opening of the last session of Assembly on the 5th of December to the proroguing of the same on the 26 instant to the 10th May next. I here transmit my speech and the addresses of both Houses [Vol. I, No. 956ii, iv-v], and can with satisfaction assure your lordship that the principal matters recommended to the Assembly have been duly considered and every step taken that the circumstances of the country would admit of towards the reformation of the abuses in the government and the restoration of the public tranquillity. Six bills I rejected and passed forty-four: these will be copied and transmitted with all expedition as well as the Journals of both Houses and the Minutes of the Council in order to lay before the King. From these materials the justest view of the present state of this country may be collected.

Hermon Husbands, the late Representative of Orange County, after having his conduct fully examined into before the House of

Assembly, was voted a disturber of the public peace and expelled the House the 20th of December accordingly, as by resolves enclosed [Vol. I, No. 956i].

The evening of the same day I proposed to His Majesty's Council the expediency of preventing him from returning into the back-settlements to inflame anew the insurgents by his seditious practices. The Chief Justice issued his warrant to apprehend him for publishing a libel against one of the Associate Judges (no testimony then being present to prove him an accessory to the riots at Hillsborough) and he was that night put into Newbern gaol and has been confined there ever since under a guard, no bail and security for his behaviour having been offered for his enlargement. It seems yet doubtful what are the determinations of the insurgents and in what manner they will execute them. An attempt to rescue Husbands is yet expected.

The returns I required from the commanding officers of the several regiments of militia of such men as were willing to turn out in defence of their King and country were in many counties unanimous in support of that glorious cause, and through the whole country very favourable on the side of government. As soon as the many beneficial laws that were enacted last session are published through the province, they will tend much to quiet the general discontents of the inhabitants and probably make it less difficult for administration to suppress the insurgents in the back-frontiers who have been greatly upheld by the seditious reports industriously spread through the whole country.

I herewith transmit to your lordship a copy [Vol. I, No. 956iii] of the Bill to prevent Riots and Tumults, being a bill of the first importance. A special Court of Oyer and Terminer is to be held next week in this town under this law where some of the principal rioters will be indicted. This I apprehend will bring the distractions of this country to a crisis as the parties must either take their trials or be in a state of outlawry. Thus you see, my lord, the situation of this country is very unsettled, and as yet uncertain what turn the public affairs will take, consequently no positive conclusions can be drawn from the present posture of affairs. They however carry a much more favourable aspect than before the session, government being much strengthened by the Acts of the legislature then ratified.

That I may be enabled on my return to England to make His Majesty a fair report of a happy termination of the disorders of this his province is the sanguine wish and earnest endeavours of, my lord, your lordship's most obedient and most obliged humble servant. *Signed.* [C.O.5/314, fo. 29]

XI

Inhabitants of Pleasant River to Governor Thomas Hutchinson[1]

[4 February]
The petition of the inhabitants of the Fifth Township granted by

1 Undated. Enclosed in Governor Hutchinson's letter of 4 February to Hillsborough, Vol. I, No. 959.

this province to eastward of Mount Desart and commonly called Pleasant River humbly sheweth to your Excellency.

That whereas there is now residing in this township upwards of sixty families and neither law nor Gospel embraced among us, everyone doing what's right in his own eyes and a great spirit of mobbing and rioting prevails, cursing, swearing, fighting, threatening, stealing, pulling down houses and the like as we can't sleep a'nights without fear, and living to such a distance from any authority that we labour under a great disadvantage of obtaining relief in such matters, being twenty miles to the eastward of Goldsboro' and upwards of twenty miles westward of Machias and very difficult passing anyway, makes us apply to your Excellency to interpose in this affair to redress our grievances; and we whose names are hereunto subscribed humbly implore your Excellency that you would appoint a Justice of the Peace at Pleasant River as it is our sincere and hearty desire to live under a proper regulation of the common laws of the land, and there is one Capt. Wilmot Woss, a man of good reputation who removed from Martha's Vineyard about three years ago and has a good interest in this township whom we recommend to your Excellency to be appointed if you in your goodness shall think proper with the advice of the Council. And we pray your Excellency to lay this our petition before our said Council as soon as possible as we flatter ourselves of your Excellency's protection of our civil rights as far as the due execution of the law will give us, which causes us to apply to your Excellency to cause them to be put in force, as we profess ourselves to be loyal subjects and are ready to spend our lives and fortunes for His Majesty's Crown and dignity and the laws and good government, as your petitioners are in duty bound to pray for.

NB. If your Excellency shall think proper to appoint any other suitable person we have no objection. *Copy*, certified by T. Hutchinson. *Signatories*, Moses Plumer and 31 others. [C.O.5/760, fo. 123]

XII

President William Nelson to Earl of Hillsborough (No. 11)

5 February, Virginia

My Lord, your lordship's circular letter of the 15th of November [Vol. II, No. CXX] I have received and lost no time in laying it before the Council for their advice. It is but too true that many abuses and violences have been committed on the Indians by the traders and frontier-inhabitants; but it happens fortunately for the colony of Virginia that the legislature last year adopted and prosecuted as far as it was in their power the very measure your lordship has so warmly recommended. For, upon the receipt of letters from several of the governors of the Northern provinces, of which I send the copies [Vol. I, No. 963i] and which Lord Botetourt laid before the Assembly, they passed the Act of which I now enclose your lordship a copy [Vol. I, No. 963iii], and in consequence of it two commissioners went from hence to New York, the place, and at the time, appointed by those letters; stayed three weeks, saw none but the gentlemen of that province, not the governor who was not in town, and did not even hear of any other commissioners being expected there; so that they were obliged to return *re infecta*. However, as soon as I can hear from Sir William Johnson, to whom I now write, or the Northern governors of any other time and place being fixed for forming a plan to regulate the Indian trade and to prevent that pernicious practice of carrying spirituous liquors among the Indians, I will prevail with the commissioners from hence to attend at the congress. But I own, my lord, I almost despair of success in any attempts to stop the traders from carrying rum to them when I consider how bewitching the passion for strong drink is among the lower and unthinking part of mankind, in so much that it is one of the greatest evils, I am told, in England which cannot be suppressed by all the wisdom of the wisest legislature in the world; and how can it be expected that any law, made by the Assemblies to stop the progress of such an abuse that is committed at the distance of perhaps an hundred miles from any magistrate who hath a power to punish, can do it? yet it is our duty to try to do something effectual.

In order to show your lordship that this government hath taken every possible method to bring to justice the perpetrators of the violences and murders committed on the Indians, I also enclose an extract [Vol. I, No. 963ii] of the proceedings of the Council on the subject of this nature. The murder mentioned therein appearing to Lord Botetourt to have been committed within the limits of Pennsylvania, his lordship sent the man thither to be tried. What became of him afterwards I have not learned. Permit me, my lord, to observe that the line between His Majesty and Mr Penn seems to be an object worthy of consideration. *Signed.* [C.O.5/1349, fo. 56]

XIII

Alexander Cameron to John Stuart[1]

8 February, Fort Prince George

Sir, I set out from Long Cane on the 2 instant and was overtaken in the night by Captain Smith and a party of men to intercept a wagon with some guns and ammunition which I had for the Indians. I however dissuaded them from it and arrived here on the 4th. No people were ever struck with a greater panic than the frontier inhabitants by the authority of some traders and packhorsemen who are continually running away from the nation and frightening each other on the smallest occasion. I endeavoured to animate the people and assured them that I did not believe there was any immediate danger, and that as I was going into the nation I would give them the earliest intelligence in case of any rupture, but all to no purpose. Some trader or packhorseman every day running into the settlement augmented their fears that they began to [?leave the] fort and run away as fast as they could, although Mr Wilkinson endeavoured to persuade them to remain in the nation and not run into the settlements to frighten the people there.

I am, however, informed that on the arrival of the Northerns in

---

1 Enclosed in John Stuart's letter of 5 March to Hillsborough, Vol. I, No. 1032.

the Cherokee nation, they proposed to the Great Warrior to strike the white people but that he would not agree. They then offered to go against the Creeks, he likewise persuaded them from it; at length they proposed the Chikesaws, which was agreed to by the Great Warrior as they had lately killed some of his people, and accordingly the Northerns and some Cherokees departed in boats down the river to strike the poor Chikesaws.

My horses are ready packed to set out immediately for the Overhills. I shall endeavour by every method to make up the breach between them and the Chikesaws and increase that if possible between them and the Westerns.

I talked yesterday to the warriors of the Lower Towns and told them that we included the Chikesaws in the last peace and that it was contrary to that treaty to strike them at this time. The Little Carpenter replied that the Chikesaws were the first aggressors and that they could not be blamed for revenging the death of their people. I wrote you before, sir, that the Cherokees promised, and particularly the Carpenter, to settle matters with the Chikesaws this spring and once more to renew their friendship, that they have been swayed by the Westerns to the contrary. More of those Indians are expected daily and the headmen of the different Cherokee towns are to be summoned to hear what they have to say. The Mankiller of Little Chote corroborates what Tuckassie informed me relative to the Creeks and that some of their headmen are actually gone to New Orleans. They threaten the English in the spring, and it is likely that if they should be supported by any nation, white or red, they will execute their design. *Copy.* [C.O.5/72, fo. 171]

XIV

Earl of Hillsborough to Governor Thomas Hutchinson (No. 4)

11 February, Whitehall

Sir, I have received and laid before the King your letters Nos. 32 and 33 [Vol. I, Nos. 774, 830].

The acquittal of Manwaring and the three other persons who were tried with him appears to have been founded in justice, and it will be very fortunate if any method can be found out for the detection and punishment of so gross a perjury as seems to have been committed by the persons who have appeared against him.

The instructions for your guidance in the administration of government are now under the consideration of the Board of Trade, and I have no doubt but that their lordships will recommend such alterations to be made from those given to Sir Francis Bernard as shall apply to the present state of the colony and be judged proper for controlling those irregularities which the disorders of the late times have introduced to the prejudice of the constitution.

I will not venture to anticipate their lordships' resolutions on this subject by suggesting everything which may be on this occasion an object of their attention, but it may be some satisfaction to you to know that they appear to be fully impressed with an opinion that there is an absolute necessity that the Crown should in these instructions declare its sentiments fully not only against the extravagant claim of the Council of acting as a Council of State separate from the governor, but also that the possession of the King's Castle at Boston by the King's troops is to be considered in no other light than that of a trust committed to them by the governor of the province in consequence of orders from His Majesty for that purpose. *Draft*. [C.O.5/760, fo. 7]

XV

Oucconnastotah to John Stuart[1]

12 February, Toqueh
Beloved Father, two days ago I was informed that there prevails a talk among our traders and their people that we were joining the Norths to go to war against the white people, and upon that strength several packhorsemen went down from the country and I suppose will alarm the settlement. It is true there came a good many Norths here to strengthen the friendship between us and them, and we are very much beholden to both our beloved fathers who had assisted us in making peace between us and them. You know when I saw you last fall we made everything straight and parted one from another well contented. If it should happen that any bad talks about us should be raised, don't believe them, there is no truth in them.

Beloved father, there is you and General Johnson who made peace for us, between us and the Norths. The Norths came here to go to war against the Choctaws. I wanted to stop them but they told me that their father, General Johnson, gave them liberty to go against the Choctaws. I want very much to know if you are as well agreed that the Norths should go to war against Choctaws, or if it is only General Johnson? I love the Choctaws as well as I do the white people. If you don't know anything about it, let me know and ask General Johnson if he gave them liberty.

The Norths came in my town with the hatchet in their hand and said their father, General Johnson, put it in their hands to make use of it against the Choctaws; therefore I could not take it out of their hands as their father put it himself into their hands. In the same time that General Johnson should have told them to get powder here of the white people, but I told them that the white people have no powder at present. In the spring I shall hear from you when you have answer from General Johnson. I hold you with both my hands, beloved father. *Copy*. [C.O.5/72, fo. 223]

XVI

Sir William Johnson to Earl of Hillsborough (No. 15)

18 February, Johnson Hall
My Lord, since I had the honour to receive your lordship's letters, Nos. 14 and 15 [Vol. I, Nos. 646, 726], the last of which came to my

---

1 Enclosed in John Stuart's letter of 27 April to Hillsborough, Vol. III, No. XXXVIII.

hands a few days since, I waited to receive such informations as I
had reason to expect from the southward in order to communicate
the same through your lordship to His Majesty. Advices I have now
received enable me to acquaint you that the great council lately held
at the plains of Sioto is ended, that the design and endeavours of the
Indians in that quarter was to promote such a union as I before apprehended and endeavoured with all possible caution to obstruct; but that
the advice given to those of the Northern alliance, joined to their
private aversion for some of the rest, had occasioned it to end after
many debates in general resolutions for promoting peace among all
the nations as a necessary introduction to a more strict alliance between
the Northern and Southern people, which is to have for its object some
particular undertaking for which matters did not appear during the
congress sufficiently ripe; and of this I can have no reason to doubt
from the present maxims of policy and sentiments adopted by the
more belligerent nations of both alliances. The deputies which were
sent from the Northern confederacy with sundry belts etc. from them
and myself, agreeable to the resolutions at the treaty I held last July
at the German Flats, met the Indians from Sioto at Fort Pitt in December last, and have agreeable to their instructions in a spirited speech
summoned them all to reassemble at Sioto without delay, when and
not before they would communicate to them the determined resolutions
of the Northern Indians entered into at the German Flats Treaty
together with the subject of the embassy on which they have one
hundred belts. As I have great confidence both in the fidelity and
abilities of several of these deputies, I have good hopes that when they
meet those nations to whom they have been sent, they will be able to
defeat any dangerous schemes or resolutions which are yet in view in
that country and awaken those nations' fears who have given offence to
the Northern confederacy which will prove a sufficient check to their
other designs, and if I am disappointed in my expectations it must be
through some accident or occurrence against which no provision can
be made at this time.

The apprehensions which I long since communicated of an union
between the Northern and Southern Indians, and which your lordship
makes particular mention of in your letter No. 14, is really a matter
of the most serious nature; for if a very small part of these people have
been capable of reducing us to such straits as we were in a few years
since, what may we not expect from such a formidable alliance as we
are threatened with, when at the same time it is well known that we
are not at this time more capable of defence, if so much, as at the former
period? This is in some measure the consequence of their becoming
better acquainted with their own strength and united capacity to
preserve their importance and check our advance into their country,
for at the beginning of the late war through the rapid advances for some
time made by the French etc. the Indians did really conceive that we
should be totally reduced; but as they discovered the increased population of this country even in the midst of its distresses, and that our
army was still recruited with fresh regiments, their sentiments altered,
they began to entertain more respectable ideas of us and of our re-

sources, and through the imprudence of our own people and their natural suspicions have gradually become more and more alarmed for themselves, though they still believe that it is in their power to give us such a check as may prevent us from attempting what they apprehend we have in view. Many will talk, some will think, and a lesser number will act otherwise, but this is nevertheless the true political state of their sentiments in general at present. As I know the nature of their unions, and that the Southern Indians found many of the rest insufficient employment during the long war that subsisted between them, so I could not help suggesting my apprehensions of the consequences of the peace I had orders to effect between these people; but the laws of humanity, the entreaty of the Southern Indians, and the earnest desire of some colonies who represented themselves as affected by that war, being powerful considerations, prevailed over what might be judged as a distant or simple apprehension. I sincerely wish it may not contribute to any ill consequence, and shall constantly and steadily use all the means in my power to prevent it; but although it may be treated as a chimera at this time, yet I can positively assure your lordship that both Spaniards and French, the latter of whom act the part of agents, did and do still continue to make presents to all the nations to whom they can have any access by the rivers which discharge themselves into the Mississippi, and that they do constantly endeavour to thwart our measures by various stories and misrepresentations, which being supported by favours and coming from a people of whom they entertain no apprehensions, against a people from whom most of the Indians imagine they have everything to fear, renders it almost impossible to prevent them from having some effect.

The Indians have for some time discovered that a war is probably at hand, many of them think that it has already commenced but that we conceal it from them on account of some advantages the enemy has gained, and in consequence of this during last week I was visited by deputations from most of the Six Nations, to whom I gave such answers as I judged best calculated for the purpose in any event that may happen in Europe. If a war commences and that any attempts are made in America, or in case the Indians should be seduced to disturb our frontiers to draw part of our attention that way, I am confident (as I formerly proposed) that I can from the measures I have taken and the influence I possess secure and attach to our interest, if empowered so to do, such a body of Indians as if not so numerous as those against us will give a severe check to their attempts; and as the distant Indians dread nothing so much at present as a quarrel amongst themselves, I am equally confident that the very appearance of some in the character of vigorous allies will in any quarrel, whether through the intrigues of a European power or of a confederacy amongst the Indians themselves, prove greatly advantageous to us and tend to defeat their purposes as much as any measures that can be adopted, which I most humbly submit to your lordship's consideration in case my apprehensions should be realised by future events or occurrences.

In consequence of a former letter wherein your lordship signified His Majesty's inclination that the Indian boundary line should be continued from where it was made to terminate by the treaty of 1768 (at Canada Creek *alias* Wood Creek) I have conferred with the chiefs of the nations interested, over whom I have in general so far prevailed that I believe they will when assembled for that purpose admit of its extension far to the northward, perhaps to the River St Lawrence. I therefore hope to be honoured with instructions respecting my conduct previous to my taking any farther steps therein. *Signed*. [C.O.5/72, fo. 183]

XVII

Governor William Tryon to Colonel Richard Caswell[1]

18 February, Newbern

Your dispatches of the 17th and 18th instant have been punctually received with the enclosures. I am much obliged to you for the prudent disposition you have made of your men and the active spirit you discover in these critical times. The assurances you give me of the cheerful resolution of your own and the neighbouring regiments in support of government afford me the fullest assurance that we shall by their united aid be enabled to chastize the insolence of any who shall dare to offer any future violence to the persons or properties of His Majesty's subjects in this province. The laws in force I trust in their operation will countenance us in that cause as well as redress the injuries already committed.

I hope to hear from you tomorrow by noon whether the insurgents are actually on their march or not, as I propose tomorrow afternoon to dismiss the Craven Regiment at present assembled if I do not hear the insurgents are on their march, concluding I shall have sufficient time to reassemble them at a short notice should there be future occasion for them. I think it is not impossible the insurgents may attempt to come down in a body with such of their party as they find stand indicted under the late law in order to protect them on their trials.

When you are upon a certainty that the insurgents are not on their march you may dismiss your men, cautioning them to hold themselves in readiness to turn out again on the first notice you may find it necessary to give them, which at the distance I am from you must be left discretionary with yourself. *Entry*. [C.O.5/314, fo. 239d]

1 From Governor Tryon's letter-book, enclosed with letter of 2 August to Hillsborough, Vol. I, No. 1434.

XVIII

John Stuart to Alexander Cameron[1]

23 February, Charleston

Sir, I am extremely glad to be informed of your being in the nation by your letter of 8 instant [Vol. III, No. XIII] which I received yesterday, being forwarded to me per express from Ninety Six, and this goes by the same conveyance.

1 Enclosed in John Stuart's letter of 5 March to Hillsborough, Vol. I, No. 1032.

The situation in which you found affairs coincides with the ideas which I had formed from the behaviour of the Cherokees at the late meetings. I could not conceive them to be such profound dissemblers as to carry such fair looks whilst mischief lurked at their hearts, but upon Mcdonald's desertion of his post and carrying off his grandchild I was alarmed. I sincerely wish you may succeed in turning the arms of the Cherokees and their allies from the Chikesaws. I wish they had chose rather to have struck the Creeks, but Oucconnastotah and his nation would rather avoid hard blows and gallantly turn their united force against a weak foe. As you have copies of both General Gage's last letters, you'll be fully informed by perusing them attentively of the confederacies formed by the Western and Northern tribes and the principles by which each party is actuated, which will direct you in pursuing proper measures for His Majesty's service. You must therefore be careful to distinguish between the Northern and Western Indians and their views. From the state of Indian affairs in the Northern District as contained in the above referred to letters, I cannot conceive that the Northern Indians should want to strike the white people, for such a step would be directly contrary to the principles of their nations who unite to support their cession of land to Sir William Johnson and to compel the Western tribes to acquiesce in it; and as you say that there were Shawnese over the mountains, I must conclude that the proposal for striking the white people was made by them, and they are at the head of the Western confederacy which is formed upon the principle of maintaining their property in the lands obtained from the Six Nations at Fort Stanwix and preventing their being settled by the white people. You'll therefore be very particular in informing yourself who those Indians are and what nations they are of, also the names of the principal persons amongst them, what tokens or credentials they bring and their errand. You will conceive it our interest to unite the Cherokees to the Northern confederacy if you find their views to be such as we imagine, and if you succeed in accommodating matters between them and the Chikesaws I doubt not but the latter would be brought to join the Northern confederacy in which event the Creeks would be awed, especially as the war between them and the Choctaws still continues.

I am obliged to Tuckassie and the Mankiller of Chote for their intelligence concerning the Creeks. The Catawbas are summoned to a meeting with the Cherokees and there will be in all probability a number of Creeks there also. If the strangers in the Overhills are Westerns the talks will be bad, if Northerns the proposal will be to unite against the Westerns.

These are my ideas: your situation will enable you to judge how far they are right or wrong, and in conducting yourself you must be directed by the situation in which you find matters. I depend on your giving me full and particular information as soon as possible, which will in some measure point out the steps to be taken by me while here. *Copy*. [C.O.5/72, fo. 169]

XIX

Governor William Tryon to Thomas McGwire[1]

27 February, Newbern

The favour of your letter reached me the 2nd instant by which I was sorry to learn you was indisposed. As I know you are a skilful doctor to your friends I make no doubt but you have been before this a successful physician to yourself. I took the liberty to retain your servant three days here in expectation that the witnesses from Hillsborough would have attended agreeable to subpoenas, but they failing perhaps through intimidation, Mr Chief Justice finishes the present court tomorrow, and immediately after I shall grant a commission for a new Court of Oyer and Terminer to open the 11th of next month when evidences will be ordered to appear, for which purpose Mr Edwards sets off tomorrow for Hillsborough. Though Mr Gordon is retained it would give me much satisfaction to have you on the spot, therefore depend on seeing you in Newbern before the 11th of March.

I this day acquainted Mr Howard in Council that I conceived His Majesty's service required and the dignity of government demanded that Mr Chief Justice, his Associates and Mr Attorney-General should all attend in person the Hillsborough Superior Court on the 22nd of March next, and that if he was of opinion the Riot Law was not sufficient to secure the court from insult any number of troops should be provided for the protection of the court that the Council should think necessary. I am therefore under an obligation to require your personal attendance at the next court at Hillsborough, being sensible it is a duty important and incumbent on you as well as the judges at this time to attend. Mr Howard purposes setting out after the indictments are found, Mr Henderson is at present ill of the flux but trusts nothing will prevent his meeting you the 22nd of March at Hillsborough though he should not be able to attend here the eleventh of next month.

The Regulators were all in Hillsborough the 16th instant, the inhabitants flying into the woods. They kept master of the town till two o'clock at noon when they marched out in triumph, drums beating, without doing any injury to the town. This forbearance I attribute to the virtue of the Riot Law, a hopeful beginning. When I have the pleasure to see you here I shall have other matters for your consideration touching the association. I have accepted Mr Jones's service on the part of the Crown for the trials of such insurgents as may surrender themselves and I have wrote to him thereon. *Entry.* [C.O.5/314, fo. 244]

1   From Governor Tryon's letter book, enclosed with letter of 2 August to Hillsborough, Vol. I, No. 1434.

XX

Affidavit of Ebenezer Cole[1]

27 February, New York City

Ebenezer Cole, aged fifty-nine, being duly sworn maketh oath that between seven and eight years ago he purchased some rights in a

1   Enclosed in Earl of Dunmore's letter of 9 March to Hillsborough, Vol. III, No. XXVI.

tract of land called Shaftsbury under a grant thereof by the late governor of New Hampshire, that he settled thereon six years ago last spring and was one of the first who settled in Shaftsbury under the grant aforesaid, that between this deponent's purchasing and settlement abovementioned Governor Colden issued his proclamation of the 28th December 1763 which was soon publicly known in that part of the country.

That he has resided there ever since and well remembers that Governor Colden and the late governor of New Hampshire notified by proclamation the King's determination of the boundary between the provinces of New York and New Hampshire, both of which pro-clamations were publicly known in that part of the country.

That at the time this deponent settled there as aforesaid, there were but two persons settled to the northward of him on any grants of New Hampshire to the westward of the Green Mountains, though this deponent's house lays within thirteen miles of the north bounds of the Massachusetts Bay. That at the time of the notification as aforesaid of His Majesty's determination this deponent believes there might be about twenty-five persons settled to the northward of Shaftsbury and not more and about as many in Shaftsbury, all but one of whom this deponent believes were purchasers and not original grantees.

That by far the greater part of the settlers at this day, which this deponent believes are at least five to one to the number of settlers at that time, are purchasers since the notification of the determination of the boundary at very small rates and who have seated themselves there under the New Hampshire grants, knowing the claim of this province and His Majesty's determination aforesaid, a considerable number of whom have purchased on condition never to pay the pur-chase-money except the New Hampshire title is made good, this deponent having been witness to some of those contracts himself, and that many of them have settled within the ancient grants of the province of New York, well knowing at the time they were within the said ancient grants and against advice given them to the contrary by this deponent and others. And this deponent saith that he doth not know that any one person is settled on the lands granted to him by Governor Went-worth.

That within a short time after the notification of the royal deter-mination as aforesaid the inhabitants in general of that part of the country claiming under New Hampshire concluded to keep up and maintain the privileges mentioned in their grants from New Hampshire and not to submit to any laws, customs or usages of the government of New York, imagining this would strengthen their pretensions, which they maintained among other things by declaring that the King's Order of Council of 20 July 1764 was not of sufficient authority. And accordingly they chose selectmen for the townships, held frequent town-meetings pursuant to their charters and made the laws of New Hampshire the rules of their conduct which in general they have per-sisted in ever since.

And this deponent further saith that he well remembers to have heard several persons, settlers in the part of the country aforesaid under grants of New Hampshire, declare that they had tied up and publicly whipped one Moore who was sent by the proprietors of Prince Town patent to settle thereon under the New York title, and according to the best of his remembrance they at the same time threatened to serve every person in the like manner who should come there on the like errand.

That he has always understood and is satisfied that it is true that the proprietors under New York have always been disposed to treat the settlers on their lands under New Hampshire with tenderness and to give them better terms than to other persons, which tenderness and forbearance has been constantly construed by the settlers to arise solely from the proprietors under New York doubting the validity of their own title and has constantly increased the spirit of opposition in the settlers under New Hampshire who took up the opinion that the New York proprietors were afraid to bring actions against them.

That this deponent's purchases under the New Hampshire grants have been saved to him by the government of New York in consequence of an order of the Governor and Council of the 22nd May 1765, a copy of which this deponent in the summer of that year carried up into that country together with orders from the Surveyor-General to his deputy, Archibald Campbell, to survey the possessions of all the settlers under New Hampshire within any warrant of survey that he had already received or should thereafter come to his hands, which order of Council this deponent made public among those inhabitants and endeavoured to persuade them to accept the benefits intended them thereby; but that in general they refused. That the said Archibald Campbell was then making surveys in that part of the country and offered to several persons in the deponent's presence to survey their possessions, and divers others have confessed to the deponent that the said Campbell had made the said offers to them, but all of them except this deponent and about a dozen persons more refused to show their boundaries or take any notice of it, declaring they would not consent to pay the quitrent reserved by the New York grants nor put themselves to any further charge about their title; among the persons so refusing was Isaiah Carpenter against whom a recovery has been lately obtained in ejectment wherein Major Small, a reduced officer, was lessor of the plaintiff in whose grant the possessions of the said Carpenter was situate.

That this deponent remembers that about a year ago nine ejectments were brought under New York for lands to the westward of the Green Mountains, one of them against the said Isaiah Carpenter, another against Justin Olin who had settled on Major Small's said grant, knowing it was granted to Major Small, having purchased under New Hampshire since the passing of the Major's grant, and upon condition not to pay his purchase-money unless his title was secured to him under New Hampshire, another against James Breakenridge who had settled on the Wallumschack patent, four against persons in Prince Town, and two against some persons on a grant of this province of New York to the Rev. Michael Slaughter, a reduced regimental chaplain; that thereupon the inhabitants of this part of the country in general declared those suits were only brought to frighten them and that they never would be tried.

That this deponent attended the Circuit Court held last June in the city of Albany when four of these ejectments were tried vizt. those against James Breakenridge, Samuel Rose one of the Prince Town defendants, Isaiah Carpenter, and Josiah Fuller one of the inhabitants on the grant to the Rev. Mr Slaughter; that Breakenridge made no defence, his possession being within twenty miles from Hudson's River; against the other three verdicts were found by special juries on trials that appeared wholly fair to this deponent and to some of the leading persons interested under New Hampshire, and particularly to one Bliss Willoughby who acted there as trustee for the New Hampshire claimants. And this deponent well remembers that after the said trials some of the defendants and many other of the leading people under the claim of New Hampshire went to some of the proprietors under New York then in Albany, owned their title to be good, confessed their moderation, and declared they could only blame the government of New Hampshire for granting these lands and themselves for contending against the New York proprietors.

That many of the claimants under New Hampshire in consequence of those trials proposed settling their dispute with the New York proprietors, but the writs of possession being delayed they in general changed their minds and declared the New York proprietors dared not to serve them, and from the common and public conversation of those inhabitants it was manifest to this deponent that they had confederated to support each other by force of arms.

That about the beginning of January last the sheriff of Albany, as this deponent hath understood in the neighbourhood and verily believes, came to execute writs of possession for the farms recovered in the said ejectments, and that he was resisted by a number of armed men who by force prevented entirely his serving his writs on the possessions of Breakenridge and Fuller, and that he returned to Albany without executing them. And that this deponent has in like manner been informed and believes that the next day thereafter the sheriff's deputy executed the processes on the farm of Samuel Rose and Isaiah Carpenter but not without a violent resistance by a number of armed men.

And this deponent saith that he has never heard of any other ejectment being brought for any lands to the westward of the Green Mountains claimed under New Hampshire except one against one Colvin which was served but not further prosecuted.

That the deponent is acquainted in general with all the inhabitants of the lands formerly claimed by New Hampshire on the west side of the Green Mountains from the line of the Massachusetts Bay to the most northern settlements and knows not of one person among them who served in His Majesty's regular forces at any time whatsoever and that very few of them ever served in any of the provincial forces.

And this deponent further saith that soon after the present governor of New Hampshire arrived in that government the inhabitants of the lands granted under New Hampshire in the neighbourhood of the deponent were animated with hopes that the royal order of 20th July 1764 might be rescinded; that messengers frequently from his arrival as aforesaid hitherto have been sent by them to Portsmouth to him and always returned with encouragements to the people that he would soon get them annexed to New Hampshire, and this deponent is well assured that if they had not received encouragements from the said Governor Wentworth they would in general long since have submitted to the laws and jurisdiction of the province of New York and the disputes concerning titles have been at an end. That something above a year ago a petition was carried about for subscription in the inhabited parts of the country within this province, formerly claimed by New Hampshire, addressed to the present governor of that province, requesting his assistance in obtaining the annexing that country to New Hampshire, which measure was commonly understood by the said inhabitants in the deponent's neighbourhood to have been undertaken by the instigation of Governor Wentworth and to have been drawn at Portsmouth and approved of by him before it circulated for subscription as aforesaid, of which besides the common report abovementioned this deponent has been informed by Samuel Robinson who was with Governor Wentworth at Portsmouth on that occasion, as he informed this deponent and which the deponent believes to be true.

That this last fall another petition addressed to His Majesty has been carried about in the deponent's neighbourhood as he understands and believes, which is generally reported there to have been done by the advice of Governor Wentworth.

And this deponent further saith that at the time of the notification as abovementioned of His Majesty's determination of the said boundary the two southermost townships were more cultivated than any other of the New Hampshire grants to the westward of the Green Mountains, and even with respect to those the cultivation was exceeding small, that the four next townships to the northward of those last mentioned had hardly any inhabitants and the clearing any part of them for cultivation was but scarcely begun, that the towns still to the northwards had no inhabitants, and that at that time [on] the lands aforesaid to the westward of the Green Mountains not one part in two thousand had had any labour bestowed on them, and that at this day the improvement and cultivation on the whole of the said tract is in comparison with its magnitude very inconsiderable. Sworn this 27th day of February 1771 before me, Daniel Horsmanden. *Copy.* [C.O.5/1102, fo. 96]

XXI

Affidavit of John Munro[1]

27 February, New York City

John Munro of Fowlis in the County of Albany, Esquire, one of His Majesty's Justices of the Peace for the said county being duly sworn maketh oath that he lives on the east side of Hudson's River about seventeen miles distant from the said river as the surveyor employed

---

1   Enclosed in Earl of Dunmore's letter of 9 March to Hillsborough, Vol. III, No. XXVI.

by him lately to measure the distance to that river informed him, that he began to build there near four years ago and has resided there near three years, that the deponent's house stands within the bounds of a tract of land called Shaftsbury said to have been granted by the late governor of New Hampshire.

That this deponent is well acquainted with the country thereabouts and verily believes that since he has lived there the number of settlers under the New Hampshire grants to the northward of this deponent's habitation have increased at least threefold, and from the general accounts he has received in that neighbourhood he is well satisfied that since the notification of His Majesty's Order in Council of 20 July 1764 those settlers have increased at least fivefold and that they are from all the information he has received purchasers for very small considerations and not patentees, and that many of them have purchased the New Hampshire titles to land which at the time of the purchases they knew had been granted by the government of New York, and particularly that such purchases have been made by about ten persons in a grant made by the said government of New York to Duncan McVicar, a reduced officer, by virtue of His Majesty's proclamation of the 7th October 1763, who have seated themselves on the said land and still hold possession under the New Hampshire grant.

That ever since this deponent has lived in that country many of the inhabitants have showed a disposition of not obeying the laws of New York or submitting to its jurisdiction and that in general they have regulated themselves by the laws of New Hampshire and the charters granted by the late Governor Wentworth, in order as this deponent hath always understood the more easy to bring about the annexing that country to New Hampshire and the confirmation of the grants of that government; that they accordingly have chosen selectmen and other officers and held town-meetings pursuant to the said charters.

And this deponent further saith that he was present at the riot and opposition made on the 19 of October 1769 to the commissioners and surveyor in the partition of part of Wallumsack patent, that he has perused the several depositions of Thomas Hun, John R. Bleecker and Peter Lansingh, the commissioners, containing an account of that obstruction and that the facts therein mentioned as far as they relate to the riotous behaviour on that day is true; that this deponent is the magistrate mentioned in those affidavits; that this deponent read to the rioters the Riot Act and commanded them in His Majesty's name to disperse, but neither that nor his persuasions to them had any effect until they had obliged the commissioners to desist.

And this deponent further saith that in the winter of the year 1770 by virtue of a law of this province he issued as one of His Majesty's Justices of the Peace for the County of Albany, on the application of two of His Majesty's subjects, process against four persons, all of whom this deponent understands live on the patent of Wallumschach and claim lands there under one of the New Hampshire grants; that the constable who had the charge of serving these processes made return to this deponent in writing which he and the other person made oath of before the deponent and a third person who was a Quaker affirmed the same, that a great number of persons, settlers thereabouts under the grants of New Hampshire having their faces blacked and otherwise being disguised assaulted him in the evening and rescued from him Moses Robinson whom he had arrested by virtue of one of the said precepts, and afterwards while he was the same evening in pursuit of the person rescued assaulted him again in the highway, that he in His Majesty's name commanded them to disperse and surrender up his prisoner, telling them they were acting against law, that thereupon they damned the laws of New York and said they had better laws of their own and finally obliged the said constable and his assistants to fly for their lives.

And this deponent further saith that since the obstruction given to the commissioners as abovementioned the universal report in that country hath been that the claimants under New Hampshire thereabouts had in general confederated to resist by force of arms the execution of the laws of New York which might affect their claims under New Hampshire and to oppose in like manner the apprehending of any of them for any offences relative thereto.

And this deponent further saith that on the twenty-ninth day of November last to this deponent's best remembrance Henry Ten Eyck Esq., the sheriff of the county of Albany, came to this deponent's house with a proclamation of his Excellency Lord Dunmore of the 1st November last by which the said sheriff was commanded to apprehend Silas Robinson and others for a second riot and obstruction to the partition of Wallumschack, that the said sheriff desired this deponent as a magistrate to attend on that service, the sheriff apprehending violent resistance, that this deponent went with him, keeping the woods as much as possible to prevent being discovered, to the house of Ebenezer Cole in whom this deponent placed confidence, that the said Cole and his son informed them that the people of Bennington expected the sheriff and were under arms, as they had been informed by many people passing the road, and one of them advised this deponent not to go. That nevertheless this deponent, the said sheriff and his deputy went to the northern bounds of Bennington where the said Silas Robinson dwelt and apprehended him at his own door, and immediately by the advice of the deponent to prevent a rescue immediately proceeded back for the city of Albany by the same road they had come, though the nearest road lay through Bennington which they thought it not prudent to follow, understanding the rioters were assembled about the house of one Stephen Fay in the town. That the same evening they lodged with their prisoner at the house of Captain Cornelius Van Ness at Sanchoick. That towards morning the house was surrounded by a number of armed men, about forty as this deponent has been informed. That this deponent asked them what they wanted and was answered they demanded Silas Robinson forthwith and that they would have him. That the persons in the house prepared for defence and this deponent sent a lad whom he put out of a window secretly to call the neighbours to their assistance, this being an old settlement. That this deponent told the rioters that if they wished themselves well they had better go off, that nevertheless they remained till dawn of day, this deponent expecting every minute they would force the house. At length as day approached they went off, discharging their arms, and soon after the sheriff proceeded with his prisoner, this deponent having procured him a party to escort him until he was out of danger.

And this deponent further saith that he remembers nine ejectments were brought by the proprietors under New York against the settlers under New Hampshire, against Samuel Rose and three others in Prince Town, Isaiah Carpenter and Justin Ollin on a tract granted in New York to Major Small, a reduced officer, James Breakenridge in Wallumschach patent, and against two other persons on a tract of land granted to the Reverend Michael Slaughter, a reduced regimental chaplain; that soon after this deponent heard frequent accounts that the claimants under New Hampshire declared the New York proprietors would never bring them to trial, and that they were only brought to frighten them into an agreement but that they were determined to make no terms with the New York proprietors.

That this deponent attended the Circuit Court last summer at Albany where four of these causes were tried; that Breakenridge made no defence and that in the three others verdicts were found by special juries for the plaintiffs; that these verdicts were to the general satisfaction of the country as well as to many of the leading men among the New Hampshire claimants, this deponent having heard Bliss Willoughby who was their agent for Shaftsbury and many others own the invalidity of their own claim under New Hampshire and acknowledge they did not suspect the New York claim was so good.

That upon this deponent's return home from the said trial and for some time thereafter he found the claimants under New Hampshire in his neighbourhood fond of coming to a settlement with the proprietors under New York, but that afterwards repeated encouragements being received in that quarter from the present governor of New Hampshire as the universal report was in that part of the country and which the deponent believes to be true, they declared they would hold their lands under the New Hampshire titles until they were defeated in England, and that soon thereafter a petition was handed about in his neighbourhood as this deponent has understood and believes for subscription in pursuance of some plan that had been fallen upon to annex these lands to New Hampshire, but to whom the petition was addressed or what were its contents this deponent knows not.

And this deponent further saith that in the month of December last he frequently heard it had been given out in his neighbourhood by the claimants under New Hampshire that the plaintiffs in the abovementioned causes in ejectment tried as aforesaid durst not serve the writs of possession.

That about the fifth day of January last the sheriff of Albany with one of his deputies and another person in his company came to this deponent's house, and this deponent having some short time before seen the said sheriff in Albany with writs of possession in his hands in the four actions of ejectment tried at Albany as aforesaid, the said sheriff now told him he had been trying to execute two of them against James Breakenridge and Josiah Fuller abovementioned but that he was opposed by a number of armed men who had shut themselves in the defendants' houses and threatened to blow his brains out if he proceeded, which as the sheriff informed the deponent prevented his executing either of them. That the said sheriff went the next day for Albany declaring his business obliged him to be there, the County Court coming on very soon. That he left his deputy at the deponent's house with the writs of possession against Samuel Rose and Isaiah Carpenter. That on Monday the seventh of January last the said deputy sheriff, with this deponent and twelve other men whom the deponent had procured to aid the deputy sheriff who feared a like violent resistance, proceeded to the house of the said Isaiah Carpenter in order to serve the said writ of possession against him. That when they came there they found the house shut up though it was early in the morning. That the sheriff knocked at the door and declared his business, upon which the said Isaiah Carpenter threatened to blow out the brains of any person who should attempt to take possession. That the deponent tried to persuade the said Isaiah Carpenter to open the door and not resist the execution of the laws but without effect. That thereupon the sheriff and his party proceeded to break into the house, which being effected in an instant, this deponent jumped in and seized the said Carpenter with his gun in his hand ready to fire, the sheriff and the rest of his party following this deponent. That they found two other men in the said house, claimants under New Hampshire, and two more guns in the corner of the room, one them loaded with powder and bullets, the other with powder and kidney-beans. That as soon as full possession was gained, it having by the attorney for the plaintiff been signified to the deponent that he might do as he pleased with the said Carpenter, and this deponent being assured the proprietor would be pleased with his showing the defendant tenderness, this deponent put the said Carpenter immediately into possession again on his giving bond either to agree with Major Small for the lands by the first day of May next or on failure thereof to surrender up the possession on demand.

That after this on the same day this deponent with the said deputy sheriff and another went to serve the writ of possession against the said Samuel Rose, and on the road picked up two other men whom they took along with them to assist them. That the sheriff went on before and got into the said house, the persons therein not knowing he was the sheriff, but by this time the neighbouring inhabitants having discovered them, this deponent observed a great number of persons making towards the house. That thereupon this deponent and one of the persons with him made their best way to the house which they found shut and was refused admittance, and about this time the sheriff in the house having discovered himself was, as he informed the deponent, attacked by a man with an axe, but a young woman interposed and thereupon the sheriff opened the door and this deponent went in.

That as soon as possession was gained here, the defendant being from home, the possession was restored to his wife and family by the directions of one of the proprietors on condition that it should be held under them; that the said Isaiah Carpenter has since voluntarily gone off his farm; and that Samuel Rose still is in possession of his.

That this complainant [*sic*] has never heard of any other ejectment brought against any of the claimants under New Hampshire except two lately sent up to be served under his direction and which he is certain are not yet served and one ejectment some time since brought against one Colvin, which though served this deponent hath understood and believes was no farther prosecuted.

And this deponent further saith that he hath never heard that any one person, claimant of lands under New Hampshire, hath been in prison in any suits brought against him by any of the New York proprietors or for any other matter than for criminal offences and for debt due to other persons, and this deponent verily believes that no such thing could have happened to any of those settlers to the westward of the Green Mountain without his hearing of it. Sworn this 27th day of February 1771, before me, Daniel Horsmanden. *Copy.* [C.O.5/1102, fo. 98]

XXII

Governor James Wright to Earl of Hillsborough (No. 55)

28 February, Savannah

My Lord, on the 21st instant I had the honour to receive your lordship's letter of the 11th of December, No. 35 [Vol. I, No. 820], and am to return my grateful acknowledgements for His Majesty's goodness and condescension in allowing me to issue writs to the four new parishes for the election of members to represent them in Assembly in case I shall think fit so to do after having taken the advice of the Council thereupon, and also for permitting me to give my assent to such an Election Bill as was proposed the last session except the clause limiting the duration of Assemblies.

But I am extremely sorry to acquaint your lordship that my apprehension of difficulties on account of those parishes not being *particularly* represented has been verified, and that on the very day before I received your lordship's letter the House of Assembly entered into a resolution that they would not order in a Tax Bill for the present year, the parishes of St David, St Patrick, St Thomas and St Mary not being represented.

They had also two days before, when I happened to be out of town, taken what appeared to me to be a very extraordinary step in ordering the Speaker to issue his warrant for committing the deputy Secretary to the common gaol during the pleasure of the House for refusing to take an oath tendered to him by a committee of the House. And on my sending for the Speaker and acquainting him that I had just received your lordship's letter and talking these matters over, I thought he (though a very strong Liberty Boy in the American meaning of the words) seemed convinced that it would be proper to reconsider their proceedings, and I did expect that they would have rescinded their resolutions of Monday the 18th and Wednesday the 20th instant. But on its being barely mentioned some of the most violent bellowed on their rights and privileges and the plenitude of their powers, which in every respect they suppose to be equal to those of the House of Commons in Great Britain, and no alteration would be listened to but they immediately adjourned till the next morning, not with an intention to consider of the matter but merely to prevent my dissolving them as I had told the Speaker I would certainly do; on which I proceeded in the manner your lordship will see by the enclosed certified papers [Vol. I, No. 1018i-iii].

This procedure, my lord, I supposed to be absolutely necessary in order to check the idea of power and importance which I find the Assembly here entertain of themselves, and their conduct and behaviour with respect to the southern parishes I conceive to be weak, insolent and every way blameworthy, and hope what I have now done will meet with approbation.

I apprehend, my lord, that the Assembly here have no other foundation for their existence and authority but what arises from His Majesty's commission and instructions to me. For this province has no charter, therefore the Assembly can claim no charter-rights, powers or privileges as in other provinces they may possibly do, and it has only been a King's government and Assemblies elected since the year 1754 when Governor Reynolds came over. Therefore, they can claim no parliamentary rights etc. by custom or prescription, but I conceive are to derive their whole power from the Crown, and by my commission and instructions they are *only empowered to join in making laws and ordinances for the public peace, welfare and good government of the colony and the people and inhabitants thereof and for the benefit of His Majesty, his heirs and successors*, and which *is the whole of the power given them*. What other rights it may justly or properly include or what parliamentary powers His Majesty may be graciously pleased to allow them I conceive wholly lies in His Majesty's breast to determine; but I cannot suppose that an Assembly thus constituted and with such limited powers can have a right, or that I ought to suffer them to claim and exercise *all the powers, laws and customs of the Parliament of Great Britain*. Nor shall I do it while I have the honour to preside here unless His Majesty shall be pleased to signify his royal pleasure that I should do so. I have in stating this matter to the Council carefully avoided touching on this point or saying anything that I thought might inflame, and shall do so until I know His Majesty's pleasure therein, unless the next Assembly should be so imprudent as to take the matter up again and by that means as it were force me to declare my sentiments as to their parliamentary rights or powers.

I only recollect one instance of their going a little out of their way or too far in point of parliamentary power, and that happened about six years ago in the case of the Provost Marshal and a prisoner, one Edmond Grey; but as that matter was entirely over before I knew of it and I was well satisfied that they had no improper intention in it, but on the contrary meant well, I suffered it to pass without any public notice but took care to let 'em know that had I been acquainted with it while depending I should certainly have put a stop to their proceedings.

And as to their behaviour relative to the writs of election, had I suffered that to pass unnoticed I conceive it would have been laying a foundation and establishing a precedent for them on all future occasions to come to a resolution of doing no business until any matter they may think fit *to demand* is granted or complied with. And therefore I judged the most proper check or mark of disapprobation that I could show to their conduct and proceedings was to dissolve them, and in this His Majesty's Council, who are really in general friends to government and very good men, clearly and unanimously agreed in opinion.

I am very sorry to acquaint your lordship by my last accounts from the Indian country it appears that a number of Northward Indians have been sometime amongst the Cherokees, where there are also some Creek Indians, and that it's much feared a junction is forming amongst them; and if a rupture should happen with the Indians, believe me, my lord, this province will stand in great need of the assurances of some of His Majesty's troops, or one of the most flourishing, and which if protected will soon be one of the most considerable, colonies belonging to His Majesty will be severely distressed if not ruined.

I hope to have the honour of waiting on your lordship in July. *Signed.* PS. 2nd March. My Lord, I humbly conceive that it will be necessary that this matter of the parliamentary power of the Assembly should be brought to a point by His Majesty's determination thereon. For they do insist that they have all the powers etc. of the House of Commons, and this being the case I thought no time more proper than the present before I leave 'em. Indeed when they persisted in their rights and refused to retract or make any alteration, I don't see how I could avoid taking the notice of it I have done, and as a proof to me that His Majesty did not consider 'em as entitled to the same privileges as the members of the House of Commons and that the matter lies in His Majesty's breast to determine what to allow them, I observe that by the 16th instruction to me it is "declared to be His Majesty's will and pleasure that no member of the said Assembly shall upon *any occasion or pretence whatever* be protected or exempted from any process of law, *civil* or criminal", and I conceive the members of the House of Commons in Great Britain were exempted or privileged against *civil* process. An explanation of this matter, my lord, may be the rather necessary lest the next Assembly should take the matter up again, in which case I must undoubtedly stop them till His Majesty's pleasure be known thereupon.

I have this day received an account that the Indians who were in the Cherokee country were in number about 70, partly Northern and partly Western Indians and that they, especially the Western Indians, pressed the Cherokees strongly to join in a war against the white people but that the Cherokees had declined it. But, my lord, the Creeks seem rather wanton, and a war with them will be near as distressful to this province as the other would be. And it is reported, but with what truth or foundation I shall not take upon me to say, although it carries an air of probability from its *policy,* that the Spaniards at New Orleans have invited the headmen of the Creeks to go there. J. W. [C.O.5/661, fo. 25]

XXIII

Lieut.-Governor William Bull to Earl of Hillsborough (No. 43)

4 March, Charleston

My Lord, on the 14th of last month by His Majesty's packet *Eagle*, I was honoured with a duplicate of your lordship's letter No. 41 and circular dated November 15 and original of No. 42 and circular December 11th [Vol. I, Nos. 723, 729, 821, 824] with His Majesty's Order in Council [Vol. I, No. 803] for the repeal of two Acts therein mentioned. On the next day I published by proclamation the King's pleasure thereupon.

As the Act for exchanging £106,500 was passed by me, I beg leave to inform your lordship that I considered it not as a new emission but merely the continuance of a former Act passed in 1748 which had exchanged bills that had been formerly exchanged by an Act in 1731; and I the more readily gave my assent to this as I knew of no disallowance signified on the former. I am sensible no provision is made for sinking this money, and I believe the true state of it is now little known here or adverted to. If it will not trespass too much on your lordship's time I will lay before your lordship what I have with some pains traced out relative thereto.

In 1723 an Act was passed for calling in and sinking, by a fund established on duties upon goods imported, all our paper bills issued under various denominations and various necessities of the province from the siege of St Augustine in 1702 till that time. And the expense of a partizan expedition by land in 1727 and of fitting a vessel to protect our coasts against Spanish *guardacostas* that insulted us, and no taxes having been raised in 1728 and 29 on account of disputes between the Governor and Assembly, with the amount of monies unsunk, left a debt on the province of about £106,500 in the year 1730; at which time His late Majesty was pleased to appoint Robert Johnson Esquire Governor of this province soon after His Majesty had purchased the soil. Under such an happy change of situation new hopes of prosperity excited the attention of people to improve it. Among other things application was made to His Majesty, and Governor Johnson received an instruction to give his assent to a law for suspending during seven years the operation of the abovementioned fund on condition it were appropriated to the better strengthening this province by encouraging foreign Protestants to become settlers here, which appears by the 24th and 25 clauses of our Quitrent Act.

The benefit of this appropriation was so great to the province and the fund so easy to the people that at the expiration of the term it was continued rather *sub silentio* than any express permission. And as the bills exchanged in 1731 to the amount of the £106,500 were obliterated and worn, in 1748 they were exchanged and for the same reason again in 1769.

I beg leave further to observe to your lordship that this branch of our paper currency was reported to the King (in consequence of an address of the honourable the House of Commons desiring a state of the American paper currency might be laid before them about the year 1751) in its true state as having no fund established for sinking it, and is as well as I can recollect the only instance [*Marginal note:* a mistake] wherein the province can be charged with breach of faith.

I proceed now to lay before your lordship the state of our disputes here respecting the King's late additional instruction, and for that purpose have enclosed several messages [Vol. I, No. 1026i-x] that have passed between the Assembly and me. Though I fear the perusal of them will give more exercise to your lordship's patience than satisfaction to your judgement, I hope your lordship will hold me excusable for not attempting the vain trouble of pursuing them through their long laborious performances in which their mistakes are too obvious to need refutation, their prejudices too deep to be removed by reasoning, while they build hopes of success upon the dangers of our present situation, the clamours of the public creditors, and the large sums due to several of His Majesty's servants which are provided for only in Tax Bills. And they express in conversation and in the course of debates a determination (though not resolved in form) not to raise any money even for years to come unless this instruction is revoked. But your lordship may be assured that their dependence upon extorting a compliance from the Governor and Council as they have formerly done, on account of public necessity or from the inconveniences His Majesty's servants may suffer, will certainly fail them. And I think it a friendly wish to the province that the Assembly may never carry any point but by reason here and a respectful application to the throne where the royal goodness is always ready to receive such petitions, to redress their grievances and protect their rights. It is possible a new Assembly may pursue new measures as many of the present seem tired and wish their triennial term were expired.

In obedience to the King's command signified to me by your lordship I have acquainted His Majesty's Council that the becoming manner in which they have exerted themselves in support of His Majesty's measures is honoured with His Majesty's approbation, and they have desired me to inform your lordship in the most expressive terms that the King's approbation of their conduct fills them with the deepest sentiments of gratitude and animates them with firmness to support every measure that can demonstrate their zealous attachment to His Majesty's person and government, and I humbly entreat your lordship will please to lay before the King their warm assurances of their affection and duty to His Majesty.

It was with great satisfaction I was informed by your lordship that Lord Charles Montagu was to embark soon after Christmas on his return to his government. I accordingly daily expected him but by His Majesty's packet *Swallow* which brought your lordship's dispatches No. 43 [Vol. I, No. 898] and duplicate of 42, I received a letter from his lordship dated December 25, which acquaints me that his departure from England would be early in the spring. As his lordship comes fully instructed in what manner he is to conduct himself in the present crisis it is not to be doubted but his lordship's address under such advantage will have the good fortune to disperse the only remaining cloud which now disturbs the tranquillity of this province. *Signed.* [C.O.5/394, fo. 46]

XXIV

Governor Peter Chester to Earl of Hillsborough (No. 10)

8 March, Pensacola

My Lord, I had yesterday the honour of receiving by the packet your lordship's circular dispatch (No. 28), and from the violent proceedings of the Spaniards in dispossessing His Majesty's subjects of their settlement at Port Egmont in Falklands Islands and the considerable naval armaments preparing at home mentioned in your letter, I have just reason to be attentive to the security of the colony which His Majesty has committed to my charge. We cannot be too thankful to our royal master for his assurances that in case matters should come to extremities the security of his possessions in America will be a principal object of his care and attention. Nor can I, lest that event should take place, be too early in my considerations of what may be necessary for the protection of this defenceless colony. We have only here at present the 16th Regiment quartered in the province (which consists of 401 men, rank and file, as appears by the enclosed return [Vol. I, No. 1042i], one company of this regiment is detached at ·Mobile) for our defence and protection against a foreign enemy and our neighbours the Indians, who for some time past have given us great reason to suspect that they have not that friendly disposition subsisting towards us which we could wish. We are by our situation environed on all sides by the Spaniards and exposed to their attacks from the Havana, La Vera Cruz or New Orleans. Three or four ships in six or eight days sail from the Havana would in our present situation make a most easy conquest of us. Our greatest security will be in a naval armament to cruise in the Bay of Mexico. Our neighbours at Orleans have there at present from the best intelligence I can procure about three hundred and eighty regular troops, fifteen hundred militia, and upwards of four thousand negroes upon whom they have great dependence, being all used to muskets and the woods. At the Dutch and Acadian settlements between New Orleans and the River Ibberville, they have about three hundred militia besides negroes and higher up the river at a settlement called Point Coupee upwards of two hundred militia and a thousand negroes. This militia is frequently drawn out, exercised and reviewed, and from their early acquaintance with the use of fire arms they must make very good irregular troops. They have about six weeks since re-established a post opposite to Fort Bute which they had abandoned, as also a post at Point Coupee, and have an officer and party stationed at each place, and I am told are in daily expectation of a regiment from the Havana, upon the arrival of which more troops are to be stationed upon the Mississippi; and I am informed by a gentleman who lately came here from New Orleans that the master of a vessel just arrived there from Philadelphia told him he had spoke three Spanish ships off Cape St Antonio who were part of eleven sail bound from Cales to the Havana with two thousand troops on board.

Your lordship will be enabled to see what works are carrying on here for the security of the harbour under the direction of Captain Sowers, an engineer sent here by Lieutenant-General Gage, and better to judge of the nature of them from the copy of a letter here enclosed [Vol. I, No. 1042ii] that I have received from Captain Sowers than from any explanation I can give.

General Haldimand and myself when we were together at Mobile both agreed in opinion that it would be an useless expense to repair the old brick fort at Mobile and that stockadoes would serve as a sufficient security to the inhabitants in case of an Indian war. As this fort is going to ruin, if it was entirely pulled down, the bricks and other materials might serve for the works carrying and to be carried on for the defence of our harbour and be of much greater use than where they are. *Signed.* [C.O.5/588, p. 91]

XXV
Affidavit of Waighstill Avery[1]

8 March, Mecklenburg County, N.C.

Waighstill Avery testifieth and saith that on the sixth day of March instant about nine or ten o'clock in the morning, he this deponent was at the now dwelling-house of one Hudgins who lives and keeps the Atkin [Yadkin] ferry at the lower end of the long island.

And he this deponent there saw thirty or forty of those people who style themselves Regulators, and was then and there arrested and forcibly detained a prisoner by one of them (who said his name was John McQuiston) in the name of them all calling him and them the people, and that soon after one James Graham (commonly pronounced Grimes) spoke to this deponent these words "You are now a prisoner and you must not go anywhere without a guard". Immediately after one Thomas Hamilton spoke words of the same tenor and purport, adding that "You must keep with your guard and you shan't be hurt". Before this deponent left the house the aforesaid James Graham desired him to step aside and then told him "You had but to call for a bowl of tody and treat the captains for they are going to ride on to the regulating camp". The bowl of tody being spent, this deponent was conducted under a guard of two men to the regulating camp (as they termed it) about a mile distant where were many more persons of the same denomination and others came there some hours after, in the whole as this deponent supposes and imagines about two hundred and thirty. Here this deponent remained for 4 or 5 hours and got leave to pass from one part of their camp to another repeatedly, as led by curiosity to hear and see what was said and transacted and discover the temper of the parties etc.; but was still deemed a prisoner by all, and many took upon them to command this deponent. That from themselves he this deponent learned the names of five of their captains or leading men then present vizt. Thomas Hamilton and one other Hamilton, James Hunter, Joshua Teague, one Gillespie and the aforesaid James Graham.

He this deponent heard many of them whose names are to him unknown say opprobrious things against the Governor, the Judges of the Superior Court, against the House of Assembly and other

1   Enclosed in Governor Tryon's letter of 12 April to Hillsborough, Vol. III, No. XXXVI.

persons in office, and while a surrounding crowd were uttering things still more opprobrious the said Thomas Hamilton stood in the midst and spoke words of the following tenor and purport (the crowd still assenting to and affirming the truth of what was said) "What business has Maurice Moore to be judge, he is no judge, he has not [been] appointed by the King, he nor Henderson neither. They'll neither of them hold court. The Assembly have gone and made a Riotous Act and the people are more enraged than ever. It was the best thing that could be for the country, for now we shall be forced to kill all the clerks and lawyers, and we will kill them, and I'll be damned if they are not put to death. If they had not made that Act we might have suffered some of them to live. A Riotous Act! there never was any such Act in the laws of England or any other country but France, they brought it from France, and they'll bring the Inquisition next".

Many of them said the Governor was a friend to the lawyers and the Assembly had worsted the Regulators in making laws for fees. They shut Husbands up in gaol that he might not see their roguish proceedings, and then the Governor and the Assembly made just such laws as the lawyers wanted. The Governor is a friend to the lawyers, the lawyers carry on everything, they appoint weak ignorant Justices of Peace for their own purposes. They had worsted the Regulators in making laws for fees but they the Regulators were sworn that they should not get them. There should be no lawyers in the province, they damned themselves if there should. Fanning was outlawed the twenty-second of March and any Regulator that saw him after that time would kill him, and some said they could not wait for that, wished they could see him and swore they would kill him before they returned if they could find him at Salisbury. Some wished they could see Judge Moore at Salisbury that they might flog him, others that they might kill him; others said neither judge nor King's attorney should come, they would be waylaid; one Robert Thomson said Maurice Moore was perjured and called him by opprobrious names, as rascal, rogue, villain, scoundrel etc., others assented to it. Thomson said Maurice Moore was partial in the trial of his suit, that when he the said Thomson obtained a recovery in a land cause Judge Moore granted a new trial, but when he was cast and the other contending party obtained a recovery Judge Moore damned himself (on the Bench) if he knew what to do and denied a trial; but that he the said Thomson was in possession, stood in defiance, and would see who would take it from him.

When news was brought that Captain Rutherfurd at the head of his company was parading in the streets of Salisbury, this deponent heard sundry of them urge very hard and strenuously that the whole body of the Regulators then present should march into Salisbury with their arms and fight them, saying They had then enough to kill them, We can kill them, will teach them to oppose us.

Taken, sworn to and subscribed this eighth day of March 1771 before me, William Harris, Justice of the Peace. *Copy.* [C.O.5/314, fo. 108]

XXVI

Governor Earl of Dunmore to Earl of Hillsborough (No. 7)

9 March, New York

My Lord, I have received by the December packet, which arrived here the 28th February, your lordship's letters of the 11th December [Vol. I, Nos. 815, 824]. I laid your lordship's circular letter before the Council and acquainted General Gage that we were ready to give him all the assistance he could require of us; and I immediately caused to be published in the usual form His Majesty's disallowance of the four Acts of Assembly according to His Majesty's commands signified by your lordship in No. 1, but I am sorry to be obliged to acquaint your lordship that the whole province except the lawyers express great dissatisfaction at it, and the more from having been accustomed to observe the laws thus repealed for so considerable a time.

The Assembly have continued sitting until the 16th of February. The chief part of their business being then finished, the members were very desirous of a recess, which I was averse from granting before the issue of the appearances of war be known unto us: however, at their request I allowed them a short adjournment, and upon their representation that they would be able to assemble again in the space of a few days, I have prorogued them for a week which is to be continued only from week to week.

The Acts of Assembly passed this sessions and the Minutes of Council could not be prepared for this opportunity; I can only transmit the Votes and Proceedings of the Assembly. They have not thought proper to discharge the arrears due upon the accounts of furnishing His Majesty's troops; I have applied, but it has not yet been under consideration, for the deficiencies of last year though I do not believe it will be complied with, and the only way we can suggest of making them good is from the savings of the two thousand pounds granted for the troops, which sum I believe will be regularly continued hereafter. Your lordship will perceive that one thousand pounds is voted for purchasing timber and plank and for making gun-carriages and platforms for the guns in the fort and battery in this city; and though nothing more be yet done in pursuance of the intimation made to them in my speech of an apprehension of war, I am fully persuaded that His Majesty may rely on having his most sanguine expectations complied with, should the event require it. The Assembly remain inflexible in their resolution of refusing to admit Judge Livingstone to a seat in their House, notwithstanding His Majesty's disallowance of the law passed for excluding the judges of the Supreme Court; they are full of nothing but the competency of their authority and the expediency of the measure, which has interested the whole province, much the greatest part in favour of the resolution, in such a manner that I did not think I ought in prudence to interfere otherwise than by endeavouring to prevail on the leading members, as a means of curing the animosities subsisting among them, to drop the affair upon his next presenting himself to the House. They seemed separately to be inclined to acquiesce with my solicitation, but I found that after they had consulted together it was determined that they were under a necessity of persisting for fear of their constituents, who as I have said above are engaged warmly in the dispute: the general opinion being that the Assembly ought to follow the wise example of the House of Commons in this case, and that besides in this country if the judges are permitted to have seats they can always secure their own elections, having so great an influence over the electors from their judgements on the bench which every man at some time or other is concerned in, and the frequent lawsuits that prevail in this country giving the judges but too many opportunities of revenging themselves on their opposers should they be so inclined, they conclude that they cannot be unbiased when engaged in party interest, the effects of which they see no other way of avoiding than by excluding those officers. It did not appear to me that it would avail anything by dissolving the Assembly as we do not know of one member that supports the resolution who would not be returned again upon a fresh election, but of the few that oppose it some would be obliged to give place to others of opposite interest. Therefore, without obtaining the effect desired, I might have occasioned a disposition among them to thwart my administration, which I have judged most for His Majesty's service to avoid by seeming to incline to neither party.

I have communicated to the Assembly His Majesty's pleasure signified to me by your lordship concerning Indian affairs, in answer to which I received the address which I herewith enclose [Vol. I, No. 1047i] and which I have likewise transmitted to Sir William Johnson, desiring him to furnish me with an account of those regulations to which the address alludes, when I make no doubt the Assembly will proceed to pass such a law as I hope on the part of this province may answer His Majesty's desires in that matter; but I must repeat here what I observed before in my letter No. 6 [Vol. I, No. 920] that the authority of Parliament alone is able to make any plan effectual for all the colonies.

I likewise enclose for your lordship the speech of the Onoide Indians [Vol. I, No. 1047ii] petitioning for certain articles of which they stand in need and which I think highly proper that they should be furnished with, and cannot be denied them without risking the friendship of people whom we ought by every reasonable indulgence to attach to us. I have wrote about it also to Sir William Johnson who I hope, from out of the money allowed by government, will be able to supply them, which if he represents to be insufficient I shall recommend to the province to do.

I transmit to your lordship the proposal [Vol. I, No. 1047iii] of a number of German people settled in this province for the forming themselves into a company to serve in conjunction with the militia of the colony in case of an emergency. I presume your lordship will think it right to give encouragement to their zeal and spirit; the emulation which is observed to actuate all national bodies of men serving with others never fails to produce good effects, and there cannot be the same objection made which is common to auxiliaries, these being established in the country and their interest concerned in its safety.

The troubled state of the north-eastern parts of this province seems to deserve your lordship's immediate attention. I speak of that large district between Hudson's River and the Lakes George and Champlain on the west and Connecticut River on the east, and between the north line of the Massachusetts Bay and the 45th degree of latitude assigned for the partition between this and the province of Quebec.

This is a fine country capable of great cultivation and of subsisting many thousands of useful subjects, but before the conquest of Canada was so exposed to the incursions of the French and the savages in their interest that very few settlements were made in it except in that quarter nearest to Hudson's River.

It is clearly within the limits of this province as granted by King Charles the second to James, Duke of York; and accordingly His present Majesty in the year 1764 was pleased to declare the western bank of Connecticut River to be the partition boundary between New York and New Hampshire.

I wish I could say, my lord, that the royal decision had been followed with that cheerful submission which was due to so express and authoritative intimation of the King's pleasure. I am obliged on the contrary to complain that there seems to be too much reason to believe that the disorders in that country owe their origin and progress to the intrigues of persons in power in the province of New Hampshire with aims of enhancing their private fortunes out of the Crown lands and the vain hope that His Majesty may be moved to annex this territory to the province of New Hampshire under which their grants were obtained.

In the prosecution of this design some of the inhabitants have lately been excited to open acts of violence as well as an immediate application by petition to the Throne. Upon procuring a copy of this petition I referred it to the Attorney-General for his report, and as his representations appear greatly to concern His Majesty's interest and to be supported by proofs of which the king ought not to be uninformed, I now transmit them [Vol. I, No. 1047iv] to your lordship for the royal consideration.

I must at the same time apprize your lordship that a great majority of the settlers are not only disposed to a peaceable submission to the decision of 1764 but very averse to the change projected in New Hampshire, as will appear by their counter-petition [Vol. I, No. 1047li] communicated to me to be transmitted in their favour.

Nor can I omit mentioning that it is in this district that many of the reduced officers and soldiers have made their locations of the bounty pledged to them by the royal proclamation of the 7th of October 1763. Besides this I find that others of His Majesty's subjects have obtained patents for many thousands of acres under the Great Seal of this province, which will be all frustrated upon detaching this country from the province of New York and greatly increase the general confusion.

Your lordship will doubtless perceive that until the order transmitted to Sir Henry Moore prohibiting grants to be made of lands before patented under New Hampshire is rescinded, there can be no established tranquillity in that quarter of this province since it is natural to suppose that the discontented settlers (countenanced as they are by New Hampshire) will flatter themselves with hopes of favour and make rapid accessions to their number from the profligate banditti of the other colonies who look for safety where government is weak and disturbed.

I have only to add, my lord, that from all the information I have been able to obtain, nothing more seems to me to be requisite for restoring peace than a revocation of a late order by which the grants of this province were suspended. The inhabitants now amount to between six and seven hundred families, of which number 450-odd have signed a petition to me which I have by this packet transmitted to your lordship [Vol. I, No. 1047lii], praying to be continued in this government. There is another petition, as I understand, sent home by Governor Wentworth signed by about 200 praying to be under the government of New Hampshire, but how these names were obtained your lordship will easily be able to conceive if you take the trouble of looking into the different papers I have sent by this packet. But surely 'tis more natural, even supposing that the New Hampshire claim was preferable to that of New York, to have a river such as Connecticut for the boundary. Add to this that the income of government would be considerably increased annually by receiving half-a-crown quitrent instead of ninepence per 100 acres for so large a tract of land as was disputed. *Signed.* PS. I have to inform your lordship of the death of Joseph Reade Esq., one of His Majesty's Council in this province. I also enclose to your lordship three affidavits which I have lately received [Vol. I, No. 1047lvi-lviii], which confirm our belief that the disorders abovementioned are promoted by people of the greatest power in the province of New Hampshire. [C.O.5/1102, fo. 49]

XXVII

Governor Peter Chester to Earl of Hillsborough (No. 11)

9 March, Pensacola

My Lord, it afforded me great satisfaction to find by your lordship's dispatch (No. 29) [Vol. I, No. 638] that His Majesty had thought fit to direct that Mr Stuart should repair to Pensacola in order to take such steps as the exigency of affairs respecting the Indians in this department should require. I shall upon his arrival here most cheerfully join with him in concerting such measures as may be thought necessary for the interests of the colony and shall be infinitely happy if our mutual endeavours to effect this end may terminate in restoring that friendship and harmony with the savages which lately seems to have been interrupted, but on which our security so much depends.

The chief reasons of that discontent which has lately shown itself among several of the tribes of Indians contiguous to this province, I imagine to have arisen from the too general and unrestricted freedom of trade that has been allowed to be carried on among them from the different colonies which has occasioned great abuses and impositions to be practised upon the savages by the traders, who are generally of the lowest class of people and very licentious, and also from the great promises and assurances which were made to the Indians soon after we took possession of this country of meeting them and their chiefs frequently at public congresses and distributing presents among them.

This they had been accustomed to during the time the French were in possession of Louisiana, who lavished such immense sums in this department for presents that most of them became firmly attached to their interests.

These presents they were taught to believe would be continued to be given to them by their new neighbours and, now disappointed, they tell us we are not to be credited and our professions of friendship do not come from the heart; and as many of them are naturally jealous and suspicious in their disposition they are afraid that without forming some strong confederacy among themselves they shall hereafter fall a sacrifice to the English.

I was informed by one of our principal traders that a chief of the Creeks told him in conversation not long since to look to the rising of the sun, to its setting, to the right hand, and to the left hand, and on all sides, says he, we are surrounded with English. You have driven the Spaniards and the French from this country and now have almost the whole possession of it, and though your talks and mouths may now be good towards us, yet as you are men they may alter, and intimated that as we had not fulfilled our promises in one point we might not in another, therefore it was prudent they should take care of themselves.

Your lordship is acquainted that the Creeks and Choctaws have been at war with each other for some time past and that Mr Stuart the Superintendant has by his mediation endeavoured to bring about a peace between them. To effect this several talks were sent by order of the Superintendant into their respective nations and meetings of their headmen proposed. And in December last a large party of Creeks who were on their way to Mobile to meet the Choctaws came within forty miles of that place but from some information they received thought proper to return without concluding the peace or effecting anything. During the absence of these Creeks, among whom there were several chiefs much attached to us, some turbulent Indians imagining that the peace would take place began to stir up the different towns to mischief, as your lordship will see by the enclosed deposition of two traders [Vol. I, No. 1046i] which I have had reason to believe is just and true. But the peace not being carried into execution, the disaffected have not as yet been able to engage any followers to take up the hatchet against us. Had this peace taken place I do not know what the consequence would have been and am very apprehensive that all our endeavours would not have prevented them from committing outrages.

I am sorry that the Act passed in the late session of Assembly for this province regulating the Indian trade has not been productive of those salutary purposes which were expected from it. Most of the towns to which the traders resort who obtain their licences from hence are in the Creek, Choctaw and Chikesaw nations beyond the limits and jurisdiction of this province, so that the breach of any regulations committed there are not cognizable in our courts nor can process issue there to apprehend delinquents until our boundaries are extended so far as to include those nations within our jurisdiction; and then a law properly framed might restrain the licentious behaviour of the traders and their impositions on the savages, of which I have had many complaints but not power to redress and prevent the constant outrages and disorders committed by those people called crackers and stragglers who come from the back-settlements of Georgia, Carolina and Virginia into the Indian country.

If there are not some measures fallen upon to curb these irregularities they inevitably will some time or other involve us in all the calamities and immense expense attending an Indian war, which must prove very disadvantageous both to Great Britain and her colonies be our success ever so great.

If the different colonies in the southern district would pass a similar bill it might be the means of preventing many abuses: the substance of which bill should be in my opinion to limit the quantity of goods and rum to be carried into the Indian nation and the number of traders in each town, and restrain them from trading anywhere but at certain proper towns to be mentioned in the Act and from selling more goods to any Indian than is necessary for his own consumption; to empower the Governor or Governor and Council to settle a reasonable tariff as occasion should require. As proof against delinquents is very difficult to be obtained it might allow Indian evidence with corroborating circumstances to be given in our courts and then left to the court and jury to convict upon if they thought proper and should from other circumstances think the prisoner guilty. It should enumerate every species of offences generally committed by traders and inflict such fines and penalties as are adequate to the offence. Each trader should enter into bond with sufficient security and take licences from the Governor within whose province and jurisdiction he is to trade and no others be allowed. And the Governor or Governor and Council should be enabled to make such orders and regulations from time to time as should be judged most suitable to the circumstances of the province. But as the best laws will prove ineffectual without proper persons to carry them into execution, therefore I submit if it would not be proper again to establish commissaries to reside in each nation who should be appointed magistrates and be also authorized with proper powers to inspect into the conduct and behaviour of the different traders that they might be enabled to issue process against delinquents and bind them over to appear at next sessions where they and their securities might be prosecuted. These commissaries would be a great check upon the licentious traders who now daily commit the greatest abuses without fear of punishment; they would also by a constant residence in the Indian towns be the best channel through which we could receive proper information of the real designs and intentions of the Indians. These are a few hints not so well digested as I could wish but may serve to show in general what the heads of such bill should be, but I am afraid that either from inattention or the private views of many of the different Assemblies no general regulation will take place but by Act of Parliament.

If government would approve of a congress being held with the Lower Creeks it would be a great means of restoring that friendship and harmony between us so much to be wished for, and we might obtain from them a greater cession of part of the interior country for the purpose of settlements: at present we are circumscribed by very narrow limits. And if the savages could be promised congresses (the expenses of which might be limited) to be held once in three or four years it would tend very much to quiet their minds and might be productive of very salutary effects. Should that plan be adopted I shall be enabled to make a considerable saving yearly out of the Indian fund allowed for the use of this province which might be applied to, and would lessen the expense of, the next congress; for the Indians would not then come down continually in swarms and make such pressing demands for presents—were I to gratify them in their requests the annual allowance of presents would be expended in a few months. I am therefore under the necessity of making use of great economy and to endeavour to satisfy them with as few things and in the best manner I can. *Signed.* [C.O.5/588, p. 103]

XXVIII

John Frohock and Alexander Martin to Governor William Tryon[1]

18 March, Salisbury
May it please your Excellency, as you have been ever attentive to the true interest of the province during your administration and have exerted every prudent method to maintain its public peace by endeavouring to quell a most dangerous and lawless insurrection that has of late disturbed this part of your government, permit us, sir, to discharge our duty on this occasion by informing you to what issue Regulation (as it is called) is brought and upon what footing it stands at present in the district of Salisbury.

The Regulators upon their return from their expedition to rescue Hermon Husband formed a design to visit Salisbury Superior Court, which hearing, one of us went down into their settlements to know the reality of their intentions and found them assembling for that purpose, though peaceably disposed beyond expectation. On the sixth of this instant they accordingly appeared to the amount of four or five hundred encamped in the woods on this side of the Axkin River. We went to them, found some of them armed and others unarmed, desired to know their designs and what they wanted. They answered they came with no intention to obstruct the court or to injure the personal property of anyone, only to petition the court for a redress of grievances against officers taking exorbitant fees, and that their arms were not for offence but to defend themselves if assaulted. These were the general answers of their chiefs, though there were several threats and menaces of whipping flung out by the lower characters among them against some particular persons but not by the general voice. We told them there was not any court, but from their late behaviour the judges did not think it prudent to hold one at Salisbury under the direction of whips and clubs. They seemed somewhat concerned and said there would have been no danger for the Chief Justice to have held a court, but as to the Associates they were silent. We farther told them if any of us were the

---

1 Enclosed in Governor Tryon's letter of 12 April to Hillsborough, Vol. III, No. XXXVI.

persons against whom they had complaints justly founded, we were always ready and willing to give them satisfaction without their disturbing the public peace. They intimated we were some of the persons against whom they were to complain, and to show their disposition for peace and that all disputes between them and us should subside hereafter they formed a committee to wait on us and to propose a plan of accommodating matters, who were Jeremiah Fields, Joshua Teague, Samuel Jones, John Vickory, Samuel Waggoner, James Graham, John Engart, James Hunter, Peter Julian, John Corry, Henry Wade, William Wilborn jnr., Samuel Low, Thomas Flack, Daniel Galaspie and James Wilson, who proposed in behalf of the people (as they said) to leave every complaint and dispute subsisting between us to men by each of us to be indifferently chosen, to which we readily agreed as equitable. Accordingly on their part they nominated Hermon Husband, James Graham, James Hunter and Thomas Person. We in turn chose Mathew Lock, John Kerr, Samuel Young and James Smith; that they or a majority of them should arbitrate and finally settle every difference between us whatsoever; and also fixed the time for the meeting of the arbitrators and every person concerned on the third Tuesday in May next at John Kimbrough's on Huwaree. By this agreement no officer is included but those of this county and those who voluntarily join in the same. Upon which the main body after being informed of what had been done went through the town, gave three cheers, and returned to their homes without using violence to any person whatsoever to our knowledge.

This, may it please your Excellency, is a short detail of what passed between the Regulators and us the sixth and seventh of this instant, and had they been insolent and daring enough to have committed any outrages there were in consequence of orders given previous to their coming three companies of the militia armed, headed by their respective officers, Major Dobbins, Captain Rutherfurd and Captain Berger, ready in town to oppose them and to protect the court if there had been any. And on the seventh day Col. Alexander and Capt. Polk appeared from Mecklenburg with seventy or eighty men for the same purpose, to whom the thanks of this county is justly due. From such appearances of opposition this deluded people begin to grow sick of Regulation and want peace upon any tolerable terms.

As the spirit of sedition has been propagated with much industry among the lower class of inhabitants here who are loud in their clamours against the officers, we flatter ourselves the measures we have taken will be approved of and acceptable to your Excellency, having a tendency to still the minds of many misinformed, misguided, though well-meaning, persons who have been inadvertently drawn in to join this faction. For we are conscious of our innocence and that their complaints are chiefly groundless, and are willing and desirous that any set of reasonable men may inspect and judge our conduct. This when the populace is once satisfied of, they will drop their prejudices and their haughty leaders will become the objects of their as well as the government's resentment. This procedure we expect will have more effect on their minds than all the formalities of law whatsoever, as they would still suggest they had injustice done them. They want, they say, to converse with the officers who have taken their money to satisfy them for what (this is surely reasonable), and they will all be quiet again. This we have undertaken to do and time must produce the effect. If our hopes and wishes be not too sanguine, perhaps this may be the foundation of putting an end to all future tumult and disorder, and would hope that our conduct by no means reflects any dishonour on the government or lessens the dignity of administration to punish those offenders heretofore guilty of outrages adequate to their crimes, but shows the desire and readiness of us to remove every complaint they may have against us without involving the government in a considerable and unnecessary expense. But should these terms not have their desired effect the aggravation of their guilt will surely be much the greater.

Upon the whole we submit these proceedings to your Excellency's wiser judgement and flatter ourselves with your approbation. We assure you, sir, we shall always be fond of whatever instructions you shall please to honour us with relative to our future conduct, in which the peace and welfare of the government is so much concerned. *Copy.* [C.O.5/314, fo. 114]

XXIX

Governor William Tryon to Colonel Joseph Leech[1]

19 March, Newbern

I yesterday determined by consent of His Majesty's Council to march with a body of forces taken from several militia regiments into the settlements of the insurgents to reduce them to obedience, who by their rebellious acts and declarations have set the government at defiance and interrupted the course of justice by obstructing, over-turning and shutting up the courts of law. That some of your regiment therefore may have a share in the honour of serving their country in this important service, I am to require you to make choice of two hundred men out of the volunteers of the Craven Regiment with officers and non-commission officers in proportion to the following regulations to which you will pay the strictest regard.

Each company to consist of one captain, one lieutenant, one ensign, two sergeants, two corporals, one drummer, a clerk and fifty private men, with a field officer and an adjutant to the detachment. The super-numerary officers that are willing to march will be entitled only to provisions and the pay of private men, if they choose to accept of that pay.

Every man to be allowed forty shillings for an encouragement to serve in this expedition and to be entitled to receive two shillings a day while on service, the eightpence per day for provisions being stopped for the commissaries who have contracted to serve the troops with provisions. Each man will also have a pair of leggings, a cockade and a haversack given him, which you are to furnish, and when delivered and

1 From Governor Tryon's letter-book, enclosed with letter of 2 August to Hillsborough, Vol. I, No. 1434.

a certificate thereof produced, signed by the commanding officer of the regiment, I will give you a warrant on the Treasury for the amount as well as for the forty shillings per man you shall advance as bounty money.

The ration of provisions to each man per day is one pound of pickled pork and one pound of wheat flour, or one pound and an half of fresh beef instead of pork, and one pound and an half of cornmeal instead of flour when ordered.

Each company to be allowed a strong commodious cart with two able horses to carry the baggage of the men, to be provided by the colonel of the regiment or captain of the company, and the owner to be allowed seven shillings and sixpence per day while employed in the service, he finding his own horses with corn. If a waggon is hired it must carry the baggage of two companies to be provided as above, and fifteen shillings per day allowed for it on the same conditions as for the carts. The waggoners will be allowed to draw their rations of provisions as soldiers but to have no pay.

The men must be made sensible the better they are provided with arms and necessaries, the better condition they will be in to serve their King and Country. No volunteers to be accepted but those who are hearty, spirited and can submit to a ready obedience to orders, nor any soldier allowed to take his horse as the whole will march on foot. The officers to take as few horses as possible.

It is not intended to move the troops before the twentieth of next month, before which time you shall be informed of the day you are to assemble your men, the time of march, and the road you are to take.

It is recommended as a Christian duty incumbent on every planter that remains at home to take care of and assist to the utmost of his abilities the families of those men who go on this service, that neither families nor plantations may suffer while they are employed on a service where the interest of the whole is concerned.

For the expenditures ordered on this expedition I shall give printed warrants payable to the bearers. These warrants will become negotiable until the Treasury can pay them out of the Contingent Fund in case there is not a sufficiency of money in the Treasury to answer the necessary service of this expedition. *Entry*. [C.O.5/314, fo. 246]

XXX

Alexander Cameron to John Stuart[1]

19 March, Toqueh

Sir, two days ago I was summoned to attend the Cherokee chiefs in council at the town-house of Chote. They began their ceremony by producing two pieces of tobacco which were sent to them by the Mortar of the Creeks, the largest of which was wrapped up in a white belt of wampum and the other with a string of black and white common beads. The Great Warrior informed me that a man who had been appointed a beloved man by the Cherokees in the Creek nation had died

1   Enclosed in John Stuart's letter of 27 April to Hillsborough, Vol. I, No. 1157.

lately and that the Mortar requested that they would send some of their headmen in order to invest another with the same honour, for which the large piece of tobacco and the belt of wampum was sent. The smallest piece with the black and white string of common beads was sent in order to clear up the bad talks which the Creeks had heard of the Cherokees joining the Norwards in a war against them.

My construction upon it was quite different. I imagined that the large piece with the belt of white wampum was to strengthen their friendship, and that the small piece with the black and white beads was to solicit the Cherokees to join them against the white people, and their behaviour soon after convinced me in my opinion. The Great Warrior being prompted by the second rank of warriors stood up and spoke to the following effect. My Eldest Brother, I am now going to talk to you and I hope you will not think hard of what I am going to say. Upon my return from the meeting at your house I told my young people what lands we had given up but they seemed surprised that I would agree to give away so much of their land that I would consent to the white people's settling so near to their towns, for which reason they never would take hold of the beads which were presented to me in token of my agreement at the congress; therefore desired me to take back the beads and wampum and that the boundary should be run by Chiswell's Mines where it was first agreed upon.

I took the wampum and told them that I never could have the assurance to return them to their father from them, that as their eldest brother it gave me great concern that they should prove so unstable in their transactions and that I should be ashamed forever to be concerned with them, that they never would be looked upon in any other light except that of liars and people void of honesty, that as to their father in Charleston he would entirely disown them. I begged therefore that they would take the beads back and not to expose themselves to public censure, that they might depend upon it that the government of Virginia would hold the land by virtue of their grant, which was maturely considered and entered into at my house, and if they would offer to oppose the execution of the boundary line as agreed upon, that we should look upon it as the commencement of hostilities, to prevent which I begged that they would consider and receive the beads again, that the grant was not only signed by the chiefs of the upper settlement but by those of the valley, middle and lower settlement. Willinnawaw observed that it was very true and that it was no wonder that I was ashamed of my brothers, that he was ashamed also and desired they would accept of the beads again; but they positively refused for that night but that in two days they would talk to me again at my own house.

Next day I went to Ouconnastotah and talked to him privately, as also to Willinnawaw who I looked upon as my staunch friend. I told them that if they did not insist upon the boundary line being run [MS: ?round] as specified in the cession, they should never be trusted to again. Willinawaw willingly consented to do what he could to assist me but said that the young men would never give it up without receiving a great many presents. They accordingly assembled on the 18th at my house where the whole settlement were present. They first demanded

that they should have 2,000 of powder and 6,000 of ball and that I
would make that demand upon the Virginians in their behalf, besides
rifles and other dry goods of all kinds, and that after they had received
such presents they would give up the land. I flatly refused to have
anything to say in it and demanded a categorical answer whether or
not they would give up the land and receive the beads again.

Willinawaw in particular spoke a great deal to the purpose in my
favour and prevailed upon them to receive the beads, but I was under
the necessity of promising them that in case the government of Virginia
did not give them 1,000 of powder I should be answerable that their
father would send it to them out of his own pocket, and that I would
represent to the beloved man of Virginia that they expected still some
more presents from them. They at first insisted that no line should be
run until they should have their answer, but at last they consented that
we should begin the line and run it to the place appointed near the Long
Island, where they would meet the commissionary and settle the
matter. I was glad to get off at any rate, for some of the gentlemen who
were present thought that I told the Indians more upon that head than
was prudent at so critical a juncture. Ouccannostotah denied having
any hand in this affair and I sincerely believe him, but he does not choose
to stand out against these young men as they have an equal right to the
land. He desires, sir, that you will believe him to be firmly attached to
the white people. He likewise desires me to acquaint you that the
Norwards are continually soliciting him to take up the hatchet and
that he is almost at a loss how to behave. I have advised him that in case
he should be under the necessity of taking it up to strike some other
nation of Indians with it but never to take it up against the white people;
otherwise that he might conclude the downfall of his people from that
very date. He has given me great assurances but they are not to be
depended upon. The affair of the boundary has given me the greatest
concern and trouble, but I cannot help it. You may be assured, sir,
that I have done everything in my power and perhaps run more risks
than many would choose by telling them of their perfidy and deceitful-
ness, particularly on that occasion. They say that they see the smoke of
the Virginians from their doors and that as they took possession of their
lands without their consent, they must either give it up for any trifle
they please to give for it or go to war against them, which they would
willingly avoid if possible; that now they have settled their lands as far
as Broad River, and they believe they were allowed so to do by the
beloved men of Virginia, and if otherwise those people would not
remove unless they took other methods with them than that of talking.
Just as we had finished matters, the Little Carpenter arrived from
Keowee. He spoke a good deal and expressed much for their having
talked contrary to what was agreed upon at Lochaber, and that their
talks could be no more depended upon. They all seem willing that the
traders should hold the land ceded to them in Savannah and said
yesterday that they would attend the running of it any time their father
thought fit, and make their titles [? free] from any claim the Creeks could
lay to it. Mr McLean from Augusta is now here: he declares that he never
was consulted about the land or any merchant at Augusta to his know-

ledge, and as the traders have given up their debts and goods upon hand, the merchants must be ruined unless through your mediation they can obtain a grant of said land. Mr Jackson or McLean will wait upon you, sir, as soon as possible to beg your advice in order to have the matter properly represented to His Majesty. I told him that he could not expect any such thing as proper application had not been made at first by the Indians. McLean told me that Governor Wright was going home this spring and that he intended to apply for liberty to purchase that very body of land which the Cherokees have ceded to the traders, he imagining the Creeks were the proprietors of it. I don't doubt, sir, but his Excellency will use every measure in his power in order to add this valuable part to the province of Georgia. Therefore if it can be obtained, I hope it will be only through your interest. It is thought by every person to be the best body of land in the three provinces, the whole being flat and the soil very rich.

I had the pleasure of receiving your letter of the 8th February on the 13th instant by Mr Richard King, by which I am sorry to learn that you was so much alarmed and that you blamed me without a cause. My intelligence from the nation was very good but I did not think that you would approve of my sending an express for every trifling report as at that time I had no reason to suspect the fidelity of the Cherokees, having daily conversation with some of their headmen at Lochaber.

The Mortar of the Creeks is expected here soon, which is agreeable to your information, but if he has any bad views I hope that I shall be able to frustrate them. Parties of the Northern and Western Indians are continually coming in and others setting off homewards. I have had conferences with them all but cannot learn that they intend to strike us. However, their private and frequent talks with each other lead me to think they are hatching some mischief. An Indian fellow and a negro belonging to the Standing Turkey were killed a few days [ago] somewhere down this river, by whom I have not been able to learn. I have endeavoured to make this affair instrumental for prevailing upon them to strike the Westerns but could not succeed. I leave it to your better judgement whether or not it would be requisite to acquaint the government of Virginia with this last determination of the Indians. However, I shall proceed with a party of them to meet the commissioners by the time appointed unless countermanding orders should be received. *Copy.* [C.O.5/72, fo. 219]

XXXI

Earl of Hillsborough to Governor Thomas Hutchinson (No. 6)

1 April, Whitehall
Sir, your dispatches of 22nd December and 17th January last, both numbered 34 [Vol. I, No. 871, Vol. III, No. VIII], have been received and laid before the King.

I have already acquainted you with the steps I thought fit to take and with the directions I had in command from the King respecting the two establishments you represented to be necessary at Castle William, and you will have the satisfaction to find that your instructions (which

I hope to be able to send you in a few days) are very full and explicit not only with regard to those establishments but also to the command over that fortress committed to you by charter and by His Majesty's commission.

With regard to the repairs of and additional works at the Castle which you have represented to General Gage to be necessary, I can only say that as what has been already done will I perceive make a very heavy article in the military contingent expenses of North America, it is very much to be wished that any further demand might at present be avoided, and not only on that account but also as it may in the execution give occasion to doubts and suspicions with respect to the authority on one side and the other, for although I have no doubt that in everything relating to the Castle both General Gage and yourself will act with that moderation and cordiality so essential to the efficacy and success of the King's instructions yet the less occasion there is in a matter of some delicacy to bring that authority into question the better.

The general disposition which you say at present appears in the people of Massachusetts Bay to promote order and submission to government has given the King the greatest satisfaction, and His Majesty, who has nothing more at heart than to see his people happy, peaceable and prosperous and has had so many proofs of your zeal to promote these objects, has the fullest confidence that you will neglect nothing that may tend to improve these pleasing appearances and to avail yourself of the good temper which you say the Assembly are likely to meet in at their next session to obtain every provision that may be necessary for the welfare and security of the colony and the advantage of its inhabitants.

Upon this occasion I cannot forbear to mention the accounts I have received through various channels of the disorders which prevail in the new settlements in the Eastern Country, and which calls so loudly for the interposition of government.

I ever thought that the encouraging settlement in a colony so remote from the seat of government and under very peculiar circumstances was imprudent and unadvisable without a previous consideration by His Majesty and his Privy Council here of a state of the country and of the means by which the advantages of such settlement could be best promoted without prejudice to the interests of this kingdom and more especially in that important one, the preservation of the timber with which that district abounds.

You will I daresay have been already informed that, in consequence of a joint report of the Boards of Admiralty and Trade to the King, the Lords of the Treasury have appointed persons to survey that country and to report for the consideration of Parliament the state of it in respect to this object, and whether there are any or what parts that it may be proper should be reserved for a supply of naval stores to this kingdom. It will be impossible therefore until this report is made to suggest any plan for the particular government of so extensive a district which will not be liable to very great difficulty and uncertainty, and therefore all that can be done in the meantime is to avoid encouraging any further settlements whatever, and to endeavour by the appointment of Justices of the Peace and other civil magistrates to restrain those violences and disorders so strongly complained of in the petitions which have I understand been presented by the well-disposed inhabitants of the new townships. *Draft.* [C.O.5/760, fo. 129]

XXXII

Lieut.-General Thomas Gage to Earl of Hillsborough (No. 59)

2 April, New York

My lord, your lordship's letter *most secret* of the 2nd of January [Vol. III, No. I] has been received together with copies of letters that had passed between your lordship and the principal officers of the Ordnance [Vol. I, Nos. 838, 878] and a copy of a letter from Sir Jeffrey Amherst to the several North American governors in 1762.

From all the accounts that have been received hitherto of the state and condition of Louisiana an attack upon that province is very practicable, and of the different ways of approaching New Orleans the river Mississippi is judged the most advantageous though feigned attacks might at the same time be of service on the side of the Ohio and West Florida.

Your lordship's letter was not received till the 21st ultimo, the packet having been out above ten weeks from Falmouth, a passage unfortunately long at this juncture, but the greatest diligence will be used to assemble a body of troops; and on due consideration of every circumstance requisite in the fitting out an expedition, I know no place in North America so proper as the port of New York. I therefore propose, till camp equipage is provided or that the weather permits to encamp the troops, to post them as near to New York as I shall be able.

Orders have been transmitted for the 64th and 65th regiments to embark at Halifax for Boston, from whence they will march into some of the colonies the most contiguous to this till farther orders; and as application has been made to Commodore Gambier to assist in this embarkation I am to hope it will be carried on with alacrity. Vessels have sailed for St Augustine to take on board the 21st regiment which I propose to post for a time at Philadelphia.

When the aforesaid regiments arrive it will be in my power to assemble the six regiments following, the 14th, 21st, 26th, 29th, 64th, 65th, and to add to them a small train of artillery. From the latest returns of their strength they may amount, sick and well, to about two thousand men, rank and file, from which a detachment to garrison Castle William must be deducted. I don't judge it advisable to send less than 2000 men on the proposed service, nor so few but in the confidence of the general aversion of the inhabitants to their present government and that few of them will take arms to defend the country against an invasion. But in all events it will be prudent they should be kept in awe by a force that shall appear to them respectable.

If war shall be decided I look upon it certain that the American colonies will be required to raise provincial troops, and take the liberty to give an opinion that considering the absence of the King's regiments, one thousand of the first troops raised in the eastern governments should be sent to join the six companies of the 59th regiment left at Halifax and that 1500 or 2000 provincial troops should be sent to Quebec for the better security of that province.

I cannot be otherwise than elated and greatly flattered with the favourable opinion our royal master is graciously pleased to entertain of my abilities and zeal for the honour of his arms, and gratefully acknowledge his goodness in the command he confers upon me.

The orders that your lordship informs me will be sent to the commander-in-chief of the squadron at Jamaica must contribute materially to the success of the enterprise proposed, which depends much upon secrecy and dispatch that the blow may be struck before the enemy has time to fortify and throw in succours. I am to mention likewise the absolute necessity that some of His Majesty's ships should convoy the troops from New York and that it would be proper some frigates should go up the Mississippi. I doubt not that Commodore Gambier will act in respect of a convoy to the utmost of his power.

I perceive by the letters that have passed between your lordship and the principal officers of the Ordnance that batteries are to be raised to defend the harbour of St John's, Newfoundland, in the manner the most expeditious; but I yet remain in doubt whether it is His Majesty's pleasure that the number of troops first required by the Board from North America should in all circumstances be employed on that service. The six companies of the 59th regiment left at Halifax will not be able to spare any men, but if they are speedily reinforced with a body of provincial troops the number required for the work in Newfoundland might then be sent from Halifax.

I return your lordship thanks for the copy of Sir Jeffrey Amherst's letter to the several North American governors; it contains some hints that may be useful though I don't recollect that it produced any great effects at that time. *Signed.* [C.O.5/89, fo. 92]

XXXIII

Governor Earl of Dunmore to Earl of Hillsborough (No. 8)

2 April, New York

My Lord, I have received your lordship's letter No. 2 [Vol. I, No. 897] and am pleased to hear that the account which I had transmitted relating to the disturbances on the borders of New Hampshire has been laid before His Majesty, and I hope that it together with the further information contained in my succeeding letters to your lordship, and particularly my last dated 9th of March No. 7 [Vol. III, No. XXVI] and the papers referred to therein, will prove sufficient to determine His Majesty to confirm his royal declaration of 1764 and that I shall speedily receive instructions in consequence thereof.

I continue to prorogue the Assembly from week to week that they may be in constant readiness to meet in case of a war.

The Acts of the last sessions of the Assembly are not yet ready to be transmitted.

A person in this town having received an account of the capture of some whaling vessels by the Spaniards off the island of Hispaniola,

I have thought proper to transmit to your lordship an extract of the letter [Vol. I, No. 1093i] which brought the report to this place.

Lieutenant-Colonel Bradstreet having discovered, as he asserts, that the patent obtained by Johannes Hardenberg and others in the year 1706, commonly called the Great Patent, was issued on false suggestions and without the forms that are necessary to make it legal and valid, and that therefore the said patent is void and the lands pretended to be granted thereby remain vested in the Crown: this the said Lieut.-Colonel Bradstreet represented in a petition to the governor of this province in order that he might obtain a grant of part of the said vacant lands, and the same has been examined before me in Council and a number of evidences as well on the part of the patentees as the said Lieut.-Colonel Bradstreet were heard, all which took up many sittings and in the end no other decision was made than, as the Council thought fit, to grant 20,000 acres of the said lands to the before-mentioned Lieutenant-Colonel Bradstreet as a compensation for the expense he has been at in endeavouring to prove the facts he alleges. The patentees however object to the said grant and determine to defend it at law, which Lieut.-Colonel Bradstreet nevertheless is resolved to prosecute and seems confident he can support and prove the whole, or nearly, to be vacant as above related. This has induced a number of officers and persons who are possessed of *mandamuses* and otherwise entitled to land by having served during the war in America to petition me [Vol. I, No. 1093ii] that I would of my own authority order their several locations to be surveyed for them upon these said lands and to grant the same to them, which they are willing to accept notwithstanding the claim of the said patentees. I have not thought proper to comply with the said petitions until I had represented the affair to your lordship, and for that purpose transmit the petition abovementioned and with it a state of the case to prove the suggestions contained therein, and in consequence of which, if orders be sent me to grant the said petitions, the Crown will be brought into no expense thereby, the petitioners being willing to carry on the suit at their own expense and risk. However, I shall not proceed in this affair until I receive instructions from your lordship thereupon.

It is necessary to observe to your lordship that the said patent, which contains about fifteen hundred thousand acres, was granted to seven persons only and no more than three pounds annual quitrent reserved, whereby a manifest prejudice is done to His Majesty's revenue, and though the patentees have been in possession of the said lands since the year 1706 yet there are not ten families settled thereon at this time. *Signed.* [C.O.5/1102, fo. 128]

XXXIV

Governor William Tryon to John Frohock and Alexander Martin[1]

5 April, Newbern

Gentlemen, I have received your letter of the 18 of last month [Vol. III,

1   Enclosed in Governor Tryon's letter of 12 April to Hillsborough, Vol. III, No. XXXVI.

No. XXVIII] respecting your negotiation and agreement with the insurgents.

If you have abused your public trust it is your duty to give satisfaction and make restitution to the injured. As for my own part, I entertain a just abhorrence of the conduct of that man who is guilty of extortion in the execution of his public character. The mode, however, of your agreement with the insurgents, by including officers who are amenable only for their public conduct to the tribunal of their country, is unconstitutional, dishonourable to government and introductive of a practice the most dangerous to the peace and happiness of society.

On the 18 of last month it was determined by consent of His Majesty's Council to raise forces to march into the settlements of the insurgents in order to restore peace to the country upon honourable terms and constitutional principles. This measure is not intended to impede nor has it the least reference to the agreement between you gentlemen and the Regulators, though it is expected in the execution of it more stability will be added to this government than by the issue of the convention ratified at Salisbury. *Copy.* [C.O.5/314, fo. 119]

XXXV

Charles Dudley to Commissioners of Customs at Boston[1]

11 April, Newport, R.I.

May it please your honours, the Comptroller gave your honours a short account by the last post of an assault and hindrance I met with while I was in the execution of my duty in the morning of the 3rd inst. By this post we give your honours a more particular relation of that affair and its consequences.

Though it appears somewhat contrary to instruction that a Collector should address your honours on any matter relating to the Customs without the concurrence of the Comptroller, though the subject of this letter may extend in some degree to the service in which I am engaged and may touch on some matters wherein the Customs are concerned, yet as it will pertain more immediately to myself I must beg your honours' indulgence to hear what I shall offer.

Your honours will know then that in the evening of the 2nd inst. about 6 o'clock a vessel called the *Polly,* whereof George Champlin was master, arrived from foreign parts in this port, I mean in the harbour of Newport, into which (it being calm) she was towed by the help of boats and there came to anchor about a cable's length from the quays. That it being universally known this vessel was expected from St Eustatius I kept a watchful eye for her arrival, and having discovered it I ordered a person in whom I could confide to give me an account of all her motions, well knowing had I been seen in the streets or upon the quays in the evening my hopes of detecting this vessel in her unlawful practices would have been totally defeated; still more likely to be so

1 Enclosed in John Robinson's letter of 13 July to John Pownall, Vol. I, No. 1393.

as there was no man-of-war in the harbour to give me assistance. I trusted too in some degree to the fidelity and vigilance of my outdoor officers. About 12 o'clock I was acquainted that the vessel in question had shifted her berth and was towing into the dock, from which I judged 'twas designed to smuggle her cargo that night, and having no doubt at all, as the vessel was under such suspicious circumstances, but that the Searcher or Tide Surveyor or both of them had boarded her on her first arrival and at least had placed proper tidesmen on her to take care of her till the morning, so I concluded these officers would be driven from their duty or prevented by some means or other from doing it, and therefore considered it as a duty incumbent on me to go to the place where the vessel was lying to examine her situation and to prevent as far as I could her too apparent design.

So secure did the owners and master of this vessel think themselves that they had not even taken the common precaution of keeping a watch on the quay to give an alarm, and I was not discovered (though the moon shone) until I was within ten paces of the vessel's side. The first person I saw was a merchant of the town, a brother of the master of the vessel. I accosted him but he made me no answer. I immediately stepped on board the vessel where instead of finding my officers on duty I found a number of men unloading her, some with lights in her hold, others upon deck hoisting up the goods.

I first asked if there were any officers of the Customs there to which I had no reply. The lights in the hold were soon put out and some of the people who were on the main deck retired to the quarter-deck. Two or three still remained, one of which I challenged so closely that he could not deny himself, he being a house-joiner whom I had employed in repairing the damages received at the Custom-house in the late fire. I put several immaterial questions to this man, some of which he answered; others more material he would not speak to. While I was talking with him I had a very good view of the goods on deck, and before the lights in the hold were extinguished I had a fair and full view down the hatchway. She appeared to me to be full-laden. The casks in general in the hold and those which had been hoisted upon deck answered the descriptive part of your honours' letter No. 1: some few were of a different construction and from their appearance I judged they contained indigo or East India piece-goods, but the bulk of the cargo I am pretty certain was tea.

I imagine about ten minutes had now elapsed from the time of my coming aboard when a man in a horseman's coat appeared up on the quarter-deck and seemed to take upon him the command of the vessel. I therefore applied myself to him, asking if he was the master? To which he answered yes. I then acquainted him with my being an officer of the Customs, that I was Collector of the port, and required him to tell me his name and the name of his vessel, to which he answered fictitiously. I then observed that the vessel was in an unlawful act and that therefore I would seize her for the King, and I accordingly did seize her and marked the broad arrow upon her mast. I had scarce time to reflect on my situation or to look round for the persons I had recognized on my first coming down to the vessel when I received a violent blow upon the back part of my head with a stick or some such weapon which deprived me of my reason. When I recovered from this blow I found myself surrounded by as many men as could well come near me, some of them striking me with their fists, some with their sticks, others kicking me. I desired they would suffer me to go ashore, that they would not add cruelty to injustice, that they might pursue their designs without murdering me etc. I had now got to that side the vessel which lay towards the wharf but found the people on shore had cast her off from it eight or ten feet. However, I used my best efforts and some man with more seeming humanity than the rest put out his hand and took hold of mine, by which help I got footing on shore; but this only preserved me for the savage fury of the people there, for I had no sooner recovered myself but I was knocked down again and afterwards was dragged by my hair along the wharf. The blows I had received on my head and stomach had now rendered me insensible either to pain or to my situation. When I recovered myself I found I was alone in the main street, my clothes torn from my back, my left eye shut up, and my right arm useless. In this wretched condition my servant (who had been waiting for me in an adjoining street and who hearing the noise and fearing for my safety had applied to the watch, who very inhumanly refused me assistance) found me and conducted me to my house where I am still confined to my room.

I am afraid I tire your honours with this detail, but as I must beg leave to make some remarks thereon I hope your honours will allow me to proceed.

I have told your honours this vessel at first arrived in the harbour so early as 6 o'clock in the evening at an hour when she might have been boarded and rummaged without any difficulty.

If she had then undergone a proper search by the proper officers detection must have followed. They could not have mistaken her cargo. They must have discovered she was laden with prohibited goods.

Now your honours will hear what the officers did. The Searcher went first on board of her the next morning. The Tide Surveyor, rather more attentive to his duty, went on board at 10 o'clock in the same evening she arrived but did not rummage her, and leaving her in the care of one tidesman. This tidesman had been on board of her from her entrance into the harbour's mouth, having gone off in a boat to meet her, and was the person the Tide Surveyor left her in care of, and he acknowledges that after the Tide Surveyor was gone on shore he went on shore too, and did not return to his duty until the next morning a little before break of day.

It appears then the vessel came into the harbour at 6 o'clock apparently laden, towed in by boats (a circumstance rather uncommon), the evening calm, the quays crowded with people, and I will venture to say (speaking comparatively) there was not a person in the whole town ignorant of this vessel's motions except the officers of the Customs who of all men ought to have known the best.

It was well known this vessel was expected from St Eustatius, and it is also well known that St Eustatius is the channel through which the colonies are now chiefly supplied with tea. The outdoor officers of this port have been repeatedly admonished on this head. They have long ago been acquainted with that part of your honour's letter No. 1 as relates to this baneful commerce; and yet here is a vessel brought into harbour in the face of day, carried deliberately into dock and there unladen in as much security and with as little fear as if she had been a sand-barge.

Your honours will find the revenue of this port decreasing without any visible decrease of its trade, and the incident expenses of it are great beyond all proportion. I have always considered myself as the responsible officer, and I have long felt with great concern my inabilities to check the abuses which are daily committed against the laws of Revenue and Trade. I have had no aid from the Navy nor support nor countenance from this government, not even a writ of assistance. Still I had some chance left: the fidelity and viligance of my outdoor officers. But here I have been most miserably deceived, and this last instance (which may prove fatal to me) will be a striking proof to your honours of the justness of sentiments I have often been bold to give. I never yet heard of an outdoor officer making a seizure in this port, and while they hold such principles as I have discovered I am satisfied they never will, though there are few ports on this extensive continent where they have so large a field. And 'tis a bitter circumstance to me to see these officers rather the servants of the people than of the Crown. I do not look for perfection in this order of men more than in others. I look only for common honesty and I look in vain, for I never yet trusted one of them with a single act of duty of any consequence in which I was not either disappointed or betrayed. But it does not comport with their views that illicit trade should be restrained, for that would lessen the wages of their corruption.

I may soon appear at the dread tribunal of Almighty God, and in that expectation I do solemnly declare to your honours, and I do believe it in my soul of conscience, that the barbarous treatment I lately met with was principally owing to base insinuations of my outdoor officers; for my abuse did not come from the hands of the lowest class of men, it came from men who are styled merchants and the masters of their vessels.

While this government remains under its present constitution, it will not only be impracticable for me to do my duty to effect but my person will be exposed to dangers which common prudence will bid me shun. I am therefore afraid I shall be forced to seek an asylum in some other country or at least withdraw myself from an office which I can no longer execute either with safety to myself or to the advantage of the Crown. The favours I have received from government I have a proper sense of, and while I am its servant I will serve it with my best powers. I am persuaded your honours in your great justice will make some note of this affair to the Lords Commissioners of His Majesty's Treasury, at which right honourable board I trust my friends will solicit my relief.

The night I was assaulted I lost my deputation which I have little chance to recover. I presume your honours will be pleased to furnish me with a new one.

Having at best but a poor constitution, this accident has reduced me to a very bad state of health. I must therefore beg the indulgence of your honours that I may transact the business of my office for a little time by a deputy for whose fidelity and good conduct I will hold myself accountable, and as far as my strength will allow my own attention shall be kept on the service. The person I would propose to your honours is Mr Richard Beale, and I entreat the favour of your honour's directions on this head. *Copy*. [C.O.5/72, fo. 283]

XXXVI

Governor William Tryon to Earl of Hillsborough (No. 70)

12 April, Newbern

My Lord, in my dispatch of the 31 of January, No. 60 [Vol. III, No. X], I informed your lordship an attempt to rescue Hermon Husbands was expected. Accordingly on the sixth of February I received intelligence by express that the insurgents were making preparations to come down to Newbern to release Husbands and to lay the town in ashes if opposed in their design, and that they were to begin their march from Sandy Creek (within their settlements) on the 11 of the same month. I immediately dispatched orders to several regiments of militia to hold themselves in readiness to march to the protection of Newbern. The Craven Regiment was embodied and kept three days in the town. The next day the 7th, the Court of Oyer and Terminer opened agreeable to commission issued the 22nd January for the purpose of receiving indictments against and hearing the trials of the Regulators. On this occasion I took the opinion of Mr Chief Justice Howard whether it would not be advisable to put Hermon Husbands on his trial for the libel he published against Judge Moore, no witness yet appearing concerning the riots at Hillsborough, that from the jealousy generally prevailing among the common people at his confinement I was apprehensive, while Husbands continued in gaol without being brought to trial and the courts of law open, no vigorous support could be relied on from the militia, but when he was found guilty of the charge there would be better grounds to keep him in prison until he had complied with the penalties of the law. The Chief Justice assured me it would be very proper that Husbands should be forthwith brought to trial and that he would take care that he was so. Accordingly the deputy Attorney-General, the principal being sick and absent from me ever since the last session of Assembly, prepared an indictment for the libel and presented it Friday the 8th of February to the grand jury, who not finding the bill and the Chief Justice not seeing cause to bind over Husbands to his good behaviour, he discharged him from his confinement the same evening.

Colonel Caswell's letter bearing date the 20th of February inserted in the minutes of the Council Journal of the 23rd of that month will inform your lordship of the sequel and consequence of Husband's release.

Not being satisfied with the temper and disposition of this grand jury nor pleased with the discharge of Husbands, and further no evidences coming down from the back-settlements to prosecute the insurgents agreeable to subpoenas sent to them, this court was dismissed and a commission issued the first of March for a new Court of Oyer and Terminer to be held here the eleventh of March. Finding the reason the evidences did not appear resulted from the intimidations of the insurgents who had threatened destruction to every man that should give evidence against them, I sent my secretary expressly up to Hillsborough with a letter requiring the attendance of the witnesses, and at the same time giving them assurance of protection by a body of forces. I also sent circular letters to the sheriffs of the several counties within this district, recommending to them on so important an occasion to make choice of gentlemen of the first rank, property and probity in their respective counties. These measures had their desired effect. Mr Edwards by his great diligence and activity brought down fifteen witnesses from Hillsborough under the confidence of the protection of government. The grand jury was formed of the most respectable persons. The court was opened. The deputy Attorney-General and Mr Gordon, whom I employed as assistant counsel for the Crown, drew out and presented sixty-one indictments, every one of which were found without a dissenting voice. The grand jury to the number of twenty-three, after the business of the court was over, waited upon me by appointment at the palace, when I made them an offer of going in person to suppress the insurgents if they thought the inhabitants of the province in general and the counties in particular in which they resided were hearty and willing to stand up in the cause of government, to compel the insurgents to obedience to the laws, to resent the insults offered to His Majesty's crown and dignity and the outrages already committed and still threatened against the constitution. They unanimously and thankfully accepted my proposal, promised me their interest and influence and instantly signed the Association, which with their presentment I herewith transmit [Vol. I, No. 1119ii-iii]. Printed copies of these have been circulated through the province.

In confidence, my lord, of such support and seeing a few days before in the *Wilmington Gazette* an Association of similar purport and intent entered into by the gentlemen on Cape Fear River, the next day the 18 I summoned His Majesty's Council, related to them some reasons that prompted me to offer my service, and took their advice on the expediency of raising forces to restore peace and stability to government. They approving the measure, I lost no time in sending requisitions to almost every county in the province for certain quotas of men, in appointing the time and place of their rendezvous respectively and ordering the necessary preparations to be made for this service. I have wrote to General Gage to request he would send me two field-pieces to cover the passage of the forces across the broad rivers on which it is expected the insurgents will make their stand.

To forward this business I went myself last week to Wilmington when I appointed Mr Waddell general of all the forces raised or to be raised against the insurgents, and expect he will get seven hundred men from the western counties to serve under his immediate command, who will march them into the settlements of the insurgents by the way of Salisbury, while I bring up the forces from the southern and eastern parts and break into their settlements on the east side of Orange County.

In my excursion to Wilmington I had the satisfaction to find the gentlemen and inhabitants at Cape Fear unanimous and spirited in this cause and the officers successful in recruiting.

On the minutes of the Council Journal your lordship may see an intercepted letter of Rednap Howell's, a leader in the councils of the Regulators. It gives the fullest proof of the wicked designs of these people. The judges' apology for their not attending their duty at the last Hillsborough Court also stands on the minutes of the Council. The conduct and proceedings of the insurgents on the sixth of March last in and near Salisbury will be best understood by the letter of Colonel Frohock and Colonel Martin to me and the deposition of Mr Avery, both which with my answer to the above letter accompanies this dispatch, as well as the general orders sent to the commanding officers of regiments [Vol. I, No. 1119i, iv-vi]. The forces in this neighbourhood I expect will march the 23rd instant and join other divisions as they move up the country.

I have communicated to Governor Bull and Mr President Nelson my plan of operation that they may prevent the insurgents from taking shelter in the provinces of Virginia and South Carolina should they retreat to those governments.

A principle of duty, my lord, has embarked me at this time in this service. The country seems willing to seize the opportunity and I cheerfully offer my zealous services, relying that the motive of this conduct will be favourably accepted by my most gracious sovereign. *Signed.* [C.O.5/314, fo. 105]

XXXVII

Governor Thomas Hutchinson to Earl of Hillsborough (No. 2)

19 April, Boston

My Lord, I shall transmit under this cover a printed paper called an Oration with a vote of the inhabitants of the town of Boston [Vol. I, No. 1137i-ii].

I have no apprehensions of any other mischief than its tendency, with other publications of the same nature, to confirm the people in a disrespect to the supreme authority and an opinion of their own independence, but this dangerous tendency makes it my duty to acquaint your lordship with it.

In their votes and in most of the public proceedings of the town of Boston, persons of the best character and best estates have little or no concern. They decline attending town-meetings where they are sure to be outvoted by men of the lowest order, all being admitted and it being very rare that any scrutiny is made into the qualification of voters.

As I shall put an end to the General Court in a few days I will not trouble your lordship with their proceedings until they are finished any further than to observe that the conduct of the Council has been unexceptionable and that although a majority of the House still continue under an undue influence they have given me but little trouble, and I hope their attempts to perplex the affairs of the government will open the eyes of the people and produce a change of members in many towns and a better temper. *Signed.* [C.O.5/760, fo. 136]

XXXVIII

John Stuart to Earl of Hillsborough (No. 31)

27 April, Charleston

My Lord, since my last letter No. 30 [Vol. I, No. 1032], I have not been honoured with any commands from your lordship.

The dissatisfaction of the Western tribes of Indians at the extensive cession of land at the congress at Fort Stanwix induced them to be active in forming confederacies and alliances with other nations. They were indefatigable in making peace with and sending messengers to the Southern Indians to balance the power of the Northern tribes who had made the cession and declared they would support by force what they had done. The success of their commissaries with the Cherokees will appear to your lordship by the extracts from Mr Cameron's letters [Vol. I, No. 1157iii, Vol. III, No. XXX] which I have the honour of laying before you, and the Mortar Warrior of the Upper Creeks seems to be in a disposition to give trouble probably from the same cause. I shall probably see him at Pensacola and hope to keep him quiet. I am humbly of opinion that the conjuncture is not favourable for renewing our applications for an addition of territory to the province of West Florida on the side of Pensacola, and our boundary on the Choctaws side is far extended; so that the lands already obtained from the Indians seems to be more than proportioned to the state of population in that country. Your lordship's instructions, which I hope to be honoured with on my arrival in Pensacola, will direct my conduct in this business.

The want of regulation among the Indian traders has given rise to many disorders in the different nations. The Indians, particularly the Cherokees, have been permitted to contract great debts. At their return from hunting the traders to whom they are indebted seize their skins and leave them destitute of any supply but what they may choose to trust them with. Under such circumstances they have been for some years past extremely uneasy and have lately proposed to give up a considerable tract of country as satisfaction for their debts, but the land which they have proposed to give up on this account is claimed by the Creeks. The traders greedily grasped at the offer and went so far as to draw up an instrument of cession [Vol. I, No. 1157ix] which they got signed by the principal chiefs, and in consideration gave the Indians all the goods they were possessed of in the nation. This irregular and very wrong step was taken without giving me the least intimation, and they have not as yet so far as I can learn digested any plan which may induce the assent of government and point out how such a cession to the Crown on their behalf can be made to answer the purposes of satisfying the respective traders for the debts due by the Indians.

The extension of our boundaries into the Indian hunting grounds has rendered what the Indians reserved to themselves on this side the ridge of mountains of very little use to them, the deer having left those lands, frightened by numberless white hunters and the settlements so near them. This the Cherokees are sensible of and therefore are easily induced to compliment away great tracts. At the late congress at Lochaber they wanted me to accept of several large tracts on behalf of individuals which I positively refused. They are, however, extremely pressing to settle their accounts with the traders by a cession of land as above mentioned, and as the matter has been agitated I am firmly of opinion that they will never think of making any other payment, which cannot fail of affecting the fortunes of the merchants engaged in the Indian trade. This is all that I am as yet enabled to submit to your lordship of this transaction.

I am so far recovered as to be able to embark on His Majesty's ship the *Carrisford* for Jamaica on my way to Pensacola: she will sail tomorrow.

Mr Cameron is gone with the Indian chiefs to mark the Virginia boundary line, which will I hope be accomplished at last to the satisfaction of the parties and meet with your lordship's approbation, which honour will render me extremely happy. *Signed*. [C.O.5/72, fo. 210]

XXXIX

Governor James Wright to Earl of Hillsborough (No. 56)

30 April, Savannah

My Lord, my last was of the 28th of February [Vol. III, No. XXII] in which I gave your lordship a full account of the proceedings of the Lower House of Assembly here, and that I had been reduced to the necessity of dissolving them. On the 6th of March I issued writs for electing a new Assembly which were returnable on the 23rd of April, and on the 24th I met them and opened the session. On the 25th they proceeded to make the enclosed most extraordinary resolve [Vol. I, No. 1165i] by which they absolutely deny His Majesty's right to put a negative upon or disapprove of a Speaker. This I was immediately made acquainted with and ordered the Council to be summoned to meet me in the Council Chamber the next morning at nine o'clock, when after stating the matter fully and observing upon the nature and tendency of such a procedure I put some questions to them for their opinion and advice, and then sent for the Lower House into the Council Chamber and dissolved them.

The particulars of the whole proceedings from the meetings to the dissolution your lordship will see from the enclosed extracts [Vol. I, No. 1165i-iii] certified by the Clerk of the Council and Clerk of the Assembly, and to which I beg leave to refer your lordship.

And here, my lord, I think it necessary to observe that the gentlemen of the Council who have always conducted themselves extremely well and with great tenderness to the people, after they had given me their opinions on the matter and advised me to dissolve the Assembly, observed that probably it might have been a hasty thing and not properly considered or attended to, and that if the Assembly was acquainted that they were to be dissolved in consequence of their resolution, possibly they might chose to rescind it, and therefore requested that I would delay sending for the House till some of them could go and have a little conversation with the Speaker about the matter; which they accordingly did but to no purpose, for so far from thinking they had done anything amiss or had gone too far they firmly adhered to their resolution.

And, my lord, they are so intoxicated with ideas of their own importance and power that it seems absolutely necessary to bring these matters to a point and settle them. For on all occasions they declare that they are well entitled to and have an absolute right to exercise all the parliamentary rights and powers that the House of Commons in Great Britain has, and now have been hardy enough to deny His Majesty's undoubted prerogative and authority.

My lord, if these people are not restrained in the parliamentary powers they claim, I'm afraid they will become petty tyrants and set up a kind of court of inquisition under an idea or pretence of promoting public justice. If His Majesty may think proper to signify his royal displeasure at their past conduct and to declare what parliamentary powers they may or may not exercise, I'm pretty certain it will entirely prevent any attempt of this kind in future and business will be done with ease and satisfaction.

Parliamentary enquiries in Great Britain undoubtedly are frequent and may be proper, but in our little sphere, my lord, seem totally unnecessary, and in the hands of such people as our Assembly generally consists of such a power with its concomitants I conceive would prove the greatest grievance.

I think it my duty, my lord, on this occasion to declare my sentiments with freedom for your lordship's better information on these matters.

I expect to have the honour of seeing your lordship the beginning of August, and when I hope I shall be able to give a satisfactory account of affairs in this province and of its importance. *Signed.* [C.O.5/661, fo. 41]

XL

President H. T. Cramahé to Earl of Hillsborough (No. 8)

30 April, Quebec

My Lord, I have the honour to acknowledge the receipt of your lordship's letters Nos. 36 and 37 [Vol. I, Nos. 823, 899]. The prospect of government's being established here upon a more firm and solid basis gives universal satisfaction to all His Majesty's new subjects, and the manner of doing it seems perfectly agreeable to their manner of thinking.

Though little attention ought to be paid to public newspapers, having seen some hints thrown out in the prints at home as if the Canadians upon the near prospect of a war had behaved with unusual insolence, I think it my duty to assure your lordship there has not appeared the least symptom of any such spirit breaking out among them, indeed the wisest and most sensible of them heartily rejoice at the late accounts of an accommodation with Spain having taken place, though we have it as yet from no other authority than the public papers.

During the course of the last winter several robberies were committed here in which from many circumstances there was reason to suspect some soldiers were concerned; they grew at last so audacious as to assault, almost murder, and rob the deputy Provost-Marshal of this district. Upon my offering a handsome reward in money and His Majesty's most gracious pardon to the informer, the gang has been discovered and three of the soldiers hanged as an example to the rest which I hope will have its due weight.

In justice to Lieutenant-Colonel Smith who commands at Quebec, to Major Skeene commanding the 52nd regiment, and indeed to all the officers of this garrison, I must declare that they gave all possible assistance to the civil magistrate upon the occasion, and I have the most sincere satisfaction in assuring your lordship that the whole winter through there has subsisted between the civil and military in every part of the province the most perfect harmony and good agreement. *Signed*. [C.O.42/31, fo. 38]

XLI

Governor William Tryon to General Hugh Waddell[1]

1 May, Col. William Bryan's, Johnston County
I have experienced much satisfaction on the receipt of your dispatches: the first from Mecklenburg met me on Sunday last near Mr Miller's on Neuse, the other dated from Salisbury the 27th ult. is just put into my hands by express.

I flatter myself the difficulties and fatigue you have struggled with in raising the troops required will be recompensed by a happy issue to our important undertaking.

I shall have in this camp tonight the detachments from the Neuse, Tar and Cape Fear divisions amounting nearly to eight hundred men exclusive of the detachments I expect to join me on the march. General Gage has furnished me with some brass cannon and the necessary ammunition which will be up here with the Neuse division this evening. The men are well-satisfied with the service and seem determined to do their duty with spirit and order. If you think, by leaving a captain or other officer behind you, you could get a few more men to follow you in a week or ten days you will use your own discretion in this point. I apprehend I shall not be able to get the troops to the place of destination before the 13th or 14th instant. They will move from this camp Friday afternoon. It may therefore be advisable that you should keep out of the heart of the settlement of the insurgents till after the first week in May so as to meet me the 13th or 14th instant at the appointed place of rendezvous. *Entry*. [C.O.5/314, fo. 259d]

XLII

Governor Thomas Hutchinson to Earl of Hillsborough (No. 3)

1 May, Boston
My Lord, in conformity to the uninterrupted usage from the first

1   From Governor Tryon's letter-book, enclosed with letter of 2 August to Hillsborough, Vol. I, No. 1434.

year of the present charter I have dissolved the Assembly and issued writs for a new election. I can find no clause in the charter which makes a new House of Representatives necessary every year, and I think if the practice had been otherwise it would have been well warranted, and it would have strengthened the government if the governor could have continued a House of Representatives that should be well-disposed; but an usage of four score years has rendered such continuance as impracticable as if the charter had been expressly in favour of it.

The party in the House in opposition have failed in many points, and on a motion for an address of congratulation they carried the negative by one vote only. Their address or answer to my speech, which I shall enclose to your lordship [Vol. I, No. 1175vii], was substituted instead of it, and falls much short of what was intended by the faction. I am not without hopes of a majority in favour of government upon the new election.

The Council during the session showed a good disposition until I communicated to them your lordship's letter which respects the lieut.-governor's conduct while Secretary. I informed them the letter was in consequence of the censure passed upon him by the Council and the present Secretary has so entered it upon his minutes. They have notwithstanding passed a vote in which they will not allow that it could refer to the proceedings of Council. Two or three gentlemen, who are of a particular connexion and were most violent against Governor Bernard, had prepared several resolves much more exceptionable than the vote which passed but they were rejected, and I expected my friends would have carried a vote for rejecting the whole motion. A majority finally agreed to the vote which I shall enclose [Vol. I, No. 1175vi], and which being matter of record after the record of your lordship's letter will I think convey to posterity greater dishonour than if the letter had stood alone.

The laws which have passed this session are of no great moment. As soon as they can be prepared I will transmit them with remarks in conformity to my instructions. There are five bills to which I refused my assent. My reasons for not assenting to the two for the governor's support [Vol. I, No. 1175ii-iii] are contained in my answer to the message of the House to me upon the subject. The other three I thought most advisable to take your lordship's directions upon, being doubtful whether His Majesty would approve of my giving my assent without a suspending clause which the Assembly will never suffer to be brought into any of their bills. That for establishing a Marine Corporation [Vol. I, No. 1175i] I refused because a bill for establishing a society for propagating the Gospel among the Indians had lately been disallowed by His Majesty after it had received the governor's assent, one reason of which disallowance I imagined to be the tendency of such an Act to call in question the power of the Crown by the governor to grant charters of incorporation without the aid of the General Assembly. I do not know that the persons interested in the bill would not be content with such a charter.

The bill respecting the militia [Vol. I, No. 1175v] is calculated to charge the disorderly state of it to a wrong cause, a defect of duty in the officers, when the true cause is want of subordination in the men. There is a clause which virtually repeals a clause in a former law altering the age when men are to be exempt from ordinary military duty from 60 to 50 years.

The bill which prohibits the importation of negro slaves [Vol. III, No. XLIII] appeared to me to come within His Majesty's 7th instruction to Sir Francis Bernard which restrains the governor from assenting to any laws of a new and unusual nature. I doubted besides whether the chief motive to this bill, which it is said was a scruple upon the minds of the people in many parts of the province of the lawfulness in a merely moral respect of so great a restraint of liberty, was well-founded, slavery by the provincial laws giving no right to the life of the servant, and a slave here is considered as a servant would be who had bound himself for a term of years exceeding the ordinary term of human life, and I do not know that it has been determined he may not have a property in goods notwithstanding he is called a slave.

I have reason to think these three bills will be again offered to me in another session, I having intimated that I would transmit them to England that I might know His Majesty's pleasure concerning them.

The two Houses elected the Speaker to manage the trade with the Indians, whom I negatived, as I did afterwards Mr Hancock and Mr Adams, as also two persons whom they chose by a very small majority in the place of Mr Goldthwait, the truckmaster. After so many negatives they would choose no more so that the two officers chosen last year must continue until others are chosen in their stead. They also renewed their votes for grants to their agents Mr De Berdt and Mr Bollan, to both which I have again declined assenting.

I urged them to repair the governor's house which is in very bad condition but they have declined it, some of their leaders intimating that if I would carry the Court to Boston they would make it a palace, but whilst they dispute His Majesty's authority to cause the Court to be held in any place except Boston I may not ask his leave to hold it there.

I have mentioned to your lordship everything which I remember to have passed of a public nature in the session. The private business does not deserve your lordship's notice, most of it is too trivial for the legislature to spend their time about and I wish I may be able by degrees to break them off from it.

I have a favourable account from the Eastern part of the province and hope shall suppress or keep under the disorderly spirit there, but the intruders multiply every day. *Signed.* [C.O.5/760, fo. 152]

XLIII

Bill of Massachusetts to Prevent Import of Slaves[1]

[1 May]

An Act to prevent the importation of negro slaves into this province.

Whereas the importation of negro slaves into this province is not

1 Enclosed in Governor Hutchinson's letter of 1 May to Hillsborough, Vol. III, No. XLII.

only found to be no real advantage to the interest of His Majesty's subjects here but also gives occasion to the most cruel and barbarous practices in Africa from whence such slaves are brought.

Be it enacted by the Governor, Council and House of Representatives that no negro slave of either sex shall from and after the first day of July in the present year of Our Lord Christ one thousand seven hundred and seventy-one be imported or brought by any ways or means whatever into this province, and that whosoever shall after the said first day of July import or bring into this province either by land or water any negro slave or slaves, or whosoever shall be the first purchaser or seller within this province of such slave or slaves so imported or brought into the same after the said first day of July, shall for every slave so imported, bought or sold, forfeit and pay the sum of one hundred pounds.

And be it further enacted that if any person shall hereafter be convicted of any breach of this Act, the negro or negro slaves so imported into or bought or sold within this province, shall be adjudged and declared free, and the person importing, purchasing or selling the same shall be obliged to maintain such negro or negroes in case he, she or they shall stand in need thereof in the same manner as by law they should be obliged to in case they should manumit them without bond being first given to the town-treasurer to indemnify the town.

Provided nevertheless that nothing in this Act contained shall extent or be construed to extend to the masters, owners or freighters of such vessels as before the making and publishing hereof shall have sailed from any ports in this province for the coast of Africa with intent to purchase negro slaves there and shall hereafter in prosecution of the same voyage import them into this province.

And be it further enacted that the forfeiture and penalty beforementioned shall be recoverable by presentment or indictment, and when so recovered shall be to His Majesty, his heirs and successors, for the use of the government; and that it shall likewise be recoverable by action in any of His Majesty's courts of record, and in case of such recovery the one moiety shall be to His Majesty for the use of the government, and the other moiety to any person who shall sue for the same.

This Act to continue and be in force seven years from and after the first day of July next and no longer.

April 24, 1771. This bill having been read three several times in the House of Representatives, passed to be enacted. *Copy*. [C.O.5/760, fo. 160]

XLIV

Earl of Hillsborough to Governor of Newfoundland

4 May, Whitehall

Sir, the King having thought fit to direct a tower or battery to be built for defending the entrance of the harbour of St John's in Newfoundland, and it being judged necessary for the greater security of that place and for rendering the said work more effectual that the cove of Quiddy Viddy should be destroyed so as to render it inaccessible, it is His

Majesty's pleasure that you do so soon as conveniently may be after your arrival in Newfoundland cause an account to be taken of such houses, fishing-stages and other buildings and possessions as may legally belong to any of His Majesty's subjects in that harbour under and according to the limitations prescribed by the Act of the 10th and 11th of William the Third for encouraging the trade to Newfoundland; and that you do ascertain by arbitration or other equitable method the sums to be paid to the proprietors in compensation of the damage which each shall respectively receive by the destruction of the said cove of Quiddy Viddy, and certify the same to the engineer employed to carry on the said works who will be authorized to pay such damages.

As the works proposed to be erected are not only of great importance to the security of the harbour of St John's but also to the commerce and fishery of Newfoundland in general, His Majesty has the fullest expectation that his subjects carrying on that fishery will give every facility in their power in a case in which their own interest is so much concerned and you will therefore not fail to urge this argument in case such of them as are settled in Quiddy Viddy should make any difficulty of parting with their possessions upon receiving a reasonable compensation for the damage they shall sustain.

It having been represented to the King that great disorders have been committed at the Magdalen Islands within your government by crews of vessels fitted out from New England and other parts of North America, to the great annoyance and prejudice of the sea-cow fishery of those islands, and which if not prevented will totally destroy the same, it is His Majesty's pleasure that you do take the most effectual measures for preventing such abuses as may disturb or destroy the said fishery and that you do not suffer any persons whatever to establish themselves on the said islands or carry on the said sea-cow fishery without licence from you, upon their agreeing to pay such consideration by way of rent to His Majesty for the same as you shall judge adequate to the advantage of an exclusive right to carry on so beneficial a fishery, which cannot in its nature be carried on in any other manner. *Draft.* [C.O.194/30, fo. 31]

XLV

Earl of Hillsborough to Sir William Johnson (No. 16)

4 May, Whitehall

Sir, I have received and laid before the King your dispatch No. 15 [Vol. III, No. XVI] containing general observations upon the state of Indian interests and repeating your apprehensions that notwithstanding the meeting of the Indians at Scioto (which had given so much alarm) had ended only in general resolutions of continuing their alliances, yet that there still remained some latent intention in the savages to form a confederacy dangerous to the King's possessions.

You will allow me, sir, however to observe that I am fully convinced as well from what has passed at this meeting as from my observations of the disposition of savages in general that those natural enmities and jealousies which subsist between one nation and another, if left to have their own operation without any interfering on our part, are a full security against any hostilities which (they well know) must in the end terminate in their own destruction, and which therefore they will never attempt unless provoked by such injuries and injustice as being common to all may make the resentment of them a common cause. To prevent such abuses, therefore, and when they cannot be prevented to endeavour to redress them, will I doubt not be the principal object of your attention, avoiding as much as possible interfering or becoming party in any councils the Indians may think fit to hold relative to their own interests. I do not mean by what I have said to express an opinion that there may not be some cases in which it may be advisable for the servants of the Crown in the Indian Department to take some share, nor would I have it understood that they ought to be totally indifferent about what passes at such meetings. On the contrary, they cannot be too active to obtain the fullest intelligence of the views and proceedings of the savages, because nothing will be more likely to defeat any designs which they may form to the prejudice of the public peace than the letting them see we know what those designs are; but if we persist in making ourselves parties in their politics, either directly or through the intervention of any particular tribe in which they know us to have a particular confidence, it is impossible to say to what consequences it may lead, and therefore I was concerned to find that the deputies which were sent from the Northern confederacy to the meeting at Scioto had insisted with the Indians whom they met returning from that meeting that the congress should be reassembled.

With regard to the continuation of the boundary line from where it was made to terminate by the treaty of 1768, it is a matter which requires much consideration; but it is impossible for me to give you any instructions upon that head without knowing precisely in what direction and to what point the Indians wish to have it carried. *Draft*. [C.O.5/72, fo. 188]

XLVI

Earl of Hillsborough to John Stuart (No. 21)

4 May, Whitehall
Sir, I have received your dispatch No. 30 [Vol. I, No. 1032] and have laid it before the King.

I hope the indisposition that prevented your intended journey to West Florida will not continue, for besides the propriety of the Superintendant visiting from time to time the different parts of his District, I must confess to you that I felt some disappointment on this occasion, and the more so as your deputy's letter of the 26th of December does not convince me that there was no cause for apprehending danger from the disaffection of the Indians; on the contrary it is one continued narrative of injuries and oppressions by the King's subjects carrying on trade with them that cannot fail of having the effect to excite the keenest resentments.

With regard to the war between the Creeks and the Choctaws, I still am of opinion that, though it might have been advisable to have removed any suspicion which they might have entertained of our acting as incendiaries, yet that we interfered further than was necessary; and I cannot but think that the best general rule of policy that we can adopt with regard to the Indians is to avoid interfering in the quarrels and disputes between one nation and another, and to confine our attention to a just observance of our public engagements with them and to the endeavouring to redress such abuses as may be committed in violation thereof.

The motions among the savages that you seem to think indicated a plan of dangerous union ought certainly to be attended to, but I have but little apprehension of the issue of a confederacy to be formed by so many different nations, having each to the other the greatest natural aversion and who have created to themselves those wants and necessities, the supply of which almost entirely depends upon their living in friendship with the King's subjects.

The influence which may be made upon the minds of the Lower Creeks by their communication with the Spaniards is more alarming; and therefore you will direct the persons through whom you negotiate with that tribe to omit no opportunity of informing you of what passes amongst them, and you will not fail to communicate to me for His Majesty's information whatever intelligence you may receive. *Draft.* [C.O.5/72, fo. 190]

XLVII

Commissioners for Trade and Plantations to Committee of Privy Council for Plantation Affairs

10 May, Whitehall
My Lords, pursuant to your lordships' order dated the 11th of February last [Vol. I, No. 976] we have taken into our consideration twenty Acts passed in the province of Pennsylvania in September 1769 and in February, May and September 1770, whereupon we beg leave to report to your lordships.

That these Acts having in general been enacted for purposes of domestic economy and convenience we have no observations to submit to your lordships' consideration thereupon, neither has any objection in point of law been reported to us by Richard Jackson Esquire, one of His Majesty's Counsel, to whom we have referred these Acts except in the four following cases.

The first and second of these respect two Acts passed in the said province of Pennsylvania in the year 1769 entitled 1st, An Act for the relief of John Relfe and Abraham Howel, prisoners in the gaol of Philadelphia, with respect to the imprisonment of their persons; 2nd, An Act for the relief of John Galbreath, a languishing prisoner in the gaol of Chester, with respect to the imprisonment of his person.

Upon these two Acts Mr Jackson observes that besides the general objection to which they are liable as private Acts of insolvency, he conceives them to be faulty inasmuch as they contain no clause excepting debts due to the Crown nor any clause in favour of landlords as to goods subject to distress nor a clause in favour of distant or absent creditors, every one of which clauses he thinks should make part of an insolvent Act. On the other hand he observes that it is probable the object of one of these Acts being confined in a country gaol is not indebted in any mercantile debt, that Relfe the bankrupt, one of the objects of the other, appears to be entitled in justice to his personal liberty, having complied with the laws of bankruptcy in this kingdom, and that these clauses having frequently as he observes been inserted in former insolvent laws of this province, it may be presumed they would have had their place here had there not been some proof given that there was no occasion for them, which is the more probable as there has been no objection made to the Acts though they passed above eighteen months ago, nor does there appear to have been any opposition to them in America.

The next case whereon Mr Jackson has stated any objection to the Acts under consideration refers likewise to an insolvent Act passed in the said province in the year 1769 entitled An Act for the relief of the languishing prisoners in the gaols of the several counties within this province with respect to the imprisonment of their persons.

Upon this Act Mr Jackson observes that it is defective in the particulars mentioned in the observations above stated, but that these defects are in a degree obviated by the trustees being required to act under the directions of the court; nevertheless he observes that he should humbly submit his opinion for the repeal of this Act thinking as he does these provisions necessary in these laws unless it should be deemed sufficient for this year to rely on the control given in the court, intimating however in such manner as shall seem fitting what should be the contents of future laws of this kind.

The fourth and last case refers to an Act passed in the said province in the year 1770 entitled An Act for the sale of goods distrained for rent and to secure such goods to the person distraining for the same for the better security of rents and to prevent frauds and abuses committed by tenants.

Upon this Act Mr Jackson observes that the greater part thereof is almost necessary in a country where lands and houses are frequently occupied by tenants, and so much of this Act has therefore long since been made part of the law of England by Act of Parliament but that there is besides a clause in this Act, empowering two Justices to deliver possession of the demised premises in case of a tenant's holding over, that goes beyond any provision in our law; that there is indeed in this Act a direction for empanelling a jury to try the fact of demise, but as it is possible the title may sometimes be in question (as for instance where the original lessor being dead, his will or the construction of it is disputed) he thinks it by no means proper such a question, perhaps a point of law, should be decided by two Justices, as it must sometimes be as the Act now stands, that therefore he wishes that an amendment of this law may be made by a further Act of Assembly enabling the tenant to allege that the title is disputed, at the same time naming the person who he alleges disputes the title, and in case such person shall on summons enter into recognizance to prosecute his claim within a limited time, the Justices to stay their proceedings, but in default of such prosecution or of the tenant's appearing judgement to be by default.

Having thus stated these observations and objections in the cases above enumerated, as reported to us by Mr Jackson, we shall submit it to your lordships' consideration to give such advice to His Majesty thereupon as to your lordships' wisdom shall seem fit. But before we close this report we think it our duty on this occasion to observe to your lordships that the proprietaries of Pennsylvania having in the laws of that colony for some time past been usually styled true and absolute proprietaries of the province of Pennsylvania and of the Counties of Newcastle, Kent and Sussex on Delaware, and it appearing that such style so far as it relates to the counties on Delaware is highly improper and unwarrantable, this Board in July last did accordingly represent the impropriety of this innovation to the said proprietaries, requiring it to be discontinued; in consequence of which intimation Henry Wilmot Esq., agent and attorney to the said proprietaries, who has attended us on the subject of the above laws, has informed us that the said proprietaries did accordingly give instructions thereupon and that the deputy governor in answer thereunto by letter dated the 6th of March last writes to the following effect vizt. That the Assembly being then on the point of breaking up, the laws passed that session must be in the usual form but that at the next meeting he shall take care to change it. *Signatories*, Hillsborough, Soame Jenyns, E. Eliot, John Roberts. *Entry*. [C.O.5/1296, p. 367]

XLVIII

Governor William Tryon to General Hugh Waddell[1]

10 May, Hillsborough

The army arrived here yesterday in good health and in high spirits. I shall be at the place of rendezvous at the time appointed, from whence I shall be happy to carry into execution in concert with you the most vigorous measures in the support of government and the invaluable rights of this constitution. The army with me is formidable from the unanimity that subsists through all ranks, independent of its numbers, which with officers included will be little short of two thousand men. I have a good train of artillery, well provided with ammunition. General Gage sent me some brass cannon from New York which fortunately arrived at Newbern the day before we marched.

Perhaps this letter may fall into the enemy's hands; if it should my operations will be the same and the principles of my actions invariable. My heart feels a generous warmth in the cause in which I am enlisted and I trust I shall pursue it with an ardour that will not discredit the confidence that is reposed in my conduct by both officers and soldiers under my command. *Entry*. [C.O.5/314, fo. 262]

1   From Governor Tryon's letter-book, enclosed with letter of 2 August to Hillsborough, Vol. I, No. 1434.

XLIX

Petition of Inhabitants of Orange County to Governor William Tryon[1]

15 May, Alamance Camp

The petition of us the Inhabitants of Orange County, humbly sheweth.

First, that we have often been informed of late that your Excellency is determined not to lend a kind ear to the just complaints of the people in regard to having roguish officers discarded and others more honest propagated in their stead, and sheriffs and other officers in power who have abused the trust reposed in them to be brought to a clear, candid and impartial account of their past conduct, and other grievances of the like nature we have long laboured under without any apparent hopes of redress.

Secondly, that your Excellency is determined on taking the lives of many of the inhabitants of this county and others adjacent to it, which persons being nominated in the advertisement we know them to be men of the most remarkable honest characters of any in our county. These aspersions, though daily confirmed to us, yet scarcely gains credit with the more polite amongst us; still, being so often confirmed, we cannot help having some small jealousies abounding among us. In order therefore to remove them, we would heartily implore your Excellency that of your clemency you would so far indulge us as to let us know (by a kind answer to this petition) whether your Excellency will lend an impartial ear to our petitions or no; which if we can be assured of, we will with joy embrace so favourable an opportunity of laying them before your Excellency with a full detail of all our grievances, and remain in full hopes and confidence of being redressed by your Excellency in each and every of them, as far as lies in your power; which happy change would yield such alacrity and promulgate such harmony in poor pensive North Carolina that the sad presaged tragedy of the warlike troops marching with ardour to meet each other may by the happy conduct of our leaders on each side be prevented. The interest of a whole province and the lives of His Majesty's subjects are not toys or matters to be trifled with. Many of our common people are mightily infatuated with the horrid alarms we have heard, but we still hope they have been wrong represented. The chief purport of this small petition being to know whether your Excellency will hear our petition or no, we hope for a speedy and candid answer. In the meantime your humble petitioners shall remain in full hopes and confidence of having a kind answer.

And as in duty bound shall ever pray etc. Signed in behalf of the country by John Williams, Samuel Low, James Wilson, Joseph Scott, Samuel Clark. Delivered to his Excellency at Alamance Camp the 15th day of May 1771, six o'clock in the evening. *Copy.* [C.O.5/314, fo. 181]

---

1 Enclosed in Governor Tryon's letter of 1 August to Hillsborough, Vol. I, No. 1433.

L

Governor William Tryon to the People now Assembled in Arms who Style Themselves Regulators[1]

16 May, Great Alamance Camp
In answer to your petition [Vol. III, No. XLIX], I am to acquaint you that I have ever been attentive to the true interest of this country and to that of every individual residing within it. I lament the fatal necessity, to which you have now reduced me by withdrawing yourselves from the mercy of the Crown and the laws of your country, to require you who are assembled as Regulators to lay down your arms, surrender up the outlawed ringleaders and submit yourselves to the laws of your country, and then rest on the lenity and mercy of government. By accepting these terms in one hour from the delivery of this dispatch you will prevent an effusion of blood as you are at this time in a state of war and rebellion against your King, your country, and your laws. *Copy.* [C.O.5/314, fo. 183]

LI

Governor William Tryon to Earl of Hillsborough

18 May, Great Alamance Camp, N.C.
My Lord, I have the happiness to inform your lordship that it has pleased God to bless His Majesty's arms in this province with a signal victory over the Regulators. The action begun before twelve o'clock on Thursday the 16 about five miles to the westward of Great Alamance River on the road leading from Hillsborough to Salisbury. The loss of our army in killed, wounded and missing amount to about sixty men. We had but one officer killed and one dangerously wounded. The action was two hours but after about half an hour the enemy took to tree-fighting and much annoyed the men who stood at the guns which obliged me to cease the artillery for a short time and to advance the first line to force the rebels from their covering. This succeeded and we pursued them a mile beyond their camp and took many of their horses and the little provision and ammunition they left behind them. This success I hope will lead soon to a perfect restoration of peace in this country, though had they succeeded nothing but desolation and ravage would have spread itself over the country, the Regulators having determined to cut off this army had they succeeded. The enclosed declaration to the troops [Vol. I, No. 1226i] will testify to His Majesty the obligations I lay under to them for their steady, resolute and spirited behaviour. Some royal mark of favour I trust will be extended to the loyalty that has been distinguished by His Majesty's faithful subjects within this province.

A particular detail of this expedition I shall transmit to lay before His Majesty as soon as I have settled this country in peace, hoping that the advantages now gained over a set of desperate and cruel enemy may meet with His Majesty's approbation and finally terminate in

1   Enclosed in Governor Tryon's letter of 1 August to Hillsborough, Vol. I, No. 1433.

giving a stability to this constitution which it has hitherto been a stranger to.

The army under my command amounted, officers included, to upward of eleven hundred men, that of the rebels to two thousand. The two field-pieces from General Gage was of infinite service to us. *Signed.* PS. General Waddell with two hundred and fifty men was obliged on the 9 instant about two miles to the eastward of the Yadkin to retreat back to Salisbury, the Regulators surrounding his forces and threatening to cut them to pieces if they offered to advance to join the army under my command. I shall march tomorrow to the westward and in a week expect to join the general. [C.O.5/314, fo. 141]

LII

Richard Jackson to Commissioners for Trade and Plantations

23 May

May it please your Lordships, in humble obedience to your lordships' commands signified to me by Mr Pownall's letter of the 16th inst. [Vol. I, No. 1221], I have taken into consideration the paragraph extracted from a letter [Vol. II, No. CX] of the Surveyor-General of His Majesty's Woods in America inserted therein, together with the two law reports accompanying the same.

The paragraph states a claim made by the proprietors of an extensive tract of land upon both sides of Kennebec River on which there is an abundant growth of the best pine timber, and which tract the proprietors allege to be private property; not as I conceive because it is parcel of the province of Main (within which only part of it lies) but because it is not the property of the province of the Massachusetts Bay nor indeed of any other corporate body but is the property of a set of private partners.

I have likewise considered the question stated in Mr Pownall's letter, namely whether by the provisions of the Statute of the second of George the Second, chap. 35 white pine trees of the diameter of twenty-four inches or upwards at twelve inches from the ground growing upon any tract of land possessed under a grant of the Council of Plymouth may or may not be felled without a licence from the Crown; and am humbly of opinion that in case the soil or tract on which such white pine trees grow was private property before the 7th of October 1690 they may be cut without a licence from the Crown notwithstanding any provision of the Statute of the 2nd of George 2nd.

That Act appears to me to have been intended to obviate the doubt that gave occasion to the question stated in 1726 to the then Attorney and Solicitor-General for their joint opinion, whose answer is contained in one of the reports transmitted to me. That doubt arose upon the 8th George 1st which was alleged to amount to a release of the Crown's right to part of the reservation contained in the charter of the Massachusetts Bay. This doubt is now totally removed and the single question that can occur on the 2nd of George 2nd is whether the soil in question was actually private property before the 7th October 1690, not whether it is within or not within a township.

The claim of the Kennebec Company (the proprietors mentioned in the Surveyor-General's letter) is founded on a grant from the Council of Plymouth long antecedent to the 7th October 1690, and I am therefore of opinion that in case their title be well-derived (of which I do not pretend to judge) they are exempt from the penalties of the second of George 2nd. I should have been inclined to think so, had that company been a corporation, but this is not now the question as they are a mere partnership.

But I think it my duty to remark to your lordships that although white pine trees growing upon the soil possessed by private persons under a grant of the Council of Plymouth are not the objects of preservation under the 2nd of George 2nd, yet in case they do not grow within the limits of some township they seem to come within the provisions of the 8th of George 1st, chap. 12. *Signed.* [C.O.323/27, p. 101]

LIII

President William Nelson to Earl of Hillsborough (No. 18)

27 May, Virginia

My Lord, I have received your lordship's dispatch No. 41 of the 11th of February [Vol. I, No. 988], which I laid before the Council as soon as I possibly could for their opinion upon the subject of the copper coinage. As the execution of the Act of Assembly is left wholly in the hands of the Treasurer for the time being it was judged proper to desire his attendance with the Speaker of the House of Burgesses at the board; and upon reading and considering the warrants [Vol. I, No. 988i-ii] which show the manner in which the kingdom of Ireland hath been supplied with copper money, the Treasurer agreed that he would appoint an agent in London, Mr John Norton, Virginia merchant, to perform the several requisites for obtaining the quantity that is wanted for this colony, and I expect that his orders to his agent will go by the ship which carries this letter.

The settlers in the back-country will be happy in relying on His Majesty's justice for a proper attention to their rights in the consideration of any propositions that either have been or shall be made by persons in England for the settlement of those lands.

I have ever been backward, and upon your lordship's caution shall be more so, in endeavouring to bring into discussion any part of the conduct of the clergy, from a doubt I have had of the legality of such proceedings; yet if faults should abound among that sacred order of men the people will be dissatisfied and religion must suffer if there should not be established some regular jurisdiction among us to enquire into their lives and doctrines. It is to me, and I believe to most men, immaterial where this power is lodged; perhaps it is most to be wished to depend entirely upon the authority of the Crown in right of its Supremacy, which will make it necessary that this authority should be delegated somewhere.

However, this matter may probably come to your lordship through another channel, as the Bishop of London's commissary hath summoned a meeting of all the clergy in the colony to be held the fourth of next month; and I am told that one principal point to be considered is the expediency or inexpediency of applying for an American episcopate. I will not take upon me to observe upon the propriety of this meeting, which is intended to determine a matter of some importance to the colony, without knowing the sentiments of the legislature and the people's in general upon it. Which way soever it may be settled by proper authority is I believe of more indifference to this colony than any other; as we have few among us who are not of the Established Church; but though upon our principles we cannot consistently oppose the establishments of bishops among us, yet I doubt much whether the laity could be brought to petition for them.

I understand that the commissary hath taken up this subject in compliance with the pressing instances of some episcopal clergy in the northern provinces who have grown warm in the dispute with some able men on the other side of the question, and however indifferent the Virginians may be (which is only my private opinion) the attempt will make a great noise to the northward where they have but just begun to cool after some former uneasinesses. As this question may possibly hereafter engage your lordship's thoughts I hope I am not wrong in letting you know how it stands here.

I flatter myself that a good progress is by this time made in marking the line between the Cherokees and this colony, of which your lordship will doubtless receive a full account when it is completed.

Mr Wormeley's appointment is I believe arrived though he hath not been with me to be sworn at the Board; however at all events I shall have his name inserted in a commission of oyer and terminer to be held the 11th of next month. *Signed.* [C.O.5/1349, fo. 98]

LIV

Clergy of Connecticut to Earl of Hillsborough

29 May, Connecticut

May it please your Lordship, the clergy of the colony of Connecticut in New England in voluntary convention, taking into consideration the distressed and truly deplorable state of the poor Church of England in America, in some parts destitute of any aid from the government at home and labouring under all the disadvantages and hardships in which a bigoted, fanatical government here think proper to involve it; and at the same time in all parts destitute of resident bishops, an order of officers which we believe Christ has set in his Church to direct, to govern, and to ordain ministers in it, and hereupon she is obliged to send her sons across the wide Atlantic to obtain Holy Orders; viewing these distresses under which the Church of England groans in America, we think it our duty to implore your patronage of, and to ask your influence towards obtaining, an episcopate for it. Under God and the King, we know of none, may it please your lordship, more able, and considering your wise and steady administration in the worst of times in matters of state, we think we have a right to presume that none can be more disposed to redress the grievances of the Church than your lordship.

A plan, may it please your lordship, has many years since been concerted by some of the principal dignitaries of the Church at home for an American episcopate, in which it is proposed that the bishop to be sent here shall have no temporal powers, that their authority shall be purely spiritual and operate only upon the clergy. Doctor Chandler in an appeal made to the public in behalf of the Church here has duly explained this plan and it is here universally approved and acknowledged to be harmless even by our bitterest enemies. This is the only plan upon which bishops are desired to be sent. A request which can injure none, a request which the truly pitiable state of the Church in America earnestly pleads, may soon be granted. It is conceived the Church in these parts labours under unparalleled hardships in this particular. Can a country of as large extent as Europe be found peopled by millions, one-third part of whom are professor of a Church which believes bishops to be of divine appointment? Can such a country so peopled, may it please your lordship, be found upon earth where no bishop resides? Can our request in favour of this Church as part of the national establishment, a request indeed so rational, so innocent and so modest, be denied? while the Moravians in one of His Majesty's colonies are allowed a bishop and the Roman Catholics in another are indulged the same favour. Nay, and every wild enthusiast in the British dominions is tolerated in the full enjoyment of all the peculiarities of his sect. If our request is denied, must not we think the Church in America singled out to bear the only frowns of the British government? and yet in point of loyalty we claim an equal standing with the foremost of any sect.

Our clergy, may it please your lordship, really want somebody to superintend them, our youth really want confirmation, and our candidates really want Holy Orders without travelling three thousand miles to obtain them. These are real wants which cannot be redressed without resident bishops; we therefore humbly conceive the suffering state of the Church here claims the attention of every good man and the patronage of every great man, and as we upon good reason believe both to be united in your lordship we presume to ask your patronage of it and hope everything from your wisdom and influence we desire for it.

The petition to His Majesty is desired to be presented by the Archbishop of Canterbury to whom it is sent, and he is desired to enforce the prayer of it. We have addressed the Archbishop of York, the Bishop of London, Lord North, the Lords of Trade and Plantations, the Bishop of Oxford, and the Bishop of Lichfield and Coventry, to afford their influence that bishops may be sent America.

May God long preserve your life and make you a lasting blessing to Church and State, is the earnest prayer of, may it please your lordship, your lordship's most obedient humble servants, the clergy. *Signed,* Jeremiah Leaming, secretary to the convention. Signed by order. [C.O.5/1284, fo. 112]

LV

Earl of Hillsborough to Governor Thomas Hutchinson (No. 8)

1 June, Whitehall

Sir, since my letter to you of the 4th ult. [Vol. I, No. 1187] I have received and laid before the King your dispatches of the 2nd and 19th of April, Nos. 1 and 2 [Vol. I, No. 1094, Vol. III, No. XXXVII], and I take the opportunity of the *Halifax* schooner which carries orders from the Lords of the Admiralty to the commander of His Majesty's ships at Boston to acquaint you that the attention you have shown to the duties of your station and the important objects committed to you is very pleasing to the King, and I have great satisfaction in finding that the publication of your commission of governor-in-chief has been attended with marks of civility and respect from every order of men except only such whose neglect you say rather does you honour; and although I cannot but lament that there are still some incendiaries in Boston who endeavour by publications of a very dangerous tendency and by inflammatory speeches at town-meetings to keep up in the lower sort a spirit of disrespect to government and an opinion of their own independence, yet I am not without hopes that the influence of the more respectable inhabitants together with the example of the good conduct of the Council will have sufficient efficacy to counteract their mischievous intentions and to preserve the tranquillity which has been so happily restored to that town. *Draft.* [C.O.5/760, fo. 150]

LVI

Governor William Franklin to Earl of Hillsborough (No. 31)

1 June, Burlington

My Lord, in my letter of the 30th of April [Vol. I, No. 1166] I informed your lordship of the Assembly's having at that time refused to grant any money for the supply of His Majesty's troops stationed in this province, but that I had hopes of their receding from their resolution at the next session. In these hopes, however, I have been greatly disappointed for they have again resolved by a great majority not to comply with the requisition. The only reason they give for their refusal is that the colony in its present circumstances is not of ability to make any further provision for the troops, which is one of the worst reasons they could possibly have invented, it being a notorious fact that the colony was never in a more flourishing condition than at present and that there is now actually in the Treasury a greater sum of paper-money unappropriated (originally made current for the use of the Crown) than is sufficient to answer the present demand. Their conduct therefore in this respect is entirely inexcusable, and I can assure your lordship that it not only appears in this light to me but to many of the principal inhabitants of this province. Some of the Members who voted against the supply had positive instructions from their constituents to grant it. The real cause of their extraordinary conduct, as I am informed and have reason to believe, is that they expect a dissolution will shortly take place in order to give the counties of

Morris, Cumberland and Sussex an opportunity of electing members agreeably to the law lately confirmed by His Majesty, and that by their refusal they shall recommend themselves to the bulk of the common people and so secure their elections. I had therefore some thoughts of dissolving the Assembly in hopes that after they had secured their seats by a new election they might be brought to grant the supply as formerly; but the gentlemen of the Council and many other friends of government were of opinion that if they were dissolved at this time it would be understood that it was on account of their refusing to burden the people with new taxes etc. which would increase their popularity, ensure the return of the same if not worse men into the Assembly, and, as they would be re-elected principally for their refusal of the requisition, they would probably still avoid a compliance.

My purpose at present is to prorogue them from time to time without letting them proceed to any business till I am honoured with His Majesty's pleasure thereupon. If it should not be thought expedient to punish them with a suspension of their powers of legislation by Act of Parliament, as was done in the case of New York on the like occasion, the same thing may be regularly and constitutionally done by continued prorogations until they consent to make the provision required. There are many matters both of a public and private nature for which they want to obtain Acts of Assembly and for which, rather than continue long without, I imagine they would give up the point. Or, if leave could be given me to consent to a Loan Office Act on condition that part of the interest should be annually applied to the support of the troops, I am convinced that the people in general would then insist upon the Assembly's compliance even though the money was allowed to be a legal tender in the Treasury and loan-offices only. But this cannot be done I suppose without an alteration in the late Act of Parliament respecting paper-currency in the colonies.

The only inconvenience which occurs to me is likely to attend the proroguing the Assembly till they are brought to a proper sense of their duty is that if they should happen to hold out any long time the officers of government would be deprived of their salaries which, small as they are, they cannot well do without. The present support of government, however, will not expire until the first day of October next, by which time I may perhaps receive His Majesty's particular directions for my conduct in this matter. *Signed.* [C.O.5/991, fo. 57]

LVII

Lieut.-General Thomas Gage to Earl of Hillsborough (No. 61)

4 June, New York
My Lord, I have the honour to acknowledge the receipt of your lordship's letter No. 42 [Vol. I, No. 1084] with a copy of the 43rd article of the King's instructions to Mr Hutchinson, Governor of Massachusetts Bay.

I shall not fail to conduct myself in the manner your lordship is pleased to recommend in the affair of Castle William; it was easy from a slight knowledge of the people to foresee that laws, constitution and

charter would be twisted to form complaints against the commit-
ment of the custody of the Castle to the King's troops, and as the relieving the provincial company and giving possession of the fortress to the
14th regiment required the most caution, I hope your lordship has
observed that the management of it was left entirely to Mr Hutchinson.
I objected indeed to one proposal which was that the King's officers
should accept of provincial commissions to empower them to do what
they were in my opinion fully authorized to do by virtue of their
commissions from the King, and it appeared to me in the light of a
degradation of the King's authority. This point was very soon settled
and I can assure your lordship that a cordiality has always subsisted
between Mr Hutchinson and me and that we have acted in concert
from the beginning of this affair and I trust we shall continue to do so.

The officer commanding at St John's, Newfoundland, will receive
orders by the first opportunity to furnish every man that can be spared
from the duty of the garrison to work upon the battery His Majesty
is pleased to order to be erected for the defence of that harbour, and
to give every other assistance in his power for carrying on the said
work.

My last letter [Vol. I, No. 1200] acquainted your lordship that I
apprehended the 64th and 65th regiments would be at or near Boston
before they could receive any counter-orders. They arrived at Boston
but received their orders before landing and have sailed since on their
return to Halifax, four companies of the 65th excepted who are accommodated in the barracks of the 14th regiment at Castle William till
the ship of war that is to transport them can be got ready for sea. The
parties that were recruiting in America are mostly returned to their
respective corps and there was time to stop several on their way to
embark for Great Britain though a few were sailed before the advice
was received of the convention with Spain.

The engineer who had been detached to West Florida is lately
returned from Pensacola which he left on the 15th of April. He makes
a bad report of the state of the storehouses, magazines and other
public buildings, particularly of the barracks or huts which are in a
miserable condition. These huts have undergone almost an annual
repair since the King's troops took possession of the province at more
expense than would have been incurred in building good barracks for
the troops that have been usually quartered there. Brigadier-General
Haldimand acquaints me that no repairs will now make them habitable
and that it would be so much money lost. Two of the batteries are
finished and three more marked out, which they hoped would be soon
completed for immediate service, which the likelihood of a war required
they should be, but they can have no duration unless they are faced
with brick and piled at the bottom. They are made with fascines and
filled in with a dry loose sand, as nothing better was to be procured.

The engineer is making out his general report of all the works in
the province with a draught of the harbour and plans and estimates
of the batteries as well as of a pile of barracks proposed for the troops,
which is referred to His Majesty's consideration and approbation.
The plans etc. cannot be completed in a manner fit to be transmitted

to your lordship by the present opportunity but I hope to lay the whole before you by the next packet.

Mr Stuart was wished for at Pensacola as it was judged necessary to assemble the nations, and I am told the Spaniards have tried to gain the Indians lately through the means of presents. There are complaints from the Indians as usual, and amongst others of the white people settling and hunting amongst the Chikesaws, a country very remote. The Creeks have plundered and drove away some settlers from beyond the Mobile River, as the Creeks pretend out of our bounds, upon lands they had never ceded. If all the Indians confine themselves to this method without proceeding further, it might save us trouble by preventing our vagabonds from strolling in the manner they do.

I continue to receive advices of councils, meetings, machinations and intrigues amongst the savages, though no certainty of any consequences likely to arise from them. I imagine this must always be the case whilst there is so general a peace as has lately subsisted amongst an active restless people who have no occupation but war and hunting; and it's probable that peace can't be of long duration but a war break out soon either between themselves or against the white people.

Several parties of Indians are gone out from the Lakes but no disturbance at our posts there. Numerous bands pass and repass Fort Pitt continually where they are very troublesome guests, and a number has been discovered near Fort Chartres, supposed to have killed or taken a soldier of the garrison who was missing.

The vessels on Lakes Erie and Huron are reported in too bad condition to be repaired but they are patching up one of them at the Detroit so that she may be navigated during the summer months, and with her assistance it will be contrived to supply Detroit and Missilimakinac with provisions for this year. I hope by next spring two other vessels will be built, artificers are set out for the purpose who will have time to perform their work, and seasoned timber being prepared for them I trust the new vessels will last three times as long as the old ones that were built in a hurry and with green wood. Two new vessels for Lakes Ontario and Champlain I conclude finished by this time, the others being quite rotten could be converted to no use but to be broke up for the sake of the ironwork.

There is scarcely any fort or post that is not in want of some repair every spring either of their defences, platforms, gun-carriages, magazines or barracks; and Castle William is likely to become far more expensive than any of the rest. I transmit your lordship a copy of a letter I have received from Governor Hutchinson [Vol. I, No. 1266i] concerning the damages the works of Castle William have sustained, and I received a demand prior to this for several new platforms and carriages and reparation of others. I have also the honour to transmit to your lordship two estimates [Vol. I, No. 1266ii-iii] given in by Captain Montresor, the engineer who was employed at Castle William, of the expense of those repairs as well of the works as of the platforms and gun-carriages; and wish to know His Majesty's pleasure thereupon, which I have informed Mr Hutchinson it is necessary I should first be acquainted with before I could undertake the repairs required. *Signed.* [C.O.5/89, fo. 113]

LVIII

Governor Earl of Dunmore to Earl of Hillsborough (Duplicate, Private)

4 June, New York

My Lord, according to the advice which your lordship is pleased to give me in your lordship's letter of the 12th of February [not found] I shall take proper steps to endeavour to compromise with Mr Colden, but in case I should not succeed I shall transmit to your lordship all the proceedings on that matter in the Court of Chancery, and I doubt not but that it will appear very evident to your lordship that there is a clear right in the Crown of disposing of that moiety for which your lordship's order was given to me.

Your lordship will have received my letter of the 9th of March [not found; ? private] before this; and as I continue in the same inclination of desiring to remain in this government, I shall not remove until I receive your lordship's answer. There can be no doubt that Mr Tryon would be pleased with the exchange: as he is perfectly a stranger to both countries he cannot have a reason for choosing other than that which is esteemed the most advantageous as to emolument, and I am persuaded he will be equally agreeable to the people of that province. I hope also he will be thought as fit to conduct His Majesty's service.

If Mr Tryon should repair to this place in consequence of his appointment, which I think cannot be before I receive an answer to my letter of the 9th of March, and I should not find him disposed to wait the issue of my application before he takes upon him the administration, I shall nevertheless remain here until I know it, which I have the greatest hopes may be conformable to my wishes. *Signed.* [C.O.5/154, fo. 10]

LIX

Governor Thomas Hutchinson to Earl of Hillsborough (No. 5)

4 June, Boston

My Lord, I am now to acknowledge the honour of your lordship's letter No. 6 [Vol. III, No. XXXI] by the April packet. I had signified to General Gage the necessity of some small repairs at the Castle, and by the last post he writes to me that he can do nothing more than represent that repairs are wanting and make the repairs when it is His Majesty's pleasure they should be made. The platforms must be new and the cost will be the same whether the work be done at one time or another, but the defence of part of the glacis against the sea being gone, if it should not be restored there is danger of great devastation from a heavy storm whenever it may happen. I had rather therefore advance a small sum in hopes of being reimbursed than the Crown should run the hazard of a much greater charge a short time hence, and I have wrote to General Gage conformably.

The new Assembly is now sitting at Cambridge. The choice of Councillors much the same as the last year; of four new elected I accepted two, of whom one has the character of being a friend to government and the other has not distinguished himself in opposition to it, the other two I had negatived the last year and, as they had not given me any reason by a change in their conduct neither could I prevail with the electors to bring in one or two who had formerly been left out of the Council, I thought it most advisable to repeat the negative. I will enclose to your lordship copy of the speech I made to the Assembly after the election was over, also of a message from the House and my answer [Vol. I, No. 1269i-ii]. I am not wholly disappointed in my expectation of a better temper in the Assembly. They have given up the claim of right in determining the place of the Court's sitting, and I think they are fully convinced that the arguments urged by the last Assembly from the form of the writ etc. were quite trifling.

There are inconveniences in holding the Court out of Boston unless the seat of government be altered, particularly I have not that advantage of knowing and making myself known to the members which I otherwise should have, and whilst there is any room to expect a return to Boston there will be room for the disaffected to make a handle of the Court's being out of town for increasing discontent and discord; and as I have both publicly and privately declared that whilst the right of the Crown to determine what place the Court should sit was disputed I would never ask His Majesty's leave to remove it to Boston, I humbly submit it whether the honour of government would not be saved although I should be allowed to prorogue the Court to Boston. I shall make the next prorogation to Cambridge and so from time to time until I am further instructed.

The two Houses will take some notice of that part of my speech which relates to the Eastern Country but I doubt whether they will take the proper measures for removing any of the intruders. I thought my intimating to them the probability of the matter's coming before Parliament would not be disapproved of by your lordship. *Signed.* [C.O.5/760, fo. 174]

LX

Earl of Hillsborough to Governor William Tryon (No. 2)

5 June, Whitehall
Sir, I have received and laid before the King a letter from the Earl of Dunmore as Governor of New York, dated the 2nd of April [Vol. III, No. XXXIII], and as his lordship continues to urge with great propriety the expediency of some speedy decision in respect to the lands on the west of Connecticut River, I presume it will be a satisfaction to all parties interested in the questions that have been agitated touching those lands to know that the Board of Trade have prepared and will in a few days transmit to the Privy Council their report on that business, and that you may expect before the fall to receive such instructions thereupon as shall without prejudice to titles derived from actual improvement and settlement open a way to immediately perfecting the grants to the reduced officers and soldiers who have been so long kept in suspense, and that after proper reservations are made of woodlands for the use of the Navy and the rights of individuals are provided for, the residue of the land remaining for settlement will be disposed

of upon such a plan and upon such terms as shall best correspond with the value and importance of them.

I have fully considered what Lord Dunmore states in respect to the proceedings at the Council Board upon the petition of Colonel Bradstreet and the step which has been taken in consequence thereof of granting to that gentleman 20,000 acres of the land patented to Hardenberg and others in 1706, and as I am equally at a loss to guess upon what ground it was that the Council took upon themselves extrajudicially to draw into question and decide upon the claims of those patentees and afterwards to grant so large a quantity of the land as 20,000 acres to one person without regard to the restrictions contained in the governor's instructions, I cannot but consider such proceedings as irregular and can on no account until that matter shall be further explained advise His Majesty to consent to the prayer of the petition for the further granting of those lands which Lord Dunmore has transmitted.

It is with great pleasure I acquaint you that the Queen was happily brought to bed of a Prince this morning, and that Her Majesty and the young Prince are as well as can be desired. I most heartily congratulate you upon this increase of the royal family, an event which gives the greatest satisfaction to all His Majesty's subjects. *Draft.* [C.O.5/1102, fo. 158]

LXI

Earl of Hillsborough to Deputy Governor Robert Eden (No. 21)

5 June, Whitehall

Sir, I have received and laid before the King your dispatch of the 4th of April, No. 9 [Vol. I, No. 1098], and most sincerely regret that anything should have happened to obstruct that harmony which it is so much for the interest of Maryland should subsist amongst the different branches of the legislature.

I can by no means think that the regulation of trade with the Indians, though an object of great importance to some of the colonies, is a business of such a nature as to require a congress of commissioners, nor do I think that the appointment of commissioners for such a purpose or indeed for any other of a general concern is strictly regular without express orders from His Majesty for that purpose, and is under all events a measure to which there are in sound policy so many objections as that it ought never to be adopted but in cases that cannot be provided for by any other means, which I apprehend is not the case of the business referred to the consideration of the colonies respecting Indian trade, as a law passed in any one colony and approved by the Superintendant would be a sufficient example for enacting a like law in another.

It is with great pleasure I acquaint you that the Queen was happily brought to bed of a Prince this morning and that Her Majesty and the young Prince are as well as can be desired. I most heartily congratulate you upon this increase of the royal family, an event which gives the greatest satisfaction to all His Majesty's subjects. *Draft*. [C.O.5/1284, fo. 96]

LXII

Richard Jackson to Commissioners for Trade and Plantations

5 June

My Lords, in obedience to your lordships' commands which I had the honour to receive from Mr Pownall the 30th of last month [Vol. I, No. 1256], I have considered the clause of the Act of the 8th of George 1st c. 12 intended for the preservation of white pine trees in several provinces (therein named) in America, and am of opinion that white pine trees growing on any lands in the province of Massachusetts Bay not erected into a township cannot under the provisions and reservations of that statute be in any case cut, felled or destroyed without a licence from the Crown.

I beg leave to add that I conceive the statute of 2 George 2 c. 35 has not removed the restriction imposed by the former Act but has on the contrary style narrowed the right of felling to such white pine trees only as grow on private property and (by an explanation of the province-charter) in the case of trees of a certain description to such as grow on land that was private property before the 7th of October 1690.

I take it that as the law now stands:

1. No man can cut white pine trees in any part of America (without licence) unless they grow on private property.

2. Not in Nova Scotia, New England, New Jersey or New York unless they grow within a township.

3. That in the province of Massachusetts Bay no man can legally cut white pine trees, 24 inches diameter, 12 inches from the ground, unless they both grow within a township and on land that was actually private property prior to the 7th of October 1690.

How far it may be expedient to continue or remove this restriction as to property without the bounds of a township or in any other respect is for the consideration of your lordships and the legislature. It is certainly obvious that though the law gives a protection to such trees growing on private property which they would not otherwise have had, it deprives them at the same time of another protection (the vigilance and care of the owner) that might perhaps have been more efficacious, as experience has shown it to be in most other cases. *Signed*. [C.O. 323/27, p. 105]

LXIII

Commissioners for Trade and Plantations to Committee of Privy Council for Plantation Affairs

6 June

My Lords, pursuant to your lordships' order of the 5th day of July 1770, we did on the 13th of that month take into our consideration the humble petition [Vol. I, No. 455i] of several officers and soldiers who served in North America during the late war and were reduced at the

peace, setting forth "That in pursuance of His Majesty's royal proclamation of the 7th of October 1763, they did obtain warrants from
the lieutenant-governor of His Majesty's province of New York for
sundry tracts of land to be surveyed and also patents for divers tracts
of land in the northern parts of the said province, which lands the
petitioners allege do yet remain unsettled owing to a claim of several
grantees under the government of New Hampshire, as also to a late
instruction of His Majesty to his governor of New York restraining
him from making any further grants in these parts till His Majesty's
royal pleasure shall be known, and humbly praying His Majesty to
permit the governor of New York to grant lands to such of the petitioners
at whose expense they have been located and surveyed and to confirm
to others the grants which have already been made". A request of such
a nature from persons so respectable and meritorious induced the
fullest attention to it. As it appeared to us by a letter from the governor
of New Hampshire to the Earl of Hillsborough [Vol. II, No. XVII],
communicated to us by his lordship, that the Council of that province
were preparing in order to transmit to His Majesty for his consideration
a full state of the claims to lands in that district under grants from the
government of New Hampshire, we thought fit to postpone any report
to your lordships on this case until that representation should be
received.[1] As no such representation has yet however been transmitted,
and as His Majesty's governor of New York has repeatedly and in the
strongest terms represented the necessity there is, as well in justice to
the case of the reduced officers as in propriety with respect to His
Majesty's service, that some speedy determination should be had
concerning that very valuable and extensive tract of land which in
consequence of those claims remains in great part unsettled and
unimproved and in which the greatest disorders are committed, it
becomes our duty no longer to delay making our report to your lordships
upon a matter which in every light wherein it can be viewed seems to
us of great importance.

Your lordships are already apprized by former reports of this Board
of the very extraordinary circumstances accompanying the grants made
within this district by the late governor of New Hampshire; and when
we consider how extravagant those grants are with respect to the
quantity of lands they contain, and combine that consideration with
the many irregularities and improprieties attending them in other
respects, we have no doubt that they would upon examination be
found null and void. But this is a matter which cannot depend upon
any opinion of ours and is a consideration which leads to questions
that cannot now be entered into without laying the foundation for
further delay in a matter that seems to require immediate decision.

We are sensible how difficult it will be, in a case where so many
opposite interests depending upon claims under very different circumstances are to be considered, to suggest any propositions that will
coincide entirely with the hopes and expectations of all parties; but
when we reflect how important it is to all to have some speedy deter-

1   See Vol. III, No. LXXXIX.

mination, we cannot but flatter ourselves that they will readily acquiesce in any reasonable conditions that can be proposed to them. And as this appears to us to be the only probable method of bringing this matter to a speedy issue, we shall beg leave in the first place to state to your lordships those claims which appear to us to be objects of consideration, and in the next place suggest what seems to us reasonable to be proposed with regard thereto.

The claim that seems to us to deserve attention in the first place is that of those persons who possess lands in this district under grants legally and properly obtained from the government of New York antecedent to any pretence set up by the government of New Hampshire to exercise the power of granting lands to the westward of Connecticut River, and before any such grants were made. From the best information we have been able to collect relative to this claim, it is confined to two or three grants, but a small part of which lies on the east of the Green Mountains, the country to the west of which was at all times, before the unwarrantable claims set up in consequence of the New Hampshire grants, admitted incontestably to be within the province of New York, and therefore we cannot but be of opinion that the proprietors of those grants should not be disturbed in their possessions on the ground of claims derived from these subsequent grants of the government of New Hampshire.

The claim that in the second place seems to us to merit attention is that of those persons who, in consequence of the grants from the governor of New Hampshire, have made actual settlement and improvement of any lands not comprehended within the limits of the possessions above stated; for however disputable their titles may be upon the ground of the grants themselves, yet there always has been and we think there always ought to be in the Plantations an attention to actual settlement and improvement that in cases where the possession does not interfere with the rights of others ought to have preference to any other consideration, and therefore we think that persons under this description ought to be left in entire possession of such lands as they have actually cultivated and improved, subject to no other condition or reservation either of quitrent or otherwise than what is contained in the grants under which they claim.

The third claim and indeed the only remaining one which appears to us to merit particular indulgence is that of the reduced officers and soldiers, as well those comprehended within the petition referred to us by your lordships as all others under the like circumstances who may have obtained warrants from the government of New York for the survey of lands to them in this district, the possession of which lands has been obstructed by the pretensions of those claiming under the New Hampshire grants; and with regard to these persons we cannot but be of opinion that no time should be lost in carrying their grants into effect, provided however that the surveys under which they claim do not include lands which were actually and bona fide settled and improved by persons claiming under grants from the governor of New Hampshire antecedent to such warrants of survey, who we think, for the reasons already given, ought not to be disturbed in their possessions on any account, but that if any such case should exist the officer or soldier claiming such land under warrant of survey from the government of New York should have compensation made to him by an adequate grant in some other part of the district.

With regard to the remainder of the lands contained in this extensive district which, if the foregoing propositions can by consent of the parties interested be carried into effect, will remain for His Majesty's disposal, they are on all hands represented to be of great value and importance not only from their natural situation and fertility but as including very extensive tracts containing large growth of white pine trees and of other timber fit for naval purposes. And when we consider the great advantage of them in this light, it is our duty in conformity to what we humbly represented to His Majesty on the 24th day of July 1767 respecting the preservation of woodlands in America to recommend to your lordships to advise His Majesty not to allow any further grants to be made or warrants of survey issued for any lands within this district until the person who in consequence of that representation has been appointed surveyor for that division of North America in which this district is included shall have carried his instructions into execution and shall have marked out for reservation to His Majesty such parts of it as shall contain any considerable growth of trees fit for the purposes abovementioned.

When this service shall have been executed we see no reason why the residue of the lands may not be laid open to settlement and improvement by grants from His Majesty; but we can by no means recommend to your lordships to advise His Majesty to suffer the Governor and Council of New York to dispose of the said lands either upon the terms or in the manner in which they have hitherto exercised that power.

The well-known fertility and particular advantage of these lands, arising from their situation in the midst of a well-settled and cultivated country, render them we conceive far more valuable than those which lie more distant and remote; and we see no reason why His Majesty may not in this case at least reasonably expect the same advantages which the proprietors of the provinces of Maryland and Pennsylvania derive from the grants of their waste and uncultivated lands, who over and above a quitrent nearly double what is reserved on lands granted by the Governor and Council of New York receive five pounds for every hundred acres, which is required to be paid to their respective Receivers whose certificate of such payment is made an indispensable requisite for obtaining a warrant of survey for the lands.

We have hitherto avoided stating to your lordships the pretensions of those persons who claim the possession of lands in this district under the exorbitant grants from the governor of New Hampshire, but who have not taken any steps towards acquiring possession of the land or for seating or improving the same. We are persuaded your lordships will agree with us in opinion that combining this circumstance of neglect of improvement with the little degree of attention which is due to the grants themselves from the manner and circumstances under which they were passed, the claims of these persons can or ought to have in a general view of them little weight in the present consideration. In order, however, to avoid all possible ground of complaint and to give facility to the execution of what is proposed in the cases already stated, we submit it to your lordships' consideration whether it may not be advisable after the reservations abovementioned for naval purposes have been made that such of the above grantees as shall before a certain day to be fixed by proclamation apply by petition to your [sic] Majesty's Governor and Council of New York for grants of land within the said district may receive warrants of survey for such parts of the said lands as they shall choose, in quantity proportioned to their ability to cultivate and improve the same, with this restriction however that no one of the said persons so applying shall either in his or her own name or in the name or names of any other person or persons in trust for him or her receive more than five hundred acres, the said grantees not to be subjected to the payment of the purchase-money above recommended or to any other terms or conditions than what are usually contained in grants from His Majesty's governor of New York under the present instructions.

We are aware that the claims of persons under this general description must vary in their circumstances, and that a greater regard and attention may be due to one than ought to be showed to another; but it is we fear impossible to distinguish any different case and we humbly conceive it is the less necessary inasmuch as these general regulations will not preclude any particular persons who think themselves entitled to particular indulgence from making such application thereupon as they shall think proper.

We beg leave further to observe to your lordships that there is another claim of interest in these lands which, as it stands upon grounds very different from those already stated, requires a separate consideration, and that belongs to the Society for the Propagation of the Gospel in Foreign Parts who claim His Majesty's consideration in consequence of their having in each of the townships granted by Mr Wentworth a reservation of five hundred acres in order to enable them to carry the laudable and pious purposes of their institution into effect.

As this claim of the above Society has already been considered as meriting His Majesty's attention and was, as we conceive, in great measure the foundation of that instruction to His Majesty's governor of New York by which the lands in this district were locked up from settlement until His Majesty's further orders were known, it becomes our duty to consider in what shape an adequate compensation can be made for it; and we beg leave to suggest to your lordships whether such compensation may not be most properly obtained, and every other religious establishment for which reservations were made in the New Hampshire grants effectually provided for, by subjecting every grant which shall be made of lands within this district in consequence of the above proposals to the payment to the said Society for the Propagation of the Gospel of one shilling proclamation money per annum for every hundred acres over and above the quitrent payable to His Majesty, and that it be recommended to the said Society that the moneys arising therefrom be applied solely to the purposes of providing ministers and schoolmasters for that district.

If these propositions should meet with your lordships' approbation and His Majesty should upon your lordships' advice think fit to adopt them, we do not apprehend that any difficulty will arise on the part of those whose different claims are meant to be provided for, or that any other measure will be necessary for the present than merely a transmission of the propositions themselves to His Majesty's governor of New York, with the signification of His Majesty's pleasure that the said propositions be made public in such manner as that all persons interested therein may have notice, and that the Governor and Council do within a reasonable time thereafter proceed to confirm to the reduced officers by grant the property of such lands for which they have obtained warrants, with exception only to such parts as may have been seated and improved by the claimants under the New Hampshire grants antecedent to the date of such warrants.

We further beg leave to submit to your lordships whether it may not be proper, in order to prevent disputes and for effectually securing the settlers under New Hampshire grants in the possession of what they have already settled and improved conformable to what is before proposed, that the actual state of such seating and improvement should be ascertained by a jury of disinterested persons to be summoned for that purpose by the sheriff of the county in which the lands lie, whose return thereof, with a plot and description thereunto annexed of the lands so seated and improved, being registered in the County Court will be a full evidence upon record of the title in case any question should hereafter arise thereupon.

With regard to the lands proposed to be granted to other persons claiming under the New Hampshire grants but who have made no settlement or improvement whatever, the execution of what is submitted in their case, as well as in the case of the residue of the lands which will remain for His Majesty's disposal within this district, must be suspended until the country has been surveyed with a view to proper reservations of woodlands for the supply of masting and timber for the Royal Navy according to the directions already given for that purpose; and we are of opinion that the instructions to be given to the governor of New York in the latter case cannot be too explicit and precise in order to guard against those irregularities and abuses which we are concerned to say have but too much prevailed in the exercise of the powers given to His Majesty's governors in America for the granting of lands, to the great prejudice of His Majesty's interest, to the discouragement of industry, and in many instances to the oppression of the subject by the exaction of exorbitant and unreasonable fees. *Signatories,* Hillsborough, Soame Jenyns, Edward Eliot, John Roberts, William Fitzherbert, Thomas Whately. *Entry.* [C.O.5/1131, p. 443]

LXIV

Extract of letter from Samuel Cornell to Elias Debrosses[1]

6 June, Newbern
A few days ago I arrived in town from the camp at Sandy Creek about

1 Enclosed in Earl of Dunmore's letter of 20 June to Hillsborough, Vol. I, No. 1326.

20 miles to the westward of the Alamance where we had the engagement with the Regulators. You will no doubt expect and be anxious to hear the fate of our campaign which I shall now communicate to you. On the 24th of April, as I wrote you per Capt. Gooding, the Craven and Carteret troops marched from this town under the command of his Excellency Governor Tryon. On the 3rd of May they reached Colonel Bryan's in Johnstone County, being the place appointed for the general rendezvous and where the southern detachment punctually joined us, making in the whole about 1000 men. From thence we marched to Hillsborough about 70 miles to the westward of Colonel Bryan's, with 8 pieces of artillery, three ammunition wagons, 20 commissary ditto with provisions, and a great number of wagons, carts etc. with baggage, sutlers' stores etc. On our arrival at Hillsborough we were joined by the Orange detachments consisting of 200 men exclusive of officers. Here a number of gentlemen from different parts of the province met his Excellency, who were properly equipped and formed in a troop of light horse and generously offered their service in support of their country and were extremely serviceable during the whole campaign. His Excellency now hearing of General Waddle being stopped by 2000 of the Regulators who had surrounded the General's camp near the Yadkin River about 7 miles from Salisbury, who had about 400 men under his command and was making down towards Hillsborough in order to join his Excellency's troops. But those insurgents being so very numerous obliged General Waddle to retreat back to Salisbury: they did him no other injury than destroying two wagons of ammunition. On hearing this disagreeable news the governor gave orders for the whole troops to march with all expedition to relieve General Waddle, but by the time we had crossed Haw River we had certain accounts of the rabble's being embodied and armed again to the amount of near or quite three thousand in order to prevent his Excellency from marching through their settlements and joining General Waddle. Upon this intelligence orders were given for the whole troops to make a forced march and secure an encampment on the Alamance, where there was both advantageous ground and a fine stream of water. This we happily effected and got everything in complete order, expecting every moment a visit from these rascals as we were then encamped within 5 miles of each other. But finding they did not attack us, and our intelligence from all quarters were that their numbers daily increased prodigiously, this was really alarming indeed, upon which his Excellency called a council of war, being on Wednesday the 15th May in the afternoon, when the board took under consideration this very weighty affair in order to speedily pursue the most prudent and spirited measures to bring it to a happy and honourable issue. His Excellency recommended to the board and gave it as his opinion that the whole troops should march next morning and attack the insurgents as soon as possible as delays were dangerous in our situation. His Excellency's motion was seconded and the whole board unanimous. Orders were then given for the troops to prepare, and in the morning of the 16th about 9 o'clock they marched, and about half after 10 we met the insolent daring rabble with drums beating and colours flying. As we

approached within about 300 yards of them they gave three huzzas, seemingly full of spirits and sure of success from their superior numbers which were quite or near three to one. The number of our troops in the field that day did not exceed 1,100 as there was a strong guard of the Johnstone detachment left at the camp with our provisions, baggage etc. The number of Regulators from the best accounts amounted to near or quite 3,000. Before the engagement began his Excellency sent to the insurgents, requiring them to lay down their arms and deliver their principals, which they refused and treated the message with contempt. The governor then sent the sheriff of the county to them, ordering them to disperse in one hour or he would fire upon them. This was to comply with a law of this province that was passed last sessions of Assembly and calculated exactly for these villains. This message also they treated with their usual contempt and insolence and cried out for Battle, battle. By this time we were within 30 yards of each other and some few within 10. Never did I see men so daring and desperate as they were, for during the expiration of the hour the governor gave them to disperse (as he would not fire on them till it expired) they would even run up to the mouths of our cannon and make use of the most aggrieving language that could be expressed to induce the governor to fire on them, for they actually seemed impatient and thought the hour too long; indeed they were so bold and hardened in their villainy as to run up to our first lines before the battle began and wounded some of our men with cutlasses. But they all met with their deserts, some were run through with bayonets and others taken prisoners, much wounded. Indeed none made their escape as soon as the hour allowed the insurgents for dispersing was expired, which our officers and soldiers much wished for. His Excellency gave orders to Col. Moore who had the command of the artillery to fire, who instantaneously obeyed the order by firing one of the cannon. This began the engagement a little before 12 o'clock, when immediately ensued a very heavy and dreadful firing on both sides, which continued about $2\frac{1}{2}$ hours when the rabble were so galled by the artillery and so hard pressed by our men, they were obliged to give way. We pursued them about a mile through the wood, took a great quantity of their provisions, baggage etc., also sixty-three horses and about 30 prisoners which were brought to our camp. The killed and wounded on our side are about 70 but of the rabble there were upwards of 300. Never did men behave with more true spirit and bravery than our troops, it must forever do them and their country honour. I am now from experience convinced that nothing but this spirited measure would have restored peace, tranquillity and a due obedience to the laws of their country. I had the misfortune to receive a slight wound by a musket ball in my thigh but not dangerous, and is now almost well. I left the camp twelve days after the battle during which time near 1,300 of the rabble had come in, surrendered themselves, laid down their arms, and taken the oath of allegiance. These were pardoned agreeably to his Excellency's proclamation. I dare say there is double of that number surrendered before this time. I expect the governor down in 8 or 10 days, and if he goes by water 'tis likely he will be with you some time the last of this month. *Copy*. [C.O.5/154, fo. 16]

LXV

Philemon Kemp to Governor of Georgia with Talks from Emistisiguo and Gun Merchant[1]

6 June, Augusta

Sir, being desired by Emistisigo and other chiefs of the Upper Creek Nation to act as their scribe at a talk that was given out 1st May last, I accordingly attended and send it you verbatim as it was delivered to me by the interpreter. *Copy. Signatory,* Philemon Kemp, clerk to Messrs. Robert Mackay & Co.

To the Governor of Georgia.

This is a talk from his friends and brothers the headmen and warriors of the Upper Creek Nation to let him know that they have not forgot their good talks and to keep their path that leads from the sun-rising always white and clean. It's true there are a great many mad young people amongst us, but notwithstanding we mean to continue the said path white and clean. We very well remember that the former talks of their old friends the white people were that no *small* breach between them and us should spoil this old white path, that the white people were always told by us that we were a mad sort of people but that nevertheless there were some sensible people amongst us that would take care to keep the path white and clean, and that this path was to lead from Charleston to the Cowities, from thence to the Tuckabatchies, from thence through the Abuccas, and from thence to the Chickasaws, which path should be always free for their friends the Indians to pass and repass upon.

We are pretty sure that the governor of Charleston has not forgot the talk that came from the Great King over the Great Water to the different nations of Indians behind. We did not know the contents of that talk before it was given out but we then approved of it very much. We remember that at that time the Cussaty King put all the different nations of Indians behind him, he being their elder brother. We therefore consented to everything he proposed. The Cussaty King then said that our land is like our flesh but that we could not cover the whole land ourselves and that when any person died they could only rot on one spot of it. He nevertheless cautioned us to take care of granting too much and told us that according to former treaties between the Indians and their old friends the white people the boundaries were fixed to the centre of the Savannah River, but now he had removed that line so far from Augusta as the firing of a small gun might be heard; but immediately the white people made a large step from that line which though it was not by our consent we are willing to have continue so. At the fixing the aforesaid boundary it was concluded by both parties that if any blood was spilt on either side, man for man must be given up. Mr John Stuart also said we should be paid one gun and three blankets for taking up and delivering to him any negro that we might catch beyond the boundaries. We have not forgot the talk respecting

1   Enclosed in Governor Wright's memorial of [12 December] to Hillsborough, Vol. III, No. CXXXIV.

one party murdering the other, especially as we have lately received three messages on that head. We are very sensible it is as it is represented in the talks, and that by our repeated delays to give satisfaction it is plain there are some amongst us who want to prolong the days of the murderers. We are informed that an Indian was lately killed by the white people upon Savannah River but we were not there to see it. We understand that the Great King over the Great Water is of the Tiger Family, so was the man that was murdered, he also took up arms in defence of his relations. He is the first man which you have killed, and we and all the headmen of the Tiger Family now send to assure you that they look upon that matter as taking proper satisfaction and hope the trade will not be stopped on that account. At the congress held by the four Governors and the Superintendant, they gave out a talk which we have not forgot and hope you will never forget. In former times the white path that came into our nation was for the use of the packhorses to bring goods into our towns. At that time the Corvity [*Sic :?* Cussaty, Cussiter] King told the Governors and Superintendant that if from that time we should find any persons trading in the woods either with or without packhorses we should consider them as French or Spaniards and should plunder them of everything they might have; and they also told us that if we found any white persons settling beyond the boundaries then fixed we should seize all their effects but not hurt their persons, which they would take care should be severely punished. They also told us that they thought we had given them a great deal of land and thanked us for it, and that if any white people's cattle should stray over the boundaries their owners should take care to drive them back again. We have not forgot what Mr Stuart then told us, that he should ask no more land from us and that he was appointed by the Great King to settle all disputes which might happen between us. We are informed by the Mountains Indians that the white people have sent cattle to the head of the Coosy River. We imagine Mr Stuart has not acquainted them with his promise to us or they would not do so. We had also a talk with the governor of Georgia and we will presently repeat it. When the boundary for the province of Georgia was fixed an Indian of the Tiger Family lived within the boundary but the white people were going to drive him out; we thought proper to insist upon his continuing there because he was an old and a sensible man who might thereby give us speedy intelligence of any ruptures that might happen between the white people and us and forward the talks from the governor to us. But we have never received any talks by the said Indian. At the same time we desired of the governor that if any Indian happened to travel in the land we had granted to the white people they might be supplied with such provisions as they should stand in need of. At the same time it was promised that no more cattle should be drove through our nation but that the path should be always kept green and we hope it will remain so. Mr McGillivray too then told us the governor said the Savannah River should be the boundary to keep in all bad talks from your nation and that your cattle should go no farther than your own yards, that he (Mr McGillivray) came very young to our nation and knew well how we lived and that the white people was obliged to be satisfied with the same coarse food that we used. The governor of Georgia also told us that 60 chalks should be paid us for every runaway negro we should catch and deliver to him. At the congress at Pensacola we gave the white people a little land but have not run the line yet for reasons you are well acquainted with: however, the days for running the line are not all gone.

We are informed that the white people have encroached two days march over the land that was given them. We suppose that these people by coming over the Great Water have not seen the path which Mr Stuart and the governor said should be like a mountain, not to be passed, or they certainly would not have done so. We are pretty sure that they have not lost the talk as Mr Charles Stuart was the man that wrote it, and we were told that our giving them that land would fix our friendship for each other as firm as a chain that cannot be broken. We also told them that we were poor and could give no other token of our friendship which we consider as a vine springing up and clinging round a great tree that would so nourish the vine as to bring it to its full growth in the space of four years. We do not blame the governors for their people settling beyond the line and we suppose the people know no better, but we are informed there is a very substantial man settled beyond the line with 40 negroes. The Indians have plundered others of some of their effects but did not hurt their persons. We mean to acquaint Mr Stuart of this immediately. We hope you will not blame us for this application for redress as it was always the intentions of both parties to make known their grievances to each other. The things taken from the white people were two pieces of small gold about 6 dollars, some pewter and one rifle-gun. We mention these particulars to convince you that it was not done with a view to rob but only to assert our native rights as we will make more fully appear when we see Mr Stuart which we hope will be soon. We do not think it necessary to say more on this subject.

We have heard that the Cherokees have given a body of land at the head of the Oconis to the white people in payment of their debts to their traders and that they are to have no more credit from them. Thomas Grierson confirmed this report and said it was true.

We also heard that Mr James Grierson carried an Indian down with him to Augusta and that this Indian saw the other who was murdered. We wonder much that an account of the murder was not sent to us as the said Indian brought letters from Mr James Grierson to his brother Tom Grierson. We hear that the man who committed the murder has a scar upon his eyelid and as we apprehend you may think of punishing him we send this to prevent it and to tell you that we are very willing to give up the said Indian by way of satisfaction.

We have had no talks from the Northern nations but have received some white ones from the Mountains which acquaint us that they expect the Northern nations will send us a talk; when it comes will certainly communicate it to Mr Stuart. A young king from this nation is expected to bring it.

Thus far Emestisigo in behalf of himself and the other headmen and warriors. The Gun Merchant now acquaints you that, as an old friend both to his country and the white people, is very glad that the above mentioned murder was committed as he hopes the cloud which has been for some time hovering over our heads will thereby be dispelled and the sky become once more clear and serene; that to prevent any mischief arising from the murder he had called a council of all the headmen together as early as possible which he hopes will convince you and all their mad young people that we desire to keep the sky clear.

He hopes also that now the governor, merchants and traders are sensible of our desire to hold fast the chain of friendship, and that they will supply us with more ammunition than they did last year, which nevertheless he cannot blame them for as there was a jealousy subsisting between us; also with plenty of other articles as the mad young people will be ready to listen to his friendly talks and decline breaking open the white people's houses. Oakchoy, Upper Creeks, 1 May 1771. *Copy*, certified by J. Wright. [C.O.5/651, fo. 115]

LXVI

President William Nelson to Earl of Hillsborough (No. 19, Duplicate)

14 June, Virginia
My Lord, it becomes my duty to acquaint your lordship that the very great calamity which hath befallen this colony by the overflowing of some of our rivers hath produced the memorial, of which I enclose your lordship a copy [Vol. I, No. 1316i], from many of the most respectable merchants and planters. The total loss of about four thousand hogsheads of tobacco at the several inspection-houses on James and Rappahannock Rivers, for which the public stand engaged to pay, will greatly affect if not wholly ruin the credit of many merchants here as well as their principals in Great Britain if a speedy remedy is not applied for the relief of the sufferers; and it would be very injurious also [to] the welfare and credit of the colony in general if some early provision is not made. Upon these considerations, after laying before the Council His Majesty's instruction by which I am restrained from holding an Assembly except for the peace and welfare of the colony, they are of opinion that the necessity of this case will justify me in convening the representatives of the people and have accordingly advised me to issue a proclamation requiring them to meet the 11th of next month in order to consider what might be done in this time of distress. Your lordship may be assured that my utmost care shall be used to prevent their entering upon any other business than this single object and that on this and every other occasion His Majesty's instructions shall be the rule of my conduct.

The public loss which I have mentioned, though it amounts to 40 or £50,000, is trifling when compared to the sufferings of individuals, their lands being destroyed for above an hundred miles upon both sides of James River, their houses, tobacco, corn, stocks of cattle, horses, hogs, sheep etc. being swept away by the torrent, besides the loss of some people in their houses. In short it is by far the most dreadful catastrophe that hath happened to Virginia since its first settlement by the English.

I enclose your lordship copies of the proceedings in Council [Vol. I, No. 1316ii] and of the proclamation in consequence of them. *Signed.* [C.O.5/1349, fo. 102]

LXVII

Governor Thomas Hutchinson to Earl of Hillsborough (No. 7)

22 June, Boston

My Lord, at the time of the date of my letter No. 5 [Vol. III, No. LIX] everything appeared fair for the removal of the General Court to Boston. What effect a very ill-judged proceeding of the House of Representatives since that time may have to prevent it, I must submit to your lordship's consideration, and I may not omit transmitting it [Vol. I, No. 1334i] as it is published in a newspaper under the name of a Protest, and this by the first opportunity lest His Majesty's pleasure should be signified before this fact comes to his knowledge. It passed the House when it was much more exceptionable but was reconsidered and some high paragraphs expunged and the members were enjoined to take no copies of them. The whole proceeding has been opposed by about a third part of the House in number and men of the best character in the House, and the majority of the other two-thirds seem to have come into it rather from ignorance than any ill intention; and the real spring of it is from the heads of the party who make the most clamour at the Court's being held out of Boston and yet secretly wish it may not return there because they will be deprived of the principal means of keeping up discontent in the minds of the people. It is so mean and pitiful a performance that when proper notice is taken of it, which I intend shall be before the close of the session, it will be of real service to government and strengthen my interest with the people, and it is already considered by many as a miserable effort of a few despairing men which will only sink them the faster. *Signed.* [C.O.5/760, fo. 184]

LXVIII

Governor Peter Chester to Earl of Hillsborough (No. 24)

23 June, Pensacola

My Lord, since the writing of my letter No. 21 [Vol. I, No. 1325], enclosed with these dispatches, I was agreeably surprised at the arrival of Lieutenant-Governor Durnford who has just returned from the Mississippi. The time appointed for the detention of the packet being nearly elapsed has prevented his giving me a full account of his proceedings to be transmitted to your lordship by this opportunity, but he has communicated to me in a letter (the copy of which is here enclosed) [Vol. III, No. LXIX] such sentiments relative to that part of the province as have immediately occurred to him.

The settling the country contiguous to the Mississippi in townships is a measure I have always thought the most advisable both for the protection and convenience of the inhabitants, but the injudicious and impolitic method that has formerly been pursued in this province of granting great tracts of land in those parts to persons, many of whom are utterly unable and others unwilling to cultivate them, who have been allowed to take up the greatest part of the front on the River Mississippi from Manchac to the Natches, will prevent my laying out townships in several places upon this river where they would be most convenient and necessary unless these patents can be considered as forfeited and revested in the Crown, the patentees having never made any improvements, paid no quitrents, or complied with one of the conditions contained in their grants.

I have here enclosed a blank form of the letters patents [Vol. I, No. 1336ii] that have passed for granting these lands except those granted in pursuance of the King's *mandamus*, some of which are different, by which your lordship will see the particular terms and conditions under which they hold. These are conformable to His Majesty's instructions, and I shall be glad to know whether I cannot regrant those lands (whereon no improvements have been made and which have all their quitrents due and unpaid) to such petitioners as will really cultivate them, without any farther process than publishing a proclamation requiring the proprietors to cultivate and pay their quitrents within six or twelve months and notifying the consequences in case of their neglect.

There being no settlements upon these lands, no distress can be made for the King's quitrents and I do not think it probable that the Assembly who are most of them interested will soon frame any law for the effectual collecting of the quitrents or authorizing the governor to regrant lands that are unimproved. Neither will a jury be easily prevailed upon, if writs of intrusion are brought for any other mode of process commenced wherein they are to determine between the Crown and the subject, to bring in any verdict against the latter.

Your lordship will see by the copy of Mr Durnford's letter that he agrees with me in opinion that there should be some assistance given to the first settlers and that they should be protected by troops from the insults of the savages, who would be also highly necessary at first to support the civil magistrates in carrying the laws into execution and assisting them in maintaining good order and decorum. I have before in my letter No. 3 been more particular on this subject and therein showed that the expense to government in supporting troops for a few years in that part of the country would not be great and would probably be very soon repaid in the acquisition of many useful colonists.

I hope Lieutenant-Governor Durnford will enable me by the next opportunity to transmit to your lordship his report relative to the cut that has been proposed near Fort Bute and a more particular account of his observations.

The complaints mentioned to have been received in the copy of the enclosed letter from the Spanish commandants at Point Coupe and Fort St Gabriel are against some of our licentious traders on the Mississippi for selling of rum to the Indians. I will inquire into the particular facts and shall not fail to use my utmost endeavours in punishing the delinquents. *Signed*. [C.O.5/588, p. 291]

LXIX

Lieut.-Governor Elias Durnford to Governor Peter Chester[1]

23 June, Pensacola

Sir, your Excellency was pleased yesterday to express a desire of having my sentiments of that part of the province under your government which I have lately visited as also my observations thereon. As it cannot be done with that clearness and accuracy I wish without being accompanied by the actual survey made, and it being a work of some time to put in proper form, I hope your Excellency will excuse my giving a general description at present. The lands are universally good from Perle River to the west, and from the junction of the Manchack or Iberville Creek with the Amit to the north the lands are equal to those of the Mississippi, if not superior, having an easy communication with the lakes and to the other seaports in the colony, which will if once settled be the most flourishing part of your province, for the lands which are situated between the River Mississippi and Amit are superior in goodness to what I have ever imagined and exceed what report says of the Mississippi, over the banks of which river these lands have many advantages. It is with some concern I have observed the front of the River Mississippi where the high land is easy of access granted to persons who have either no ability or no inclination to become settlers and the very lands which should have been reserved for townships are in the possession of private persons; for this reason I would recommend it to your Excellency that an application be made to Parliament for an allowance per annum to be employed in making real and not imaginary surveys of the interior parts of your government which hitherto is very imperfectly known.

Townships are in my humble opinion the first object worth attention and to induce people to assemble together every needful assistance should be given to the first settlers, for be assured, sir, after the first township is settled on a proper plan very little difficulty will happen in settling others, and this is the only means I can foresee of procuring any kind of security to new settlers against the savages. At the first settling and for a few months a little Indian corn, rice, powder and ball, nails and a few tools ought to be furnished them, for which indulgences they should be obliged to build a place for divine worship and any other public building necessary as soon after they become settled as possible.

It would surprise your Excellency much to see how few settlers are resident on the various lands granted on the Mississippi, for leagues not an inhabitant, and many who are inclined to settle are prevented by this means; even of those few who are resident, many are of a very licentious behaviour and who defy all law and good order. Whenever it may be thought proper to lay out a township it will be necessary to have a party of the military to assist the magistrates in supporting good order until the township is well settled which will be the speedier done

---

1   Enclosed in Governor Chester's letter of 23 June to Hillsborough, Vol. III, No. LXVIII.

by this means as it will carry the face of protection with it.

As yet it is not in my power to speak positively of the cut proposed to open a communication from the forks of the Ibberville to the Mississippi as the various levels I have taken as well as the survey itself is not committed to paper; but if I am to speak from appearances I have every reason to hope something may be done to answer the purpose but it will be attended with some considerable expense.

I cannot help observing to your Excellency that the small tribes of Indians formerly in our interest named the Pascagoulas, Mobiliens and Tensas lately settled on the River Amit have by some means been induced to remove to the Spanish side of the River Mississippi, and is a detriment to us as these Indians although small in numbers are very useful and would be more so if that river was once well settled.

I have received complaints from the Spanish commandants at Point Coupe and Fort St Gabriel, Ibberville. The nature of their complaints will appear by their letters which with my answers I take the liberty of enclosing to your Excellency, who I doubt not will pursue every measure to prevent the evil consequences they forbode from happening. The Spanish inhabitants at Point Coupe were very much alarmed when I left Manchack and in great dread of a sudden rupture with the savages which will be equally terrible to our few settlers.

I have now communicated to your Excellency the most material incidents which have fallen under my notice in the western part of your government during my residence there. *Copy.* [C.O.5/588, p. 295]

LXX

Memorial of Traders to Creek and Cherokee Nations to Governor James Wright[1]

[? June]
Sheweth, that your memorialists have traded unto the Creek and Cherokee Indian nations for upwards of ten years in which time they have acquired a confidence with them, and as far as it was possible for men circumstanced as they were have adhered to the rules and regulations laid down to them from time to time; but from various causes according to the exigencies of the different nations and as unforeseen incidents intervened they have been under an indispensable necessity of deviating so far as respected the trusting Indians and purchasing from them skins in the hair.

With respect to the Cherokee Indians, that in the year 1761 when peace was concluded between His Majesty's subjects in South Carolina and them, the Cherokees had suffered so much during the course of the war particularly by two expedition carried into their country by His Majesty's troops that they were reduced to nakedness and extreme poverty; therefore it became necessary to trust them not only with ammunition but with guns and clothing also before they could go out to hunt even for a bare subsistence. That to add to the miseries which

1 Enclosed in Governor Wright's memorial of [12 December] to Hillsborough, Vol. III, No. CXXXIV.

that war subjected them to, the Northern and Western Indians soon after fell upon them in swarms and harrassed them in their own hunting-grounds for several years so much that their debts with their necessities increased annually. And with respect to the Creek Indians who are a turbulent as well as numerous, bold and warlike people.

That the traders to the Creek nation before the year 1760, when several of His Majesty's subjects were plundered and murdered by them in their towns, were few in comparison to the present number and generally consulted together for their mutual benefit. That the apparent fortunes made by sundries in that trade who died or declined business about that time tempted so many others to become adventurers that they were too numerous and their interests too widely dispersed and disunited to act with unanimity for the common good, and each endeavouring to acquire to himself as great a share of the trade as possible, carried a greater quantity of goods into the nation than was necessary for the general trade of it. That those goods being once in the nation, the Creeks who for a long time have scorned control look upon them as effects that they had an interest in, and unless they had been trusted with them the traders would have been in constant alarms for the safety of their persons as well as property.

That a war between them and the Choctaws for five years past has greatly prevented them from hunting, nevertheless being used to large supplies they could not be curtailed without giving up the prospect of ever recovering what was already in their hands; and what contributed to the loss and disappointment of the traders was that the Creek Indians could not be prevailed on for several years past to dress their skins so that if the usual quantity of hides had been taken they were not equal in value to what they would have been dressed, although the Indians obliged them to take them at the same rate.

That a general agreement among the traders to stop the importation of goods to these two nations for a season, had it taken place, might have produced fatal consequences and been regarded by these savages in the same light as a declaration of war against them, which they would have the more readily interpreted it into as they are of opinion that a war rubs off all scores, therefore and from a natural reluctance to sit down with a certain known loss and in hopes of retrieving their losses from year to year your memorialists continued their supplies to these Indians until they have insensibly involved with themselves their creditors in their misfortunes.

That at last seeing no other way of averting the impending ruin and enabling them to continue in the trade, your memorialists proposed a mode of extricating themselves and other debtors both from a burthen too intolerable to both parties, which the Cherokees partly from a motive of justice and partly to encourage an ample supply in future adopted with eagerness and earnestly persist in, as your Excellency will have seen by the talks addressed to you on this occasion, namely a cession of land on Savannah River to the Crown to be disposed of as His Majesty shall think fit for the purpose of paying off their debts contracted since the conclusion of the war with them in the year 1761.

That the lands proposed to be ceded are claimed by both nations, not occupied by either of them, nor of any use to them as a hunting-ground, being so near to our settlements that the upper line will reach no higher on the south side Savannah River than the Carolina settlements on the north side already do.

That this tract contains upwards of three millions of acres of as fine lands and as fit for the culture of indigo, tobacco, hemp, flax, wheat and other valuable produce as any in America, having the advantage of the Savannah, Okony, and Great Ogetchy Rivers bounding or running through it.

That the lands to the norward are much worn out and very insufficient for the increase of population in those parts as appears by the number of immigrants that flock from thence into the upper parts of South Carolina and Georgia where they are obliged to remain, being unable through poverty to transport their families by water to the Floridas and prevented from journeying by land by the several nations of Indians they have to pass through.

That if the lands proposed to be ceded are exposed to sale or otherwise granted in small tracts for a moderate or even a small consideration per acre, a sum much more than sufficient to discharge all the Indian debts and every expense attending it would be presently raised and they would be settled with a great number of industrious poor white families that would cover the more opulent plantations nearer the sea coast and prove an acquisition of the utmost importance to His Majesty's province of Georgia in particular.

Your memorialists then confiding in your equity and readiness to assist them as innocent sufferers as well as your discernment in seeing the necessity of relieving the Indians from a load of debt that is grown irksome to them most earnestly entreat that you will be pleased to lay their distressful and indeed ruinous situation at the feet of our good and gracious Sovereign in whose wisdom and paternal care of his most distant subjects they firmly and humbly hope for relief. *Copy. Signatories*, George Galphin; James Jackson & Co.; Robert Mackay & Co.; for Martin Campbell & Son, Woodgion; Rae, Whitefield & Co.; Edward Bainard; J [?]. Waters; James Grierson; James Spalding & Co.; Edward Keating. [C.O.5/651, fo. 127]

LXXI

Governor Earl of Dunmore to Earl of Hillsborough (Private)

2 July, New York

My Lord, I received your lordship's private letter dated the 4th of May [not found]. I am perfectly sensible your lordship could have no other motive for interesting yourself in my removal to Virginia than what your lordship expresses, and it is not inconsiderately that I differ in opinion with your lordship. I grant the advantages in point of emolument but the climate is such that it will oblige me to live without my family, which will make my residence in that country where there is little or no society so tiresome that I cannot be certain I should be able to stay there any time, and therefore it might be more advantageous for me as well as my family that I should remain in a place where there is a harmony between me and the people, and at the same time suits so well with my disposition that I cannot foresee anything which may interrupt the design I had in coming to this country at first, but may continue here as long as His Majesty shall judge proper. In consequence of which I have referred your lordship's letter to Mr Tryon, and if he agrees to the change I shall be pleased with being indulged in my desire of remaining in New York. *Signed.* [C.O.5/154, fo. 20]

LXXII

Additional Instruction to Governor Guy Carleton

2 July, St James
Whereas it hath been represented unto us that the terms and conditions under which you are by our royal instructions to you authorized and directed to make grants of lands within our province of Quebec under your government have been found to be inconvenient and inadequate, and that it would be more for our advantage and for the benefit of our subjects inhabiting in and resorting to our said province if the ancient mode of granting lands which prevailed under the French government before the conquest and cession of the said province was to be adopted; we therefore taking the same into our royal consideration and being desirous to promote as far as in us lies the welfare and prosperity of our said province have thought fit to revoke and do hereby revoke and annul all such parts of our said instructions to you and every clause, matter and thing therein which contain any powers or directions in respect to the granting of lands within our said province, and it is our will and pleasure and you are hereby authorized and empowered to grant, with the advice of the Council of our said province, the lands which remain subject to our disposal in fief or seigneurie as hath been practiced heretofore antecedent to the conquest thereof, omitting however in such grants so to be made by you the reservation of the exercise of such judicial powers as hath been long disused within our said province. And it is our further will and pleasure that all grants in fief and seigneurie so to be passed by you as aforesaid be made subject to our royal ratification and also be registered within our said province in like manner as was practiced in regard to grants held in fief and seigneurie under the French government. *Entry.* [C.O.43/8, p. 93]

LXXIII

Earl of Hillsborough to Governor Thomas Hutchinson (No. 9)

3 July, Whitehall
Sir, I have received and laid before the King your dispatches of the 1st and 15th of May, Nos. 3 and 4 [Vol. III, No. XLII, Vol. I, No. 1217].

His Majesty approves of your having dissolved the Assembly and issued writs for a new election; for although it may as you observe be doubtful upon the true construction of the charter whether an annual election is requisite, yet the practice has been so established by usage that it may not be advisable, for the present at least, to attempt an alteration.

With regard to the vote passed in Council in consequence of my letter signifying His Majesty's approbation of Mr Oliver's conduct, I think it no otherways material than as it must remain a proof to posterity of a conduct in the present Council equally dishonourable and disingenuous.

The three bills to which you withheld your assent until His Majesty's pleasure was known are certainly of such a nature as required that caution; and if the King's governors would in all cases show the same attention to their instructions it would be of very little consequence whether the Assemblies did or did not insert in their laws the suspending clause.

I observe that the bill for establishing a Marine Society is not liable to the same objection upon which the law for establishing a society for propagating the Gospel amongst the Indians was disallowed, and therefore His Majesty does not think there is any material objection to your assenting to such bill if it should be again proposed. But it is His Majesty's pleasure that you should not assent to any bill prohibiting the importation of slaves, nor to a militia bill so long as the provisions of it are introduced by a preamble containing assertions that you think are not founded in fact.

Your conduct in putting a negative upon the persons elected to manage the trade with the Indians and upon the votes for payment of money to Mr De Berdt and to Mr Bollan is approved by the King, as well as in refusing to move the General Court to Boston so long as the Assembly continues to dispute the authority by which you are directed to cause it to be held in any place except Boston; but you may assure them that whenever they shall cease to dispute that authority, and it shall not be found inexpedient for other reasons, His Majesty will most graciously comply with their wishes.

In your letter No. 4 you say that the judges of the Supreme Court were struck with the informality of the instrument enclosed in my dispatch No. 5 [Vol. I, No. 986], by which I presume you mean the warrant for the pardon of Ebenezer Richardson.

As you do not explain yourself as to the nature of the informality I am at a loss to guess whether the doubt refers to the mode of doing it by warrant to the Recorder of London or to the omission of the christian name of the boy. If it refers to the former case I can only say that the same mode of pardoning persons convicted of murder in the colonies has been in all cases invariably pursued almost ever since the Revolution; and therefore though I have always had great doubt of the propriety of it, yet it was not fit for me to make any alteration in a practice against which the law-servants of the Crown had reported no legal objections. If the doubt on the contrary refers to the omission of the name of the boy, it was an unavoidable defect as I was not able either from your letters or from the fullest enquiry to procure his christian name. *Draft*. [C.O.5/760, fo. 170]

LXXIV

Earl of Hillsborough to Governor Peter Chester (No. 4)

3 July, Whitehall

Sir, by the last packet which arrived from Charleston a few days ago I received your dispatches numbered from 10 to 19 [Vol. I, Nos. 1042, 1046, 1051–2, 1054, 1057–9, 1100–1, 1121], and having laid them before the King I have the satisfaction to acquaint you with His Majesty's entire approbation of your conduct in every part of it.

I am sensible that had the dispute with the Court of Spain terminated in war the colony of West Florida must have been from its situation, which you very justly describe, exposed to great danger without the protection of a naval force; but its principal security would I conceive have in that case depended upon such offensive operations as might have counteracted any designs which the enemy might have formed against it.

There is not I think at present the most distant prospect of any disturbance to the public tranquillity; but at the same time I see with satisfaction the steps that are taking to fortify the harbour of Pensacola, and if the demolition of the old brick fort at Mobile and the making use of the materials for the batteries that are constructing at Pensacola would facilitate that service I see no objection to it, leaving however to your consideration whether it may not be advisable to consult General Gage upon it before any step is taken.

I am glad to find you approve of the orders given to Mr Stuart to repair to Pensacola, and indeed from your representation of the present state of Indian affairs it seems to have been in every light a very necessary measure; and your conferring together upon the variety of arrangements you point out is the more to be wished as I observe that there is upon some of them a difference of opinion between you.

In the present temper of the savages as described in your letter No. 11 it appears to me that we ought carefully to avoid every measure that is likely in its consequence to increase the jealousy and suspicion of our integrity which you say they have so strongly entertained; and therefore though I think an enlargement of the boundaries of West Florida might be desirable yet it seems to me that it would be a dangerous attempt at this time.

With regard to the engagements entered into with the Indians when we first took possession of West Florida that frequent meetings should be held with them and proper presents distributed, I see no reason why those engagements are not inviolably preserved since the same provision which was at first made for these services is not only continued but also a very large allowance made to the Superintendant on that account.

The unsettled state of Indian affairs arising from the want of a proper plan for regulating our commerce with them is indeed a circumstance very much to be lamented; but you will see from the paper which I now enclose to you for your private information that the proper Offices here have not failed in a due attention to so important a matter, and it will be at least some satisfaction to you to observe how nearly the ideas of the Board of Trade in respect to the proper regulations for the Indian trade correspond with your own.

You will naturally ask how it came to pass that a proposition of this nature in respect to a matter that was on all hands agreed to be equally urgent and important should have remained so long without any decision upon it; but when you recollect the questions that have been agitated in respect to the authority of Parliament over the colonies, and more especially in taxation, and the countenance given to those opinions which tended to encourage these questions, you will see at once the difficulties which stood in the way of such a plan, and which together with the request of almost all the colonies that they might be allowed to regulate the Indian trade themselves entirely defeated that measure and induced the Crown to leave this service to be provided for by provincial laws; and whenever those colonies which are connected with the Indians in the Southern District can be induced to agree upon similar bills for the regulation of the trade they may rely upon a ready concurrence here in whatever shall be found to be just and reasonable for that purpose.

Your ideas, expressed in No. 12, of the necessity of keeping the House of Assembly in a state of due subordination as well as of the proper mode of appointing an agent are perfectly just; so long as you regulate your conduct by those sentiments you cannot err.

The reasons you give in your letter No. 13 for deferring your tour through those parts of West Florida which are adjacent to the Mississippi are very satisfactory, and as I have a good opinion both of the ability and integrity of Mr Durnford I entirely approve of your having in consequence of Brigadier Haldimand's request sent him to survey that country, and shall be very glad if his report shall enable me to lay before the King any propositions that may have the consequence to remove the obstructions which have hitherto attended the improvement of so valuable a part of His Majesty's possessions.

Your appointment of a deputy in Mr Hannay's office in the place of Mr Doig, giving notice thereof to the patentee, was equally necessary and proper, and corresponds I conceive exactly with the letter and spirit of your instructions.

I was very much concerned to find by your letter No. 19 that the advices contained in Mr Charles Stuart's dispatch to you had created so great an alarm; but as you say that you could not, after waiting for some days for fresh intelligence, learn that any considerable mischief was done and had good reason to believe that what happened was only the act of riotous young Indians accidentally passing through the settlement from whence the alarm came, I hope the fears of the inhabitants will have subsided, but I think it exceedingly necessary that the course of the boundary line should be ascertained and have wrote to Mr Stuart upon that subject.

I have not had time to examine so fully into the claim of Mr Le Fleur as to be able yet to see how far his pretensions are or are not well-founded, but I will make a further enquiry and will send you such directions thereupon as shall appear to be necessary.

Enclosed I send you by the King's command an Order of His Majesty in Council of the 7th of June last [Vol. I, No. 1295] for disallowing three Acts passed in West Florida in 1767 and 1769, and that you may know the reasons that have induced such disallowance I send you enclosed for your own information a copy of the Board of Trade's representation thereupon. *Draft.* [C.O.5/588, p. 201]

LXXV

Earl of Hillsborough to John Stuart (No. 22)

3 July, Whitehall

Sir, I have received and laid before the King your dispatch of the 27th of April No. 31 [Vol. III, No. XXXVIII].

The advices contained in Mr Cameron's letters [Vol. I, No. 1157ii-iv, vii, Vol. III, No. XXX] are in many respects interesting and important but I cannot after the closest attention find in them anything to alter the opinion I have already expressed to you of the improbability for the present at least of a general Indian war.

I am very much inclined to agree with you that the present conjuncture is not favourable to an extension of the limits of West Florida but I observe from Governor Chester's correspondence that he thinks such a measure would on many accounts be expedient, and therefore I shall wait the result of your conference together upon this subject before I take the King's pleasure for any positive instruction upon so important a question. I think it fit however to observe to you that there is one matter which I trust will have been an object of your immediate attention on your arrival in West Florida, which is the ascertaining with precision the courses of the boundary lines already agreed upon with the Indians, the evidence of which is so very defective as to have occasioned great embarrassment to Governor Chester in some late transactions with them; and I cannot avoid upon this occasion again reminding you of the great utility that would attend the having the course of the lines agreed upon with the Choctaws, Creeks and Cherokees throughout the whole of your district accurately delineated upon some correct map of America, one copy of which should be transmitted to me to be laid before the King and one copy lodged in a proper office of record in each of the colonies through which the lines pass.

The want of a proper regulation for the Indian commerce has long been the subject of very just complaint and the source of disorders that cannot fail to have the most fatal consequences; but as the King has thought fit, upon the grounds of the representations of the several colonies that they were themselves the best judges of what those regulations should be, to leave this matter entirely to them and to lay aside a plan which the Board of Trade had with unwearied attention prepared for that purpose, it is an evil that now admits of no other remedy but that of the several colonies interested passing similar laws in each colony for that purpose. And if the plan of such a law was framed by you and communicated to the governors of each colony separately it might have the consequence to facilitate so desirable an object.

With regard to the cession of land proposed to be made to the traders by the Indians in payment of debts, it is a transaction that ought to be discountenanced as much as possible; it will therefore be your duty to represent to those traders who inadvertently grasped at any proposals of this nature made to them by the Indians that His Majesty does entirely disapprove such proceedings, and in case they shall persist therein you will not fail to give me the earliest notice of it in order that the necessary steps may be taken to put a stop to such dangerous and unwarrantable practices.

In the meantime I rely on your attention that nothing of this sort is countenanced or carried on by your officers from any interested views of their own, which I mention to you in caution as I observe that there has been some suspicion of this sort with regard to Mr Cameron. *Draft.* [C.O.5/72, fo. 240]

LXXVI

Governor Thomas Hutchinson to Earl of Hillsborough (No. 8)

6 July, Boston
My Lord, I have the honour of receiving by the May packet your lordship's letter No. 7 [Vol. I, No. 1187] with His Majesty's instructions to me as Governor of Massachusetts Bay. I had then before me a Tax Bill and a bill for supply of the Treasury, both of them incompatible with His Majesty's 27th instruction. I informed the House of Representatives of this instruction and that I could by no means give my consent to the bills unless they would comply with the requisitions in the instruction. The heads of the opposition are glad upon every occasion of new dispute, and the next morning after my message to the House I received an answer which discovers the influence they had to bring the House to the most open denial of the authority of Parliament to appoint Commissioners of the Customs or to raise any monies from the colonies. It is not the first time this principle has been avowed. It has for some years been gaining strength among the people in this and other colonies, which made it less difficult for the representatives of the people of this province to avow it in this open and public manner.

Notwithstanding the principle had been propagated, there has been of late a disposition in the body of the people to be quiet and to make no opposition to the Acts of Parliament which are now in force. I will do all in my power to counteract the party who will take fresh courage and use their utmost endeavours to raise new disturbances. I have not had time to judge what success they will meet with.

I received the answer of the House yesterday morning, and as soon as I could make a short addition to a speech I had before prepared for the two Houses I ordered the Court to be prorogued. I will cover such papers [Vol. I, No. 1380i-ii] as can be prepared before this ship sails, and as soon as the laws which are passed can be transcribed or printed I will send them according to my instructions. *Signed.* [C.O.5/760, fo. 188]

LXXVII

Upper Creeks to John Stuart[1]

15 July, Tallassies

A talk from the headmen and warriors of the Upper Creek Nation to John Stuart Esq., Superintendant etc.

Emistisiguo speaks.

Friend and Brother, listen to my talk. I heard a little talk. You told me the last time I saw you if I heard any talks to acquaint you with them and that you would do the same to me, though you have not informed me concerning the cession of land by the Cherokees. You remember the great congress at Augusta when the Cherokees, Chickasaws, Choctaws and Cattawbas were present, you said you'd never forget what conclusion we came to about the line; as for my part I have not nor never will. After the land at Augusta was given up the line was not run for three years. In running the line there was a great dispute but it was made up. Some time ago you called a meeting at Augusta at which the Second Man attended and you told him that the Great King over the Great Water was glad to hear we had given up so much land to our white brothers. You then told us that it was the last land ever you would ask of us and if any red men should offer to give up any of our lands you would not harken to it. I have heard a little of the Cherokee talks but they are only like a puff of wind. When I see you we will talk of it. There is a great deal of disturbance about this land but I will go there myself and show the white people the line. When the trees are already marked, I think no white man will go over it. I am not the only man will go, the kings and headmen of all the towns will go. This, my friend, is with an intention to confirm the line that we may not be always troubled about it. After we have settled the line towards Mobile and Pensacola I hope my white brothers will all go to their own land. If they do not I will think they are mad and will not hear their beloved people's talks. There is a path from Pensacola to Tensa which I told you, the Governor and Charles Stuart, should be the line. It should be like a stone wall, never to be broke. When we gave up that land you told us that we were chained together in friendship never to be broke. For my part I still hold the chain fast and hope you do the same, and we hold our brothers the white people fast as a vine holds a tree, the longer the faster it holds.

I sent down a talk before to have four hogsheads of rum for the people who shall go to mark the line but now I expect you'll add two more which will make six. I have nothing more to say till I take you by the hand when we will have a long talk. Signed on behalf of the headmen and warriors of the Upper Creeks by Emistisiguo. *Copy.* [C.O.5/72, fo. 348]

---

1 Enclosed in John Stuart's letter of 24 September to Hillsborough, Vol. I, No. 1525.

LXXVIII

Governor Thomas Hutchinson to Earl of Hillsborough (No. 9)

18 July, Boston

My Lord, I have communicated at a general Council His Majesty's 5th and 16th instructions and have ordered copies thereof to be entered upon the Council books. The Council do not pretend any right to meet without the governor but say it is a hardship to be obliged to determine suddenly upon any matters of importance which may be laid before them. I told them I knew no better precedent than the practice of His Majesty's Council in England, and when any matters came before them which appeared to me proper to be considered in that way I should have no objection to a reference to a committee of Council who might consider and make report to me in Council, but the committee should have no power to act upon anything more than was committed to them, nor should any of their doings be of any validity until reported and accepted. This they said was all they desired, and unless His Majesty shall disapprove of it I shall as often as there may be occasion admit of this practice.

The other instruction which relates to the agents for the Council and House of Representatives I endeavoured to convince them was only a restraint upon them from departing from their constitution which they had done in this affair of the agent as much as it was possible for them to do in any case whatsoever, for they not only appointed a person to be their agent without any authority so to do, but in their legislative capacity whilst the General Court was sitting substituted a committee to correspond with and instruct the agent in the recess of the Court, which was in effect continuing one branch of the Assembly after the governor had by his authority declared their discontinuance, and I had no doubt the instructions would have extended to this practice if it had been known, but being contrary to all rules of parliamentary proceedings I supposed it was not suspected. I advised them to proceed no further in this way which they could say nothing to justify. The correspondence which both Council and House carry on with their agents has contributed much to keep up jealousies in the province of designs to oppress and enslave the people. I hope when the agents find they are not like to be paid this correspondence will cease.

I send under this cover a newspaper [Vol. I, No. 1399i] which gives an account of Mr Tryon's arrival and reception at New York. *Signed.* [C.O.5/760, fo. 196]

LXXIX

Earl of Hillsborough to Attorney and Solicitor-General

19 July, Whitehall

Gentlemen, the Lords Commissioners of the Treasury having communicated to me a representation [Vol. I, No. 1393i] made to the

Commissioners of His Majesty's Customs in America by the Collector and Comptroller of Rhode Island relative to the office of Naval Officer in that colony, and their •lordships having requested that I would consider what remedy can be applied to the evils therein complained of, I am commanded by the King to send you the enclosed copy of that representation and to desire you will take it into your consideration together with the charter of the said colony and the Acts of Parliament made for regulating the Plantation Trade, particularly the Act of the 15th of Charles 2d, cap. 7, sect. 8 and the 7th and 8th of William the 3d, cap. 22, sect. 5 and report to me with as much dispatch as may be your opinion in point of law whether there is anything contained in the said Acts of Parliament and charter to warrant the claim set up by the governors of Rhode Island of being the Naval Officer thereof, and consequently of a right to appoint any person they think proper to execute that office, and whether the Crown may not of its own authority appoint such officer within that colony.

If you shall be of opinion that the right of appointment is by the said Acts of Parliament or by the charter vested in the governor for the time being in exclusion of the authority of the Crown to appoint, you will be pleased in that case to report your opinion whether by law the persons so appointed by the governors can or cannot be subjected to any further checks or comptrol than those they appear at present to act under, and if so what those checks ought to be. If on the other hand you shall be of opinion that the Crown has a right to appoint such officer you will be pleased to report your opinion in what manner such appointment may be legally made so as to supersede and set aside the appointment made by the governors.

Upon this occasion I think fit to observe to you that it appears to me that the officers known by the name of Naval Officers in the colonies were originally established for the execution of those duties which are required of the governors by the Acts of Parliament made for the regulation of the Plantation Trade and were for some time after the passing the Act of the 15th of Charles the 2nd appointed by such governors; but except in one or two instances they have for many years past been appointed by the Crown either by letters patent under the Great Seal or by warrant under the royal Signet and Sign Manual, that is to say in all those colonies the governors of which are appointed by the Crown; but I know of no instance of an appointment of Naval Officer in those colonies where the governors are either elected or appointed by the proprietaries, except in the case of the colony of Rhode Island for which a Naval Officer was appointed by the Crown in 1743 as will more fully appear to you by the enclosed commission to Leonard Lockman.

Mr Lockman has, as I understand, been dead some time, and the only information I am able to give you of what passed in consequence of his appointment I collect from a memorial of his amongst the papers in my office, in which he states that he was refused admittance into his office by the government of Rhode Island, the General Assembly of that colony having voted that the King was mistaken in his appointment, and that though the Attorney-General here was ordered to advise in what manner the patent should be enforced yet he never had any satisfaction made him. *Draft.* [C.O.5/1284, fo. 135]

LXXX

Earl of Hillsborough to Proprietaries of Pennsylvania

19 July, Whitehall

Gentlemen, the Lords Commissioners of His Majesty's Treasury have communicated to me several papers [Vol. I, No. 1393 and enclosures] received from the Commissioners of the Customs in America relative to certain outrages committed on their officers and the neglect of the governors and civil magistrates in giving them assistance and protection; and their lordships have desired that I would take such measures as I shall judge most expedient to prevent in such governors and civil magistrates the like neglect of their duty for the future.

From these papers it appears that some of the most violent of these outrages have been committed in the city of Philadelphia, particularly in the months of April and October 1769 on occasion of lawful seizures made by the officers of the Customs, when such seizures were rescued by force and violence, and the officers and those from whom they received information of breaches of the law were treated with the greatest cruelty and inhumanity in the presence of the magistrates who gave them no assistance.

It has given me great concern to find that such acts of violence and inhumanity should have been committed with impunity in a colony from which I have received such strong professions of loyalty and duty to the King and in a city hitherto deservedly commended for the regularity of its government. But after the repeated signification of the King's pleasure to the governors of all His Majesty's colonies that they should use their most strenuous efforts and exert themselves in the most effectual manner for the support of the Commissioners of the Customs and their officers and for enabling them to carry the Laws of Trade into due execution, any further exhortation on that subject would probably be useless, and it must remain with those to whom the powers of government are entrusted in Pennsylvania to consider what must be the consequences if, after such repeated admonition, the laws of this kingdom are suffered to be trampled upon and violences and outrages of so reprehensible a nature are committed with impunity. *Draft.* [C.O.5/1284, fo. 19]

LXXXI

Governor William Franklin to Earl of Hillsborough (No. 32)

20 July, Burlington

My Lord, since my last I have been honoured with your lordship's letter of the 4th of May (No. 30) [Vol. I, No. 1186]. It gives me pleasure to find that His Majesty has been pleased to approve of Mr Coxe for supplying one of the vacancies in the Council of this province and I shall be happy to hear that Mr Lawrence is appointed to fill the other.

Enclosed I send your lordship a printed copy of the Votes and Proceedings of the Assembly during the two last meetings at Burlington. They contain nothing particular (besides the messages I before transmitted relative to the Assembly's refusal to grant money for the supply of the troops) except three messages which passed between us on the subject of a member having resigned his seat in the House on account of his having become insolvent. The House accepted his resignation and ordered their Speaker to issue his warrant to the Clerk of the Crown to make out a writ for a new election, which the Clerk accordingly did and applied to me to have the Great Seal affixed to it as usual. But as I had some doubts of the legality of such a resignation, I consulted the Council upon it who were of opinion with me that it was by no means regular or constitutional. It appears to me indeed that if it was once admitted that the Assembly have an uncontrollable right to permit the members to resign whenever they think proper it would be nearly the same thing as allowing them the power of dissolving themselves, as a dissolution might by such means be brought about at any time when the House should incline to have one though against the inclination of the governor. The law of the province which directs the qualifications of members and gives the House a right to judge of their qualifications is similar to that in England. I apprehend that when the person elected is judged to be duly qualified and admitted to take his seat, it cannot be vacated merely on account of his afterwards becoming a bankrupt or insolvent; and if I mistake not, there are more than one who hold their seats in the present House of Commons though they have long since become bankrupt and consequently not possessed of the qualification required by law to entitle them to be elected. But the Assembly contend that in such a case, if a member does not resign, that they have a right to expel him as being the sole judges of the qualifications of their members. There are instances of resignations being admitted where it has been clearly proved that a member was absolutely disabled by bodily infirmities from attending his duty in Parliament but not otherwise that I can find; and I imagine if resignations in other cases could be accepted by the House of Commons it would not be so much the practice as it is for members to accept of places under the Crown for the purpose only of vacating their seats. However, as it appears to me to be a matter which nearly concerns the prerogative I have refused to seal the writ for a new election until I can obtain farther light on the subject or receive His Majesty's directions for my conduct. I beg leave to refer your lordship for the particulars of what passed between me and the Assembly on this head to pages 11, 21, 22, 23 and 24 of the Votes and Proceedings sent herewith. *Signed.*

PS. I have received from Mr Pownall ten printed copies of the account of the process used in Sweden in the manufacture of pitch and tar, which I shall not fail to distribute in such manner as may be most likely to answer the good purposes intended. [C.O.5/991, fo. 68]

LXXXII

John, Thomas and Samuel Freebody to Earl of Hillsborough

22 July, Newport, Rhode Island

My Lord, for the supporting and maintaining the honour and dignity of the King and Council and their judgements against the scandalous contempt and indignity two judgements of the King and Council we obtained in the year 1769 against Jahleel Brenton and others in cases of mortgage has been treated by the Governor and Company and Courts of this colony, and the cruel injustice done us respecting the said two judgements, has laid us under the necessity of making our address to your lordship as one of His Majesty's Principal Secretaries of State and to acquaint your lordship that upon our receiving the said two judgements of the King and Council in 1769 we presented the same to the Governor and Company with the King's *mandamus* strictly commanding them and all concerned to carry said judgements into execution immediately, which we prayed might be done according to the true intent and meaning thereof; upon which the Governor and Company (i.e. the General Assembly) passed a vote and order that the Justices of the Superior Court of Judicature etc. should in their session in March Term 1770 carry the said judgements into execution, but added the words Judicially according to the laws, custom, usage and practice of the Courts in this colony etc., which words were added by the Governor and Council for they would not concur with the vote of the Lower House of Assembly without that addition, from which it appears they were determined the King's order should not be obeyed. At March Term Superior Court 1770, we entered the two judgements of the King and Council and prayed the court the said judgements might be carried into execution according to the true intent and meaning of them. Upon which Henry Marchant Esq., counsel for Jahleel Brenton and others, prayed the court he might be heard, for he had reasons to offer why the said judgements ought not [to] be carried into execution. We objected to the court's hearing any reasons they had to offer, for by law the judgements of the King and Council was final judgements, but the court overruled our objections and suffered them to plead. Upon which Mr Marchant did aver and say the King and Council had made up said judgements contrary to law, reason, equity and justice, and when the King and Council made up such judgements the King was no King, therefore the court ought to set the said judgements aside and pay no obedience to them and make up a judgement of their own according to law, and then produced the depositions of Stephen Hopkins Esq. and others who had been judges of courts in this colony to prove what had been their custom and practices of making up judgements. We objected to the court's receiving their depositions, for that the court had no causes upon trial before them, the court was only to carry the final judgements of the King and Council into execution, but the court overruled our objection and received the depositions; then they brought into court and made a tender of the same sums they did in 1756 before ever there was a trial had in this colony, which they said was sufficient for the redemption of lands.

The pleadings lasted two days when the Chief Justice James Helme Esq. put the question to the court, to wit, if the judgements of the King and Council should be carried into execution according to their true intent and meaning or not. Two judges, to wit Searle and Comstock, gave judgement that the judgement of the King and Council should be carried into execution, and two judges, to wit Hall and Green, gave judgement they should not. Upon which it rested with the Chief Justice to determine, who said by the law of the colony the judgements of the King and Council are final judgements, therefore no court of this colony has any right to alter or set aside the judgements of the King and Council, and therefore he was in duty bound to carry the said judgements into execution.

Upon which the defendants said, as the court had determined against them they must submit, and therefore prayed the court that they would not issue execution immediately for the possession of the lands and that if the court would allow them a little time they would pay the redemption moneys. Upon which the court fixed the first day of the next September Term for the payment of the redemption moneys, and on failure of payment execution to be issued for the possession of the lands; and the court then appointed five gentlemen to calculate the interest on the principal sums of the paper-currency up to the said first day of next September Term in silver according to the pro- clamation of the 3rd of Queen Anne agreeable to the judgements of the King and Council, and to make a report to the court at their next sitting of the sums the interest amounted to in silver. Accordingly the gentlemen made the calculation and made their report to the court, the sums the interest amounted to in silver. But before the next Sep- tember Term, to wit in May 1770, came on the annual choice of officers for the colony when the General Assembly turned out every one of those judges that gave judgement that the judgements of the King and Council should be carried into execution, and then chose Stephen Hopkins Esq. Chief Justice of the Superior Court as a suitable judge who gave his deposition in March Term of the custom and practice of the courts' making up judgements when he was a judge several years before, and more especially as he had previous to his being chosen Chief Justice said that the said two judgements of the King and Council ought not to be carried into execution, and it is apparent that our opponents looked upon Mr Hopkins who was of so base principles to be the most suitable person for a judge to serve their purpose, by their making all the interest they could to get him appointed Chief Justice and more especially as he had several years past publicly declared that the King and Parliament had no more right to pass any Acts of Parliament to govern us than the Mohawks (i.e. a tribe of the Indians) as was proved by the evidence of Job Almy and William Richmond Esqs., gentlemen of the first rank, on a trial at law at the court of Worcester in the province of the Massachusetts Bay between Stephen Hopkins Esq. and the Hon. Samuel Ward Esq., late governor of this colony, as will appear by a pamphlet containing a narrative of that trial which we have sent to our agents, Messrs. Lane, Son and Fraser, in London with the copies of records of the court's proceedings respecting the two judgements of the King and Council and have requested of them to prefer a petition in our names and on our behalf to His Majesty of complaint against the government and courts, and a prayer that His Majesty would be graciously pleased to grant us speedy relief in the premises by compelling the government to carry the said judgements into execution by such ways and means as His Majesty in his great wisdom shall think right and just. The General Assembly for some political reasons, after they had turned out James Helme Esq., the Chief Justice of the court in March Term 1770, they now chose him second judge; they also appointed some other judges, men of the same principles with Judge Hopkins, so that we despaired of justice being done us. At the Superior Court in September Term 1770 we made application to the court that as the Superior Court in March Term 1770 had given judgement that the said judgements of the King and Council should be carried into execution, and that at the prayer of the defendants for allowing them a little time to pay the redemption moneys the court had fixed the first day of this September Term for the payment of the moneys, and on failure of payment execution was to be issued for the possession of the lands, and as they had failed paying the redemption moneys, we prayed that execution might be issued for the possession of the lands. To which the court replied that as the Chief Justice Hopkins was absent they would not proceed to do anything in the affair without the Chief Justice, therefore they continued the consideration thereof to their adjournment in October. At the adjournment in October the Chief Justice being present, we again made the same request to the court as we did in September, praying that the judgements of the King and Council might be carried into execution. Upon which Henry Marchant Esq. desired the court would hear him, for he had reasons to offer to the court why the said judgements ought not [to] be carried into execution. To which we objected to the court's hearing of him, for that the Superior Court in March Term had given judgement that the said two judgements of the King and Council should be carried into execution, and that the Superior Court of September Term could not without doing of violence alter or set aside the judgements of the Superior Court of the preceding term of March 1770. But the court overruled our objection and allowed Mr Marchant to proceed in his pleadings, and he did again treat the judgements of the King and Council with as great contempt and indignity as he did in March Term by averring and saying the King and Council had made up the said judgements contrary to law, reason, equity and justice etc., and that they never had a hearing on the causes before the King and Council, their counsel having deserted them, and therefore the court ought not to regard as paying any obedience to the King's order but ought to set the said judgements aside and make up judgements of their own according to law, and then had read the Chief Justice's own deposition with the others that they had given in the court of March Term, and made again the same tender of the same sums they tendered in the year 1756 before any trial was ever had in this colony, which they said was sufficient for the redemption of the lands. To all which we objected for that the court had no right by law to admit of any pleadings or tenders, the judgements of the King and Council being final judgements; and that they had a hearing on the causes, for the Lords Committee of Council had reported to His Majesty that they had fully heard counsel learned in the law on both sides, to which Mr Marchant replied there was nothing in their lordships' report, it was only a matter of form for they never had a hearing, so that Mr Marchant made the Lords Committee of Council the authors of reporting to His Majesty a falsehood, all which contempt and indignity the court suffered Mr Marchant to treat the judgements of the King and Council with. And after a day's hearing the court continued the causes over to the next March Term in the year 1771 to keep us out of our right and to harass and perplex us in order, we think, to bring us to accept of the tender made. The court being sitting in March Term 1771, we then prayed the court that the two judgements might be carried into execution, there being four judges (Judge Hall being absent). The Chief Justice Hopkins put the question to the court, to wit, if the said two judgements of the King and Council should be carried into execution or not. The Judges Helme and Bowler gave judgement that they should be carried into execution in obedience to the King's order and the judgement of the Superior Court of March Term 1770. The Judges Hopkins and Potter gave judgement they should not. The court being divided, the Chief Justice then proposed to carry the causes to the county of Providence, where they did contrary to law, and ordered that the parties should attend there with their pleadings, which we would not do as the Chief Justice had given judgement that the said judgements should not be carried into execution, therefore we expected no justice would be done us from men of such bad principles, as we knew Judge Hall would attend the court at Providence who had given his judgement in March Term 1770 that the said judgements should not be carried into execution. At Providence Superior Court the Judges Stephen Hopkins, Benoni Hall and Stephen Potter took upon themselves the power and authority of disannulling or setting aside the judgement of the Superior Court of March Term 1770. They also assumed to themselves (contrary to law) the power and authority of reversing or setting aside the judgements of the King and Council and did take upon themselves the power of making up judgements which by law they had no right to do; for all judgements that any court in this colony had a right to give was given before our appeal to His Majesty and Council. By which judgements they have made up, they say that as the defendants in the year 1756 made a tender of the sums specified in the judgements before any trial had in this colony, which is considered by the court sufficient for the redemption of the lands, and that if the defendants refused to pay us the sums that was tendered we should be entitled to have execution for the possession of lands in three months, provided we shall give the defendants notice a month before that we are ready to receive the sums tendered and are ready to reconvey the lands. By which judgements they have cut us off of one-half of the redemption moneys decreed by the King and Council, beside the cost of about £700 sterling they have put us to in the law in suing out a forfeited estate, all which costs by the rules in

Chancery they ought to pay before they can have a redemption; against which judgements Judge Helme entered his protest, for that the court had no right to alter or set aside the judgements of the King and Council. So that we despair of justice being done us but only through the royal interposition of His Majesty, for which purpose we have transmitted the copies of record of the court's proceedings to our agents as aforementioned for obtaining justice and redress of our grievances by an humble petition to His Majesty, from whom we have not the least doubt of justice being done us. It appears very plain that the Governor and Company approves of what the court has done in disobeying the King's orders, for if they did not they would have exerted their authority in carrying the judgements of the King and Council into execution; instead of obeying the King's orders his Honour the Governor has been endeavouring to persuade us to compromise the affair by naming the sum we would take up with or else leave the affair to three men to determine what we should receive, and if we would he would engage in it; to which we replied we would not treat the judgements of the King and Council with such indignity for we expected His Majesty would order justice to be done us if the government refused to obey His Majesty's orders, upon which his Honour the Governor refused to authenticate the first copies of records of the court's proceedings we sent home by certifying under the colony's seal that John Greala jnr. Esq., was Clerk of the Superior Court, so that we was under the necessity of authenticating them by other testimonies. So cruelly are we treated, as Judge Helme has expressed himself since the rising of the court and that he never can believe His Majesty would suffer his judgements and orders to be treated with such contempt and disobedience, and that it was his opinion His Majesty would enforce his judgements either by force or at the risk of the charter privileges, but Judge Helme is called by many a prerogative man in contradistinction to too many in this charter colony who think themselves under no obligation to pay any obedience to the authority of Great Britain. But Mr Marchant (that Son of Liberty as he calls himself) has said since the determination of the court that if the King was to carry his judgements into execution by force they should soon get a court to dispossess us again as soon as the force was withdrawn. And it is also said that if the King should send over another order it would be treated in the manner the last was; but Mr Marchant having a high opinion of his own abilities gave out that if his clients would retaliate him for his trouble and service he would undertake to go to London and would convince the King and Council that they had made up erroneous judgements and would get the King and Council to alter or set aside the judgements they had given and make up other judgements that would be agreeable to Mr Marchant and his clients. Upon which his clients has agreed with him for a certain sum and he is actually embarked on his voyage, and the government has (as he had engaged to go home) appointed him a joint-agent with Mr Sherewood, their agent in London. We imagine one of their views was that Mr Marchant might appear at the Court of Great Britain in a public character which would give him the greater credit at Court in his endeavours to convince the King and Council that they had made up such erroneous judgements as he is pleased to call them, so as to prevail with that august Court to set aside or alter their judgements (which we look upon as vain and idle). Another grievance we have to complain of is a fraudulent Act of Assembly passed in their sessions in September 1770 for obliging all those who are possessed of any of the bills emitted by the government to bring them into the General Treasurer who is empowered by said Act to give them his notes for the same payable in one year without interest, to wit for every eight pound old tenor he shall give his note for six shillings lawful money, which is $17\frac{1}{2}$ pennyweight of silver, which is not $\frac{1}{6}$ part of what the government promised on the face of the bills the possessor should receive out of the Treasury for said bills of forty shillings, which the government rated at eight pounds old tenor, they promised in said bill the possessor should receive out of the Treasury 5 oz. 18 dwt. 12 grs. of silver or gold equivalent, by which Act of Assembly they defraud the possessor of above $\frac{5}{6}$ parts of what they promised he should receive, and what is more unjust they have by said Act excluded all who do not bring in said bills to the Treasurer by the first day of July 1771 from ever having any redemption for said bills. By which Act of Assembly we are excluded of ever having any redemption for the whole principal sums decreed us by the judgement of the King and Council for the redemption of the lands, if ever we was to be paid, as it will fully appear by the copy of the Act we sent home with the copies of the records of the court's proceedings respecting the judgements of the King and Council. From the force of said fraudulent Act of Assembly, we humbly beseech His Majesty's royal interposition that we may not be defrauded by the government of this colony out of our right, and that His Majesty will support the power and authority of an Act of Parliament passed in the 23rd or 24th year of the reign of His late Majesty George the Second, restricting the colonies of New England from emitting any more paper currency and for obliging them to call in and sink the bills they had emitted agreeable to the Emitting Acts, without any alteration, postponing or reissuing, and if any Assembly should pass any votes or resolves contrary thereto are declared null and void; and that any governor or deputy governor that should preside in any Assembly that should pass any votes or resolves contrary to the said Act [of] Parliament should suffer the pains and penalties expressed in the said Act. But this government has treated the Act of Parliament with the same contempt as they have the judgements of the King and Council by their continuing out their paper bills of credit many years after the time that they should have sunk by the Emitting Acts and the Act of Parliament. As Mr Marchant has been suffered here to treat the judgements of the King and Council with such scandalous contempt and indignity, we have enclosed sent your lordship our depositions [Vol. I, No. 1418i] of Mr Marchant's conduct and behaviour here that he may answer for his contempt when he arrives in London. We humbly entreat the favour of your lordship as being one of His Majesty's Principal Secretaries of State that for the supporting and maintaining the honour and dignity of the King and Council and their judgements and the supporting of the power and authority of Parliament and the cause of justice, that you will be pleased to communicate our depositions to His Majesty respecting Mr Marchant's conduct and the cruel treatment and injustice done us by the government and courts of this colony by disobeying the King's positive orders and taking upon themselves the power and authority of reversing and setting aside the judgements of the King and Council, from which injustice we humbly beseech His Majesty's royal interposition for our relief, and that justice may speedily [be] done us. Your lordship's favour and assistance in the support of justice, and that we may have speedy relief from such cruel injustice, will ever be gratefully acknowledged by us who are with great submission and due respect. *Signed.* PS. We knew it would be in vain to make application to the governor to certify under his hand and seal of the colony that Charles Bardin Esq. is a Justice of the Peace in any affair that concerned Mr Marchant's conduct. But as we had sent certificates under the seal of the colony in a case of appeal of Thomas Freebody versus John Holmes, that Charles Bardin Esq. was a Justice of the Peace, will be sufficient to obtain credit to his attestation of the enclosed declaration. [C.O.5/1284, fo. 150]

LXXXIII

Colonel Thomas Goldthwait's Talk with Mataugwesannack Indian[1]

July

Colonel Goldthwait's talk with a Mataugwesannack Indian who is now among the Penobscot Indians. This talk was in July 1771.

Q. What nation of Indians do you belong to?
A. I am a Mataugwesannack.
Q. Where is the Mataugwesannack country?
A. Very far off.
Q. Can you describe to me where it is?
A. I will do as well as I can. There's a lake which you call the Great Lake (meaning Lake Superior). The nation of Indians to which I belong are beyond that lake towards the setting of the sun.
Q. Do you know the sun sets in different places at different seasons of the year?
A. I speak of this season. The sun is our guide when we travel in unknown countries.

---

1 Some of the Indian names in this document are either so eccentrically spelt as to be unrecognizable or sufficiently rare not to appear in John R. Swanton, *The Indian Tribes of North America*, Smithsonian Institution, Bureau of American Ethnology Bulletin No. 145 (U.S. Government Printing Office: Washington, 1952). No suggestion is offered for 'Mataugwesannack.' The 'Counawangas' are the Caughnawagas. The 'Counasodogas' may be the Conestogas and the 'Wousaugas' the Osages. The 'Pannegn' could be the Pawnee and the 'Pannooks' the Pouanak. The 'Annundoswesauwacks' are probably the Nadouessioux (Sioux). The 'Widowanks', mentioned later in the document, are perhaps the Ottawas, Udawak being the Penobscot name for Ottawa: Swanton, p. 244.

Q.   Are your Indians numerous?
A.   They are very numerous and they occupy great space of country.
Q.   Have you been at Montreal?
A.   I have been there often.
Q.   Are there many Indian nations between Montreal and the Mataugwesannack country?
A.   There are a great many.
Q.   Can you name them?
A.   I will name some which have come to my knowledge. There are the Counawaugas and Counasodoggas near Montreal. There's the remains of some nations of Indians near Michilimacanack and at Meromona. There's an Indian village called Winnebago and another of the same name. There's the Wousaugas and Ottawaus and Woutaugamases. These nations I haven't much knowledge of but have been acquainted with some Indians belonging to them. From my country to Canada we pass by a great many Indian nations. Some of the names I remember and some I do not. I can describe that country to you better upon a bark. When we get upon the track of my country we pass by many great nations. There's a nation called Ann,un,do,wes,au,wacks which is a powerful nation and is most always at war with the nations round about them. Another nation called Pannegn and another called Pannooks and many more which I'll mark upon the bark. We fight one battle every year with some of them.
     (This nation of Annundowesauwacks appears to me by his account to lie west from the head of the Mississippi River)
Q.   What is the occasion of those wars?
A.   It's pride, nothing but pride, it's to see which are stoutest men.
Q.   Maybe you interfere upon the land of each other?
A.   If it was so, that need not occasion any ill will, for all that country greatly abounds with everything good for food and the fruits of the earth are produced without labour except only to gather them in proper season.
Q.   What is produced there?
A.   Everything, rice in abundance, corn, beans, pease, apples, plums, grapes, pumpkins, tobacco and almost everything that I have ever seen in Canada or here and many things which I have not seen there or here.
Q.   Are the rice and corn like what you have seen here?
A.   No, it is not exactly. The corn is a small ear not a quarter so big as what grows here, and the rice is much larger than your rice and a darker colour. All the things I mention differ more or less from yours but they are of the same kind.
Q.   Is your winter cold like ours?
A.   No, they are not, it's rare to see any snow lay long upon the ground.
Q.   What meat do you eat there mostly?
A.   I can't number the fowl and beasts that inhabit that country and which are taken for food with little or no trouble. There are cows of the same kind of yours, but smaller and in greater plenty. There are buffaloes which are good meat. There are sheep and goats, but our sheep are bigger than two of yours and the goats too are larger than yours.

Q.   Are the sheep like ours except only in size?
A.   The sheep have but little wool. The flesh tastes like your sheep. There is horses too in great plenty but much less than yours. The goats are much bigger than these goats I see here but have the same actions, they rise upon their hind legs, butt with their heads, and make the same noise.
Q.   Do you eat horse-flesh there as the Indians do here?
A.   No, the principal use of horses is when we go to battle.
Q.   Do you fight on horseback?
A.   Some on horses and some on foot.
Q.   Are your horses tame and familiar?
A.   No, all run wild and when we catch them we take a party of men and surround them.
Q.   What fowl are there in your country?
A.   Turkeys, ducks, geese, hens, pigeons and all sort of fowl and in great plenty.
Q.   Do you keep any about you tame as we do?
A.   No, all are wild but we can kill them or take them at any time.
Q.   Is your country healthful?
A.   It is more so than this. It is not cold as it is here nor it is not hot as it is here.
Q.   How could you forsake such a fine country?
A.   I have often wished myself back again but I am married to a woman and she won't go with me and she says I must not leave her. In my country I might have ten wives and I might leave them all without a word being said. Here I find it difficult eno' to maintain one. It isn't here as it is in my country. There the women do all in gathering and laying up stores, and the men only go to war; but here the men do more than the women for the support of the family.
Q.   What brought you away?
A.   I was taken in battle by the Annundowesauwacks when I was a young man and was sold for a slave as is the custom.
Q.   Are all the captives made slaves?
A.   If they are young men and not much wounded, but those who are old and disabled are killed immediately.
Q.   To whom was you sold?
A.   I was sold to an Indian of a distant nation.
Q.   Do you know what was given in pay?
A.   I don't know, but it is a trifle that purchases a captive from the first sellers, maybe a bundle of arrows. I was sold from one nation to another and for various things. I was at last purchased by a Widauwank and he paid in knives and some iron utensils and some such things. This nation had intercourse with the French and gave Governor Vaudrille some assistance when Canada was last besieged by the English: every town in the Widauwank country was to furnish a certain number of men to assist the French. My master sent me for one and it was there I got some acquaintance with the Penobscot Indians.
Q.   Did you understand the language of the Penobscots? or could you talk with them?
A.   I could not understand them any other way but by signs.

Q. Did you understand the Widauwank language?
A. No more than I did French or English.
Q. Can you describe where the Widauwank country is?
A. I cannot, but it is a cold mountainous country and the Indians are clothed and have but little sun in the winter.
Q. Don't you wear clothing in your country?
A. No, we wear none, neither men or women. When we sleep we cover ourselves with a skin of leather (that is a buffalo's skin dressed) which we sometimes carry about us and which upon occasion serves to make a canoe to cross a river.
Q. What do you carry when you go to war?
A. We carry a bundle of arrows slung upon our backs, a bow and a club.
Q. How are your arrows pointed?
A. They are pointed with stone and sometimes the stone is poisoned. Some lately are pointed with iron which they get in return for their slaves.
Q. What is the club you carry?
A. It is a short club made of a very heavy wood and will most certainly kill a person it fairly strikes.
Q. You say you was on the French side last war?
A. I was in the battle at Quebec on the side of Mr Montcalm but I was there but a little while before the battle.
Q. Are the armies in your country when they meet to fight any way to be compared to those you saw there engaged?
A. Do you mean in number?
Q. Aye, in number. What do you laugh at?
A. The number of men at Quebec were but a handful. Our armies are innumerable, I don't know how to tell you their number. The armies meet upon a vast plain which appears to have no end and are at a distance from each other. Each side engages with one line in the front and the main army is in reserve behind. Between this line and the body of the army is the officers' post: they ride continually from one end of the army to the other giving orders, and I have heard it said it is a day's journey for them.
Q. Is this ground level?
A. It appears to be as level as your parade.
Q. Are there any trees upon it?
A. There is not a tree to be seen. I believe trees don't grow upon it.
Q. Don't the battle soon become general?
A. No, the officers prevent it.
Q. How can they prevent it?
A. The persons of officers are sacred. It is immediate death to anyone who aims an arrow at an officer. This is the custom of all those nations.
Q. If officers are so secure they needn't have a brave man for an officer?
A. If he isn't brave he cannot be an officer.
Q. How then is he appointed?
A. By the people.

Q.   Pray tell me the manner of the appointment?
A.   One is named for an officer upon a day appointed for that purpose. The people give a great shout and he is chosen.
Q.   What must be his qualifications?
A.   That he made no account of his life in former battles, that he has great activity, and is expert with his bow. There are some other qualifications but I don't exactly understand them.
Q.   How can you provide subsistence for so great an army?
A.   It is done by the women and laid up in places at a distance from the field of battle and none eats till the battle is ended, or it is agreed to respite for a time.
Q.   Are there many killed?
A.   A very great number.
Q.   How often are these battles?
A.   A year don't pass without one at least.
Q.   Are your women spectators on these occasions?
A.   As many as like it are, and those women who lose their husbands in battle offer their persons to such warriors as distinguish themselves most.
Q.   When you return from a great victory do you give thanks to God as the author of your success?
A.   No, we take all the glory of it to ourselves. The people of my country have no knowledge of God, not the least idea of such a being.
Q.   Don't you worship the sun, moon, or stars, some animal or something or other?
A.   No, we worship nothing. I never heard of worshipping anything till long after I came from my own country. When we return from victory we chew a root which exhilarates the spirits and makes us sing and dance.
Q.   Have you any marriage-ceremony or do [you] take as many women as you like?
A.   If a woman offers herself to a man and the man likes her, he offers a present to her friends, and if they accept the present he takes her, and in the same manner he takes as many women as he likes.
Q.   You say you know nothing of a God or the worship of anything when you came from your own country? Do you still continue in such ignorance?
A.   No, I have embraced the Christian religion, I worship God as this tribe do, I have been baptized.
Q.   Don't you think you have made a good exchange of countries?
A.   I like the religion better than I do the country. It's very hard to get our living here.
Q.   Has there ever been any attempt of white people (French or Spaniards) to introduce religion among you?
A.   I know of none. There is a memorial that two white people were burnt in some part of that country. It's likely they might go there with some such intention. [C.O.42/87, fo. 207]

LXXXIV

Annonymous Letter to Earl of Hillsborough[1]

[Newport, R.I.] [? July]

Right Honourable, for such thou art in regard to thy office as councillor to a King.

As thou professeth thyself a servant to the present King, thou canst not dispense with discharging that duty which every good servant oweth to his master.

This being the case thou wilt no doubt deliver the enclosed [not found] according to its address.

Thy ears have long been accustomed to the clamour of the people for the redress of their grievances. The purport of the letter entrusted to thy care is for redress of grievances of another kind, grievances which call loudly for redress, the attention or neglect whereof will without fail be productive of either of these two: a blessing or a curse.

Thou art a servant to an earthly King. Should any presume to infringe his prerogative thou wouldst make loud complaints for immediate satisfaction. I am a servant to the most sacred majesty of heaven, the one, only true God. Should any (however dignified on earth) dare to usurp his attributes it becomes me equally to complain and demand an immediate restitution.

In full hopes of a compliance to so reasonable a request I conclude with desire that the things belonging to thy master's welfare may not (till it is too late) be hid from his eyes. *Signed,* A Servant. [C.O.5/1284, fo. 154]

LXXXV

Governor William Tryon to Earl of Hillsborough (No. 77)

1 August, New York

My Lord, on the 18th of May last I had the honour to transmit to your lordship an account [Vol. III, No. LI] of the victory obtained on the auspicious 16th of the same month over the rebels of North Carolina. I shall here with as much brevity as possible relate the principal events that attended the success of that day. On the 17th, the day after the battle, I took the opinion of the gentlemen of the Council present, vizt. the Hon. John Rutherford, Lewis De Rossett, Robert Palmer and Samuel Cornell Esqs., whether it would not be advisable in order to leave a door open for mercy to issue a proclamation of pardon to all of the rebels who should come into camp, surrender up their arms, take the oath of allegiance and oath of obligation to pay all taxes as well due as those that shall become so, and to support and defend the laws of the land. This measure was unanimously advised and a proclamation issued accordingly. The happy effects of this proclamation, extended from time to time for a few days, soon disarmed all opposition. The inhabitants came in by crowds to surrender themselves and by the 19th of June three thousand three hundred had come into camp and took the oaths of allegiance etc. to His Majesty, and upwards of five hundred

1 Postmarked Newport. Received 8 November.

arms were surrendered up. Many of those that surrendered asserted they were not in the battle while others pretended to be in the battle without arms.

As soon as I found the force of the rebellion was broke I detached parties in the neighbourhood of the army and made requisitions to the settlers to bring in a certain quantity of flour and beeves according to the strength of the settlement of necessities of the army, which requisitions were generally strictly complied with insomuch that the commissary had not occasion to purchase any provision for the troops from the 16th of May till they quitted those settlements the 20th of June.

On the 19th of May the army proceeded westward in order to join General Waddell with his troops, then entrenched near Salisbury, and on the 4th of June we effected the junction about eight miles to the eastward of the Yadkin River and marched the same day to the Moravian settlement, where on the sixth we commemorated His Majesty's birthday and celebrated the victory at Alamance. Intelligence being brought that the counties of Tryon, Mecklenburgh, and north-west part of Rowan, westward of the Yadkin, were meditating hostilities, it was judged proper by a council of war that a strong detachment from the army should march through those parts and compel the inhabitants to take the oath abovementioned and to suppress any insurrection among them. Agreeable thereto I appointed Genl. Waddell for that command with the troops he brought with him, amounting to three hundred and forty men from the counties of Mecklenburgh, Rowan, Tryon and Anson, reinforced with the four companies of the Orange, the company of light infantry from Cumberland County, and the artillery company of sailors raised at Wilmington, with one of the brass field-pieces and six half-swivel guns. The General marched the eighth of June to the westward with orders from me after he had performed the service aforesaid to disband his troops. Since his first day's march I have not had any intelligence of his measures or success, which will be communicated to your lordship by Governor Martin. On the ninth of June I returned with the army through the northern part of Orange County to Hillsborough, where the judges were waiting at a especial Court of Oyer and Terminer to try the prisoners taken in battle, twelve of whom were capitally convicted as traitors and two acquitted, of which twelve, six were executed the 19th of June near the town of Hillsborough, and by the solicitation of the officers of the army I suspended the execution of the other six till His Majesty's pleasure should be known. As soon as I can transmit their names I shall solicit in their behalf, having in the hurry of obedience to comply with His Majesty's commands to repair to this government left many papers at Newbern for Governor Martin relative to this service which I now find I stand in need of. The executions being over, on the 20th the army marched to the southward, and as I had received the 13th of June by one of the judges your lordship's dispatch requiring me to take upon me without loss of time the government of New York, I left the army early the 20th, arrived the 24th at Newbern, and on the 30th I embarked with my family for this country.

Benjamin Merril, a captain of militia, at the hour of execution left it in charge to the officers to solicit me to petition His Majesty to grant his plantation and estate to his wife and eight children. He died under a thorough conviction of his crime and the justice of his sentence, and addressed himself to the spectators to take warning by his suffering. His Majesty's indulgence to this request would I am persuaded be dutifully and affectionately received by his unhappy widow and children.

This service, my lord, with all the impediments and difficulties under which it was undertaken and prosecuted, has been attended with every desired success. The inhabitants cheerfully pay their taxes, are satisfied that Husbands, Hunter and a few others have by misrepresentations misled them, and are convinced that they are much happier by losing the victory than they would have been had they defeated His Majesty's forces. The eastern counties raised no men owing to the Northern Treasurer refusing to answer my warrants on him payable to the colonels of those counties to enable them to pay each volunteer forty shillings bounty money and to furnish them with necessaries for the expedition, or even to issue his notes as the Southern Treasurer had done to the sum of six thousand pounds (without which credit no men could have been raised) to be received by him in the payment of the contingent tax.

I shall leave to your lordship's reflections the tendency this expedition has had on the frontiers of every colony in British America as well as on that of North Carolina. When His Majesty is informed that this service was undertaken without money in the Treasury to support it, no armoury to furnish arms nor magazines from whence we could be supplied with ammunition or draw provisions, and that his new-raised troops acted with fidelity, honour and obedience to their King and Country, I am sanguine enough to believe they will receive some favourable testimonies from their Sovereign. They have had no other immediate encouragement than the forty shillings bounty money which was necessary to leave with their families to hire husbandmen to plant their corn in their absence. The pay of the troops, the provisions, waggons and every other contingent service remains a demand on the public, a sum I estimate at not less than forty thousand pounds currency, a load the province is absolutely incapable to discharge unless by a new emission of currency or an aid from Parliament, both which I humbly beg leave to submit to His Majesty's wisdom. As the orders delivered to the troops will be explanatory of this service I have the honour herewith to transmit them [Vol. I, No. 1434iii], also the petition of the insurgents to me, delivered the evening before the action, with my answer thereto [Vol. III, Nos. XLIX-L]. The particular returns of the strength of the army was left for Governor Martin. If your lordship will turn to the orders of the 23rd of May you will see £126 distributed among the non-commissioned officers and soldiers of the army, a sum calculated (by the returns) at 2s. 6d. per man which in the whole amounted to 1,109 men exclusive of officers, thirty light horse and the nine men that were killed. *Signed.*

PS. I should have mentioned that one Few, an outlaw taken in battle, was hanged the next day in camp, and that the houses and plantations of the outlaws we came near were laid waste and destroyed and that the owners fled out of the province. [C.O.5/314, fo. 175]

LXXXVI

President James Hasell to Earl of Hillsborough (No. 2, Duplicate)

9 August, Newbern
My Lord, I am to acknowledge the receipt of your lordship's letter No. 1 [Vol. I, No. 1180], directed to Governor Martin and in his absence to the commander-in-chief of this province. As he is not yet arrived, I apprehend indisposition has detained him at New York.

When Governor Tryon left this province he acquainted me that he intended to inform your lordship of his procedure against the insurgents. They appear at present thoroughly convinced of their having been deceived and imposed on by the seduction of a few turbulent villains who had formed a distracted scheme of overturning this government and thereby throwing the country into anarchy and confusion, but under the gracious protection of the Almighty, his Excellency's vigorous and prudent conduct has frustrated their infernal designs so that this province is now restored to peace, the preservation of which shall be my constant study and endeavour.

By a letter I received by express from Governor Eden of Maryland, dated the 9 last month, he acquaints me he had information that Hermon Husbands, the chief ringleader of the rebels, with eight or ten of his associates were in that province and that the difficulty of proving the identity of his person made him delay attempting to arrest him until he heard from hence. I answered his letter by the same express and sent with him a young man I had obtained of good character who lived many years among the insurgents and knew most of their ringleaders and could swear particularly to the identity of Husbands. I also sent the copy of two proclamations issued here offering large rewards for taking them and informed Governor Eden that I had wrote by the same express to Mr President Nelson of Virginia, acquainting him with the intelligence I had received and requested his endeavours to procure the *Magdalen* cutter or the man-of-war that was then in Virginia, to proceed to Maryland in order to bring them securely to Newbern should they be taken. I also wrote to Mr President Hamilton of Pennsylvania, requesting his assistance in having them apprehended in case they should fly from Maryland with an intention to shelter themselves in his government. By these precautions I rest in full expectation that Husbands may be taken and brought to suffer at that tribunal which he has so daringly insulted and opposed, an event which would effectually restore and permanently establish the peace and tranquillity of this government.

Your lordship may be assured that for the short time I may have the honour to be entrusted with the administration I shall constantly use my utmost endeavours for its support and most punctually obey every command I may have the honour to receive from your lordship. *Signed.* [C.O.5/314, fo. 273]

LXXXVII

Sir William Johnson to Earl of Hillsborough (No. 16)

9 August, Johnson Hall

My Lord, I was lately honoured with your lordship's letter (No. 16) [Vol. III, No. XLV] which I delayed for some days that I might at the same time acquaint your lordship with the issue of a congress I was then about to hold with the Six Nations, which was occasioned by informations received by my deputy at Fort Pitt from a Shawanese Indian and others. The substance of which was that the Six Nations were concerned in exciting the Shawanese, Delawares and many others to make war upon us, and although this had been formerly propagated without any just grounds or foundation, I judged it best policy to call the chiefs to a congress thereon in order to show that such designs by whatsoever nation carried on could not be totally concealed from us, which might prove a check on the nation that first excited it and render them suspicious of each other. The chiefs only were summoned, but many more attending to the number of 350, I opened the conference the 14th ultimo which held for several days.

I began by acquainting them with the obligations they were under to give me the earliest information that was anywise interesting, and that I was surprised to hear from another quarter of some dangerous transactions which might prove the ruin of those concerned, adding that I expected to have the certain particulars from them. On their appearing ignorant of what I hinted at, I gave them to understand that I had received an account of their being engaged in promoting a rupture with the Indians, the event of which must have proved very fatal to themselves. They gave me many assurances to the contrary and requested to know their accusers, on which I related to them what I thought sufficient to convince any that might have been privy thereto that no designs of any ill tendency could long remain secret to the English. This produced many speeches on both sides, the last of which being the most material I herewith enclose [Vol. I, No. 1457i], as I did not judge them of sufficient importance to give your lordship the trouble of perusing the whole. After this I told them that I should not think their answer satisfactory until the belts mentioned in their speech were delivered up, which they promised to see strictly performed, and after renewing the covenant chain the congress ended. On this congress I have only to observe that although there is some cause to doubt of the friendship of the Senecas on the Ohio and at Chenussio, for reasons formerly given, yet I had not neither have I any reason to suspect the rest of the Senecas or any other of the confederate nations. Besides I know it to have been before the practice of those nations more remote from us and who are apprehensive of the Six Nations to propagate stories much to the disadvantage of the latter, with a view to exasperate us against them and thereby draw them into their association, and I am confident that if an opportunity offered I could give a demonstrating proof of their fidelity from the part they would take in our quarrels if required so to do.

I have always been entirely of your lordship's opinion with regard to the advantages we may expect from the jealousies subsisting between one nation and another, and I have more than once observed the like to your lordship. I have been also always averse to entering into any of their private concerns. It would therefore give me great pain could I have the least reason to accuse myself of deviating from your lordship's sentiments and my own so repeatedly expressed, and I am persuaded it can be sufficiently made to appear that no part of my proceedings, if they had been justly expressed in my pacquets, could have a tendency so contrary to the political practice I have always adopted. Indeed it is extremely necessary and gives the Indians a favourable idea of our justice and friendship to appear concerned at their private divisions or differences and desirous to see them composed, but I never interfere in any where His Majesty's interest and the public tranquillity is not materially concerned, which was peculiarly the case in the affair of the deputies sent to Sioto where the chiefs of the most powerful nations on the continent were assembled for purposes that were too interesting to be overlooked, so that it appeared highly necessary to me that they should know we were not ignorant of their designs and that they should be reprimanded for their past conduct and cautioned against any future undertakings. And the means by which this was ordered to be effected as well as the agents made use of were in my judgement the best calculated for that purpose, as well as for keeping up that jealousy which contributes so much to our security. Those deputies are shortly expected home, when I shall transmit the result of their embassy, and I flatter myself that my long experience in these matters and zeal to acquit myself an useful servant to the Crown will continue to me your lordship's favourable opinion. Could my authority extend to the redress of grievances in anything material, we should have much less apprehensions from the Indians, but as my authority cannot be so far extended your lordship may rely on my doing everything in my power for the interests of the Crown and the public within the limits prescribed to me, and that faithfully according to the best of my judgement. *Signed.* [C.O.5/72, fo. 310]

LXXXVIII

Governor Thomas Hutchinson to John Pownall [Private]

[? 13] August, Boston

Dear Sir, I enclose to you Sir Francis Bernard's newspapers that you may see what sort of a correspondence is carried on between the House and their agent. The clerk of the House is the reputed writer of the illiberal and seditious pieces in the newspapers and furnishes these letters to serve the same, though he knows their agent cannot be pleased with it. This doctrine of independence must sooner or later become a serious affair and the same spirit which denied the authority of Parliament to make laws now denies the authority of the King to give instructions to his governor. I have so often wrote my sentiments of the danger of suffering such doctrine in any part of the legislature especially to pass without notice that I need not repeat them.

In the paper of the last date you will see an account of a verdict for two thousand pounds sterling damages in an action brought by Mr Otis for an assault and battery by Mr Robinson, Commissioner of the Customs. Both parties have appealed to the Superior Court. It is not impossible that a jury there may have as little regard to law and evidence as they seem to have had here. Robinson may appeal to the King in Council but the charter provides that the judgement shall be first satisfied and security given to refund in case the judgement shall be reversed. Besides, will there be no difficulty in the taking cognizance of an action of this nature which wholly depends upon evidence? Has not an appeal in an action of the same nature from New York been dismissed? There is however this difference that by our charter all personal actions without distinction, where the value exceeds three hundred pounds, are subjected to an appeal. I will endeavour that the action may be continued at the Superior Court to another term.

As Mr Robinson is now in England he will be able to judge whether it is advisable for him to return, for keeping out of the province he may prevent the judgement having any effect, no special bail being given.

If it be thought best to bring it before the King in Council he may as well be here as not, for the money must be paid, and if the appeal is not claimed in fourteen days after judgement it cannot be received.

Neither the Judges nor the Attorney-General are clear in the discharge of Richardson without some further evidence of His Majesty's pardon which it does not appear to them ever has been done. If a copy could be procured of the Newgate pardon attested, I hope it may be sufficient. I am not acquainted in what manner pardons are passed for such persons whose sentences are respited in the several counties in England, but if it be usual to insert the names of such persons in the Newgate pardons I wish to be furnished with a certificate that it is so. It is a hard case upon this poor fellow to lie so long in a horrid jail, but I can do no more for him than I have done, and it is compassion which moves me to ask this further trouble from you. *Entry.* [C.O.5/246, p. 25]

LXXXIX

Council of New Hampshire to Governor John Wentworth[1]

16 August
May it please your Excellency, in pursuance of a vote of Council of the 20th December 1768 appointing a committee to draft a just representation of the grievances of more than a thousand grantees of land granted by the late governor of this province with the advice of His Majesty's Council on the west side of Connecticut River in consequence of a petition of John Wendell Esq., their agent, and that the committee exhibit a report to your Excellency in Council, we beg leave upon mature and faithful examination to report as follows.

First, that Benning Wentworth Esq., late governor of this province, by his commission was authorized and by instructions required to grant (with advice of Council) the unappropriated Crown lands in said

1 Enclosed in Governor Wentworth's letter of 20 August to Hillsborough, Vol. III. No. XCI.

province under certain reservations and services to His Majesty's subjects.

Secondly, that between the years 1749 and 1764 the petitioners with many others solicited and obtained grants of sundry tracts of land westward of Connecticut River to a line twenty miles east of Hudson's River of the aforesaid Governor Benning Wentworth Esq., with advice of Council and under the Great Seal of this province.

Thirdly, that by His Majesty's Order in Council of 20th July 1764 the jurisdiction of the district westward of Connecticut River (the property of the soil ungranted equally vested in the Crown under either provincial jurisdiction, as we humbly presume) was rescinded from the province of New Hampshire and annexed to the province of New York, unheard, unexpected and without consciety of error or forfeiture, although extremely detrimental to the province, and unless relieved by His Majesty's most gracious clemency, will be entirely ruinous to the petitioners and others in like circumstances, who with their numerous, innocent, loyal and industrous families must be reduced from hard-earned competence and quiet diligence to all the horrors, disorders and desperations of unmerited extremest indigence; for the petitioners allege and (for them) too plainly prove that their grants under New Hampshire being perfected, they rested satisfied of their title to the premises, as it was never made a doubt by any person in New England or even suspected but that the jurisdiction of New Hampshire extended to a line twenty miles east of Hudson's River. They therefore proceeded to remove themselves, their families and all their property upon the premises, where for many years they peaceably pursued their laborious cultivations, complying with the terms of their patents and populating an immense wilderness with useful subjects. These lands being thus settled and improved excited the cupidity of their neighbours, and in the year 1763 or early in 1764 this desire to acquire or rather seize the New Hampshire well-cleared plantations first broke forth in the proclamation of Lieut.-Governor Colden requiring a return of all those names that did or should hold possession of any lands westward of Connecticut River under the grant of New Hampshire that they might be proceeded against according to law. Hereupon surveyors were sent from New York who avouching the authority of that government surveyed the premises including the houses, barns and every other valuable improvement of the petitioners, to grant them to other people, which was actually done by Mr Colden soon after the proclamation aforesaid was published. The petitioners waited on Mr Colden, remonstrating to him the injury they suffered by these proceedings and the unprecedented barbarity of such divestments; but they say a day was appointed by the lieut.-governor to hear their claims in Council and they were promised that grants should be suspended until that day. However, they experiènced that grants were made previous thereto and all relief totally refused. Upon enquiry it appeared that forty grants had actually passed of the premises which were known and probably many more, containing from two to twenty-seven thousand acres of the most fertile and best cultivated lands possessed by the claimers under New Hampshire, and these grants to single persons of Mr Colden's own family connections or to officers, the largest tract not exceeding to five or six grantees, under no services or conditions of settlement or cultivation except of quitrent, not even a reservation of pine timber for masts with which this country is well clothed. It is now reported that some of these grants have been altered, bearing a reservation of mast timber and requiring some cultivation or settlement. Immediately the grantees under New York proceeded to demand a relinquishment of the claims under New Hampshire, although settled, possessed, cultivated and built upon from ten to fourteen years. Letters were sent wherein these new patentees menaced violence to some, actions of ejectment to others, and others proposing leases for ten to fourteen years at the rate of sixty bushels of wheat per annum for every hundred acres of land, others demanding three pounds York currency, equal to thirty-four shillings sterling per acre to release the possessors. Such exorbitances, cruelties and injustice amounted to a total prohibition.

Whereupon some were actually driven off from their possessions, others sued in actions of ejectment and harassed through different courts at a great distance until the cost had swelled above their personal estates and then their persons thrown into gaol, there to starve and rot until the remainder was satisfied while their more miserable families ousted from their possessions had the choice to starve in the wilderness or rob and become a prey to that law which had not protected them from the oppression of powerful avarice. Some of these people were taken by the sheriff as trespassers, though residing upon and holding their lands granted by royal authority under the seal of New Hampshire, their persons hurried to Albany gaol, all bail refused; and when the day of trial came in which they were to be ousted and perhaps fined for presuming a refusal to yield up their whole and honestly-acquired estates to those who had unworthily obtained new grants of them under New York, the patent under New Hampshire upon which that title was professedly grounded was not permitted to be given to the jury in evidence, upon which strange event every case went against them. Indeed it is a sure method, and by the like there is not the least doubt but every other patent or grant may have the same fate. It has an admirable brevity and extremely facilitates an entire eradication of all property unless sanctified by a grant under New York at the enormous expense of £330 sterling for a tract of six miles square, which sum was actually paid by those few whose ability, cooperating with the distress of impending ruin, enabled and compelled them thus unreasonably to purchase peace and quiet possession of their own property. But had the patent or grant under New Hampshire been admitted to be given in evidence to the jury, yet the petitioners were reduced to the most extraordinary disadvantages, torn away from their friends and families from sixty to eighty miles, confined in a loathsome gaol, bail refused upon a civil process, their little monies wasted, without a friend to protect or lawyer to advise and direct them; thus to have a trial at law for all the property they had on earth before a court and by a jury in effect interested in their defeat, opposed by the most ingenious and weighty lawyers who had almost universally directly or under cover of other names been shrewdly made grantees under New York and located upon these desirable farms; under such untoward circumstances the event required no divination to foresee, and accordingly the petitioners suffered, being poor people and strangers, sunk under the frowns of government and interest, they could neither sustain the cost of an appeal nor procure bondsmen to respond the event. Thus unsurmountably oppressed, their adversaries cautiously avoided laying their actions at such a sum as justifies an appeal to His Majesty in Council and consequently forecloses that only sure and just relief. Having thus stated the facts as they have been strongly proved to us, it now remains that some observations be offered which we humbly presume will recommend the petitioners to an establishment in their property, and this province to His Majesty's most gracious condescension and favour, in restoring to them a district so essential to their welfare, contiguous to and otherwise convenient and desirable for the settlement, prosperity and orderly government of that people, now groaning under and heavily complaining of every outrage, disseizin and wretched confusion, in a degree not known even in the hour of conquest.

The government of New York evidently proceeding upon some title to these lands previous to His Majesty's Order in Council, 20th July 1764, which expressly says "Considering a representation of the Lords Commissioners for Trade and Plantations relative to the disputes that have some years subsisted between the provinces of New York and New Hampshire concerning the boundary line between the two provinces, His Majesty taking the same into consideration was pleased with the advice of his Privy Council to approve of what is therein proposed and doth accordingly hereby order and declare that the western banks of Connecticut River as far north as the 45th degree of latitude to be the boundary line between the said provinces"; it may be answered the province of New Hampshire by royal authority was to run from a point in Merrimack River due west until it met some other government. The province of Massachusetts and Connecticut claimed and possessed to a line of twenty miles east distance from Hudson's River; and as the eastern boundaries of New York were not determined by royal authority, by public claim, or by acts of jurisdiction, or even by common popular supposition further eastward than the said twenty-mile line, it was surely the duty of this province to extend their jurisdiction thereto in obedience to His Majesty's commission. We are further supported herein by His late Majesty's instructions to Benning Wentworth Esq., governor of this province upon a report of Lords of Council, 28th August 1744, requiring him to move the Assembly to provide for and support the garrison called Fort Dummer situated on the west side of Connecticut River or in default the district adjoining should be granted to the Massachusetts Bay, who could not with reason be required to maintain a fort no longer within their jurisdiction. Accordingly it was proposed to the Assembly who, disapproving the situation, refused and were dissolved. The next Assembly conceded and made proper grants for its support, which monies with other instances of obedience to the royal requisitions this province is now paying interest for and has a tax of three years yet unexpired to reimburse. This of itself cannot fail to ascertain the jurisdiction to New Hampshire previous to the royal decree in 1764. In a report of His Majesty's Attorney and Solicitor-General, 14th August 1752, it is said that sixty thousand acres of land on the western side of Connecticut River, called equivalent land, by the determination of the boundary line in 1738 is become a part of New Hampshire. The district here reported upon is part of the land the petitioners complain of being ousted from. These we presume are the highest and fully sufficient authority that the case can require or admit in favour of New Hampshire, and perfectly conclusive in support of the petitioners' claims of property. But we find it most particularly justified by the treaty between the commissaries of Massachusetts Bay and New York, held at New Haven anno 1767, in consequence of His Majesty's recommendation officially signified by the Right Honourable the Earl of Shelburne. In that treaty the commissaries for New York proposed a line, after many intermediate proposals, about thirty-seven miles west of Connecticut River to be the boundary line between those two provinces; wherefore we conclude that in their own opinion New Hampshire did extend to the same line before the decree of 1764 had altered it, for it is plain beyond a doubt that every reason in behalf of the Massachusetts having this line is much stronger in favour of New Hampshire, and consequently that the grants to the petitioners by the governor and under the seal of New Hampshire are valid and legally convey a legal title to the premises, which no alteration of jurisdiction can abrogate or nullify.

We have purposely neglected considering the stale pretence of claim under the Duke of York's patent, that title being universally supposed merged in the Crown; or if this is waived yet it is surely obsolete and vacant from non-user, and absurdity in itself. If not, and that patent is still a private and valid existence, it equally includes more than half the patent to the Council of Plymouth and can operate to the removal of at least half a million of British subjects after near a century's quiet possession.

An idea so repugnant to the civil law (the common law knows nothing of settling new countries), to good policy, to common justice and even to commonsense itself, that we forbear to enlarge our report with the abundant refutations that title unalienably suffocates itself with. As this province has not been informed of the cause that occasioned the defalcation of so large and valuable a district nor were ever cited to defend themselves, nor were in the least apprised thereof until the arrival of His Majesty's Order in Council, and to this day are entirely at a loss therein, it is impossible for us to enter fully into our justification or properly to represent thereon to your Excellency in Council; but as some misrepresentation alone could have occasioned a measure so grievous to a loyal province, and so uncommonly replete with eventual injury and distress to a numerous body of His Majesty's subjects, we would hereby confute such things as have occurred during our enquiry into the petition.

It has been suggested that Lieut.-Governor Colden had represented the inconvenience of this district appertaining to New Hampshire, and that for distance and situation it could never be well-governed but in New York, of which the inhabitants were very desirous. It is with great reluctance we find it our duty to contradict such assertions. The district in question is nearer to Portsmouth than to New York from sixty to three hundred and twenty miles, and it is evident that the nearer an estate to the capital of its government, the more convenient, more especially in America where upon most occasions of law recourse must be had to the capital where all appeals are heard and which in the present extent of New York is almost impossible, at least it must be ruinous for from many parts of the district taken off from New Hampshire the directest course to New York must forever be through New Hampshire, Massachusetts and Connecticut, in which provinces there are no laws to conduct a prisoner through them under a precept issued in any other, consequently these poor people are deprived of this court and the Court of Chancery in said province unless they travel without the limits of New England, a journey of at least five hundred miles which in time and expense would swallow almost any American farmer's estate and render law and justice the greatest violence and mischief to him. And here it is worthy observation the bounds proposed vizt. the western banks of Connecticut River, which we are told was represented to bear a north and south course into the country, whereas it appears by a survey of Samuel Holland Esq., Surveyor-General of the Northern District of America, taken officially and without the intervention of the parties, though a fact well-known for twenty years past, that the course of said river is for many miles east and west, and in many places to the south of east, insomuch that for more than five-eighths of the river there is no west nor east banks and therefore no bounds that can be known. Besides this in the spring and upon freshets, the river dilates more than a mile in many places, upon which as being the most fertile there are the best farms and most inhabitants, and by this means are in New Hampshire half the year and the other half in New York. As to the inhabitants' preferring to be in New York, their continual petitions both here and in the public offices at home, their agents in England appointed to solicit their restoration to New Hampshire, and the manifold grievances they daily suffer and complain of in that province, testify the contrary beyond a volume of representations. Nor can we imagine with what spirit it could be offered or how any person could presume to utter such gross and palpable fictions which we humbly conceive are detrimental to His Majesty's service by causing a mutilation of a small province, at the best but scarcely able to support the government, although from the beginning to this day both in war and peace they have approved themselves faithful and loyal subjects to the King and who by their blood and treasure defended this very territory from the enemy, annexing it to the province of New York, already of immense extent and opulence, who neither in the last war dared to defend it from the savages nor in the present peace gave the strongest testimonies of veneration and obedience to the laws, except the receding from an agreement to distress the British commerce, when it was no longer tenable, can be called an adequate renovation and an all-meritorious obliteration of their former conduct.

It is also said that Mr Colden represented that the grants under New Hampshire were clandestinely obtained by enormous fees, and that a man no better in appearance than a common pedlar travelled through New York and New Jersey, offering for sale many townships. The first part of this calumny Mr Colden well knew was false. It is contrived to injure the Governor and Council of New Hampshire. The grants were made in Council and recorded in the Secretary's office, whereto all persons have uninterrupted and open access with a full right to demand copies of record which was never yet denied to anyone.

It is therefore plain that these grants were not made in the least clandestinely neither could they be in the very nature of the thing. Therefore this assertion is highly unjust, untrue and injurious to His Majesty's Council of New Hampshire. As to the enormous fees insinuated, we can only say they are unknown to and unparticipated by the Council and that we believe it might be proved that Mr Wentworth did not receive more than thirty pounds sterling for passing a patent of those very townships, which we know after the decree of 1764 the same grantees were for each township compelled to pay at New York three hundred and thirty pounds sterling to obtain, notwithstanding they had performed all the conditions in the patent under New Hampshire. We are surprised at the nugatoriness of his asserting that a man of no better appearance than a pedlar offered to sell many townships. Be it so, we justly may suspect that such a person had no right to them, or may it not be reasonably apprehended that some such tool was employed merely to defame and degrade the government of New Hampshire, seeing that even Mr Colden presumed to lay such groundless positions before His Majesty's ministers of state, though from his present rank and appearance so highly remote from the pedlar, we heartily wish we were not called upon to be jealous of either. But had those grants been obtained clandestinely and at enormous expense, how could a poor pedlar-like man have acquired them? The absurdity and malice of the anecdote are equal and evident.

We also are casually informed that it was by him represented that officers would not locate in New Hampshire. If it was true it might have been our misfortune but by no means a matter of accusation or criminality; but the fact is otherwise, many officers did and do daily locate in New Hampshire, and it might be more reasonably complained of on our side that these did not claim in New York. Yet this is not all the insidious cruel secret. It was suggested to many officers and other people of respectable rank who had obtained the royal *mandamus* for grants of land that they might locate in the cultivated tracts of the New Hampshire settlers, which were rendered valuable by their labour. By this means many, not knowing the injustice of the case, did locate upon the premises which undoubtedly answered the purposes of those who wished to have the poor settlers ousted under the misused name and countenance of the royal proclamation. These being all the matters of complaint against New Hampshire preferred by Mr Colden that have been suggested to us, and the province having had no official or other citation nor the least notice of these or any other complaints against their jurisdiction in the premises before the arrival of His Majesty's Order in Council in 1764 whereby they were deprived of this district, we beg leave further to represent that this unexpected decree, obtained ex parte and without a hearing of New Hampshire as was formerly granted in a similar dispute with Massachusetts Bay and is now in agitation between New York and New Jersey and between New York and Massachusetts Bay, though immediately obeyed with the utmost minute punctuality, yet it conveyed the greatest surprise and grief through the province, not only on the loss they sustained of a country maintained and defended by their men and money as part of the province by express command of His late Majesty, but more especially that it appeared as a censure inflicted for misconduct they know not to have incurred and without an opportunity to vindicate themselves; whereby many innocent subjects, the petitioners, are involved in the most distressful circumstances, far more to be regretted and marked with infinitely greater calamity than the Canadians, whom they assisted to conquer, were subjected to by the change of government that ensued, under which they were mercifully quieted in their possessions while the petitioners complain and lament that they are disseised and ejected solely under the pretence of an alteration in the boundary lines of two provinces. But as the petitioners were now excluded this province, the Council entertained the greatest reluctance to hear their petition nor were prevailed upon until through repeated representations that the grievances complained of were in some degree innocently occasioned by their official advice and that the event extremely affected the honour and prosperity of this province, which in duty to His Majesty and faithfulness to their fellow subjects they are bound to pursue.

From the same motives we have delayed returning our report, daily hoping that the petitioners would be relieved and that their petitions would be laid before His Majesty from whose paternal care of his remotest subjects the most solid relief will undoubtedly result.

We therefore beg leave to report as before expressed and that an humble address be presented to His Majesty representing the injury sustained by his loyal and obedient province of New Hampshire by the alteration of the boundary line of said province in favour of the province of New York, also of the sufferings resulting to many thousands of His Majesty's good subjects thereby, most humbly praying that His Majesty will be graciously pleased to restore and reannex the premises to this province; which event we humbly conceive will give peace and relief to the petitioners, highly promote population and improvement of that district, facilitate and augment the revenue of quitrent, preserve the pine timber fit for mast, accommodate the inhabitants in the mode, situation and distance of their provincial government, and be in every other view and tendency a blessing to that country and plant an everlasting gratitude for such an instance of the royal benignity of His Majesty's most happy government.

All which is humbly submitted to your Excellency in Council, by Daniel Peirce, George Jaffrey, Daniel Rogers, committee. August 16th 1771.

Province of New Hampshire. In Council the 16th August 1771. The foregoing report having been read, voted and resolved that the same be accepted and presented to his Excellency the Governor, praying his Excellency will be pleased to transmit the same to be laid before His Majesty, humbly imploring the royal condescension to reannex the district on the west side Connecticut River, taken from this province and added to the province of New York by His Majesty's Order in Council in the year 1764, and that his Excellency will be pleased to recommend the same, being for His Majesty's service and for the just benefit of this province by such further explanations and observations thereon as to his Excellency shall seem proper and just. Theodore Atkinson, Secretary. *Copy*, certified by Theodore Atkinson. [C.O.5/937, fo. 51]

XC

John Stuart's Instructions to John Thomas[1]

17 August, Pensacola

Sir, as you have the opportunity of Mr Bryan's sloop for New Orleans, I am to desire you will proceed thither in her with the proportion of presents which I have purchased for the annual expense of your district.

Upon your arrival at New Orleans you will wait of the governor and after delivering Governor Chester's letters with one from me, you will ask his permission to land the presents etc. that they may be put on board the batteau which Mr Forrestal will provide for you in eight days after your arrival there. Upon your acquainting me that you are furnished with a batteau properly equipped for carrying the presents etc. with 12 rowers, a patroon and the necessary provisions for them etc., I have engaged to pay Mr Monsanto 250 dollars for the use of said batteau one month. Immediately after you shall have been furnished with said batteau you are to proceed up the Mississippi as far as Natchez. On your voyage you are to be particularly attentive to the situation of the small tribes that you may be enabled to report to me fully of their numbers, disposition and places of abode, the state of the trade with them, whence they are supplied and at what prices, the number and names of the traders residing among them, whether or not licenced and by whom. After you shall have made the necessary remarks at Natchez you will return in the same batteau to Iberville and Manshac, in the neighbourhood of which place I think it will be for His Majesty's service that you do reside. You will be pleased to mark what rivers fall into the Mississippi and the number and situation of the inhabitants on our side.

Your business in your district must be to cultivate a good understanding with the nations of Indians within it and to conciliate them to His Majesty's government, to take care that justice is done them by the traders or inhabitants under the laws of this province and His Majesty's instructions to me.

1 Enclosed in John Stuart's letter of 24 September to Hillsborough, Vol. I, No. 1525.

As many small tribes, who after the cession of Eastern Louisiana and Florida to His Majesty by the Crowns of France and Spain were settled on lands within the British territories, have been induced to remove to land in the Spanish dominion, if you find any of them inclined to return you are to give them all the encouragement in your power, giving timous notice to the governor of the province that lands may be allotted them.

You are to be particularly cautious not to give umbrage to the Spanish government by encouraging or inviting any of the nations who resided on lands reserved to the Crown of France at the end of the last war to remove to our side of the River Mississippi, and you are not to interfere with them or their concerns except so far as may be necessary for maintaining a good understanding with them that the public tranquillity may not be disturbed.

You are to inform yourself fully and report to me in the clearest manner concerning the claims and pretensions of the different small tribes to the lands on the eastern bank of the Mississippi and of the Lakes Pontchartrain and Maurepas, that I may be enabled to judge how far it may be necessary to treat with those Indians for said lands before they shall be settled by British subjects.

You are regularly to keep the governor of West Florida informed of every matter in your department which may concern the said province. You are also to communicate to Brigadier-General Haldimand every occurrence which may respect the public tranquillity and give him all the intelligence which may be useful to His Majesty's service in the military department, and in all matters relative to peace or war between His Majesty's subjects and the savages you are to be governed by his ideas. But you are not to undertake any service by which an extraordinary expense may be created until a fund be pointed out for discharging the same as I shall not approve of or defray any expense exceeding the estimated fund.

You are by every opportunity to advise me fully of your transactions with the Indians in your district that I may lay the same before His Majesty's ministers. Your letters for me on His Majesty's service after I shall have left this province must be sent under cover to Mr Charles Stuart, my deputy here, and left open for his perusal who will have my directions concerning them.

You are to draw upon me every six months for your salary and your interpreter is to draw in the same manner, taking care to transmit me your receipts, also receipts from your interpreter signed by himself, and your certificate of his service and behaviour, without which no bill or order for your or his salary will be paid.

As you are now furnished with the estimated sum for all contingencies in your district for a year, that is to say from 1 July 1771 to 30 June 1772, I recommend the utmost economy and that all unnecessary expenses may be avoided. Your interpreter must be paid by you out of the money you have received until the last day of June next and you are to consider that the sum paid you stands charged to you as an imprest until you shall have accounted and transmitted to me vouchers for the payment of the same.

You will please not to detain the batteau longer in pay than 30 days agreed for.

I wish you a successful and prosperous voyage. *Copy.* [C.O.5/72, fo. 362]

XCI

Governor John Wentworth to Earl of Hillsborough (No. 37)

20 August, New Hampshire

May it please your Lordship, His Majesty's Council of this province having presented me their report upon the state of private property and jurisdiction of a certain district west of Connecticut River to a line 20 miles east of Hudson's River, which report they have requested me to transmit to your lordship and that I would add such other explanations as appertain to the cause of their humble petition to His Majesty for a confirmation of the property and restoration of the jurisdiction to the province of New Hampshire: I have therefore the honour to beg leave herewith to enclose the said report [Vol. III, No. LXXXIX] and most respectfully to entreat your lordship's favourable representation thereon to His Majesty.

As this matter originated before my appointment to the government of New Hampshire, and the whole appears to be so largely considered in the report, I am not furnished with many observations thereon nor much matter of explanation. From the best information I can obtain the claimants or *bona fide* proprietors under the seal of New Hampshire are and have been exceedingly distressed and are most undoubtedly real objects of royal clemency. The law and equity which they think justify their possession and title I presume not to consider, but I hope will prove effectual to recommend them to your lordship's protection. Their peculiar distresses find an only remaining comfort in a reliance on your lordship's universally known humanity and extensive delight in the prosperity of all His Majesty's subjects, more especially of those who are happily the immediate objects of your lordship's administration. In considering the petition of the inhabitants of the aforesaid district it is most humbly entreated that the jurisdiction may also be annexed to New Hampshire, without which a confirmation of property cannot fully relieve the inhabitants, who in every instance of manners, interest, situation and interior police, are and must ever be strongly connected with and bound to this province. Perhaps it may appear the more necessary when it is considered that the property has already been often changed and the records of its origin and mutations are in New Hampshire, which must entail perpetual cost and confusion upon the altered jurisdiction. In the patents of these townships was also granted sundry incorporated privileges unknown to the laws of New York, though consistent with and established by laws in New Hampshire. But if the patents under New Hampshire are vacated and property originate *de novo* under New York, although it might be open to the present possessors, yet the unavoidable expense, time and difficulty in taking out new titles would be such a burthen to the greater part of those poor people as would be utterly impossible for them to surmount.

The public benefit that would redound to this province from the recovery of this district would be very great indeed. It is the country that must either enrich or impoverish New Hampshire, being a soil capable of raising corn for the use and export of the present province, and will ever be their only resource for this indispensable article. It cannot be so important to New York which already abounds and is still further capable to an immense degree, exclusive of the premises. Neither can this district so greatly affect the extent or revenue of New York as it does of New Hampshire. The former is large, opulent, numerous and plentiful without this addition, but the latter are in all these instances exceedingly confined and diminished by the loss of almost a third part of their former estimated bounds, which with the uncommon geographical form of both provinces in their present state will strongly appear to your lordship upon the first view of an exact and faithful map of the two provinces. *Signed.* [C.O.5/937, fo. 48]

XCII

Students of King's College, New York, to Governor William Tryon[1]

[before 20 August]
The human heart at some seasons is agitated with mingled rapture and anxiety. These emotions this moment rise high in my bosom. I feel exalted pleasure in beholding your Excellency within these walls, I feel distinguished transport from the honour of addressing you for my fellow-students. But my bosom beats at the same time with anxiety lest my feeble tongue should not be able to express the sentiments of affection and reverence with which we are so deeply affected. The remote advantages of science are too delicate and distant to strike the youthful eye: the attention, the advice, and fostering smiles of the generality of mankind will often kindle up this flame. To what height will it not rise when cherished by the countenance of persons as superior for their abilities and virtues as for the splendour of their actions and the dignity of their stations? 'Tis the glory of Britons to excel in arts as well as in arms, to be equally eminent in enlarging the happiness of mankind as they are superior themselves in the enjoyment of private and public felicity. While we are indebted to our mother country for protection, support and defence, our obligations have been increased by the streams of munifence which, flowing from our gracious Sovereign and augmented by the generosity of the benevolent and noble, have yielded us the power of tasting the fruits of science in this before-uncultivated soil. To express our sense of such unrivalled bounty exceeds the reach of our feeble disruption [*sic : ?conception*], but it shall never be forgotten while we have hands to write or tongue to speak or a soul to think, though removed at a distant from our benevolent Prince, we have constantly rejoiced in the beams of his paternal favour; but our joy is on this day complete when we behold his influence immediately reflected upon us by so just a representative of his royal person and virtues. To encourage an early application to

1   Enclosed in Governor Tryon's letter of 30 August to Hillsborough, Vol. I, No. 1481.

wisdom is to promote the general welfare of society; to extend the happiness of their country is the object of the good and great, and goodness accompanied with greatness is the brightest jewel in the hero's crown. We behold them shine with unparalleled lustre in your Excellency's character. We hail the future splendour of this, our infant university, under your benign auspices. We feel the generous flame of emulation already intwined by your presence and forcibly stimulating us by humbly imitating your virtues to become in some degree worthy of your attention. Inexperienced and separated from the stage of active life, we can yield no adequate compensation for your Excellency's kindness but our strenuous endeavours shall be exerted (which we are confident will be the acceptable returns to your Excellency) to become faithful subjects of His Majesty and useful members of society.

                                                                    Roebuck

Pacatum reget patriis virtutibus orbem

Stanza 1st

When Tryon led his loyal bands
O'er pathless wilds and barren sands,
Crimson'd with crimes a bloody train
Rush from their haunts and crowd the plain,
Dark o'er their ranks rebellion's banner flies,
And shades the blushing fields and blots the conscious skies.

2nd

The generous chief with pity view'd
Their legions thirsting for his blood:
Stern Justice sheath'd her shining blade
And Mercy wide her arms display'd.
The rebel hosts with tow'ring pride advance,
And spurn the gracious call and shake the threatening lance.

3rd

My muse whom peace and order charms
Starts at Bellona's loud alarms,
Nor paints the hero in his car,
Serene amidst the waste of war;
Or fierce as tempest sweep the angry main,
Bursting through hostile ranks and thund'ring o'er the plain.

4th

Where faction stretch'd her wide domain
And rapine led a numerous train,
Auspicious chief, thy conq'ring sword
Has laws and harmony restor'd,
The stormy waves of civil discord hush'd,
And calm'd seditious rage and foul rebellion crush'd.

5th

Just to your prince, a patriot try'd,
Opposed to meanness, vice and pride,
Brave, candid, vigilant, sincere,
Thy virtues ev'n thy foes revere.
Malice and envy aid the voice of fame,
Repeat the strains of truth and echo Tryon's name.

6th

How shall my cold unpolish'd verse
Thy boundless gratitude rehearse?
O favor'd land! to whom is given
This friend to virtue, truth and heav'n.
My tim'rous muse with trembling pinions flies,
Thy sons in deeds sublime shall sound it to the skies.

                                                          Edward Stevens

Pacatum reget patriis virtutibus orbem

While suppliant crowds in grateful zeal contend,
Their wishes pour and hail their country's friend,
Humbly the Muse her tribute too would bring,
Humbly illustrious Tryon's virtues sing,
Kindly for him indulgent heaven implore,
And hail his presence on our happy shore.
This happy day in Time's renew'd career
Shall shine the fairest of the circling year.
Well-pleased each bard shall make the sounding lyre,
Each grateful tongue the glorious theme inspire,
Each gen'rous breast with ardent love shall glow
And the high notes of joy in general chorus flow.
Now lovely peace around her banners spreads,
The Arts enliven'd rear their beauteous heads,
Domestic toils and civil tumults cease,
And smiling Concord views her fair increase.
Offspring of Heaven! sweet Wisdom, Virtue, Love,
Blessings which polish, comfort and improve,
Whose secret charms with power resistless bind
The jarring passions of the human mind,
In tender friendship ev'ry heart unite
And dictate always what is always right.
Tryon, thy praise what tongue can celebrate?
By thee we know what's truly good and great,
From thee we learn our country to defend
And make Rebellion to bright Justice bend.
But while thy steady calmness we admire,
Who can attain thy courage and thy fire?
Who learn that martial skill to deal the blow,

And pour destruction on a desp'rate foe?
Well didst thou gain a people's just applause;
Well didst thou fight and in a noble cause;
But still the Muse her heartfelt grief must own,
And bless the conquest with a pitying groan,
While rises to her sight the insanguin'd field
Which daring rebels scorn'd to thee to yield,
Unhappy men who 'gainst their country's good
Rush't on their fate and madly spilt their blood.
But now wild war has hush'd her dire alarms
And disengaged thee from the weight of arms.
Indulgent ease shall crown thy happy days,
Thy rich reward a grateful people's praise.
No envious tongue shall dare to blot thy name,
Pure and unspotted in the rolls of Fame.
O mayst thou long the helm with safety guide,
With wisdom rule, and justice by her side,
No storms to fear, no base ungrateful jars,
The sad presage of intestine wars,
But peace and plenty spread thoughout the land
And Heaven propitious smile on thy command.

                                                      Barclay

Pacatum reget patriis virtutibus orbem

Beneath their vine and fig-tree shade,
By sad experience wiser made,
Two youths thus sang and mourn'd their crime
Tho' pardon'd in alternate rhyme.

Corydon:

Now peace, with all her smiling train,
Visits our drooping land again;
No more wild licence spreads dismay,
While deeds of frenzy mark her way;
Yet not unmix'd with woe our joy,
The fruit of guilt the sad alloy,
As sunshine mild doth oft attend
When gently vernal show'rs descend,
So doth fair Caroline appear,
Her smile attended with a tear.

Thyrsis:

O happy when with guiltless mind
We think of dangers left behind,
But woe the while when we review
Escap'd from punishment, our due!

Corydon:

Our fears the conquer'r hath remov'd,
While stubborn justice scarce approv'd,
Our farms remain, our happy bow'rs,
Those laws we spurn'd ensure them our's.

Thyrsis:

When forth his sword the hero draws
To assert his country's dying laws,
If in his breast sweet pity lives,
That mourns and feels the wounds he gives,
Still shall the Muse his worth proclaim,
And sound to distant times his name,
Still shall the farmer from his toil
In peace behold his harvests smile.
That happy boon is your's and mine,
The high applause, O Tryon, thine.

John Jauncey

Pacatum reget patriis virtutibus orbem

Cease calumny, ye heirs of envy fly,
Discord avant or hide thy head and die!
Her sacred form let smiling virtue raise,
With joy exult and pour the notes of praise,
For to the Chief appears, by Heaven design'd,
The scourge of vice and friend of humankind.
When bloody rapine's stern unpitying band
Roar'd high to ravage o'er a feeble land,
When fetter'd Justice mourn'd her dread disgrace
And Order totter'd to its firmest base,
Then ran the hero, danger threats in vain,
He smiles at toil, disease and sickening pain;
Health, pleasure, fortune, safety, ease invite,
And call him from the fatal fields of fight.
But health and ease and pleasure vainly charm
When bleeding Justice asks the hero's arm;
Joyful for her, he'd pant his latest breath,
And for his country's service smile in death.
Victorious Tryon! faintly speech imparts
The love to thee which blazes in our hearts.
As the strong eagle's tender nestling brood,
While their fond parent wings abroad for food,
With anxious bosoms for his safety burn,
And pant impatient for his wish'd return,
Eye the vast fields, and at his homeward flight
Swell their young breasts with rapturous delight,
So while a country's welfare claim'd thy stay,
Anxious we trembled at thy long delay,
Impatient number'd ev'ry moment passed,
And wish'd each long expected hour the last.

Fond hopes and fears, the fruits of anxious love,
By turns superior in our bosoms strove,
Till Heaven propitious gave our hearts to see
Their bliss complete by blessing us with thee.
Patron of good! with each fair virtue bless'd,
Who bear'st thy Sovereign's image in thy breast,
Like him our welfare watchful to extend,
Like him a foe to vice, religion's friend,
Prompt like thy Prince to act in virtue's plan,
The patriot, ruler, and the honest man.
Ungird thy sword, thy years shall peaceful move,
Blest like thy Sovereign in his people's love,
No arms he needs, no forceful pow'rs of art,
Whose sword is justice and whose throne the heart.

Frederick Philipse

Copy. [C.O.5/1102, fo. 231]

XCIII

Governor Thomas Hutchinson to Earl of Hillsborough [*Private*]

25 August, Boston

My Lord, Mr Henry Barnes who lately arrived from England has requested me to cover a letter from him to your lordship and to make a representation of his services and sufferings in the cause of government. He has not acquainted me with the contents of his letter. He certainly has suffered greatly by his refusing to comply with the scheme of non-importation and by his endeavours to support the authority of the magistrate; but in his solicitations for compensation he discovers more impatience than I could wish, which I am willing to attribute to a mind chafed with the troubles he has met with and impressed with a strong sense of his merit which he supposes to exceed that of many others who have received the favours of government. He complains of my neglecting him in not particularly recommending his case to your lordship when he went to England, and though he did not ask it of me yet concluded that I had done it in the course of my public correspondence as governor of the province. I transmitted an account of the incendiary letters sent him and I would have been more particular if he had desired it of me.

For his general character, which is very good, I thought he depended on Sir Francis Bernard who I know held him in esteem and to whom he was more particularly known than to me. If there was anything in the province in my disposal worth his acceptance I would give it him, but there is not.

Permit me, my lord, to take this opportunity of making my grateful acknowledgements to your lordship for His Majesty's warrant to the Commissioners of the Customs for the payment of my salary. The fund upon which this warrant is charged would rise to a very large sum if the illicit trade with Holland could be prevented.

The consumption of tea in America exceeds what anybody in England imagines. Some persons capable of judging suppose five-sixths of what has been consumed the two last years has been illegally imported, and in Philadelphia and New York it is judged nine-tenths.

In my letter to your lordship of the 14th inst.[1] I expressed my hopes that a vigorous pursuit of the illicit traders by the cruizers would discourage the trade but I am informed they make such an extravagant profit that it will require more frequent seizures to discourage it than we have any reason to hope for.

If the India Company had continued the sale of their teas at 2s 2d. to 2s 4d. as they sold them 2 years ago, the Dutch trade would have been over by this time; but now that teas are 3s. and upwards in England the illicit trader can afford to lose 1 chest in 3 whereas I am very sure not one in a 100 has been seized.

The Custom-house officers on shore have strong inducements to do their duty but they are really afraid of the rage of the people. The sea-officers have of late been more active than formerly, and Admiral Montagu appears disposed to keep out his cruizers. I doubt, notwithstanding, whether this trade will ever be discouraged in any other way, especially in New York and Philadelphia, than by reducing the price of tea in England to the exporter very near the price in Holland. For want of this, the revenue by a moderate computation has lost the last and present year at least £60,000 sterling from the 3d. duty only, besides what it would have left in England over and above the drawback.

Your lordship has encouraged me when anything occurs for His Majesty's service, though out of my immediate department, to suggest it. I believe the cruizing vessels are capable of doing more towards suppressing the illicit trade than the officers ashore: they should therefore be excited to do their duty by a reward in proportion to their activity.

The commanding officer of the squadron may very well retain the same share of the seizure which he is now entitled to, because the direction of the whole depends upon him, but it seems that a greater proportion is necessary for the particular officer who makes the seizure under a commission from the Customs than what he is now entitled to. If the officers on shore were not entitled to $\frac{1}{3}$ or a large proportion we should have no seizures made on shore, and I believe the remissness of the sea-officers is very much owing to the small share which he who makes the seizure is entitled to, which might be $\frac{1}{3}$ of the whole with as much reason as to the officer on shore.

I the rather suggest this to your lordship because I have discovered when I have sworn some of the Navy officers to qualify them for their commissions from the Customs a great indifference and a disinclination to make themselves obnoxious to the people without any great advantage to themselves. *Entry.* [C.O.5/246, p. 31]

---

1 Not found, unless No. LXXXVIII above, which is addressed to J. Pownall and does not mention cruisers.

XCIV

John Stuart to Governor Peter Chester[1]

30 August, Pensacola

Sir, as I have advice that the Creek Indians may be soon expected here to mark the boundary line dividing the lands ceded to His Majesty in this province from those reserved by them for hunting-grounds, it becomes my duty to request of your Excellency your opinion and advice with respect to the business relative to this province to be transacted with them, which I apprehend is to be considered under the following heads.

1st. Whether a further extent of territory on this side of Mobile Bay as well as upon the Alibamon and Scambia Rivers be really necessary in the present state of population of this province.

2nd. Whether upon considering the temper of Indians in general respecting lands as well as the present state of this province it will be advisable to renew our application for land at this time.

3rd. Upon what principles are we to account to the Creeks for having made settlements so far beyond the stipulated boundary upon the Alibamon River.

That your Excellency may be enabled to consider these questions in a proper point of view I think it necessary to acquaint you with the temper of the Indians with respect to their lands.

The extensive cession obtained by Sir William Johnson from the Six Nations not only contained the hunting grounds of many Western tribes but also of the Cherokee Indians who took umbrage at seeing settlements made on their lands without their consent; but as the Six Nations declared their intention of supporting their grant the Western tribes formed themselves into a general confederacy, to strengthen which they are soliciting the Southern tribes to join them, and deputies are continually going into the Cherokee, Chickasaw and Creek nations for that purpose; and although great pains have been taken to remove the complaints and jealousy of the Cherokees by fixing their boundary with their approbation in November last, yet the machinations of the Western tribes have kept up a spirit of discontent in them and my deputy Mr Cameron found the greatest difficulty to persuade them to stand to their solemn agreement and attend him in marking the line agreed to by all the chiefs.

The traders in the Cherokee nation having suffered the Indians to incur large debts have thought of obtaining payment by taking land. Those Indians, uneasy under the load of debt, agreed to give up a considerable tract on the western side of Savannah River and I have late intelligence that they have actually run and marked it. This has been transacted without my knowledge and concurrence, is irregular and contrary to the King's proclamation, and will of course be disapproved by Government. The lands so ceded by the Cherokees is claimed by the Creeks, and I have always understood it to belong to

---

1 Enclosed in John Stuart's letter of 24 September to Hillsborough, Vol. I, No. 1525.

them. It gives them much uneasiness, and although the transaction was unknown to me and without my approbation and consent, yet it serves to increase the general discontent as the ignorant Indians cannot distinguish this irregular act of the traders from a measure of government. In acting for any particular province we must not lose sight of the general good which is still to be principally attended to. At this very time there is a great and general meeting at Sciota, where the encroachments on Indians' lands is the great object of their deliberations; it is a very general and interesting concern to all Indians, and however they may quarrel about other matters they will unite and make this a common cause, for which reason I submitted it as my opinion to Lord Hillsborough before I left Charleston that the present is an improper and unfavourable conjuncture for renewing our applications for land; but if I am wrong I am open to conviction and shall pay the greatest attention to any reasons your Excellency shall be pleased to offer upon the subject. *Copy*. [C.O.5/72, fo. 350]

XCV

Governor William Tryon to Earl of Hillsborough (Private)

31 August, New York

My Lord, upon my arrival in this province I was warmly solicited by the Earl of Dunmore to make the exchange of governments with him. To strengthen his solicitations he showed me a private letter of your lordship's to him signifying that the exchange might be easily made. He had wrote me, he said, two letters on that subject but neither of them arrived in Carolina till after I had left that country. I acquainted his lordship that in obedience to the King's commands I had removed to this government to receive the commission His Majesty had been graciously pleased to honour me with, that I thought I was bound in duty to the Crown to qualify to the commission of governor, nor could I after coming into this country with any possible colour of decency retreat from a province to which I was appointed to preside over. Exclusive of these public reasons, I assured his lordship I was in too crazy a habit of body voluntarily to return to the southward climates without first going over to England to re-establish my health. My family and baggage was also with me and Mrs Tryon at that time in so weak a state of health that she could scarce bear the voyage from North Carolina and has continued very ill ever since her arrival here. These circumstances did not seem to carry any conviction with his lordship of the impossibility of exchanging governments with him, and I own I was sorry to see his disappointment at my not being able to comply with his sanguine wishes to remain here. Your lordship must be sensible that I entertained the most favourable opinion of the government of Virginia by my writing to you, my lord, on the death of my very valuable friend Lord Botetourt to solicit your lordship's good offices in procuring for me that government. Had it been His Majesty's pleasure to have cast my lot in that dominion I should have been very happy in receiving so distinguished a mark of royal favour. I shall be satisfied here if I can carry on the King's and the country's business. As yet I can make no judgement but from the public addresses, which however give me encouragement. Most of the principal inhabitants are at their country-seats. Lord Dunmore has made a trip up Hudson's River and returned to this town last Wednesday. I understand he very shortly sets out by land to his government of Virginia. I am sorry I have been the innocent means of his disappointment and heartily wish he may meet with as much happiness in his new government as he experienced in this.

Having a thorough sense of your lordship's favourable regard towards me, I am induced to give you this detail on the rather awkward manner in which I entered upon my administration as it was the prevailing opinion here that the then next packet would bring orders for my removal. *Signed.* [C.O.5/154, fo. 25]

XCVI

Governor William Tryon to Earl of Hillsborough (No. 5)

2 September, New York

My Lord, as doubts have arisen respecting the appointment of Surrogate and Register of the Prerogative Court within this government, I beg leave to submit the equity and propriety of the claims to His Majesty, the one claiming the appointment of the officer of the said court under the King's commission as commander-in-chief in and over the province, the latter under the patent of secretary of the province.

Mr Banyar's memorial in behalf of Mr George Clark, Secretary, with a copy he delivered me of an Order of His late Majesty in Council at the Court of Kensington the 8th of May 1758, I have the honour to transmit to your lordship together with my letter in answer to Mr Banyar's memorial [Vol. I, No. 1491i-iii] wherein I required the Prerogative Seal to be delivered up to me. The rights of this court, my lord, I was in the exercise of in North Carolina, with this difference that the crown of the Great Seal was used to all instruments as the Prerogative Seal, and that wills were by the direction of a particular Act of Assembly recorded in the County Courts. Finding therefore on my arrival here that the principal perquisites which were appropriated in North Carolina to the support of the Governor's private secretary were received by the Surrogate and Registry in question, and also finding the Earl of Dunmore had actually given to Mr Banyar, the deputy Secretary, the commission of Surrogate and Register, and after receiving opinions both in England and in this town from gentlemen of the first eminence at the bar that such appointment was vested in the Governor, I gave the commission in question to Mr Fanning, my private secretary, as an honourable testimony of his public and distinguished services in the late rebellion in North Carolina where he commanded the Orange detachment of two hundred men, and in recompense for the loss he sustained by his house and furniture being destroyed in the riot at Hillsborough Superior Court in September last. I shall not trouble your lordship with any law points but rest my conduct in this instance on the equity of the case. *Signed.* [C.O.5/1102, fo. 245]

XCVII

Governor Peter Chester to John Stuart[1]

10 September, Pensacola
Sir, I had the honour of receiving your several letters of the 30th [Vol. III, No. XCIV] and 31st [Vol. I, No. 1525viii] of last month, and in answer thereto am to acquaint you that as it required a perfect knowledge of this country and of the temper and disposition of Indians in order to furnish you with the information you desire, and as the subject-matter contained in your letters is of great importance to the interests of the province, I thought proper immediately to refer them for the opinion of the members of His Majesty's Council, many of whom have been long resident here and therefore the better enabled to assist me with their sentiments, and I yesterday received their report and opinions upon the same, a copy of which is here enclosed. This report in a great measure coincides with my sentiments but I must beg leave to make a few observations thereupon. With regard to the answer of the first question mentioned in the report, I think that if the lands which were formerly in possession of the French and ceded to us by the Treaty of Paris can for this reason be considered as our property, the Creeks have never as yet granted us any lands either on the Bay of Mobile or Alibama River, for they in that case instead of granting have only confirmed to us the quiet possession of lands they had formerly ceded to the French, and therefore we may with more propriety ask them for an extension of boundary; and although I shall be glad to procure an extension on the Alibama River yet I think it would be more advisable and more for the interest of the province first to ask them for the increase of boundary (mentioned in the Council's report) on the River Escambia which has by my direction lately been examined, and I am informed that at some distance up the river they are very proper for cultivation. The Creeks come here frequently in great numbers and expect to be supplied with provisions and other presents. The purchase of the former from the dearness and scarcity makes it very expensive to government. Therefore, if we had lands that will produce rice and corn etc., we should be able to purchase them at a much cheaper rate than at present. And by these lands being so contiguous to this town they will if settled prove of greater advantage to us than those so distant as the Alibama. The soil within our present boundary on the Escambia is so barren that several industrious persons who have some property were ruined by their attempts of making settlements in this part. Should we succeed in this first object without difficulty, I would then recommend the asking for an extension on the River Alibama, but this must depend upon the temper and disposition in which we

---

1 Enclosed in John Stuart's letter of 24 September to Hillsborough, Vol. I, No. 1525.

shall find the Indians upon their arrival. As to the second question, I am in hopes that a renewal of our application for lands at this time will not be attended with any bad consequences or tend to excite resentment in the Creeks who have hitherto given us nothing but sands; and that they may be told with propriety that as their brothers provide them with provisions whenever they come down to see them, it is but reasonable they should furnish us with some proper lands to grow them upon as they have done to all the provinces, and not to put us to the necessity of bringing them here by sea from other parts.

The best reason in my opinion that we can assign to the third question and account to the Creeks for having made settlements so far beyond the stipulated boundary upon the Alibama River, is that it was owing to a mistake in the persons who run them out and not done with the approbation and consent of government, and that upon my receiving the first intelligence of their parties warning off the settlers who had encroached, I directed them to withdraw, who have not since returned to take possession of them, and sent up a talk into their nation assuring them that I would never allow of any such encroachments; that they proceeded from ignorance in the settlers, and for the future to avoid disputes desired they would send down some of their chiefs to assist us in marking the line.

The treaty with the Creeks in 1765 which contains the boundary line is upon record in the Secretary's office. How so many tracts came to be surveyed and run out beyond it or from what cause this neglect proceeded, I will not take upon me to say as these surveys were all made and the grants passed before my arrival in the province, but as all the warrants of survey direct the Surveyor-General to observe the King's instructions in laying out tracts which forbid any encroachments on lands reserved to the Indians, I must rather impute this proceeding to ignorance than any wilful breach of His Majesty's instructions.

I agree with the Council in their answer to the first question contained in your letter of the 31 August and think they have given many weighty reasons why a congress with the Choctaws should be held at this time. To these I would add that as it seems agreed on all hands that congresses have been promised them, they will naturally imagine when they hear of your arrival, which they expected, that you have come for this purpose and to fulfil our former engagements. An Indian cannot distinguish whether the persons making these promises are properly authorized to do it or not. If they are made them by white men whom they conceive to be vested with authority they believe they will be performed and if they are deceived will tell us we are liars and never put confidence in us. I am informed that they have already said they had given us their lands upon a promise of having congresses, and now we are in possession of them we think no more of performing our agreements. I believe they have been deceived by gentlemen authorized to make those promises, and therefore to remove all jealousy and in order to secure their friendship I think it advisable to gratify them at this time. I also think proper to acquaint you that in the month of June last, when Lieut.-Governor Durnford was upon the Mississippi, he received letters from the commandants of the Spanish posts at Fort Gabriel and Point Coupee representing the great fears and apprehensions the Spanish settlers were under of an attack from the Indians, and complaining that the savages had been excited to it by some of the English; and shortly after I received a letter from the governor of Orleans on the same subject. Their fears were groundless, as I informed the Spanish governor, but their apprehensions were great and there is probable cause to imagine that they began negotiations with the Choctaws, for Lieutenant-Governor Durnford was informed immediately after, and before he left the Mississippi, both by the French and Indians that emissaries were sent by the governor of New Orleans to the Choctaws inviting them down. And I have lately seen a deposition of one Andrew Kearns, an Indian trader, who left the Choctaw nation about the 20 of last month, who swears that it was then currently reported that the Spaniards had sent a Frenchman into the Six Towns of the Choctaws with invitations to the chiefs to go down to Orleans; and that Mingo upa, a chief who formerly lived at Tombeckby, and the Hulloso King or Writing King, a medal chief, with a party were then about setting off for Orleans. All these circumstances corroborating leave little room to doubt but that the Spaniards are or have been tampering with them, and I think with General Gage that we should endeavour to conciliate their affections so as to depend upon their support, for had matters come to extremities in the dispute with Spain those Indians with the Chickasaws would have secured to us almost the whole trade of the Mississippi and must have been of the greatest service in any of our attacks upon Orleans. This nation I am told are full three thousand men fit to carry arms, that they are treacherous in their dispositions, and many of them still retain a great regard for their old neighbours, that their friendship is not to be obtained or depended upon otherwise than by presents or compulsion. This latter method we cannot carry into execution and the former appears to me to be a proper measure for the reasons before mentioned and lest our neighbours should take the advantage of our neglect and draw them over to their interest, the consequences of which, should their desires be refused them whilst you are upon the spot, may prove fatal to this province.

With regard to the question "whether or not Indian affairs with respect to the Choctaws are at present better settled than when Governor Durnford reported upon them to His Majesty's Secretary of State" I think that it is impossible for me to give a direct answer as I cannot know what disturbances were among the Indians or what transactions happened that might alarm Mr Durnford at the time he reported upon these Indian affairs to the Earl of Hillsborough; but since I have been in the province I have never seen or heard of any sufficient cause that could induce me in the least to apprehend that the Choctaws had any real hostile intentions against us. The young men will often get drunk when they can get liquor and have then been guilty of irregular behaviour, but I have never heard that these irregularities have been approved of by the leading and headmen of the nations.

I think that the people and traders who supply them with rum are more to blame than the ignorant savages, and in order to restrain the traders and others from furnishing them with such quantities of rum as they do in the nations, of which the chiefs complain so often, I think it advisable that application should be made to the Earl of Hillsborough for commissaries to be appointed in the Creek, Choctaw and Chickasaw nations, that they may keep those licentious unruly traders under some restrictions, for I am of opinion that most of the disputes and misunderstandings between the white people and the savages are owing to the irregularities of the traders which proceeds from there not being any persons in the nations who have a power to regulate and adjust the differences that too frequently arise between them and the savages, owing in a great measure to their imposing and cheating the poor ignorant Indians, which might easily be prevented if commissaries were appointed among them.

To the last question in your letter of 31 August, I think that the Choctaws should not be treated with for any lands upon the Mississippi at present, as they have never made any claims to those we have surveyed in that part. The small tribes who were in possession of them when Louisiana was ceded by the Crown of France to His Majesty should be paid for them when they demand it. *Copy.* [C.O.5/72, fo. 352]

XCVIII

Governor Thomas Hutchinson to Earl of Hillsborough [*Private*]

10 September, Boston ·

My Lord, your lordship does me great honour by your private letter of the 30th of May [not found] which I did not receive until after I had closed my last letter to your lordship of the 25th of August [Vol. III, No. XCIII].

· Having made the illicit trade with Holland the principal subject of that letter, I beg leave now to submit to your consideration an estimate of the consumption of Bohea tea in America.

From the best accounts I can obtain from the dealers in teas the two towns of Boston and Charlestown consume a chest or about 340 lbs. per day one day with another. These two towns are not more than $\frac{1}{8}$th, perhaps not more than $\frac{1}{10}$th part of the province. Suppose they consume only 300 chests in a year and allow that they are $\frac{1}{8}$th, it will make 2,400 chests for the whole province.

This is much short, for in the country towns there is more tea drunk in proportion than at Boston. This province is not $\frac{1}{8}$th part of the colonies, and in other governments, New York especially, they consume tea in much greater proportion than in this province. If it be $\frac{1}{8}$, the whole continent consumes 19,200 chests, which at £4 per chest the 3d. duty only amounts to £76,800, but my computation is short in every part.

In New York they import scarce any other than Dutch teas. In Rhode Island and Pennsylvania it is little better. In this province the Dutch traders are increasing and I have frequent informations of large quantities after it is too late to take any measures to discover and seize them, and sometimes such persons are concerned as I thought could not have been capable of countenancing perjury or fraud.

I cannot help repeating to your lordship my opinion that unless the East India Company bring the price of their teas so near to the price in Holland as to make the profit of importing teas from thence not equal to the risk, in a short time there will be scarce any teas imported from England.

Upon intimating to the acting Collector at Falmouth in Casco Bay that I was informed the Acts of Trade were broke every day in his district, he acknowledged it to be true but added that the officers on shore had it not in their power to prevent it and he suggested that the only way was to increase the number of small schooners and to keep one or more constantly cruizing in that bay, rigged and fitted to appearance like fishing-schooners. This he said would be no additional expense to the Crown except the first cost of the schooners which need not exceed £300 sterling each as they might have men and stores from the ships.

We have not virtue enough to become obnoxious to the people merely from a sense of duty. It seems therefore that it would be best to have one officer only in each vessel with a commission from the Customs, and he to have the command and be entitled to all but the King's half of the forfeiture which would give him a good chance of making a small fortune and stimulate him to his duty. There does not seem to be the same reason for sharing any part among the crew or other officers as in case of prizes taken in war where all their lives are exposed, for in the present case there is no danger of resistance to an armed vessel, seeing all our smugglers are themselves unarmed and depend entirely upon concealment.

There may be inconveniences from this proposed measure which I do not foresee, but as I have no interest in the seizures made by the sea-officers I hope your lordship will pardon the suggestion and attribute it to my sincere desire to promote His Majesty's service whenever there is the least room to hope for success. *Entry.* [C.O.5/246, p. 34]

XCIX

Report of Committee of Council of Massachusetts to Governor Thomas Hutchinson[1]

12 September, Boston
Pursuant to your Excellency's instructions you will permit us to make the following remarks.

1st. The quality of the land at Machias is very good, capable of making extraordinary farms, from the produce whereof the grantees may live very comfortably and have a surplusage for market, and considering the great improvements in so short a time which they have made we believe that will soon be the case, provided they meet with no obstructions.

1 Enclosed in Governor Hutchinson's letter of 9 September to Hillsborough, Vol. I, No. 1508.

2dly. We cannot by our view which was very considerable or by the best information we could get find that the pine trees growing there are capable of making masts for His Majesty's Royal Navy, they being what is called saplings. There is an extraordinary harbour with several ways of entrance into it and a number of navigable rivers within the bounds of Machias. About four miles up the river called Castern River on one branch of it, there is a very large pond which they call a lake about twelve miles in length and three or four miles in width, with a variety of fish in it as well as in the river aforesaid: the rivers abounding with salmon and salmon-trouts etc. of large dimensions. The rivers there all communicate with the main river which empties itself into the ocean. There are a considerable number of mills in said place, the people very notable, sober, peaceable and industrious, a few excepted who though not so peaceable are very industrious.

3dly. That there might be as much peace and good order at Machias as in the other twelve granted towns, we would humbly offer it as our opinion that the authority which is now there should be strengthened. This we believe would be greatly for His Majesty's service and the honour of government. It was with great pleasure that we had an opportunity of swearing Mr Sinkler, an inhabitant there, into the office of a deputy sheriff. That there should be such an officer there was absolutely necessary, especially as there neither was nor could be a constable in that place, it not being incorporated; but there being but one gaol in the country wherein it lies, and that gaol near 70 leagues distant by water and for several months in the year inaccessible, involves in it a thousand legal difficulties which might be removed if there was a gaol at and in Fort Pownall where there is a convenient room which would extremely well answer that purpose and in no wise hurt the garrison. But this cannot be done with[out] your Excellency's permission, which we doubt not will be granted as it will be so much for His Majesty's real service. And if we should be so happy as to have your Excellency view it in the same point of light, we persuade ourselves for the reason aforesaid that you will be pleased to express your sentiments with your permission to the Court of General Sessions of the Peace at Pownalborough, that the same by them may be made a gaol during the governor's pleasure. Machias is about 36 leagues from Fort Pownall and about 90 from Boston.

4thly. It was with pleasure and at the same time with grief we heard the good people at Machias express their ardent desires that they might be in a legal capacity to maintain the preaching of the Gospel among them and that they and their children might be taught to fear God and honour the King. That they are sincere in it we have abundant reason to believe when we consider that whilst we were there the reverend gentleman that went down with us preached twice a day the two Sabbaths we were at Machias and one lecture to an audience consisting of about 150 or rather two hundred persons, and baptized 13 children. We are sure your Excellency feels for these people and for those in the towns abovementioned and will do everything for them touching the premises that possibly can be done consistent with your duty to His Majesty.

5thly. The number of males at Machias from sixteen and upwards are about 150, and of families upwards of sixty.

6thly. As to the quality of the land at Gouldsboro, what bounds upon the harbour we thought not very extraordinary, but we were informed that that was the worst of the land. At Frenchman's Bay, part of Gouldsboro where Mr Justice Nathan Jones lives, the land is very good, but no pines fit for masts grow there, being chiefly saplings. Whilst we were at Gouldsboro Capt. Smith in a ship from and belonging to Bristol in England and bound there was in the harbour, which is a mighty good one (though dangerous to enter without a good pilot, having some ledges of rocks near the entrance), informed us that he had either lost a mast or wanted a spare one and that he could not get one in the whole township. The people in general we are informed are honest, sober, and peaceable. The lands in the other granted townships by what we saw of them and by what we heard are good, very much improved for the time, and very much in the same situation with respect to pine trees fit for His Majesty's Royal Navy as at Machias and Gouldsboro. The people in general are sober, industrious, peaceable and wellaffected to government and make great improvements of the lands granted them. This we had ocular demonstration of when we came between the islands and the main from Mount Desart to Fort Pownall, which is about 20 leagues. We anchored on a Saturday (24 August) near Naskeeg Point within the reach called Egamogging Reach 18 miles in length, very straight and about a mile wide, extremely pleasant, good improvements in many places on each side thereof, one inhabitant having about 100 cocks of fine English hay upon about five acres of land as we judged. This is in the township No. Four. We were detained here by reason of a calm and the tide against us till Lord's Day noon; the people ashore, upon their knowing there was an ordained minister on board, entreated that we would go ashore and that the minister would perform divine service amongst them and baptize their children, there not having been a sermon ever preached there. It gave us great satisfaction to see such a disposition in them and that providence had given us such an opportunity to oblige them. We went ashore, divine service was carried on, and nine children baptized and one adult though these people had only one hour's notice. We apprehend there are 500 families at least in the thirteen granted townships. Notwithstanding the pine trees aforesaid are generally of the sapling kind, yet as we are informed in the rear of said townships there are some very fine trees fit to mast the Royal Navy, the land there being stronger and better; but without the clearing of the land in said granted townships, they cannot be transported to the waterside without very great expense. We were at Mount Desart, the land there is extremely good saving the mountains, which are a desert from whence Monsieur Champlain gave it that name. We suppose there was or might have been mowed there a thousand tuns of fine salt hay this year and a vast quantity of fresh and English grass. There are on it many stately trees fit for royal masts.

7thly. It is most certain that the people who have settled and are settling in the 13 townships have this intention to make further improvements and to spend their days there; but that they went there only for the sake of the timber and when they have cut that off intend to quit the lands is without the least colour of truth, for can it be conceived that persons who have laid out their money and strength upon these lands by clearing and making such profitable improvements thereon, so that in fact they now support themselves and families, should ever voluntarily quit the same especially when a great number, perhaps far the greatest, never was concerned in logging, masting or a saw-mill? This your Excellency may depend upon as a fact; and it is the opinion of the most thinking amongst them, and their practice is accordingly, that upon the whole and in the conclusion those who are least concerned in logging will be the richest. They gave us numbers of instances to support their sentiments by way of comparison and we must confess that we were entirely of their mind.

8thly. We do not find that there hath been much if any spoil or waste made on the lands aforesaid by cutting trees fit for masts for the Royal Navy, and we are so far from apprehending that the settling these townships with inhabitants can, supposing there was a number of trees fit for the Royal Navy therein, have any tendency to destroy said trees, that we believe quite the contrary; and for this plain reason that there is less hazard of detection in committing trespasses where there are no settled fixed inhabitants than in a place where there are numbers of such inhabitants, many of whom from a sense of duty or for a reward would turn informers; and we are from our own observation certain that there is no trading maritime town destitute of informers, and the reason of the thing holds equally good with respect to informers in the above case.

Lastly, when we consider the description given by Monsieur Champlain who we apprehend was the first European that reconnoitred the eastern shore and gave the River St Croix its name, we are convinced that the River St Croix mentioned in the royal charter can by no means be the River Passamaquoda, but that the River Passamaquoda being an Indian name was then known thereby; when we consider also that there is a living witness (whose deposition we wish might be taken *in perpetuam rei memoriam*) who will swear that about sixty years ago he used to trade at St Croix, that by the Indians he traded with (who were born there and always lived there and by the oldest of them who had it from their fathers) the River St Croix aforesaid was known by that name and that St Croix River was east of Passamaquoda; when we consider these things and many more we could mention, it is plain to us that the River St Croix which we call by that name and which is east of Passamaquoda is the true River St Croix and the eastern boundary of this province as mentioned in the charter. Notwithstanding which we are well informed that there are grants made by the governor or government of Nova Scotia of Grand Nanan, some of the islands of Passamaquoda Bay, and of land upon the main and settlements thereon, all west of St Croix, and we are also informed that the same lands are very good.

The above remarks are humbly submitted to your Excellency by William Brattle, James Bowdoin, Thomas Hubbard. *Copy*, attested by Thomas Flucker, Secretary. [C.O.5/760, fo. 279]

C

Samuel Wells to John Tabor Kemp[1]

18 September, Brattleborough

Sir, as I presume information of every movement of the government of New Hampshire to obtain the lands on the west bank of Connecticut River to be annexed to that government will be agreeable to you and the better enable this government to disconcert their plans of encroachment, I give this information vizt.

The governor some time the forepart of last winter requested the General Assembly to make a grant to defray the charge of exploring Connecticut River to its source and making a plan of it to send to England (as I am informed) to show that the river comes more from the east than has hitherto been imagined, and so much from the east as not to joint the 45th degree of northern latitude; that the Assembly declining to make the grant, the governor at his own and the charge of some others who subscribed sent Mr Benjamin Whiting and Mr Grant on the business with a letter from his Excellency recommending it to all persons on Connecticut River (friends to the government of New Hampshire) to contribute towards enabling the party to proceed and effect the business, representing that it was likely the effect of the survey would be the extension of the jurisdiction of New Hampshire to those lands etc.; that in consequence of this letter considerable contributions from divers persons near the river bank was obtained by Whiting, and he proceeded on the business.

The manner of his proceeding and the probability of a fraud in Whiting's chart of the river is in few words expressed in the enclosed deposition [Vol. I, No. 1549v]. The deposition perhaps might have been more particular had there been time, but the secrets of this supposed fraudulent survey was unknown to me until this morning when Mr John Grout came here with Mr How the deponent and gave me the information, and as I was obliged to beg the favour of a gentleman on a journey through Springfield to tarry until the deposition was made and these lines wrote, will account for the reason why neither the one or the other is more particular, as I am unwilling to omit this opportunity of leaving this information in the post-office there (vizt. at Springfield). I have nothing further to add only that the plan of the survey is gone to England and Governor Wentworth informs the friends of that government that there is not the least doubt of the lands on the west bank being annexed to New Hampshire, that if you apprehend anything can be done by me in favour of this government shall be glad of the information. PS. Grant who assisted Whiting is a person within age and a servant of Captain Holland. Copy, certified by G. Banyar, deputy Secretary. [C.O.5/1102, fo. 303]

---

1 Enclosed in Governor Tryon's letter of 2 October to Hillsborough, Vol. III, No. CVI.

CI

Governor John Wentworth to Earl of Hillsborough (No. 38, Duplicate)

23 September, New Hampshire

May it please your Lordship, the provincial Acts, Journals and other public transactions being perfected and transcribed to the terminations of the last Assembly, I beg leave to have the honour to transmit them to your lordship [Vol. I, No. 1523 ii-iv], also very respectfully to submit such explanations as appertain to them, together with those other observations respecting the state of this province that have arisen since the last general report which I had the honour to lay before your lordship.

No. 1, an Act for the more speedy recovery of small debts and to save the cost usually attending the recovery thereof etc. The preamble of this Act having been long very severely felt by the greater part of the people and the evil increasing with still more grievous circumstances, particularly among the infant settlements, extremely to the unnecessary distress of all except lawyers, therefore every care has been used in constructing this remedial law which hath hitherto proved highly beneficial and unattended with any public or private inconvenience. The long and advantageous practice upon a similar law in the other New England colonies gives me reason to hope this will be equally useful here if upon examination it should happily be favoured by His Majesty's most gracious approbation.

No. 2, an Act in addition to an Act made in the 5th year of the reign of King George the 1st entitled an Act for regulating townships, choice of town-officers etc. Many difficulties and expensive lawsuits daily arising from contested settlement of paupers, wherein towns were exposed to frequent impositions from the too contracted limitation of time in the former Act, this is intended solely to relieve that general inconvenience, and I apprehend will prove very useful in the regulation of those matters.

No. 3, an Act for granting to His most excellent Majesty fifteen hundred pounds lawful money in the manner and for the purposes therein directed etc. Notwithstanding the former grants for redeeming paper bills of this province, it appearing there was still outstanding an uncertain quantity, the Assembly have generously passed this Act which finally closes the paper currency of New Hampshire upon the most equitable terms.

No. 4, an Act to authorize and enable the Treasurer to borrow the sum of fifteen hundred pounds for the payment of the like sum borrowed this year etc. This Act being grounded on local necessity specified in the preamble and proceeding upon the consent of the creditors of government, it is of essential convenience to the province at this period when the circulation of specie is so reduced as to be an evident detriment and distress both upon its commerce and cultivation.

No. 5, an Act to enable three Justices of the Peace *(unus quorum)* to determine all disputes concerning the maintenance of the poor. The reasons for and general use of this Act being described in the preamble I have only to observe further thereon that it cannot fail of being particularly beneficial as it safely contracts the time and expense of such processes, which in a new and thinly inhabited country is in all cases peculiarly requisite as the settlers for many years very hardly struggled to establish themselves in comfort. Hitherto these suits have generally engaged whole parishes merely for want of an early and local determination, which by this Act is provided and so carefully ascertained that it promises a general good to the province, in which view I beg leave to present it to your lordship.

No. 6, an Act for establishing a light to be kept at Fort William and Mary for the benefit of vessels arriving or being upon the coast in the night-time. This harbour being greatly frequented by all the coasting trade quite from Nova Scotia to New England, for whom and all other navigation bound into the bay it is a commodious and safe retreat in storms, the necessity of a lighthouse has been long felt. This Act having incompetently provided, and experience proving the impossibility of sustaining a useful light on the Flagstaff, I erected a proper and cheap building for the purpose which has already preserved three vessels and their crews who made this harbour in safety by means of the light in a violent storm wherein the whole must otherwise have perished. It will be of eminent use to His Majesty's ships cruizing on the coast of New England and render their navigation much more secure as well as all other His Majesty's subjects trading to New England. The benefit is now so plain and universally seen that I doubt not the General Assembly at their next meeting will provide for the sum expended over and above the grant in this Act.

No. 7, an Act for granting unto His most excellent Majesty the sum of two thousand five hundred pounds for the uses and purposes therein declared. This Supply Bill being expressed as usual and the sum thought to be adequate to the support of government, I have not further to observe thereon than that it was cheerfully granted.

No. 8, an Act for settling the charges of building the lower bridge in Dover etc. The reasons for this Act are so fully expressed in the preamble that I may not intrude longer on your lordship's time thereon only to observe that the bridge established is manifestly more convenient for that town and all the country adjacent, and that upon a full hearing it appeared requisite for the public and of immediate importance to the well-being of the town that this Act should be formed, which is consistent with former practice in this province, peculiarly equitable in this case, and has been productive of peace and harmony among the people.

No. 9, an Act to dissolve the marriage of Greenwood Carpenter of Swanzey in this province with Sarah Leathers formerly of Charlestown in the County of Middlesex in the province of Massachusetts Bay. It appears in this Act that the cause of separation is fully sufficient and that the parties were regularly notified, but the crimes charged were so incontestably proved that the offending party would not appear nor make any defence, it being also proved that by her residence in another province the man was daily in danger of eminent ruin, and this being the only method of divorce known in this province: these with every other circumstance renders this an Act of specific undeniable justice to the man, and therefore I thought it my indispensable duty that it should pass to be enacted.

No. 10, an Act in addition to the law already in force for the regulation of swine. The raising of swine being very general in practice, though small in quantity and number, through the province, the regulation thereof especially in large and more populous towns has hitherto been attended with much uncertainty and trouble, notwithstanding the very trifling value. For remedy hereof the present additional law is passed and being wholly directed to and embracing this purpose without any other possible operation, it is my duty to represent it to your lordship as safely beneficial for this branch of regulation of property belonging to His Majesty's subjects of New Hampshire.

No. 11, an Act to enable the inhabitants of such towns and parishes in this province as have not had a regular method to call town or parish-meetings or at present have no such method to direct and establish a rule and method for that purpose. The people of new townships from their dispersed situations and want of information being exposed to frequent error and lapse of their parish-meetings, which throws them into great confusion and in such cases ever delays and renders more difficult and expensive the collection of taxes, to rectify which disorder there are constantly many petitions to the General Assembly which tend only to augment the public expense, therefore this Act has been formed which clearly and with the greatest safety provides a general remedy for this deficiency.

Nos. 12–16. These Acts are only declaratory of the present value of the fines and penalties imposed in the respective laws to which they apply and in no matter or manner altering any law but only usefully explanatory thereof.

Nos. 17–18. These Acts being solely to revive sundry laws therein mentioned which have hitherto been transmitted and the practice thereon found advantageous to the province and to His Majesty's service, I have therefore only to observe thereon that their revival and continuance cannot fail of being equally necessary as were the original Acts.

No. 19, an Act to enable John McDuffee and Richard Jennys Esqs. to recover certain sums of money from the towns of Barrington, Barnstead and Gilmantown, for making the province road through said towns. The former or original Act to which this is an amendment being deficient in directing the individual mode of collecting the cost of making the roads therein ordered to be made though the said expense was therein generally laid on the respective towns, therefore this Act was necessary to explain, liquidate and specifically to enforce the former in the manner consistent therewith and according to the usual custom and law of this province in like cases. Through the whole Act it will appear that the utmost care has been taken both for the public and the respective towns, on the one part that the duty is well and reasonably done, and on the other that the commissioners should not be delayed or defrauded under any defective pretence of the original Act whereby they were employed.

No. 20, an Act for establishing and making passable a road from the Governor's house in Wolfborough to Dartmouth College in Hanover. The road established by this Act is almost central through the province and must ever be of the great importance, more particularly as by means of Lake Winnipisioket the general commercial intercourse with the sea will naturally be facilitated besides the distance diminished, and the road passing through an excellent tract of country now rapidly populating will be immediately of the most essential use, more especially as it is certain troops from the seacoast may hereby march into Canada at least five days earlier than any other passable route.

No. 21, an Act for the ease and relief of prisoners for debt. This temporary law having been passed in this province and transmitted in the year 1767, since which it has expired, and the reasons at that time assigned in its behalf not only subsisting but being much augmented in degree, I have thought it proportionately expedient for the public good and His Majesty's service to assent to the temporary re-enacting the same, more especially as the oath of liberation is herein still more clearly expressed.

Nos. 22–23 are the Journals of the General Assembly, which being the reciprocations on forming the Acts above recited and on many others that were not perfected, also the usual votes of allowance for the civil and incidental expenses of government, therefore do not require further explanation.

The salary to the Chief Justice, £48 15s. sterling per annum, to the assistant Justices £45 sterling, and to the Clerk £7 10s. sterling, are undoubtedly too low and inadequate to the trust and dignity of the office, especially as the fees do not exceed twenty guineas per annum. Nevertheless my utmost endeavours were insufficient to obtain a more competent grant. Indeed the Assembly say that the salaries may be increased as the province shall be more able and populous; it is true that at present the province is exceedingly distressed for currency, but I also fear that a further view is by annual augmentations to keep all officers so far dependant, an effect which every day convinces me must more and more injure, retard and embarrass the administration of government in America.

In this province I believe much less detriment has been thus sustained than in any other, yet the strong influence it has is but too evident, as also the unremitting attention to extend it as the fortress, the very essence and life of those who vainly imagine popular subserviency to be the fountain of rectitude. These principles speciously promising the reduction of taxes and divided power, although in fact pregnant with the cruellest reverse, so naturally coincide with popular ideas that they readily obtain, nor can even experience of their futility, much less reason, eradicate or suppress them. I have hitherto happily prevailed in counteracting their violent operation to the overt disorder or contempt of the government in any instance. The great evil is in the rooting such principles in the minds of a growing country, which so surely though slowly tends to the subversion of government. Hence it is my duty to present to your lordship this suggestion thereof.

The grant of £150 sterling for repair of His Majesty's Castle William and Mary has been faithfully applied to the most necessary repairs, and I am in hopes by this means to obtain another allowance for that purpose, as also an augmentation of the garrison now consisting of an officer and eight men. The castle is extremely well-situated and may be capable of great defence. It has 120 excellent good cannon from 4 lbs. to 40 lbs. shot, well-stored with shot and powder about two hundred barrels, but are as much deficient in muskets, having only seventy complete and about thirty more without bayonets and of an inferior sort not to be depended on. This great defect must be of the most fatal consequences and render the castle with all the ordnance an easy conquest. I am utterly at a loss to obtain a sufficient supply for this purpose. It is impossible to prevail upon the Assembly until an enemy appears, and then it's too late. I can at any time within six hours muster above two thousand able volunteers, exclusive of a volunteer battalion of 600 sailors to fight the cannon in the castle. I cannot therefore but regret the want of arms to put into the hands of such a body of good men for the safety and defence of His Majesty's castle and province when necessity may require.

Upon this occasion I most humbly beg leave to entreat your lordship's favour towards this province. In the fort at Crown Point it is said are many thousand stand of arms, unused and perhaps daily growing worse. If your lordship would be pleased favourably to represent the benefit that would result to His Majesty's service from an application of three thousand of those arms for the use of His Majesty's castle, it would surely confer the greatest and most permanent cause of gratitude upon this province to your lordship in an instance of the highest importance to their safety and His Majesty's service.

No. 24 are the Naval Office transcripts to the last quarter [Vol. I, No. 1523v-x]. The use of this important office towards the regulation of trade or the collection of His Majesty's revenue is so extremely inadequate to its original intent that I am bound in faithfulness to lay before your lordship the causes that produce this effect.

The Naval Office, originally the only preventive and inspecting one over the trade of the colonies, seems to have been considered, since the establishment of a revenue and officers of the Customs, by many to have become obsolete as to its general powers of control and to be at present confined to the particular objects pointed out by several statutes; these are registers of vessels, bonds for enumerated goods, bonds for rum, reports of masters inwards and outwards. The Act of the 4th of His present Majesty, which gave an entire new face to the Custom-house business of the colonies and established a variety of new forms and documents to be observed in discharging vessels inwards and dispatching them outwards, in no part expressed any alteration or newness of duty in the Naval Officer; but on the contrary seemed to express that the validity of permits, sufferances, certificates, cocketts and other dispatches consisted in the proper seals and signatures of the Collector and Comptroller or other principal officers of the Customs solely; and the same may be observed of all subsequent Acts which have further regulated the Customs in America. It is true that the governors are required to make oath that they will do their utmost to see that this as well as other regulating Acts of Trade be strictly observed within their respective provinces, and in neglect of it incur heavy penalties. But if neither Governors nor their Naval Officers have any legal power to examine, control and pass the papers and documents of every sort and kind which are directed to be used by this or other Acts in the entering, discharging and dispatching all vessels and goods without exception, then does the law deny governors the power of performing according to the oath it enjoins.

The want of express directions for the Naval Office in the late regulating Acts has been the real occasion of the complaints and clamour raised against it. For the merchant finding the dispatches for his vessel and merchandise valid without the seal or signature of the Naval Officer was led to treat it with contempt and neglect, concluding it, except in particular cases as abovementioned, to be without use or authority. The fees therefore of that office, whenever they could not be evaded, were deemed oppressive, made the subject of complaint and often refused. But the most fatal stroke to the Naval Office is that the officer as such is not empowered by any statute to make seizures: the Act of 13th and 14th of Charles 2nd confines it to the officers of the Customs or such as have special commission under His Majesty's Great or Privy Seal except in cases of ships that land enumerated goods in foreign countries and hats transported from one colony to another; in these instances any persons may seize and prosecute. Quere, Whether the governor may not seize in all cases by virtue of his commission under the Great Seal and whether that power is not legally and officially delegated to his Naval Officer? The contrary is however universally taken for granted and the office suffers the greatest disadvantages from it. It is the Naval Officer's duty to transmit accompts quarterly of ships' tonnage etc. together with the particulars of all goods imported and exported within his province to the Lords of Trade and Plantations, and another to the Commissioners of His Majesty's Customs, and whenever there has been wanted by government an aggregate state of the trade of the colonies it has been required of the Naval Officers, from whence it is obvious that it was expected that the Naval Officers should be privy to every transaction of commerce and that their accounts should be a complete check on those of the Custom-house. But the many great disadvantages they now labour under must unavoidably render the most vigilant deficient in both these respects.

This decay of the governors' power in matters of trade and decline of authority in their Naval Officers requires such an effectual support and regulation as to declare expressly by statute that the signature and seal of the Naval Officer should be necessary to the legal validity of every dispatch or document officially issued by the Collector for the entering inwards or clearing outwards any vessels or merchandise. To enable him to seize in all cases, and to establish his just fees, would place his authority on a proper foot, constitute him the most complete because the most independent check on the Custom-house, and put an end to clamour and discontent.

Immediately upon the receipt of your lordship's letter No. 33, I communicated His Majesty's most gracious approbation of the Acts which your lordship was pleased therein to signify to me.

Nothing could have given greater or more universal satisfaction than the confirmation of those Acts, more particularly the County Act for which the province were so eagerly anxious that they seemed to place almost their existence upon it. The operation hitherto has not disappointed their hopes and I am convinced will still further justify my expectations of its eminent utility in establishing and spreading a more perfect subordination to the laws than otherwise could have possibly obtained.

I have also most effectually executed His Majesty's Order in Council in regard to the proclamation for the rates of foreign coin which was directly declared to be void and its operation finally determined. The House of Assembly formed a bill to prevent any detriment that might arise by means of that proclamation, but upon examination the Council thought it too imperfect and thence rejected it. They also judged that at present there did not appear any prospect of uncertainty in what had been transacted, and therefore that it would be most likely to answer His Majesty's gracious intentions for the good of his subjects to form a bill as permitted when any circumstance arose which might lead to its particular application.

A general gratitude and good temper having prevailed through the province upon the confirmation of the Acts abovementioned, the Assembly were prevailed on to grant a Supply Bill referring the currency to the proclamation and the Act of Parliament of Queen Anne. All judgements of court are now made by consent of parties as to the currency; and the great scarcity of money makes creditors glad to recover their debts by any means. However, this cannot last long; the Assembly upon the first disquiet will embarrass the Supply Bill with this difficulty, and I expect every court, when the lawyers will move for and recover costs against the defendant who cannot plead a tender as it is the universal opinion of all the judges and lawyers in the province that there is not any legal tender which can be justified or plead in these courts.

Such a situation I am very apprehensive must be pregnant with endless confusion and disorder, almost to rendering the judicial administration of justice impossible. Every branch of the government, every order and denomination, express their readiness to cooperate herein in any mode agreeable to His Majesty's pleasure, which I most humbly entreat your lordship will be pleased to signify to me for our guide and obedience.

I am under many obligations for the honour of your lordship's letter of 22 January 1771 [Vol. I, No. 935]. This province is extremely interested in the happy continuance of peace both from their unarmed state and the peculiar dispersion of the people in settling and cultivating the wilderness; whence they are doubly benefitted by this fresh instance of His Majesty's paternal care of all his subjects.

The royal instructions requiring an exact map of this province, I embraced the opportunity of Captain Holland (His Majesty's Surveyor-General of the Northern District) his winter residence in New Hampshire through his means to carry that instruction into effect with more accuracy and less expense than could reasonably be expected in any other mode. To this good purpose Capt. Holland exerted himself with the readiest alacrity; but upon recommendation, the Assembly refused any supply for the contingent expense. His Majesty's Council and some few others voluntarily contributed the necessary aid, which enabled Capt. Holland to survey Connecticut River from the Massachusetts Corner to its source, also some part of Merrimac River, Winnepesioket Lake, and one intermediate road from the sea to Merrimac River. In the ensuing winter I am in hopes to procure aid for the survey of the remaining parts and thereby to have the honour to transmit your lordship a perfect plan of the province; although I cannot but assure your lordship that the greatest and most servile difficulties almost ever attend the obtaining any grant of money from the Assembly, for they make all election interests and opposition to rest upon this one principle of withholding or diminishing supplies, which the uninformed husbandmen are apt eno' to think is the perfection of legislators.

There has not been any new manufactures set up in this province in the year past nor are any, before that time begun, increased; but on the contrary every mechanic branch has diminished, some in part and others totally consumed except the linen, also the pot and pearl ash business which daily increases. This last article, linen, has hitherto been chiefly exported from Boston for want of roads to bring it down to Portsmouth from the interior country where it is chiefly made, which difficulty that province were able and ready to remove, being more populous and opulent and furnished with a plentiful currency by means of His Majesty's army and navy; they have thus drawn off the best trade of commodities and provisions to the impoverishment of this province, but I am now in hopes soon to rectify and recover this misfortune by the many roads now made and making through the province, for the encouragement and support of which I have applied the sum of £500 sterling moneys received for arrearages of His Majesty's quitrents in New Hampshire, whereby I have procured more than two hundred miles of road to be opened and made passable from the western limits of the province to the seacoast in parallel directions. The people absolutely unable of themselves to do the whole, and were in much distress for want of communications, but are now relieved in a great degree by thus giving a bounty or aid that would buy provisions for the time which the inhabitants could give in labour for this purpose. By this means also the recovery of this sum of arrearages has been voluntarily complied with and has put the receipt of His Majesty's quitrents into an habitual and easy method which in any other way would have cost the Crown much more money.

Indeed not one-fifth of the sum would have possibly been received, and that through lawsuits which must have opened a door to have consumed in future litigation and evasions a larger sum annually, beside the vexation and disquiet it would have excited in the country; whereas it has now been collected by persuading and informing the proprietors who are thence led to see the unavoidable necessity and honesty of making regular payments and so to establish this custom through the whole, as will demonstratively save a much more considerable sum, besides the great encouragement it has been and will be to settling and populating the interior parts of this province with many families, each of which consume at least six pounds sterling per annum in British manfactures, as the improvement of wild lands for the first twenty years are entirely pursued and maintained with imported materials (provisions excepted) while on the other hand in the populous colonies of Massachusetts Bay, Connecticut and Rhode Island these very families would not consume one guinea per annum but of their own produce. It is positively certain that every family drawn from the old settled parts of New England and employed in cultivating the wilderness of New Hampshire are in the first instance a discouragement to every manufacture from whence they came, by augmenting the price and difficulty of obtaining labour and rendering agriculture more the interest and in the power of those that remain; and in the second instance they are profitably increasing the consumption from Great Britain.

The encouragement to agriculture in this province is the most irresistible impediment to every species of manufacture in this and the other three New England colonies. Daily experience and the resentful complaints of those who there make efforts to establish them prove the advantage of thus leading off their growing numbers to an employ which may be mutually beneficial and yet in the whole amount promotive of British commerce.

From these motives and being perfectly convinced the vast and certain benefit that must result to His Majesty's service therefrom, I have judged it my duty thus far to proceed in this measure, which I had the honour to represent upon in my official letter dated 25th March 1768 to the Right Honourable the Earl of Shelburne etc.

The militia of this province, 12,000 foot in ten regiments, also one regiment of one thousand horse, are now complete with able effective men, exclusive of the alarm-list which upon emergency could turn out about four thousand men. The whole are very insufficiently armed and two-thirds the number totally unarmed, neither is it possible to remedy this evil as there are not three hundred stand of arms to be purchased in the province; and were there eno', yet 1000 of the deficient men cannot be found who can afford to purchase them. Hence I am again induced to solicit your lordship's favour in behalf of this poor but well-disposed province that they may receive such a number of His Majesty's arms as may enable them to be as useful as they are in fact ready and cheerfully disposed to His Majesty's service.

Having in the preceding pages collected the most faithful state of the provincial transactions to this day, and the province being in the perfectest tranquillity and obedience to law, I most humbly beg your lordship's favourable representation thereof with the profoundest deference, hoping for His Majesty's most gracious approbation, every part having been conducted with the most dutiful, zealous and successful views to His Majesty's service to which my heart is devoted with increasing fidelity, entertaining the highest happiness and increased obligation in every opportunity, with the most respectful duty, to have the honour of being in all things, my lord, your lordship's most dutiful,

truly devoted, much obliged and ever faithful, humble servant. *Signed.*
[C.O.5/937, fo. 62]

CII

Governor Peter Chester to Earl of Hillsborough (No. 36)

28 September, Pensacola

My Lord, in my letter No. 24 I transmitted to your lordship the copy of a letter [Vol. III, No. LXIX] that I had received from Lieutenant-Governor Durnford containing observations on the western parts of this province from whence he had then just returned, and I therein promised when furnished by fuller information to give your lordship some farther accounts of that part of the country, together with Mr Durnford's sentiments of the cut that has been proposed between the River Mississippi and the River Ibberville. I now transmit five maps [*Marginal note :* These maps will be found in Collection of Maps] of the lands near Fort Bute, the River Mississippi, Ibberville, Amit and Comit, which have now been more perfectly examined than heretofore. These maps also contain remarks on the rivers, soil and situation of the country, and I believe are done with more accuracy than any others heretofore transmitted from hence. Your lordship will observe in one of these maps the plan of a town laid out on the Mississippi near to the Ibberville which we propose to establish and to call it Harwich. This spot is universally thought to be very proper for the building a town as it will be a magazine (if the Mississippi settles) for supplying the upper country with British manufactures and the Indian traders with goods, many of whom are now supplied from Orleans. The produce of the country will be exported from hence and all the furs and peltry that comes down the Mississippi (great quantities of which now go to Orleans). The communication may be either through the Mississippi or the River Ibberville, which last and so through the Lakes may be made easy at no great expense for small vessels drawing five or six feet water, and for such would be preferable to the communication by the Balize. If the establishing of this town is approved of it will be necessary to give the inhabitants some protection and in the plan four redoubts and brick blockhouses are proposed which should be supported by troops. Mr Durnford's observations on the River Ibberville are that "The logs which were formerly cut have sunk to the bottom some few excepted which appear in the Amit. The sunken logs help to cause obstructions in different parts which require much trouble to remove. When these rafts are loosened they float a small distance and form others until they enter the River Amit which is too wide to be blocked by logs. Some few trees have fallen across the Ibberville since the attempt was made to clear this river. Nothing appears now wanting but to destroy by fire when the River Ibberville is dry the remaining logs which fill up the bed of the river and prevent the purpose first intended in cutting up this wood from being answered, for were these logs removed the body of water issuing into this channel from the Mississippi might annually deepen it, and more especially if the proposed cut should be made, as the Mississippi water would then enter into this river with a far greater violence and more than twice the quantity of water which now doth by the present channel, and is only eddy water, therefore cannot act with great force, being also stopped by very considerable rafts at the entrance of the Ibberville. When the Mississippi is high the current is very strong and will be greater if the channel is made, the Ibberville will probably deepen and widen or both, otherwise the current will be too strong to row against it. The River Ibberville near Fort Bute was within two or three inches of the bank, but lower down the bank increased and near the forks was above six feet high". Your lordship will observe that the ground is marked out between the River Mississippi and Ibberville in one of the maps through which the proposed cut would pass. Mr Durnford's sentiments on this cut are that it is practicable, but his estimate of the expense which will attend it is much greater than the immediate advantages that can arise to the province from the carrying it into execution. The remarks which he makes on the River Amit are as follows: "This river as far as the Comit is navigable for vessels drawing five feet water but for some distance upwards it is extremely shallow, in many parts there is not more than two feet and a half water. The river was low at the time that I visited it but it raises five, six or seven feet after rains. The Comit lately raised twelve feet in twenty-four hours and fell as soon. The face of the country as far as came under my notice is small hills intersected with little gullies which immediately receive the water and pour it into the large streams which cause their sudden rise after rains. The lands are everywhere rich and fertile north of the junction of the Ibberville. Southward towards Lake Maurepas the land seems gradually to descend and also appears less rich, the canes diminish in their size, the hard wood is inferior in quality and height to that up the river. Near the lake the lands are more adapted for rice than any other produce. Bear, deer, and wild fowl are plenty on the banks of this river which abounds also with plenty of fine fish of various kinds. In general these lands are valuable, being easily cleared as great part is cane-land. This river and its branches if well settled would produce many valuable commodities, in particular indigo, rice, hemp and cotton. The soil in some parts is a brown fat earth and high up a whiteish earth mixed with marl and a clay bottom. The branch of the Ibberville as far up as the forks is supplied with its water from this when that river is dry: about the end of September this river is low but rises again with every rain".

Mr Durnford acquaints me that he has received information from Indians that there is a communication from the Amit a small distance above the junction of the Comit, which runs in an east course near the north-west branch of a large river called Niatabinie, and which empties itself into the north side of Lake Maurepas and runs into some of the Choctaw towns, and that there is reason to believe with very little land-carriage a communication may be found to the Bay of St Louis, as from the interior part of that bay the Indians pass to the River Perle from which a branch communicates with a river which empties itself into the Lake Pontchartrain; and as many rivers empty themselves into this lake which run from the north some of their interior branches very probably draw near each other, and the distance from the River

Tanchipahoe to Lake Maurepas is very trifling. By the assistance of some of the Choctaw Indians who usually hunt on these rivers it may be easily known if such a communication can be had, and in case of a rupture with Spain we might with more safety communicate with the River Mississippi by such an interior passage than any other way, and by being in strict friendship with the Choctaws this passage would be very secure as the Spaniards would scarcely venture to interrupt us from Orleans and they might be greatly annoyed by the Choctaw Indians who are not far from the Lakes and whose friendship we must be careful to obtain. If this inland navigation is found practicable it will be of great utility to a township which is recommended to be laid out near to the junction of the Comit and Amit. The distance is only about 15 miles to the Batton Rouge, and the lands between the Rivers Mississippi and Amit superior in goodness to those on the banks of the Mississippi contiguous to this part. If the township of the Amit is approved of, it is thought a post should be also established there to contain a church, to be defended by forty men or occasionally a greater number, as they would be able to give assistance to the Mississippi and keep the Choctaw and Mississippi Indians in order who hunt near these lands. The expense of this establishment in putting up a redoubt is estimated at £400, and two batteaus have been recommended to be kept here capable of rowing ten oars and to carry 30 men, the one to maintain the communication with Lake Maurepas and the other for the River Amit.

Enclosed I also transmit to your lordship an estimate [Vol. I, No. 1535i] of expenses thought necessary to be incurred in establishing ourselves on the Mississippi, but I cannot agree in opinion that all these expenses are necessary at present. Our first attention should be to draw inhabitants together and form a settlement. Canals and inland navigations may afterwards be effected when they will prove useful to an inhabited country; and I think that instead of incurring the expenses that will attend the cut it would be more advisable for government to grant an annual sum for the use of the province to be expended in transporting gratis such settlers as are desirous of coming from Europe or the Northern Colonies to the Mississippi, who should be settled in townships and protected by troops and in a very few years we should have such formidable settlements in the western parts of this province and such numbers of inhabitants as not to require the farther protection of government. These would also be so great a check on the Indians in those parts that by a little management we should secure the interests of all the savages on the Mississippi.

I am confident that the great objection which has been raised to the settling of the Mississippi is that a communication through the Lakes cannot at all times be kept open between this place and that part of the country, except strong posts are erected upon the Lakes and at other places to keep the communication open or a more secure inland navigation can be discovered, as the inhabitants on that river and their properties would in case of a war with Spain fall as sacrifices to the Spaniards. But should a rupture with Spain ensue it is possible that the navigation and communication with the Mississippi through the Lakes might for a short time be interrupted unless posts were established in proper places to keep the communication open. Yet if the Chickasaw, Choctaw and Mississippi Indians are kept in our interest (an object that will always be attended to) the inhabitants in these parts would still be secure at home both in their persons and properties, for no force that the Spaniards could collect at Orleans, was this country settled, would attempt to proceed up the river or attack the inhabitants. On the contrary all the settlements on the west side of the River Mississippi would be abandoned and every Spanish settler in Louisiana must take refuge in the town of Orleans or suffer their lives and properties to be destroyed by the savages. It is universally allowed that if the Mississippi was settled West Florida from its situation would soon become one of the most flourishing colonies in America and would be of such consequence to Great Britain that it is generally imagined, should a war be commenced against Spain, that an expedition would very soon be undertaken against New Orleans as the acquisition of that place would secure to us the whole of Louisiana together with the immense interior country to the northward, and we should then soon be acquainted with the various inland passages on the west side of the River Mississippi which lead towards Mexico. I am informed that the best method of attacking New Orleans in case of a war would be by an army of the King's troops and irregulars to assemble at Fort Pitt in Pennsylvania, from whence they might proceed unmolested down the River Ohio to our settlements on the Mississippi. The distance is great but they will have a rapid current in their favour, and when they arrive if this country is settled may be supplied with all kinds of provisions and necessaries and then, joined by the savages who previously may be prepared, will with greater ease attack New Orleans than any army coming by sea through the Balize and up the river. But as I am not master of the geography of the country through which such an army would pass I can only give the sentiments of others. The commander-in-chief from his information of the country would be better enabled to judge of such a measure. But at all events great attention should be paid to the Indians on the Mississippi.

The best information that I have of the number of the small tribes of Indians on the Mississippi who were settled there when this province was ceded to His Majesty is as follows: Pascagoulas, 25 warriors; Mobilliens, 4; Chactow, 7; Allabamont, 33; Tensa, 12; Chittamasha, 27; Houmas, 25; Appalusas, 40; Tonicas, 12; Oufoe, 7; Biloxi, 45. Total, 237. Several of these small tribes were settled on the River Amit but since our taking possession of this province have retired to the Spanish side of the Mississippi. The chief of the Allabamonts applied to Lieutenant-Governor Durnford when he was at the Ibberville to come over again to our side, and Mr Stuart has directed Lieutenant Thomas, the Indian commissary on the Mississippi, to acquaint such of the tribes who were under our protection after the peace that if they chose to return they shall be taken care of. This I think a very proper measure for they alone in time of war might annoy us much on the Mississippi if disaffected to us, and on the contrary if attached be of great service in disturbing the Spaniards. Should these tribes be prevailed upon to return and we preserve our friendship with the

Choctaws, their interests may be with very little attention firmly secured to us.

I have also herewith transmitted three maps of the different parts of this province on which the several grants that have passed in this province are marked, and the grantees' names with the quantity of acres in each tract are mentioned by one of these. Your lordship will see that the greatest part of the front on the Mississippi from Manchac to the Natchez has been granted, and that to persons who have never made any improvements whatsoever. Should these tracts continue to lay uncultivated it will prove detrimental to the settlement of this country; and as most of the grantees are incapable of cultivating such large quantities of land as have been granted to them, it would be much more for the interests of the colony that these lands being now forfeited should be regranted in small tracts to such persons as will really make improvements. This I before mentioned to your lordship in my letter No. 24, and if you should agree with me in opinion I will take care to observe such directions and proceedings in vacating these grants and in regranting to others as I shall hereafter receive. *Signed*. [C.O.5/588, p. 499]

CIII

Lieut.-General Thomas Gage to Earl of Hillsborough (No. 65)

1 October, New York

My Lord, I understand by letters from West Florida that Lieutenant-Governor Durnford has finished the plans of the Ibberville and part of the Amite, and hope they have been transmitted to your lordship with every explanation that is necessary to enable the King's ministers to judge of the practicability of a junction of the Mississippi with the Ibberville. Your lordship has appeared anxious to receive Mr Durnford's report which makes me wish it was in my power to send a copy by this opportunity, but Brigadier-General Haldimand waited to get some parts more clearly explained and omitted it in his last dispatches. If I hear of any remarks or observations upon it worthy your lordship's notice, I shall not fail to transmit them as soon as received.

Mr Stuart arrived at Pensacola the end of July, and it was proposed to try to save the expense of a congress, at least to avoid the ceremonies and name of one, that the Indians might lose the idea of a regular congress which they expect every year.

The new batteries in the harbour of Pensacola have suffered so much by storms that it was found necessary to face them immediately with planks and slabs till a more durable work can be undertaken for their preservation. Ensign Hutchins, assistant engineer, is lately arrived from Fort Chartres and embarks for Pensacola in a few days to assist in the works. I had sent him orders to go there by the Mississippi in the hopes of obtaining some useful intelligence but he had left Fort Chartres and taken the way of the Ohio before his orders got there, and he received them some leagues below Fort Pitt.

I find by this officer that it will require a constant expense to secure Fort Chartres. He is certain from its present condition that it will cost

£250 the first year and that £100 annually afterwards will not be more than sufficient to preserve the fort, but that the annual expense would have been reduced to about £60 if the stones had been regularly placed at the proper seasons. Through that neglect and two violent floods in April and May last, he thinks it probable if the flood in July has been very considerable that part of the south-east bastion is washed away. Mr Hutchins has been twice at the Ilinois, the last time two years, and has now given me a paper of his remarks on that country. I transmit your lordship such parts of it [Vol. III, No. CIV] as I judge worthy your notice, omitting descriptions of countries, mineral and vegetable productions etc. He assures me that I may depend upon the enumeration of the inhabitants on the English and Spanish shores and upon the estimation of the exports from both, and though he has taken the description of Cap au Grais and of the Ilinois River from report, having never been at those places, he obtained the account given of them from people well-acquainted with those parts of the country.

Many accounts of the Ilinois country have been transmitted to the King's ministers, but it is not easy to get a true and perfect knowledge of those distant countries. Some are deceived by reports, believe too lightly without examining into things, and write accordingly; others are warped by interest or inclination and magnify or detract as it suits them. Mr Hutchins from his situation should not be biased by either, and his report appears to agree in general with others that I have thought mostly to be depended upon. If the estimation of the exports of peltry is as he asserts very accurate, it is plain that the expense of forming a new settlement at Cap au Grais, erecting a fort upon the Ilinois River, and supporting them afterwards, would exceed the profits of the trade. The commerce of the Missouri would still remain with the Spanish subjects and we must remain in the same uncertainty we do now whether any of the peltry gained in those parts would ever enter a British port. Much has been written concerning the dislike of the French to the Spanish government, but I can't learn that any except deserters from the troops and a few fugitives have come over to us.

In my last, No. 64 [Vol. I, No. 1493], your lordship is informed that a nation called the Kikapous had killed three or four people at the Ilinois, and I find they did more mischief on the 17th of July on a plantation within six miles of Fort Chartres where they murdered a white man and a negro slave and took another white man prisoner. The intelligence comes from the prisoner who since his captivity found means to get a letter conveyed to the officer commanding at the Detroit. He relates that he had been sentenced to be burned but was saved by the intercession of the French, that the Indians there, meaning on the Ouabache, were fully bent for war against the English and that some parties were then out. The latter is confirmed by other accounts, which inform that forty Kikapous went in the design of intercepting the boat that carried Ensign Hutchins and another officer up the Ohio but they had the good fortune to escape them. The Pouteatamies of St Joseph also killed some of our people in the spring above Fort Chartres, and neither they or the tribes upon the Ouabache suffer an English trader amongst them, which gives some reason to suspect that the French traders have instigated those nations against the English. They are thick upon the Ouabache and the settlement formed by the vagabond French upon that river at Post St Vincent appears to increase and to demand their being kept under some government or dislodged. I am informed that all the French soldiers enlisted with the Spaniards, of which the Spanish company at the Ilinois was composed, have deserted and joined the above settlement.

The messenger sent by the Six Nations to speak to the Western Indians is not yet returned but an account of his proceedings is brought to Fort Pitt by one of the interpreters. Sir William Johnson will give your lordship a particular detail of all that passed at the meeting, it is sufficient for me to tell your lordship that the boldness with which the messenger delivered himself and the threats he used threw those Indians into confusion who expected proposals to confederate against us; and they were so much in the opinion that he had exceeded his powers that they have sent to the Six Nations to know the truth. It is now discovered that there was a foundation for the intelligence transmitted to your lordship in my letter No. 58 [Vol. I, No. 1091i-ii] and that the Western nations had been deceived by messages privately sent them in the name of the Six Nations, without the knowledge of that confederacy, by a troublesome tribe of the Senecas, inviting the whole to unite against the English. The Western nations formed schemes accordingly and are now confounded at the message delivered to them.

I fear that we shall find it indispensably necessary to fall upon means to reduce the Pouteatamies and Ouabache Indians to peace by forcible measures. As long as their disposition is hostile the communication with Fort Chartres will be precarious and many of our traders be murdered and pillaged in other parts of the country. They affect to despise the threats of the Six Nations and to set them and the English at defiance, and give out that their friends the French are building forts to protect them should they be drove from their habitations. I have no intelligence that any forts are building, and though it is consistent with the old savage policy of Canada I am to hope the Spanish governor of Louisiana is too well-informed of the bad consequence that must attend a measure of the kind and that instead of giving any encouragement to the Indians to commit hostilities upon each other, he will be sensible that it is our mutual interest to prevent it. A contrary conduct would be productive of frequent murders both on the English and Spanish frontiers without advantage to either, and could only tend to satisfy the avarice of a few traders and the thirst of the savages for blood and plunder at our mutual loss and expense.

Sir William Johnson will as soon as possible let the Six Nations know of the message they are to expect from the westward, and seriously consider of the properest means for chastizing the disturbers of the peace. In the meantime I have given directions for the troops of the Ilinois to be marched and trained for the service of the woods, and the Indians of the country spirited up to join them; and propose also if requisite to concert with Mr Stuart about obtaining aid of the Cherokees and Chikesaws.

The Indians continue to complain of the vast quantities of rum carried amongst them, and that the white hunters interrupt them frequently in the chase, and I am told it is a fact that people have already passed the boundary settled in 1768 and are building in the Indian country over the rivers Susquehanna and Ohio.

Lieutenant-Colonel Wilkins of the Royal Regiment of Ireland and commanding at the Ilinois, having leave to go to England, I am to acquaint your lordship that Major Hamilton of said regiment is appointed to relieve him in the command of His Majesty's forces, forts and settlements in the country of the Ilinois. *Signed.* [C.O.5/89, fo. 170]

CIV

Remarks on the Illinois Country[1]

[1 October]

Extracts from remarks upon the Illinois country made by Ensign Hutchins, 60th Regiment, Assistant Engineer.

Kaskaskias, which as already mentioned is five miles and one-half up a river of that name: that village contains eighty houses, many of them are well built, several of stone with gardens and large lots to each. It consists of five hundred inhabitants who have between four and five hundred negro slaves and large stocks of cattle and hogs.

Three miles further to the northward is a village of Illinois Indians of the Kaskaskias tribe, inhabited by two hundred and ten persons who can raise sixty warriors. They were formerly a brave and warlike people but are now a lazy drunken set. Idleness has so far got the better of them that they scarcely hunt peltries sufficient to purchase clothes for themselves and families.

Nine miles further is a small village called La Prairie du Rocher (the Rock's Meadow) consisting of one hundred inhabitants and eighty negroes.

Three miles north of this place stands Fort Chartres close to the bank of the Mississippi. The village near the fort containing a few houses is scarcely worth mentioning.

One mile up the Mississippi above the fort is a village of Peorias and Metchegamias, two other tribes of the Illinois Indians, who can turn out one hundred and seventy warriors, and in their vicious habits and way of life are similar to those of the Kaskaskias already mentioned.

Four miles further is St Philip's village. It was formerly inhabited by about a dozen families but now only by two or three.

Forty-five miles further northwards, one mile up a small river, on the south side, stands the village of Cahokia containing fifty houses, many of them well built with wood and very commodious. It consists of three hundred inhabitants who have eighty negroes and large stocks of black cattle and swine.

Four miles above Cahokia, on the Spanish side the Mississippi, stands the village of St Louis on an elevated piece of ground, the most

---

1   Enclosed in General Gage's letter of 1 October to Hillsborough, Vol. III, No. CIII.

healthy and pleasant of any known in the country. There the Spanish commandant, as also the principal Indian traders, reside who pursue such measures that the trade of the Missouri, apart of that of the Mississippi northwards and of the nations of and near the Ouisconsing and Illinois Rivers, is in a great measure brought to them. The unparalleled activity and indefatigable perseverance of the French traders, added to the incredible influence they have over the natives, will be the occasion of much trouble, danger and expense before the parts of the trade belonging to the English are wrested out of their hands. In this village are one hundred and twenty houses, the best in the country, mostly of stone, large and commodious. It consists of eight hundred inhabitants, some of them very genteel and well-educated, who have about one hundred and fifty negroes.

Twelve miles below Fort Chartres on the western bank and nearly opposite to Kaskaskias village is situate that of St Genevieve or Misere, containing one hundred and fifty houses, four hundred and sixty inhabitants, besides three hundred and seventy negro slaves. This and St Louis are all the villages in the Illinois country on the western or Spanish side the Mississippi.

Four miles below St Genevieve, near the mouth of a creek formed by two islands in the Mississippi and the mainland, is a hamlet called the Saline, from a salt-spring there, from which all the salt used in the Illinois country is obtained.

A list of gun-men in the aforementioned villages; on the British side, French 300, negroes 230; on the Spanish side, at St Genevieve, French 208, negroes 80, at St Louis, French 415, negroes 40.

Before describing the Illinois River it may not be amiss just to take notice of a spot called Cape aux Gris about eight leagues thence up the Mississippi. It is acknowledged by the French themselves that should a settlement be made at Cape aux Gris those on the French side would be ruined as it would draw and intercept all the trade of the Upper Mississippi.

On the top of the ridge already mentioned, at the mouth of the Illinois River, is *by report* an agreeable, airy and advantageous situation for a fort. If an agreeable healthy air, a pleasant situation, rich luxuriant soil, a variety of timber, and good wholesome water, with the certainty of an extensive valuable trade with the natives, are desirable advantages, they will be experienced by the very first settlers themselves at the mouth of the Illinois River and at Cape aux Gris. A [MS: As] species of marble, earth fit for bricks, lime and freestones are contiguous to these places, and copper, lead and iron ore with pits of coal have been discovered not far off.

An account of the exports from the Illinois from September 1769 to September 1770. From the British territory: flour to New Orleans, 120,000 weight, which may yield 4 dollars per cwt, £1,120 sterling; peltries, 550 packs which on an average, if no damage happen to them, may yield at London ten pounds each pack, £5,500 sterling. Total, £6,620.

From the Spanish territory: flour, 15,000 weight, £150; peltries, 835 packs, £8,350. Total, £8,500.

Total value of the exports in the year 1769, £15,120.

The peltries in general that are sent from the British side are obtained from the French traders on the Spanish shore as no Englishman can with safety venture among the savages. A post up the Mississippi at or near the Illinois River might secure to us the greatest part of the trade that is now carried to the settlements on the other side.

There are from New Orleans to Fort Chartres five hundred computed leagues by water when the river is low, but when it is high the distance is lessened near one-third. The navigation is extremely tedious, difficult and dangerous, not so much owing to the distance, which is very considerable, as the rapidity of the current and the immense number of logs and shoals with which it is interrupted. For though it may be thought next to impossible to navigate against this stream, yet the benefit of the eddies found almost everywhere on either side the channel is such that boats of twenty tons are brought by towing and rowing from New Orleans to the Illinois in sixty days. These boats have commonly a passage of about twelve or fourteen days on their return.

Notwithstanding the difficulties attending the navigation of the Mississippi, it is found from experience that merchandise may be brought cheaper to the Illinois by New Orleans than by the way of Fort Pitt. For instance, Continent rum brought by Orleans costs from eight to nine shillings, Pennsylvania currency, per gallon according to the original price at the place sent from; but it can't be sent for less by the way of Fort Pitt than from 9/6 to 10/6 per gallon. This article is commonly sold for four dollars a gallon. The consumption on the British side for these last three years may amount to 10,000 gallons annually and much more on the western shore. *Copy.* [C.O.5/89, fo. 174]

CV

Governor Thomas Hutchinson to Earl of Hillsborough (No. 12)

1 October, Boston

My Lord, I received from the committee of Council their report of the state of the Eastern Country and covered it [Vol. III, No. XCIX] with my last letter to your lordship but too late to make any remarks. It is evidently calculated to excuse or justify the two Houses in their refusal or neglect to take any measures to remove intruders, and it will tend to encourage further intrusions. Notwithstanding the favourable account of the improvements made by the settlers upon the lands there, I have no doubt that by far the greater part of the inhabitants are employed in felling trees, hewing timber and sawing boards and plank with which I am informed more than 20 sail of ships have been laden every year for several years past. There is in that country great plenty of fine beech trees, many hundred cords whereof are annually brought to Boston and consumed for fuel. The value of it for plank and timber for ships is not known here: I have heard that it has been found as serviceable as the best oak. If the state of this country should come under consideration I think this report may be of some use, and this was my chief motive in obtaining a copy of it to transmit it to your lordship. I expect nothing from the General Court. In private conversation the members excuse themselves by alleging that the settlement of all parts of the province ought to be encouraged, that they are obstructed in the regular way of doing it by the disallowance of the grants which are to originate with them, and that it is better settlements should be made in this irregular way than not made at all. I have done everything in my power by declaring in my public speeches and messages that I considered them as intruders and that Parliament would first or last interpose. I am informed that these settlers were much alarmed with this declaration but have been since encouraged that it will have no consequences. *Signed.* PS. Mr Story who was one of the persons that felt the resentment of the populace in 1765, being a passenger in this vessel, desired to be the bearer of my dispatches to your lordship. [C.O.5/760, fo. 283]

CVI

Governor William Tryon to Earl of Hillsborough (No. 7)

2 October, New York

My Lord, I have the honour to transmit to your lordship the minutes of His Majesty's Council of this province in the State department from my taking upon me the administration of this government to the twenty-third of September, also the minutes of the said Council in the department of Land etc. commencing the 7th of August and ending the 18th of September following [Vol. I, 1549i-ii]. As these minutes so fully set forth in general the several matters that came under the deliberation of the Council and are abstracted in the marginal notes, I have but few observations to make on them.

The proclamations sent to Canada to call in the claimants of land on Lake Champlain under French grants have been received at Quebec, and I expect this month the parties will attend New York agreeable to the intent of the proclamation.

The forcible entry that was made on the lands of Donald McIntire and others was effected by some settlers on the New Hampshire grants on the west side of Connecticut River. The daring insults of these people will in a short time lead to serious consequences if His Majesty does not in his wisdom speedily and finally determine the contests between the two governments, the merits of which on both sides I am informed have been fully transmitted to your lordship. The New Hampshire people of some of the townships have of late opposed all civil process. On Monday last I received a letter and deposition of such a nature that it was thought advisable by the Council that I should communicate the substance of them to the governor of New Hampshire, accompanied with a letter to him, a copy of which I herewith transmit with copies of the abovementioned letter and deposition [Vol. I, No. 1549iv-vi; Vol. III, Nos. C, CVII]. I propose shortly, when I am better informed of facts, to offer your lordship my sentiments of the measure that may appear to me the most probable finally to settle the controversy, so dangerous in its progress. The New Hampshire settlers are masters of that part of the country claimed under New Hampshire grants and are daily strengthening by invitations to the inhabitants of Connecticut and Massachusetts governments so that it is evident the longer the matter remains unsettled the more prejudicial to this government.

A copy of the petition and memorial of Daniel Frisby, mariner, I have transmitted to the governor of St Domingo, requiring satisfaction for the injuries he sustained by reason of the seizure of his vessel by a Spanish *Guada de Costa*. A copy of my letter to the governor I transmit with this dispatch [Vol. I, No. 1549vii].

I have granted His Majesty's letters patent to Frederick Philips, Esquire, for the royal mines of gold and silver in the manor of Philipsburgh agreeable to His Majesty's additional instruction for that purpose, a copy of which will be transmitted to your lordship by the next opportunity. *Signed*. [C.O.5/1102, fo. 258]

CVII

Governor William Tryon to Governor John Wentworth[1]

2 October, New York

Sir, a few days ago I received information [Vol. III, No. C] that during the last winter your Excellency formed the design of exploring Connecticut River to its sources; that the Assembly declining any provision for the expense, Mr Benjamin Whiting and Mr Grant was sent on this service with a letter from your Excellency urging the people near the river, friends to New Hampshire, to contribute to the charge, in which many engaged from a persuasion that the line prescribed by His Majesty's order as the northern limits of New York would in no part intersect Connecticut River and that His Majesty might be induced from this circumstance to alter and extend the jurisdiction of New Hampshire.

With this intelligence I received an affidavit [Vol. I, No. 1549v] declaring that Messrs. Whiting and Grant instead of tracing to its source the northerly branch, which is manifestly the head of the river, pursued an easterly branch above the township of Lancaster that falls into the main river and denominated the farthest extent of this easterly stream as the head of the river.

Had your Excellency thought fit to apprize this government of your design, they would I am assured readily have adopted the measure, defrayed their proportion of the expense and joined in transmitting the map which my intelligence says has actually been sent to His Majesty's ministers and which will now be considered as an ex parte act not deserving that weight it might otherwise have had in the contest.

Though unacquainted as yet with the merits of the dispute I am no stranger to the disturbance it has produced since my arrival in this

---

1 Enclosed in Governor Tryon's letter of 2 October to Hillsborough, Vol. III, No. CVI.

government and see with the uttermost concern the consequences still likely to ensue if the refractory and disorderly behaviour of the grantees under New Hampshire is not speedily checked and punished. Regardless of justice and in open defiance of the laws they have lately by force dispossessed several persons settled under titles derived from this province prior to the commencement of the controversy, and seem to be greatly encouraged by the assurances they ascribe to your Excellency that the jurisdiction will be altered so as to comprise within your government the lands they hold which in some places lie at no greater distance than 16 or 17 miles from Hudson's River. Ill grounded as these reports I am willing to believe must be, yet as they are propagated with a view to exasperate a people already too much bent on mischief, and appear to have had the intended effect, I hope your Excellency will by some public act undeceive these deluded persons, and by so necessary a measure cooperate with me in pursuing the peace and tranquillity of that part of the country until His Majesty's pleasure shall be signified in respect to the New Hampshire grants within this province. *Copy.* [C.O.5/1102, fo. 307]

CVIII

John Thomas to [John Stuart][1]

5 October, New Orleans

Sir, Mr Bryon's sloop arrived here the twenty-sixth day of September after a long and tedious passage occasioned by the heat of the weather, maskettos and other troublesome insects. Your letter was delivered to the Spanish governor without loss of time. In consequence I obtained leave to land the Indian stores and gave orders to get the batteau in readiness which is to proceed for Ibberville tomorrow morning, and when Mr Monsante has fulfilled his agreement with you as may be necessary for the good of His Majesty's service, I shall inform you by the first opportunity. I could perceive a jealousy that prevailed through the town from a report of your being in the river with a very valuable quantity of Indians' presents. The Spanish governor has promised me to do everything in his power with the Indians to support the tranquillity of the provinces of Louisiana and West Florida and he seems well-pleased with my former good conduct among the savages, to the satisfaction of the late French and Spanish governors consisting with the honour of my profession as an English officer and place of employment in the Indian department.

The Arkansa chief has been here and received presents. The Tallapus have likewise been here and some other Indians of small nations. I cannot tell the quantity of presents they have received but I tell you from ocular demonstration that several Indians have passed by my lodgings very well loaded with blue strouds, blankets etc.

Mr Barbar has been here from the Natchez and informed that the great chief of the Grand Jacapas was there with the head warriors of

---

1 Enclosed in John Stuart's letter of 12 June 1772 to Hillsborough, Vol. V, No. XLIX.

seventy towns on the western side of the Mississippi. This nation of Indians have at least twelve thousand gun-men according to the best accounts I can get. It is remarkable that those Indians were clothed with skins only and that they said the Spaniards could make nothing but money, which was useless to them as it would neither fill their bellies nor keep them warm; therefore they would be nearer neighbours to the English in hopes to be furnished with English goods and would not fail to have a friendly talk with me as all the Indians know and expect my arrival among them, and I am happy to tell you that they are well pleased on the occasion. This information is given me by the above gentleman who is much esteemed as a very good man. I put the question to the Spanish governor concerning the English Indians that have gone to settle on the Spanish side of the Mississippi. His Excellency's answer was that it was best for the Indians that traversed the Mississippi to settle on either side as it was a matter of no consequence. Therefore, I should be glad to receive your further orders on the occasion. I cannot discover any foundation for a congress of the Choctaws to be held by the Spanish governor, but I am informed that a congress for the Mississippi Indians was held at Point Coupee on the report of a war. Mr Barbar tells me that several of the Choctaw towns nearest the Natchezs are great enemies to the English, they have burnt down the fort and are very insolent to the English in that country, which are about seventy families, which I hope will be taken notice of at the congress at Mobile. I wish to hear of a peace between the Lake Indians and Talapus's.

Fergy is sick, if he recovers I shall not forget his name as mentioned in Mr Ogilvie's letter. I could wish to answer him by this opportunity but as I am in great pain in writing this letter, having the gout in my hand, I hope it will plead my excuse.

General Haldimand intends to recall me but I hope it will be mutually considered that I have been at great expense in embarking for America, likewise suffered much in the Indian department by mistake and plunder. Therefore, I hope that you will both approve of my appointment, especially in respect to the conclusion of a polite letter from a nobleman so high in office as the Earl of Hillsborough, as it was not the intentions of his lordship (or any other friends) to fix me on the pine-barrens in the circumjacent country of Pensacola.

Mrs Thomas joins me in compliments to yourself, Mr Charles Stuart and Mr Ogilvie. NB. I expect to meet Lafluer or the man he recommends to be my interpreter (as by him recommended) every day, so I do not mean to speak to the savages on matter of consequence till I see one of the above interpreters. *Copy.* [C.O.5/73, fo. 192]

CIX

Clergy of New York and New Jersey to Earl of Hillsborough

12 October, New York

May it please your Lordship, we, His Majesty's dutiful, loyal and affectionate subjects, the Clergy of the Church of England in the colonies of New York and New Jersey, beg leave to address your lordship in behalf of our distressed Church in this part of the world, which through the want of bishops labours under many difficulties and hardships.

The case of our Church in the colonies, may it please your lordship, is peculiarly hard. It exists only in a maimed, imperfect state, being destitute of the highest order of its clergy, whilst all other religious denominations fully enjoy their respective forms of church government. Even the Moravians and Roman Catholics have their bishops; the various sects of Dissenters completely exercise the discipline and possess the privileges of their several systems. The national Church only, which is an essential part of the constitution, is excepted from this general indulgence and is denied the privileges that are granted to others. This mortifying distinction marks them out as the only sufferers in this way.

We can have no ordination but at a heavy expense; and the hazard to candidates for the ministry and the time lost in crossing an ocean 3,000 miles in breadth are very considerable. The expense amounts at a moderate computation to £100 sterling to each candidate: and the risk may be estimated from this circumstance—that according to an exact account taken in 1767, out of fifty-two persons who had gone home for Holy Orders from these Northern Colonies, ten had perished either in the voyage or by sickness which it occasioned. We are deprived of that regular discipline over the clergy which is necessary to the welfare and prosperity of every church, and of the apostolic ordinance of Confirmation which we esteem to be highly beneficial.

These grievances are very great, besides their being peculiar to us and become daily more obvious and more sensibly felt. Under these circumstances, esteeming it to be a duty we owe to God, to His Church, and to the State to use every justifiable method in our power to have them removed, we have by this conveyance humbly supplicated the Throne and laid our case before His Majesty. From his paternal goodness we entertain the most sanguine hopes of redress; and that he will graciously interpose his royal authority and power for the removal of these hardships from near a million of his loyal subjects belonging to the Church of England in these parts by appointing one or more bishops for America. We also most earnestly request your lordship's countenance and assistance in promoting this measure which is dictated by every motive of good policy as well as piety. The relation in which your lordship stands to the colonies points you out as the properest person, next to our gracious Sovereign, to whom we should prefer our complaint and request. And it is a pleasing circumstance that our duty on this occasion should coincide with our inclination to address a nobleman whose many amiable qualities and whose zeal in the service of the best of kings as well as his warm attachment to the constitution we cannot but look upon as very favourable to an application of this nature.

The only plan on which an episcopate is requested, as the public has often been assured, is that bishops may be sent to the colonies with purely ecclesiastical powers, without any temporal authority, and without any jurisdiction over the Dissenters of any denomination. From hence it is evident that we only desire an exemption from the peculiar hardships we have hitherto suffered and to be placed on an equality with other religious denominations. We wish not to interfere with the rights or privileges of others or to abridge that ample toleration they already enjoy. With this disposition we conceive it to be no more than reasonable that we should be indulged with the same religious privileges which are granted to them, especially considering our relation to the national establishment. Yet notwithstanding the equity of our claim, it has met with opposition from a certain quarter. Objections against it have been publicly offered, but these have been minutely discussed and refuted to the entire satisfaction of the impartial. And we submit it to your lordship's wisdom whether even waiving the justice of our cause the Church in America should be sacrificed to the perverseness and unreasonable clamours of its adversaries.

The members of the national Church are from principle and inclination firmly attached to the constitution. From them it must ever derive its surest support. We need not enter into a formal proof of this as the reasons are sufficiently obvious. Omitting all other arguments that might be adduced, let past experience decide. Independency in religion will naturally produce republicans in the state; and from their principles, too prevalent already, the greatest evils may justly be apprehended. The Church must inevitably decrease in the colonies if bishops are not sent to relieve its necessities; and the Dissenters will in time gain an entire ascendancy. How far it may be consistent with good policy and the safety of the state to permit this, we are willing that your lordship should determine.

We would not trespass too far on your lordship's time, and therefore beg leave to refer you for farther intelligence to the bearer, our worthy brother the Reverend Dr Cooper, President of King's College in the City of New York. He has an extensive acquaintance with the affairs of our Church in America, and in him we repose an entire confidence.

We shall only add that were the measure we now earnestly petition for carried into execution through your lordship's interposition, it would reflect peculiar lustre on your administration and ensure the grateful applause of millions to the latest posterity. With sincere prayers for your lordship's long life and happiness, and that all your endeavours to promote the honour of our Sovereign and the prosperity of his subjects may be abundantly rewarded. *Signed*, Samuel Auchmuty, D.D., Thomas B. Chandler, D.D., John Ogilvie, D.D., Charles Inglis, A.M., the committee. [C.O.5/73, fo. 4]

CX

Governor Josiah Martin to Earl of Hillsborough (No. 4, Duplicate)

18 October, Newbern

My Lord, I have the honour herewith to transmit to your lordship for His Majesty's information a list of the names of the six rebels [Vol. I, No. 1570i] who were sentenced to death by the special Court of Oyer and Terminer held at Hillsborough on the seventeenth day of June last and respited by Governor Tryon, that gentleman having just informed me by letter that he had not made report of them. And at the same time, my lord, I humbly beg leave to join in his recommendation of them for His Majesty's most gracious pardon, hoping that the examples already made will be sufficient.

Among the six criminals who were executed pursuant to the sentence of the same court, my lord, was one Robert Matear, an egregious offender but the only child of a very aged father and mother who are good people and whose case much moves my compassion. The poor superannuated man in confidence of his son's dutiful attachment transferred to him his whole property not long before he entered into rebellion, and it is now by his treason become forfeit. Thus, my lord, these most wretched parents must at once lose their all unless His Majesty in his great mercy shall be graciously pleased to grant them possession of the son's lands and goods during their lives. It is therefore a boon, my lord, that common charity engages me most earnestly to implore of His Majesty's goodness.

By a letter I received this morning from the sheriff of Guilford County, many of whose inhabitants took part in the late insurrection, it appears that the spirit which raised that dangerous commotion is not yet totally extinguished there. He says he has met with some resistance in the execution of his office, that magistrates and officers are odious to the people who have so long lived in a lawless state, and that their hearts seem much inclined towards Hunter, one of the outlawed leaders of the insurgents. It is not I think, my lord, to be expected that the systematical opposition which has been so long forming in this province against government should be instantly dissolved in the mind of every individual. Time and a steady and exact execution of the laws, it may be hoped, will effect it; in the meantime some acts of violence may be apprehended. The sheriff I am inclined to think sees things in the worst light, as all other accounts I have received from that country assure me of the people's ready obedience to the laws. Your lordship may assure His Majesty that I will vigilantly attend to the disposition of the lately disaffected parts of this country and take every measure in my power to support the honour of His Majesty's government and to secure the peace of this colony.

I received about a month ago by the wives of Hunter and two other of the outlaws petitions in behalf of their husbands from some of the inhabitants of Orange and Guilford Counties: among the subscribers I understand there are very few people of character and by the number they do not by any means appear to have the general countenance of those counties.

It is said that Husbands, the great promoter of sedition in this country, finds sanctuary in Pennsylvania but I cannot learn certainly where.

I transmit herewith to your lordship copies of six proclamations issued by Governor Tryon after his action with the insurgents that His Majesty may be informed of his exceptions in his overtures of mercy to those deluded people.

I am of opinion, my lord, that an act of grace, as extensive as His

Majesty in his great wisdom and clemency shall see fit to make it, will be attended with good effect and I therefore most humbly submit it to His Majesty's royal consideration. *Signed.* [C.O.5/315, fo. 7]

CXI

Governor Lord Charles Montagu to Earl of Hillsborough (No. 2)

21 October, S. Carolina

My Lord, when I had the honour of writing to you last [Vol. I, No. 1528] I expected by the next opportunity to have been able to have sent you the Tax Bill of this province to receive His Majesty's assent without any of those clauses in it that have so long impeded its passing, but I find that time may still be very distant as the disputes in the House of Assembly in regard to the form of the bill continue very warm. The public credit in the province is at present very low and the King's officers suffer from their salaries here and other expenses for the province remaining so long unpaid.

I am now particularly sensible of the inconvenience arising from the want of a provincial house for the governor to reside in, for I am at present without a house notwithstanding I sent orders some months before I left England to endeavour to procure one. The House of Assembly have indeed appointed a committee to find one for me but as yet their search has been vain. I shall not trouble your lordship any more about this matter as you will readily conceive how improper and how expensive this situation for one of His Majesty's governors and his family to be obliged to reside either in lodgings or at a public tavern. *Signed.* [C.O.5/394, fo. 104]

CXII

Proceedings of Congress with Upper Creeks[1]

29 October–2 November, Pensacola

At a congress of the principal chiefs and warriors of the Upper Creek Nation, held at Pensacola in the province of West Florida, by John Stuart Esq., His Majesty's sole agent for [and] Superintendant of Indian Affairs in the Southern District of North America.

Present, His Excellency Peter Chester Esq., Governor of West Florida; Frederick Haldimand Esq., Brigadier-General commanding His Majesty's forces in the Southern District; the Hon. Elias Durnford Esq., Lieut.-Governor; Charles Stuart Esq., Deputy Superintendent; the members of His Majesty's Honourable Council; Captain Carkett of His Majesty's ship *Lowestoft;* Major Dickson and the officers of the 16th Regiment of Foot.

And the following Indian chiefs: Emistisiguo, Great Medal Chief;

---

1 Enclosed in John Stuart's letter of 29 December to Hillsborough, Vol. I, No. 1700.

Neothlocko or the Second Man, Tipoy or the Fighter, the Beaver Tooth King, Small Medal Chiefs; with the other ruling chiefs and principal warriors of sixteen towns of the Alibamous, Abikas and Tallipousses. Joseph Cornell, John Simpson, interpreters.

After the usual ceremony of smoking the calumet of peace, Neothlocko (or the Second Man) spoke as follows:

This is the day allotted us by the master of breath to meet our father on this land which was originally made for the use of us red men. I am rejoiced to see so many of my white brethren here. Before our white brethren came to this land our situation was much worse than it is at present. We were originally a poor people and should have remained so but for your assistance. We were like one who sees a good thing at a distance but cannot reach it, however it pleased the supreme being at last to send our white brothers to our assistance.

Although we set off from the nation in a hurry and unprovided with the necessaries for paying the usual compliment to you in our way, yet we meet you with hearts white and clean. We intend to pay you and the other two great men here present the greatest compliment we are capable of paying, and I wish it were in our power to do it with more ceremony than circumstances will admit of.

The Appallachicola tribes were the original proprietors of this land. We therefore hope the Governor will accept of the title of Appallachicola Mico as the highest title we can confer.

The Cussitaw tribe were always noted warriors and the Cussitaw Town is the greatest war-town in the nation. We hope the General will accept of the title of Cussitaw Mico.

As the Alibamas are great in war and in peace and solicitous for the good of all the tribes, and as you are the father of all the Southern Indians and constantly employed in taking care of their interests, we call you Alibama Mico.

The place and circumstances of this meeting will not admit of the ceremonies with which we commonly confer such titles, we therefore hope you will excuse the want of them.

He then addressed his people and desired they would bear in remembrance what was said.

The Superintendant approved of the Second Man Neothlocko's sentiments, and thanked him for his title, then proceeded.

Friends, brothers, the great giver of breath has permitted us to meet here this day that we may smoke the calumet of peace and brighten the chain of friendship which has so long and happily united us together. Your white brethren meet you with hearts free from malice and bad design. We do not doubt but you are come in the same good disposition. I gladly embrace the opportunity of introducing you to the Governor of the province and the General of His Majesty's forces, and I desire you will listen to any talk which the Governor or General may have to deliver you. I will afterwards declare to you the business of this meeting.

His Excellency the Governor then addressed the Indians as follows vizt.

I am heartily glad to see my good brothers the Creeks at Pensacola. Before I crossed the Great Water I received orders from the Great Beloved King that whenever I should meet any of his good people, the red men, to assure them of his friendship and protection and that he had given orders to his governors, and other leading men in the several provinces in America to treat them as brothers so long as they should behave peaceably and well-affected to his white people, which I have the strongest reason to hope will be for a long continuance.

I wish I had it in my power to be more liberal to the red men when they come to Pensacola but the land about us is poor, nothing but a barren sand, incapable of producing either corn or other provisions, that it is not in my power to supply them with what I most sincerely wish to accomplish. Therefore, it is with you red men of the Creek nation to grant us lands for the obtaining those necessaries for your support, the limits of which I leave to the management of the Beloved Man now here present to settle with you, and I flatter myself you will readily comply with what he shall ask of you or you must often return without receiving what I should at all times be glad to furnish you with.

As to any encroachment made by the white people on your lands, it was entirely unknown to me. As soon as it came to my knowledge that they had gone beyond the boundary-line, I gave orders to them to withdraw, which they immediately did and they have not returned since, which shows that it was not done with any design of encroaching upon your lands, but it must be attributed to their not knowing where the boundary-line was for the want of its being marked out, but as you are now here I hope that affair will be settled that there may be no room left for any further dispute.

I shall at all times exert myself to see justice done to my good brethren the red men. And if any of the traders in your nation or other white men infringe upon the laws made for their guidance or in any other manner act so as to endanger the breaking of the chain of friendship between us which now subsists, and which I hope is never to be broken, I will order them to be punished with the greatest severity in hopes of deterring others from committing the like offences as well as in justice to yourselves. There is one thing I must beg leave to recommend to you, that if you think yourselves injured by any of the traders or their followers in your nation, which may often be imaginary grievances, that you are not of yourselves to take satisfaction but you must make your complaint to the governor of the province nearest to you or to such other great man in power as the Beloved Man now here present, and you will have justice done you.

You say the path is now straight and white. Your observing this recommendation is the way to keep it so, for it is a liberty the Great and Beloved King does not allow to any of his subjects. We have many salutary laws for the protection of the innocent as well as for the punishment of the guilty, and if any white man injures a red man in his person or property he will be punished in the same manner as if he had committed it against one of his white brethren. The several treaties entered into between the red men and the white people I shall always pay the greatest attention to, and I hope on your part you will continue to do the same, the strict observation of which will always keep us in harmony and friendship. I now take you by the hands and assure you that I am very sincerely your true and faithful friend.

The General then acquainted them that his sentiments exactly coincided with the Governor's, and desired they would be attentive to what he had recommended as the only means of keeping the chain bright, and thanked them for the compliment in conferring a title on him.

The Superintendant then addressed the Indians.

Great chiefs and warriors, friends and brothers, I have often met you upon business of the utmost importance to your nation as well as to your white brethren who are settled near you. Our talks have always been good and calculated to maintain peace, to prevent violence, and to obtain mutual justice. It was for such great purposes that by the King's order, you with the chiefs of the other nations were met by the governors of four provinces and me at Augusta in Georgia in 1763. With a view to the same desirable objects I met you here in 1765, the chiefs of the Lower Creeks at Picolata in East Florida in 1765, the chiefs of the whole nation at Augusta in 1767, 1768 and 1769, where we renewed the agreements which had been entered into at the general congress; and in order to remove every stumbling block from the way, boundary-lines have been agreed upon, dividing the lands which your nation has reserved as your own property from what you have thought proper to cede to your white brethren. The boundary-line between you and Georgia has been actually marked some years ago through a long extent of country across rivers and morasses. It was a very laborious but a very necessary work, and although many difficulties arose yet by perseverance we conquered them and effected it. The line between you and this province, although a cession was made by treaty in 1765 and the limits specified, is still unmarked. It is now our as well as your desire and wish that it may be accomplished. With this view I am come hither from Charleston and you have travelled from your nation. I trust it will be accomplished to our mutual satisfaction. You are the chiefs and rulers of a brave nation, you are qualified to govern in peace as well as in war, you must be sensible of the advantages which you derive from the neighbourhood of your white brethren, you have incontestable proofs of their friendship for you and your people. You will therefore consider the bad policy as well as the ingratitude of confining them to a piece of barren sand, incapable of producing any of the necessaries of life. Without you give them land that will produce corn and maintain their creatures, you cannot expect to be entertained here when you come to see them. We do not want to get your hunting grounds, we are not hunters, we are planters, an hundred miles of pine land would be of no value to us, what we ask you can easily spare. It is the lands on both sides the Scambia as far up as a boat can go, and we want no more than five miles back from the river and as far up as the river is navigable. This I hope out of friendship and gratitude you will grant us and that you will appoint persons to see it marked in company with a surveyor from this province before you return to your nation.

A string of white beads.

At the congress in this place with Governor Johnstone and me you said that friendship between us was new. It was like new fallen snow which hardly whitened the ground, that we were united like two new-planted vines whose tendrils had just interwoven but were not firm, that in the space of four years if no accident happened the snow of friendship would be deep and cover all black spots and the interwoven tendrils would grow strong like iron, that at the end of said period you would have something to tell me. Seven years have elapsed during which I have taken my brothers by the hand but they have not as yet mentioned anything particular to me. I must now desire you will declare if any promise made you by me remains unperformed and whether or not I have upon all occasions kept my word with you.

A string of white beads.

At my arrival here I received the copy of a talk from the headmen and warriors of the Upper Creeks sent to Charleston and dated at Oakchoys the 1st May last. I remember well the different public agreements which you allude to in it, but I know nothing of any message sent you by Governor Wright and delivered you by Mr John McGillivray. I must here set you right where you are mistaken with respect to straggling cattle. At the great congress at Augusta you proposed that no cattle should be suffered to stray beyond the line. It was then observed to you that you could not expect that an ox or a cow could know a boundary-line, that to kill such straggling creatures for their ignorance would be cruel with respect to them and unkind and very unfriendly with respect to your brothers since it would always be in your power to drive them within the limits. On the other hand any such agreement would be leaving an opening for your mad young men, of which you confess you have a great many among you want only to kill and destroy the cattle of poor people settled near the line. Surely, my brethren, no damage or prejudice can arise to your nation by a few cows straggling into your woods and eating your grass. If settlements are not made over the line, I hope my brothers will not take offence at such trifles, especially as you yourselves observe that we with great reason complain of infractions of treaty and at same time say that a small breach should not spoil the old white path. I hope my brothers will never make a complaint of this nature any more or seem to begrudge a little grass to our creatures that may straggle beyond the line, as your friends may one day or other have an opportunity of relieving you when oppressed with hunger at the expense of those creatures' lives.

As Governor Wright has thought proper to answer your talk to me, copy of which was sent him by Mr Kemp, I refer you to what he says respecting the Indian said to have been murthered at Augusta. He must from his situation know that matter better than I do and has a right to judge how far he considers it as satisfaction. He likewise knows the particulars of what happened to St [?] Tago, that being within his government, and I again refer you to what he says on that subject as well as the stipulated reward for runaway negroes.

A few days after my arrival here I received your message of 15 July.

I have heard that the Cherokees wanted to pay their debts by a cession of land on the west side of Savannah River but whatever has been transacted in that business is without my knowledge and concurrence. It is not my business to determine whether you or the Cherokees have a right to that land; that point you must settle between yourselves. I can only tell you that as I received no orders to ask the Cherokees for a further cession no such requisition was made and no land can be taken without His Majesty's permission and the intervention of the Superintendant. I hope we shall have no misunderstanding about the boundary-line now to be finished, and as I have complied with your request in providing for you the rum you wrote for I expect you will also comply with our reasonable request in granting the lands upon the Scambia.

A string of white beads.

I have no more at present to say, I wait for your answer, and if you have any complaints to make this is the proper time.

Emistisiguo speaks:

Father, the great being above has ordered this meeting. The day is clear, so is my heart. The road I travelled to meet you is white and I now meet you in confidence and friendship. Your talks have always been good and I have on all occasions listened to them with pleasure, and after having travelled so far am rejoiced to see so many of my white friends who are here present.

I have often talked with you upon former occasions and promised to meet you again. This is the day appointed for that purpose. At former meetings I spoke for my people, it is my intention to do the same now.

Since my first meeting you at this place the talks between us have been white. At that time you told me that till then you seemed to hold me by the point of the fingers but for ever afterwards we should be tied together as with an iron chain, but as we have no iron or chains I said that my nation was like a vine newly planted near a strong tree to which I compared the white people, that the branches by which the vine clung to the tree were still tender but if the vine should continue to embrace the tree for seven years they would be as strong as iron. Seven years have elapsed since, and I cannot now doubt but our friendship and union will continue for ever.

I remember the boundary-line which was agreed upon at our last meeting in this place. You then said it should be like a stone wall, not to be removed without mutual consent. You now propose an alteration in the line then agreed upon. My nation is numerous and every child in it has an equal property in the land with the first warrior. Making any alteration in the boundary without the consent of the whole will be improper. You know what has so long hindered our marking the boundary-line, however I engage to come down here and to finish that business in the month of May next.

I understood that the Choctaws had given you a tract of land in the forks above the confluence of Tombeckby and Coosa Rivers. At a meeting at Augusta some time afterwards I objected to that cession because the land is our property. I now object to it again, the Choctaws are our younger brothers and not so considerable as we are, they may give lands on the other side Tombeckby River but on this side of it the land belongs to us.

I now again see my father and so many warriors face to face with our hearts clean and white. I hope it will remain so for ever and that when occasion offers we shall be ready to assist one another. I hope the great giver of breath will strengthen our friendship that we may live and die like brothers. I have at present no more to say. Tomorrow we shall meet early and finish our talks.

Wednesday 30th October

Present as the day before.

After smoking the calumet of peace, Emistisiguo speaks:

Our forefathers first took the white people by the hand at Charleston. This I have heard in my nation and shall always remember. I am now come to strengthen the friendship that then began. When our forefathers first met the white people the path was dark and crooked, but since that time it has always been straight. It has and ever shall be my endeavour to keep it open and clear of thorns and weeds. Perhaps I may fail, for I think the people of the present age are not so sensible as they were formerly. It was recommended by an English governor at Charleston to open a great and broad path from Charleston to the Abekas and thence to the Chickesaws. We did not receive this talk from a Frenchman or a Spaniard but from an English governor, and I have accordingly preserved it in my mind for English governors have always agreed with our ruling chiefs that every matter should be conducted for our mutual advantage and that we and they should be considered as the same people. I now meet my father and the governor here in a new place, and I hope we shall be able to settle matters in such a manner as to prevent any misunderstanding for the time to come. You, the Governor and General, are now three chiefs of our nation, and we expect that you will interest yourselves for the good of our people and that this talk will always be in remembrance. The lands are not the property of the head warriors but of the whole nation in common; every boy has a right in the disposal of them; but as we are now met and you have spoken to me on the subject I will not be deaf to what you have requested. It is true the limits have been settled by a former treaty, when it was agreed that no alteration should be made, yet I consider what you represent, and as the governor is now a chief of our nation and I hope will be careful not to suffer any future encroachments on our lands, I will lend him a little more land and I hope he will be careful of it and see that it is improved, that it may be useful to this town and that such of us as visit him may reap some advantage by it. I have told you how little it was in my power, yet as a testimony of my friendship I will take upon me to give a little. You may make your plantations on both sides the River Conica or Scambia as far up as the old Spanish cowpen. The Spaniards upon their first coming to this land settled a boundary with us, but they did not take care to keep within the limits. They made a fort upon Conica beyond the line, the consequence of which was a war between them and us and the quarrel was never accommodated till a little time before they left this place. The Spanish old fort is upon our land and it is our intention to build a town at the old field opposite to said fort upon Conica as soon as peace can be concluded with the Choctaws. I again explain the distance I now offer, which is to the old cowpen, and further we cannot take upon us to give.

The Superintendant speaks:

My brothers, I have in my hand a plan of the country near this place which I caused to be made since my arrival here that you and I might understand each other clearly in settling the boundary. The old cowpen to which you propose extending our boundary is marked upon it. The addition you propose making to the former cession is only four miles of very poor land upon the banks of Conica, and it is not worth the trouble of altering the old lines and drawing a new treaty for such a trifle. When I met you here before we were unacquainted with the quality of the lands you then ceded to us. Upon examination we find them to be nothing but sand, incapable of producing any of the necessaries of life. In seven years that they have been possessed by white people, they have not produced so much provisions as your party will consume at this meeting. Your hunting grounds we do not want to interfere with, our request of a little land on both sides the Conica or Scambia as far up as it is navigable for a boat is very reasonable and moderate, and such a cession cannot be attended with any inconvenience to you. It is absolutely necessary for your brothers here and would be more useful to you in their possession than in your own. I hope you will consider my readiness to comply with your desires as well as the benefit you receive from the neighbourhood of your white brothers and their friendship for you upon all occasions, and grant our request.

Emistisiguo speaks:

Father, if you had sent us word before we left our nation that this was to be a talk about giving more land we should not have come down without first having consulted our people relative to it, and then I could have given a proper answer to your proposal.

Superintendant speaks:

Brother, I sent for all your principal chiefs to confer upon matters of consequence to us both, particularly to establish firmly and mark the boundary-line. You chiefs never met me before without being authorized to treat of and transact all sorts of business with me. I expected you would have met me now here with the same authority.

Emistisiguo speaks:

Our chiefs could not all attend, some were at war and some were employed abroad upon business of consequence to us. I cannot therefore take upon me to say any more but I will consult the other chiefs here and take their advice which I will communicate to you.

Superintendant:

I desire then that you will retire and consider of the matter, and about four o'clock in the afternoon we will again meet you and hear the result of your consultation.

The congress broke up and the chiefs retired to consult. In a short time afterward, Joseph Cornal the interpreter was sent by them to acquaint the Superintendant that as the chiefs after consultation and mature deliberation found that they could not take upon themselves to gratify us fully in our request for lands on the Scambia, and as we had rejected the offer they had taken upon them to make of a small addition, they would not give us the trouble of another meeting and therefore desired the Superintendant would order boats to carry them across the bay that they might return to their nation. The Superintendant returned for answer that as upon consultation they thought themselves not authorized to comply with our request, he was far from blaming them for not doing it; on the contrary he thought their conduct highly to be commended in choosing to avoid the censure of their nation and in not deceiving us, their friends, by giving lands the property of which might afterwards be disputed and create bad blood, that he was not going to differ with his friends about a piece of land and desired they would entertain no such thought, that he had other business of moment to transact with them, and desired they would meet him at the appointed time; to which they agreed and met accordingly at the usual place.

October 30th, afternoon

Present as in the morning.

The Superintendant opened the conference by repeating what had been said in the forenoon, acquainted them of his having received their message by the interpreter, approved of their steady behaviour in not choosing to exceed their commission or in not taking upon themselves to make cession without authority, represented the situation we were in for want of planting-lands and as he proposed applying to their nation by a letter to be sent by them, he expected that they would back his application to obtain the cession so much wanted, and begged they would consider and represent to their nation the benefit that would accrue to themselves from those lands being in our possession, that he should expect an answer to the talk which he intended to send to their nation by them on this subject as soon as possible by the interpreter, thanked them for the offer of a small addition on the Scambia and assured them that although he did not think proper to accept of it, he did not slight their offer for that the governor and all their white brethren present looked upon it as a stretch of their power to show the straightness of their hearts, that he was ready to attend to any answer they should think proper to give or to anything they might have to say.

Emistisiguo speaks:

Father, I am still the same man I was and not like a child varying my opinion every instant. My sentiments still remain the same they were. I formerly spoke about the boundary-line at Tassa old field, not to go above Mr Farmar's plantation. I now desire again you will consider the lands in the forks above the confluence of Coosa and Tombeckby Rivers as our property. If the Choctaws have a mind to give lands they may give it on the other side Tombeckby River.

I hope you will never more allow any settlements or hunters to go above the old field at Tensa or Tassa. We have no other method of subsisting but by hunting, for which that land is well calculated, and at every meeting you have always promised that no encroachments should be made for the future. I have always upon my return home from such meetings repeated these promises but they have always been broken and new encroachments made. You have always told us as well as the governors that you wanted lands for planting not for hunting, and that the deer belonged to us, notwithstanding which there are white people who tell us they intend hunting on our lands in spite of us. You ordered that there should be no trading in the woods but I understand that it is in agitation to fix stores in the woods, so that I find you and I have talked to no purpose and that our agreements have fallen to the ground. There is a person settled on the Chatahootchies named William Oates at a place called Tuckpaska. I am informed that the Cherokees have allowed a man to make a settlement in the uppermost forks of Coosa River and to drive cattle there. Everything goes now contrary to our agreements, and I am sorry that Mr Jackson and our merchants at Augusta should break the rules which were made and agreed to in their presence. It was agreed at the congress at Augusta that all persons found trading in the woods should be considered as infringers of treaty and treated as French or Spaniards. I caused some such to be plundered to show them their error, for which I incurred much reproach from both white and red people. It was also agreed that no half-breeds or Indians should be employed as factors in the nation, yet there are many such employed. Some time after all these matters were settled at Augusta I received a letter said to have been written by you telling me I had forgot the agreements. John Francis was the interpreter, and I answered that I thought you had either forgot or mistaken the talk. I believe the letter was written by Mr Galphin. However, I then said I would speak to you concerning it the first time we should meet. I therefore have embraced this opportunity of doing it and have mentioned all these matters to show you that I perfectly remember what passed, although some white people who were present when these regulations were made say that they are all laid aside and of no force. I hope no offence will be taken at my being particular in mentioning those matters as I mean to show that I had not forgot the different agreements entered into.

Superintendant:

My friend Emistisiguo, I have listened very attentively to all you have said and shall now answer the different matters you have stated in order. The boundary-line agreed upon when Governor Johnstone and I met you here before is very clearly understood by me. It was to terminate at Coosa River so as to cover all the French settlements at Tassa Old Field, beyond which you now desire we should neither settle nor permit people to hunt. But I must here observe to you that the small tribes of the Nanniabama and Tome Indians who were settled on the western bank of the great river formed by the junction of the Coosa and Tombeckby Rivers have always considered the lands on the opposite shore as well as on the island above as their property and planted upon them, and they have only removed since the war between you and the Choctaws broke out; they likewise claimed a certain extent in the forks above the confluence of said rivers as their hunting-grounds. The reason is clear, their villages was on the high barren banks to the westward, a healthy situation but the soil unfit for agriculture, and all the rich lowlands lie in the islands and on the eastern side of the river. It is likewise a truth of which you may be sensible that the French inhabitants near Mobile and upon the western banks of Tombeckby River had no other planting-lands but what lay in the islands and upon the eastern side of Tensa branch of Coosa River. Now most of the old French inhabitants still retain their property under the British government and still plant upon the islands and rivers as usual. Supposing the property of all the eastern side to be really yours, will you refuse us the same advantage you allowed the French and same said tribes? Your expectations of friendship and assistance from us exceed any you could have entertained of reaping from the French, yet you mean to dispute this trifle with us. I shall say no more upon this subject but refer you for the truth of all I have said to Tipoy who is well acquainted with it.

Now with respect to the cession to His Majesty of lands in the forks above the confluence of Coosa and Tombeckby Rivers, it is most certain that a cession was made by the Choctaws as far as Chickiannoes in 1765 and it is as true that you objected to it at Augusta in 1768. The war which had in the meantime broken out between you and the Choctaws prevented our coming to any settlement about your pretensions. The property of said lands we cannot determine, that is a matter of discussion between yourselves, they are not granted away, we are in no hurry, they may remain as they are until circumstances will admit of your settling the dispute with the Choctaws.

It is very true that by the regulations for carrying on the trade made and communicated to you at Augusta by me, provision was made for discouraging and preventing the destruction of your game by persons residing in your nation, but those regulations ceased to be of force when the management of the trade reverted to the different provinces, and although my intentions were good yet they were frustrated. The King enjoined the different governments to give your grievances all possible redress, and although laws for that purpose have not as yet been enacted yet there is no doubt but proper attention will soon be paid to your complaints. In the meantime when you meet white hunters in the woods you have a right to the skins of your own deer and the guns with which they were killed. As to persons unlicenced carrying on an illicit trade in the woods, your people have in their power to discourage that practice by taking their skins, for men breaking the laws of their country are not entitled to their protection. Settling stores in the woods, distant from any town or settlement, is contrary to the King's orders and an infringement on your right, which is in your own power to prevent by obliging such offenders to remove. You therefore ought immediately to order William Oates to remove as well as the person who you say the Cherokees have permitted to settle and drive stock to the upper forks of Coosa River, which is in the middle of your hunting grounds. With regard to the letter said to have been written by me I assure you I know nothing of it, it is probable Mr Galphin may have wrote it as you surmise. Upon the whole, my brothers, these regulations were made by me when I was entrusted with the management of the trade, but as soon as it was put into other hands I could no longer enforce the observation of them, and no imputation of promises broke will lie against me upon that account. I am happy to hear these matters mentioned which has given me an opportunity of clearing them up, I hope to your satisfaction. I am at the same time much pleased to hear how distinctly you remember the substance of the regulations. I must again desire if you know any promise of mine unfulfilled in any respect that you will point it out.

Emistisiguo observed that it was late in the evening and that he would defer saying any more till the morning following at nine o'clock.

October 31st, morning

Present as the preceding days.

The Superintendant speaks:
My friends, we are now met again to resume our conferences of yesterday which were interrupted by the approach of night; I shall listen with attention to whatever you shall say and desire you will not smother any complaints you may have reason to make, this being the proper time to make them known.

Emistisiguo speaks:
[Marginal note: NB. Emistisiguo appeared at the congress this day with his face painted white] It is true the evening interrupted our talks yesterday. We are now met again all white and I will proceed in my discourse. Yesterday you asked for some land on the Scambia which we could not gratify you in, and assigned our reason for refusing. You also explained the situation of the Tomees and Nanniabas, and the right they claimed of planting on the islands opposite to their villages and on the eastern bank of Coosa River. They are gone and you have now succeeded to their right. I have attentively considered what you said and we consent that the boundary shall henceforward run etc. (vide treaty or cession).

Emistisiguo proceeds:
[Marginal note: NB. As the lands on the Coosa River belong to the Alibama tribe, all the chiefs of which being present, they could with propriety make this cession] You complain much of the poorness of your land near this town. We have now given some very fine land, we hope you will improve it and that its produce will answer your wishes. We expect that those who shall settle on that tract of valuable land will use us kindly when we shall happen to go and see them. It

abounds with fine timber, we hope you will make the same use of it that the French did and that you will not encroach upon us any more.

At Mr Galphin's house in 1768, you and I had some conversation. I know not if I understood well what you meant. You told me, at least I understood that you wanted a high piece of land opposite to Mobile as you thought it a good pleasant situation for a house, and if you could get it you would choose to have some cattle, hogs and other stock upon it. You asked me if we would have any objections to your driving such stock through our nation. You then said you sent this message by me and when you should receive our answer you would send a talk to the Choctaws about the land. It was the talk that no cattle should be driven through our nation. You and Governor Johnston agreed to it at this place, yet soon afterwards Mr Galphin drove a great many for the Mobile market without our consent. Upon my return home at that time I delivered your message to the nation who agreed that you should have any piece of land you should pitch upon and that they would send people to drive your cattle; but as I have never heard more from you since, I must conclude the whole to be a mistake.

The Superintendant:

I am extremely obliged to your nation for their readiness to grant what they imagined to be my desire. What I said was, I find, badly interpreted. I must therefore now explain a matter which was made a handle of, although it had entirely escaped my memory. When I was last here I expressed an inclination of having a spot on the east side of Mobile Bay, which was not granted me till after I left this province; it was that land I meant when I spoke to you. The situation is pleasant and healthy though the soil be barren. I told you that I either intended to go there myself or to send my deputy as a place contiguous both to your nation and the Choctaws. I never did ask you or any other nation for land beyond the boundary-line. I afterwards laid aside all thoughts of driving cattle thither because I thought it would be setting a bad example. I am obliged to you for the pains you have taken in this matter, and I look upon it as a fresh proof of your friendship.

Emistisiguo proceeds:

Besides Mr Galphin who was the first who drove cattle through our nation, there are many others driving cattle and settling cowpens on our land without our consent vizt. Robert Anderson has drove cattle to the Kaialeagus; William Cousins to the Abekoutchies; Nicholas Blake to the Oakchoys; Thomas Graham to the Wakekoys; Thomas Grierson to the Eufallies; Richard Baillie to the Ottassies; Thomas Scott to the Hillabies; and James McQueen has in opposition to every talk not only brought up cattle but also negroes and has made a settlement near the Great Tallassies, by which it appears that our talks have been thrown away. I want to know whether it should be so or not. I am now far advanced in life, and this is the first time I ever saw plantations settled in my nation. The reason of my complaining is that formerly our old women and motherless children used by exchanging a little corn for goods to be able to cover their nakedness, but they now are deprived of this resource, and often obliged on the contrary to purchase corn from the traders. I remember it was formerly agreed that we should take the skins we found in the possession of white hunters we should meet in the woods, but notwithstanding that agreement there are many white men in our nation who follow no other business but that of hunting, such as McFall, Humphry Hubbard, John Stripes and Adam Taply, who declare to our faces they will hunt on our land in spite of all opposition or regulations to the contrary.

The Superintendant speaks:

Governor Johnston and I at the last congress held here asked the liberty of driving cattle through your nation provided it should be found necessary for the good of the colony. You objected to it and said it might be productive of many disagreeable consequences and might probably be the means of involving your nation in a dispute with the white people; that if such a permission was given it would be a precedent for making your nation a thoroughfare for all sorts of people. It was at last agreed upon that no person whatsoever should be allowed to drive cattle through your nation without a pass from the governor of a province or the Superintendant. No person ever applied to me for any such pass, and I never gave any. The traders who have driven in cattle and made settlements in your nation are very culpable. I shall represent the matter to the governors of the provinces from which they trade, and I hope they will find means to redress these grievances. And as your complaints will be laid before His Majesty I probably may have some orders relative to them.

His Excellency the Governor then addressed the Indians as follows:

Friends, brothers, great chiefs and warriors, I am sorry that this meeting has not been so favourable to your white brethren as we had a right to expect. You may think we were angry but I do not blame you for refusing us the lands we asked for as you tell us you were not authorized to give them; on the contrary, if this is the case I think you have acted like wise and prudent men in not granting what might give umbrage to the rest of your nation and cause disquietude amongst yourselves, which might endanger the friendship now subsisting between us. The small tract which you so kindly made us an offer of convinces me of your gratitude and friendship. I am obliged to you for your good intentions and I have strong reason to hope that what the Beloved Man mentioned to you yesterday about granting these lands will make such an impression on you that when you return to your nation you will use your utmost interest with your brothers to induce them readily to comply with our requests and join with you in granting us the small tract that has been applied for, as you must be sensible that we have no land near us fit for cultivation and that this grant will be of as great advantage to yourselves as to your white brothers, for without this cession it will not be in our power to give you those assistances that you require when you come to this place. I shall not say anything more to you upon the subject, this was not the only business that we sent for you upon. You may remember that last summer I sent a talk into your nation acquainting you of several settlements made by your white brethren on the Alibama River having been broke up by some of your people for having settled beyond the line, and desiring you to send some proper persons down to assist us in marking it out; and as you are now here I hope that affair will be accomplished. It has been generally understood that the boundary-line included all the old French settlements at Tassa which I hope you confirm to us. With regard to what you mentioned yesterday concerning white men who have settled or hunted on your lands, traded in your wood, and who have committed other abuses, I must tell you whenever these come to my knowledge I will exert myself to have your complaints redressed, and if such offences are committed within the limits of this province I will punish the offenders agreeable to the laws. I must now mention to you the many injuries that have been committed by the Lower Creeks upon the plantations of the white inhabitants in the western part of this province, which oblige me to take notice of them. Several parties frequently go out under a pretence of going to war, which is far from their thoughts, for without going to seek for their enemy they go to our plantations, destroy our cattle and plunder the poor inhabitants of their all, and then return home with their booty. These are grievances that must be put a stop to. We are the people of one Great and Beloved King, therefore let us live like brothers and not as enemies, for what is a man that robs me of my property but my enemy? It behoves you leading men of the Creek nation to exert your power and authority so as to prevent any of the like transactions for the future, and I think in justice you ought to oblige those who have thus transgressed to make restitution to the poor people whom they have plundered and in a manner ruined. I do not blame any of our red brethren here present for these offences but I must desire that you will send talks to the Lower Creeks to prevent them from such practices for the future. There is another thing I must also observe to you which is, as you are now at war, your young people frequently come into our towns with arms in search of their enemy, which is not agreeable to the white people, neither is it usual in any of the provinces. The frequent complaints of the misbehaviour of the red men, who often get drunk with rum which they get for their skins and then are riotous, make it necessary that I should acquaint you with it in hopes that you will give such advice to your young men as to make them avoid giving any offence for the future. I hope what I have now said will make that impression on you and that you will use your influence with your young men that their future conduct will be such as to make us esteem them as welcome friends and not look on them as plunderers of our property.

I have not forgot to thank you for the distinguishing mark of your friendship which you was pleased to confer upon me at our first meeting, appointing me to a high rank in your nation. I shall always consider you as friends and brothers and shall retain a grateful remembrance of the honour you have conferred upon me.

The Indians thanked his Excellency for his talk and friendly advice and assured him that they would pay the greatest attention to what he had recommended.

Emistisiguo speaks:

I must not omit to acquaint you that one John Miller, a trader, lately brought a talk into our nation said to have been sent by Governor Wright of Georgia, which he said contained a threat to stop our trade if we did not acquiesce in the cession of land by the Cherokees to their traders.

The Superintendent replied that the assertion of Miller's was a falsehood for that he had Governor Wright's talk in his possession, which contained no such threat or even desired their consent to the cession and that he would not fail to represent Miller's behaviour to the governor of Georgia; and proceeded:

Friends and brothers, I have now heard all your complaints with great attention and must observe to you that on our parts we have likewise great reason to complain. You must be sensible of many capital infringements of treaty which as yet you have never given any satisfaction for. It would be needless here to repeat what happened to a slave you carried off from Mobile; it is very recent and you must remember what the governor wrote you upon that subject. Many inhabitants of this province have Indian slaves brought from a great distance on the other side of the Mississippi. These cannot be enemies of yours, nor can any honour redound to you as warriors from killing poor defenceless slaves; yet your parties frequently insult the plantations in search of such people, an instance of which happened very lately at Mr Wegg's plantation on Mobile Bay where they pursued and fired several shots at a very valuable slave of his. Had they killed him they would have derived no honour from it and it would have been doing great injustice to his master. If you will consider how contrary such proceedings are to your professions of friendship for us, and with how little reason you can expect redress of grievances you complain of on our part, without you also exert yourselves to prevent such insults, I am convinced that upon your arrival in your nation you will immediately give the necessary orders for that purpose.

You complain of a number of lawless white people residing in your nation, who contrary to all order and regulation hunt on your land and put you to open defiance. I am obliged to you for your tenderness shown to your white brethren in not hurting the persons of such offenders, but as they are often bad people who, having fled from justice, take refuge in your nation, in case the governor of any of the provinces should send to apprehend them, I expect that you will not oppose but on the contrary be aiding and assisting in apprehending them.

I thank you for the addition you thought proper to make to the former cession on Coosa River, and as I am come here with a view finally to accomplish the importance service of making the boundary-line I hope you will appoint a sufficient number of your people to attend the persons to be sent from this province to execute it.

We met in friendship, we will part in the same disposition, we will therefore smoke the pipe of friendship, and if anything black remains, let it fly away with the smoke.

Emistisiguo speaks:

I am sorry I cannot comply with your request and mark the boundary-line at this time as it is our hunting season and there is no grass in the woods for our horses; but I am the man who will come and accomplish this in the month of May next. I have now talked a great while and will give up my place to any of my people who may have anything to say.

The Superintendant acquainted them that he had a token of the King's bounty to bestow and would order the presents to be got ready as soon as possible.

The Conferences then ended

Copy of the affidavit of Joseph Cornal and John Simpson, interpreters for the Creek language.

West Florida. Personally appeared before me E. Rush Wegg Esq., Attorney-General of the province aforesaid, Joseph Cornal, interpreter for the Creek language in the Indian department, and John Simpson, interpreter for said language for this province, who being duly sworn make oath that they were present at the different conferences between the Superintendant and the Indian chiefs of the Upper Creek nation during a congress beginning the 29th day of October and ending the third of November current, at which the said Joseph Cornal did truly and faithfully interpret the speeches made by the Governor and Superintendant to the said Indian chiefs as well as the answers of the said Indian chiefs to said speeches, truly to the best of their knowledge and judgement, and the said Joseph Cornal and John Simpson were present when the treaty of cession was signed and executed by the said Superintendant and Indian chiefs when Joseph Cornal did also explain to the Indians the course of the line agreed upon and specified in said treaty, and to which they the chiefs assented and agreed; and further that the Superintendant did then by the interpretation of the said Joseph Cornal ask the said Indian chiefs whether they or any of them remembered any promise said to have been made by Governor Johnstone and the Superintendant or either of them at the meeting with their chiefs and warriors at Pensacola in the year of Our Lord 1765 of a congress to be held at the expiration of three years from that time, or whether they or any of them expected such a congress or complained to any person of a breach of promise on the part of government or Superintendant for want of such a congress; to all which the Indian chief Emistisiguo on behalf of the whole answered in the negative and declared their total ignorance of any such promise by the said Governor and Superintendant or of any such complaint having ever been made by him or any of his nation, all which the said Joseph Cornal interpreted truly and faithfully to the best of their knowledge. Sworn at Pensacola, this 4th November 1771, signed E. R. Wegg, Attorney-General. The mark of Joseph Cornal; John Simpson.

Copy of a letter from John Stuart Esq., Superintendant of Indian Affairs, to his Excellency Peter Chester Esq., Governor of West Florida, dated Pensacola 2 November 1771.

Sir, I herewith send for your Excellency's perusal a treaty of ratification and cession of land at different times within this province, that your Excellency with the advice of His Majesty's Council may if agreeable signify your concurrence and approbation thereof. I have the honour of being, sir, your Excellency's most obedient and most humble servant, (signed) John Stuart.

His Excellency's answer
Pensacola, Council Chamber, 2 November 1771. Sir, Immediately upon receipt of your letter dated this day enclosing the articles of treaty and cession of lands proposed to be made to His Majesty by the Creek Indians, I laid it before His Majesty's Council and I am to acquaint you that they have advised me to concur in the cession of lands mentioned in the articles of the said treaty, and I do hereby signify to you my approbation of the same. I have the honour to be with great regard, sir, your most obedient humble servant, (signed) Peter Chester.

West Florida. At a congress of the principal chiefs and warriors of the Upper Creek nation of Indians held at Pensacola in the province of West Florida on the twenty-ninth day of October and continuing to the second day of November 1771 by John Stuart Esquire, His Majesty's sole agent for and Superintendant of Indian Affairs in the Southern District of North America.

A treaty for the ratification and confirmation of a former cession and for a further cession of land within the limits of said province to His Most Sacred Majesty George the Third, by the Grace of God, of Great Britain, France and Ireland, King, Defender of the Faith and so forth. By the several chiefs herein named and who are authorized by their said nation.

Whereas at a congress of the said Creek Indians held by the said John Stuart Esq. in conjunction with his Excellency George Johnstone Esquire, Governor of West Florida, at Pensacola in the said province on the twenty-eight day of May in the year of Our Lord 1765, it was agreed upon between the Governor and Superintendant and the several ruling chiefs and warriors, deputies from the said Creek nation there present, that the lands reserved by the said Creek Indians for their own use should be distinguished by the following boundaries vizt. By a line running from the River Choctaw falling into Santa Rosa Bay, westward to the Bay of Pensacola, and round the said bay to the River Scambia opposite to the mouth of a creek known by the name of Boundary Creek, said line from the River Choctaw to the Scambia to run across all the rivers, creeks and bays as far as the flowing of the tide, and from the confluence of Boundary Creek with the River Scambia up by the course or channel thereof to the place where it is crossed by the old path or road leading from Pensacola to Mobile, and afterwards to run along said road across the river called by the Indians Cassapa and by the Spaniards Perdido to another branch or Black Creek called by the French Roche Blave, then up the main stream or channel of [MS: or] said creek or branch to its source, and thence to the branch of Coosa River called Tassa or Tensa River, so as to cover all the French settlements at Tassa Old Fields.

Article 1st. Pursuant therefore to His Majesty's orders to, and power and authority vested in, the said John Stuart Esq., His Majesty's sole agent for and Superintendant of Indian Affairs in the Southern District of North America, it is agreed upon by the said John Stuart in behalf of His Most Sacred Majesty George the Third by the Grace of God of Great Britain, France and Ireland, King, Defender of the Faith and so forth, and the subscribing Upper Creek chiefs and warriors on behalf of their nation, that in consideration of His Majesty's protection extended to the said Indians of the Creek nation, and for a valuable consideration in goods now given them, the above recited boundary-lines be ratified and confirmed, and they are accordingly by these presents ratified and confirmed. And they the said chiefs and warriors do of their own free will and accord and for the abovementioned considerations further cede and grant unto His Majesty and his heirs for ever all the lands lying between Coosa River and a line to run from Briar Creek above Major Farmar's plantation at Tassa [ ] miles distant from and parallel to the Tassa branch of Coosa River to the Great River formed by the confluence of Coosa and Tombeckby Rivers, and then to extend along the high land by the edge of the swamp on the eastern side to Coosa River above its confluence with Tombeckby River, and afterwards the line is to run by the eastern bank of the Coosa River to the mouth of the branch called by the Choctaws Byuck Connonga and by the Creeks Hitesia. And the said contracting chiefs do cede to His Majesty on behalf of themselves and their nation all claims, pretensions or rights to the lands, creeks and rivers lying to the westward of said line, and they further engage to send proper authorized persons on behalf of their nation to see the above specified boundary-line surveyed and marked as soon as possible and this further cession of land agreed upon and stipulated, provided His Majesty shall be graciously pleased to accept of and confirm the same and not otherwise.

Article 2nd. And it is further stipulated and agreed upon by the contracting parties that no alteration whatsoever shall henceforward be made in the boundary-line above recited and now solemnly agreed upon, ratified and confirmed as aforesaid, except such as may be hereafter found necessary and expedient for the mutual interests of both parties, and which alteration shall be made with the full consent of the Superintendant or such other person or persons as shall be authorized by His Majesty as well as with the consent and approbation of the Creek nation of Indians at a congress or general meeting of said Indians to be held for said purpose and not in any other manner.

In testimony whereof the said Superintendant on behalf of His Majesty and the underwritten Creek chiefs on behalf of their nation have signed and sealed this present treaty at the time and place aforesaid. (Signed) John Stuart, Superintendant, S. District; Emistisiguo, mark; Neothlockto, mark; Othlopoye Hajo, mark; Yahatamico, mark; Estonnake Opaye, mark; Siahoula, mark; Opay Hajo, mark; Wectomke Mico, mark; Ashcahoula, mark; Opaye Atke, mark; Neomatco, mark; Testnnake Upage, mark; Tacussa Mico, mark. By order of the Superintendant, William Ogilvy.

The following gentlemen were present when the within treaty was signed by the Superintendant and Indian chiefs and heard the questions and answers referred to in the preceding affidavit: Major Dickson of the 16th Regiment; Jacob Blackwell Esq.; E. Rush Wegg Esq., Attorney-General; Major Hutchinson of the Royal Americans; Charles Stuart Esq., deputy Superintendant; Lieut. Carrique, 16 Regiment; Doctor John Lorimer; Mr Urquhart; Mr Falconer. *Copy*, certified by William Ogilvy [C.O.5/73, fo. 26]

CXIII

Lieut.-General Thomas Gage to Earl of Hillsborough (No. 66)

6 November, New York
My Lord, as soon as I had the honour to receive your lordship's letter No. 48 [Vol. I, No. 1402], I dispatched Captain Montresor, engineer, to Boston to begin the repairs at Castle William recommended by Governor Hutchinson, but I learn by a letter since received from the governor that he is of opinion the season is too far advanced to enter upon works of consequence, particularly mason's work which will be better done and at less charge in spring and summer, though the present time is best for providing all the materials that are wanted.

I am to acknowledge also an extract of your lordship's dispatch to Governor Franklin [Vol. I, No. 1403], enclosed in your letter above mentioned, and have the honour to inform your lordship that the King's service has of itself caused the measure of withdrawing the troops out of the colony of New Jersey to be adopted without any prejudice to His Majesty's affairs. Your lordship has been made acquainted in my former dispatches that a regiment was to be sent to St Augustine to replace the 21st regiment, removed from that garrison in the spring. The 26th and 29th regiments drew lots for that station, and the lot fell to the 29th quartered in New Jersey. This has been publicly known a long time, the regiment is embarked and I imagine at sea.

When the transports were nearly ready to take the troops on board I acquainted Governor Franklin of their embarkation approaching, and I enclose an extract of his letter to me in answer [Vol. I, No. 1596i]. Your lordship will see by it that he regrets the departure of the troops, and I find that most of the better sort of people in the province have the same sentiments about their going away. I was a good deal surprised at that Assembly's late disobedience to the Mutiny Act because from the time that the Act was passed there has never been any difficulty till now to procure quarters for any troops in the province of New Jersey, whether they were to be stationed in it or marched through it. I am told the reason is the present Assembly's being composed of more low people than was ever known in it before, who are trying by popular arts to make themselves of consequence, telling the people they have been imposed upon and that the gentlemen have given away their money to supply the King's troops without occasion, for that other provinces had refused such supplies and they would incur no prejudice in refusing. The better sort wish the supplies granted and would have it contested to the last, in which they are supporting their own cause with that of government, fearing if they yield that all influence over the common people will descend to those of the lowest class, and I believe would not be displeased if the province suffered some inconvenience from the Assembly's late disobedience.

By the removal of the regiment there will be no demand for future supplies for the barracks but there is an arrear due for quartering from the time the Assembly refused to make provision to quarter the troops till the regiment embarked. I have been applied to and desired not to omit writing to Governor Franklin on this point that he might press it upon the Assembly in the strongest manner, but it must be left to his better judgement how to act, who knows his province better than I can pretend to do. If his demand to discharge the debt is complied with all will be well, and the troops being removed prevents all contest for future supplies. But if it is rejected the proceeding will be a strong indication of a fixed resolution in the Assembly to condemn the authority of Parliament, which will make things worse. And again should no demand be made to discharge the debt contracted for quartering the troops, it will be construed as a tame acquiescence in the Assembly's former refusal, and the faction will gain the point they assured the people they would obtain. The management of this affair must be left to Governor Franklin's better judgement to whom I mean to write upon the subject in the hopes that he will find means to gain a majority upon the question or, despairing of that, devise some method to evade it in such a way as to avoid the appearance of yielding to the disobedience of the Assembly.

By letters received from Governor Byron and Captain Debbieg, engineer, employed in the works at Newfoundland, I find the works were not begun till the 12th of August and that the engineer previous to the receipt of my letter upon the subject had fixed the payment of the soldiers, sailors and marines employed on the works at the rate of ninepence per diem for common labour. But my letter to Governor Byron concerning those matters arriving soon afterwards, the price was reduced to sixpence. The reduction naturally occasioned much murmur and discontent, I understand so much as to impede the carrying on the works with the alacrity to be wished. Captain Debbieg is returned to England where he will of course make his report and give in a state of everything at Newfoundland which shall be proper for His Majesty's information.

Sir William Johnson has been some time in the country of the Six Nations in order to settle some important points with that confederacy. His return from thence is daily expected and I am in hopes very soon to hear that his negotiations has been attended with success. There are late letters from the forts upon the Lakes and Fort Pitt which contain nothing of moment but that everything in those quarters was quiet.

Since my last to your lordship, I have reviewed His Majesty's regiment of Scots Fusiliers at Philadelphia, and have the pleasure to inform your lordship that I saw a good regiment in very good order and that they performed their military exercises to great satisfaction. *Signed.* [C.O.5/89, fo. 185]

CXIV

Governor Josiah Martin to Earl of Hillsborough (No. 6)

10 November, Newbern
My Lord, I have the honour to acquaint your lordship that a rumour of a boundary line being determined by His Majesty between North and South Carolina on the representation of Lord Charles Montagu gives great alarm to the people of this province, which they conceive much injured by such a partition, and it seems the more to hurt them as they had formed sanguine expectations of defeating Lord Charles's plan of division by the intervention of Governor Tryon in consequence of the remonstrance of the Assembly at the last session when his lordship's proposals to that gentleman were communicated. This, my lord, is a subject-matter of dispute between the two provinces that I conceive it impossible to settle to their mutual satisfaction. It is certain that by such a division as is talked of this province will be dismembered of a large tract of well-peopled, flourishing country that hath been long deemed to belong to it; but if His Majesty hath been pleased to determine it otherwise it cannot be doubted that his royal decision is made upon the justest principles. My present meaning therefore, my lord, is only to inform your lordship of the manner in which the report of this matter has been received here. The governor of this province will I believe be the greatest sufferer by such an arrangement which will very much diminish the little emoluments that arise to him from granting the King's lands, that portion of country taken off by it being what is most in request with new settlers and almost the whole field of his profit.

The proprietary right of the Earl Granville in the heart of this province I learn from all hands, my lord, to be a very principal cause of the discontents that have so long prevailed in this country. The superior excellence of the soil in this district, which includes by far the greater share of the fair and fertile part of this province, invites emigrants from all the Northern Colonies who many of them bring money to take up lands, but Lord Granville having empowered no person here to give them titles, they set themselves down where they please, and because they cannot establish freeholds under these circumstances they refuse to pay taxes which has been and still is a source of perpetual discord and uneasiness. I am informed, my lord, that this proprietary may be purchased upon very easy terms. I submit to your lordship's consideration whether it is not an object that deserves the royal attention. It seems here an universally acknowledged principle that this country will never enjoy perfect peace until that proprietary which erects a kind of separate interest in its bowels is vested in the Crown. The quitrents of that district, which would be immediately settled, would produce a revenue that would very soon reimburse the purchaser who should pay much more for it than sixty thousand pounds sterling, the price at which I hear it is valued.

I have from time to time forgot to mention to your lordship that the province seal was broke when it was put into my hands, and that I was obliged to have it repaired before it could be used without doing it further injury. It is awkwardly mended but in such manner as to answer all purposes.

A report obtaining here that Mr Mercer, lieutenant-governor of this province, is promoted to a new government erected on the Ohio, I most humbly beg leave to remind your lordship of the long and faithful services of Mr Hasell, President of the Council of this province. His merits have been often represented to your lordship by Governor Tryon and were particularly conspicuous during the operation of the Stamp Act. *Signed.* [C.O.5/315, fo. 17]

CXV

Governor John Wentworth to Earl of Hillsborough (No. 39)

15 November, New Hampshire

May it please your Lordship, since I had the honour to write your lordship, No. 38 [Vol. III, No. CI], an unfortunate and illegal event has happened in the port of Piscataqua in this province which is my duty to represent, both that your lordship may have timely information and also be assured that every care is taken to bring the delinquents to legal punishment so effectually as may in future prevent any such violences.

On the 26th October the brig *Resolution*, Richard Keating master, was entered at the Custom-house of Piscataqua. The Collector, being dissatisfied with the quantity of molasses reported, on the 28th of October seized said brig and part of her cargo for breach of the Acts of Trade. This, although very proper and right, was yet a new thing here and threatened deserved ruin to the owner who thereon became an object of undistinguishing compassion among maritime people.

This was manifested by an universal refusal of labourers to work or assist the Collector in removing and securing the vessel and cargo until a trial at law should determine the matter, and in other circumstances of conversation which induced the Collector to apply to me on the 29th October, setting forth that he had but two Custom-house waiters who were afraid to remain alone on board the vessel, though not the least abuse to them was complained of; that he the Collector was not apprehensive of any violence but desired I would order the captain and four soldiers from His Majesty's Castle William and Mary to be on board the seized vessel that night, thereby to give comfort to the waiters.

This I immediately ordered and was obeyed punctually, leaving in the castle only four men. Captain Cockran was directed to obey the legal command of the Collector and all magistrates. At 9 o'clock the officer and soldiers went on board; about midnight or later, instantaneously appeared on deck upward of fifty men from the quays and adjacent vessels, armed and disguised; they suddenly locked the cabin doors where the waiters were, then proceeded to Capt. Cockran and ordered him with his soldiers to leave the vessel, which he positively refused, putting his small party in the best manner of defence, determined although he could not possibly expel the trespassers and there was no revenue-officer to direct him further yet to maintain his post on the deck; which the rioters finding could not possibly be carried until every man of the party was killed, they went to work to hoist out the cargo which was not lawfully entered, of which Capt. Cockran took account and rendered upon oath before the Judge of Admiralty upon the trial. The Collector having obtained notice of the trespass notified the High Sheriff of the County, then came and informed me, whereon I ordered the sheriff to call the magistrate of the town and proceed with them to aid and assist the Collector as he should require, which was performed with all the dispatch possible at that time of night. In the streets were found a few scattered people who dispersed instantly at the appearance of the magistrates and were unknown under cover of night and from the speed with which they separated without speaking a word or in any way offending the magistrates or breaking any law in their presence or knowledge. However, the vessel in this time was robbed of forty or fifty hogsheads of molasses.

The Collector complained in writing hereof, which I laid before His Majesty's Council for their advice, who unanimously advised a proclamation offering a reward of two hundred dollars for a discovery of any of the rioters, which proclamation I pray leave herewith to transmit to your lordship [Vol. I, No. 1607i].

In a few days the Collector discovered and took possession of part of the molasses stolen on the 29th inst., which was secured without the least difficulty. On board the vessel was still remaining that part of the cargo which was legally entered and had paid the duties. This under care of the marshal of Admiralty (and is reported) was forcibly taken away by unknown men in the night of the 7th November, no complaint having been made thereof to me. In due course of law the cargo was condemned, also seven hogsheads of sugar and two hogsheads of wine seized in a storehouse, all which were peaceably sold at auction by judicial decree of the Court of Vice-Admiralty.

Immediately on this robbery the Collector ordered one of His Majesty's ships of war into this port from Boston, which is safely arrived and pleasantly moored near the town, who have formed such hopes of profit from their expense as to wish the number was increased.

The 14th November was appointed for the trial of the vessel, during which one Jesse Saville, a waiter in one of the out-members of this port, who had been odious in some part of Massachussetts Bay as an informer, this man was called to testify in this case, which being done he indiscreetly expressed some fears of being ill-used if known, which was soon carried from the court-house to the people in the street below, which then had many sailors, labourers and boys, as it was just in the dusk of the evening when such are retiring from the navigation and daily employ to their respective dwellings.

The cry of an informer being thus given by himself, the idle people hallood him, the noise gathered more, and in ten minutes 500 sailors, boys and slaves, were together pursuing the waiter and setting one another on, they knew not why.

They found the man and were hustling and knocking him about when casually two or three gentlemen of the town came by, and enquiring the cause found the man in danger, went in among the crowd, dispersed them and rescued the waiter without the least difficulty or abuse. These gentlemen aver that these fellows were to a man common sailors or people of that order and degree who seemed disposed for any noisy mischief rather than designing an injury or resentment. This lasted about twenty minutes, by which time the magistrates in the town and many of the principal inhabitants, hearing a noise and suspecting a riot which they exceedingly detested, were convened together upon the spot with their peace-officers, and with laudable spirit and resolution commanded and preserved the public peace.

That nothing might be wanting to discourage and suppress such tumults and that I might know exactly the whole matter, upon the first notice from the Collector of the affair I walked unattended and publicly through the midst of those remaining, for the magistrates had dispersed many on their coming. I found about 300 people gathered in little knots of 6–8 to 10 and 12 who upon my appearance instantly gave way and discovered every possible testimony of respect; neither were they in the least noisy or contumacious or did they attempt any injury or disorder, as is evident for my chariot passed uninterruptedly through them four times. The Collector and all the other Custom-house officers were in the street during the whole time and were not even abusively spoke to. This I report from my personal knowledge, being resolved at all times to call forth every officer in this province for the support and execution of His Majesty's laws and to countenance them by my personal example. I am hence very happy to assure your lordship that through the zeal, firmness and resolution of the magistracy a sudden riotous attempt was effectually suppressed in the beginning, and in so spirited a manner as will probably prevent such excess for the future.

Hitherto there hath not been any information of the trespassers, but I've not the least doubt whenever they or any of them are discovered and informed against they will be brought to a legal and exemplary trial.

Through the whole course of this reprehensible trespass it has evidently appeared that the provincial officers and the principal merchants disapproved such conduct, and in their respective stations readily afforded their aid to the Collector; and that this matter was an unlawful violence of sailors and labourers artfully contrived and suddenly executed, most probably through the influence and direction of those interested in the vessel and cargo, who are exposed to the penalty of the laws which I apprehend the Collector will avail himself of as soon as he has gathered evidence proper to institute and sustain his process.

At present there does not appear the remotest idea of riot, mob or rescue or any other interruption in the execution of the laws of trade, that I am in hopes this representation will contain the whole relative to this affair, but if not I beg leave to assure your lordship that nothing shall be omitted which may be in my power to enforce due subordination and obedience to the laws and to transmit to your lordship the earliest and most perfect account that events may require. My ardent desire of fidelity and diligence in His Majesty's service has caused me to presume on your lordship's time with this minute and exact detail of an event which in itself or its probable consequences to government could scarcely justify such an intrusion. In the rectitude of the principle I most humbly ground my reliance on your lordship's condescension and goodness to pardon the prolixity of the effect. *Signed.* [C.O.5/937, fo. 104]

CXVI

Robert Rogers to Earl of Hillsborough

17 November, Spring Gardens, at Charing Cross
My Lord, as immediate guardian to the colonies I presume upon your lordship's patronage and protection, my services having been confined to North America and the little private interests I have being there located.

No man, my lord, has gone through more vicissitudes of alternate hardship and persecution than myself, and if I have now remained two years in England without formally claiming your lordship's protection, I did so that I might urge my case with greater confidence now that prejudice has had time to subside and the world is disposed to be just to my character.

From the time at which I was first called to the service of the King to the end of the French war, my career through difficulties, perplexities and dangers of every sort, was uninterrupted and successful. I had fewer obligations to the chapter of accidents than anyone and if there be any reward in the universal eclat of the day I certainly had a most ample proportion.

When the corps of rangers which I was entrusted to command was thought to have been rendered of little use by the cessation of hostilities and was disbanded, Sir Jeffrey Amherst thought that a more substantial reward ought to follow my services, and that General who is politic and judicious but was never profuse in apportioning bounty to desert gave me one of the independent companies, the fair annual value of which was £560 and has often been improved to much more. As they had been long established permanency in the provision for me was his object; he did not foresee the subsequent reduction; I am persuaded he regretted my loss; nor is he unjust to the alacrity with which I, though on half-pay, put myself forward upon the recommencement of hostilities to repel the savage enemy under an inferior officer nominated to a periodical rank for the occasion, it being matter of indifference to whom the credit of a dangerous enterprise might be intended so that I stood signalized in a prompt obedience to the calls of my country.

Since that I was nominated to a command in the interior country of great trust which invested me with the management of affairs of all the central Indians, in which I have a right to say because it is universally acknowledged that I acquitted myself with a fidelity and address beyond all former example. And though crimes of such prodigious magnitude as a breach of that trust and of my allegiance were formally exhibited in charges against me, upon the scandalous deposition of a wretch twice recorded for perjury and who though he ought never to be believed boasted the promise of ample reward for the service, yet did my full acquittal demonstrate my innocence, and the checks since given to the wonted profusion in the Indian department evince that His Majesty's ministers cannot be ignorant in whose jealousy that absurd, wicked and profligate prosecution originated.

And though I submitted without repining to unexampled severities, though standing in a civil capacity I waived my right to the habeas corpus writ and my liberty on bail to suffer a rigorous previous confinement, though I forewent my right to a jury and was content to take my acquittal from a court of which each member individually depended for his promotion on the man who stood forward in the unwarrantable prosecution, yet was I without cause assigned dismissed from employ, and do now stand consigned to inactivity and almost absolute want, with an enormous responsibility for my expenditures on credit in the Indian and ranging services.

I have, my lord, presumed to trespass thus far in particulars that I might dispose your lordship to consider and to commiserate my situation, and to ground an humble request that you would be pleased to move the King to grant his standing warrant for a provision from year to year of fifteen shillings per day without deduction as major in His Majesty's service as a reward for past and retainer for future service; and I farther humbly request that your lordship will give order to renew my commission as major granted in the late reign, which I take the liberty to leave at your lordship's house for that purpose. *Signed.* [C.O.5/154, fo. 29]

CXVII

Arthur Savage, Comptroller of Falmouth, to Commissioners of Customs at Boston[1]

19 November, Boston

Honourable Gentlemen, it becomes my duty to inform you that on the evening of the 12th current, being sitting in my house in company with Mr William Savage, my wife having just left the room, a violent stroke was given at the door, upon which I desired my nephew, the abovementioned William Savage, to open the door who took a candle in his hand and went; upon opening of which I heard a rushing in the entry, and turning my head towards the door see a number of disguised persons coming into the room. Upon which I rose from the chair and asked them their business with me. They replied they had come to know who the informer was and immediately seized me. I told them that I could not tell them who it was. They told me I should tell, and forcibly hauled me out of the house, upon which I told them they need not treat me ill, as if I must go with them I would walk without hauling. Being in the street I desired my nephew abovementioned to

---

1 Enclosed in Hutchinson's letter of 28 November to Hillsborough, Vol. I, No. 1631.

call Mr Benjamin Titcomb, a coroner who lives opposite to me; after endeavouring to keep them in conference some little time, Mr Titcomb came out. I told him "That a number of persons in disguise, armed with clubs, had entered my house and forced me out and I desired his assistance". Immediately one of the disguised persons replied We come to know the informer, and I must and should tell who he was. Upon which Mr Titcomb said We want to know who the informer is, which we shall be glad to know, and left me. Upon which I desired my nephew not to leave me; the disguised persons then pushing me and violently hauling me by my arms down a lane leading to the water, my nephew soon disappeared and I was left in their possession, who hurried me along to a part of the town by the side of the river where no houses are but at a considerable distance, and frequently stopped and with horid oaths demanded of me whether I would let them know who the informer was, at the same time threatening me if I declined. I still refused satisfying them and asked them whether I had in any way injured any of them. They told me I had not, but by the Almighty God they would know from me who the person was that had given the information. I told them again I would not tell them, let the consequences be what they would; upon which with horrid yells they forced me along the side of the river with often repeated threatenings; soon after which there was a hoop and they encircled me, when the person who appeared their leader told me that by the living God I now should let them know, and that they were armed. I replied I could not help it, upon which a pistol was presented towards me by the said leader, and three or four others shew[ed] them, when they held me and said that by the great God I must now tell them or take the consequence. Upon which I let them know what I was acquainted with respecting the matter, which they obliged me twice to swear to; the person who appeared the leader then asked Shall we take his word and dismiss him or carry him to Mrs Pribble? Carry him to Mrs Pribble, was the general cry. Upon which I asked them what I must go there for; they replied I had there said that a written information was lodged in the office. I denied it and they hauled me along back up the lane towards my house and stopped at the door of the beforementioned Benjamin Titcomb and desired him to give them some liquor and directly before his door made me again swear to what I had before done, upon which after mentioning my swearing to them that if I knew them I would not discover them, they in the most solemn manner called God to witness that if I knew any of them and should discover them they would destroy me or words conveying that meaning. They then fired two or three pistols in the air and left me, after being in their custody about three-quarters of an hour.

The next morning in company with the Collector and the deputy Collector, I waited on the justices of the Inferior Court then sitting and made known the circumstances above related. They remarked that it was a high-handed riot, bore testimony against it, and told me all they could do was to issue warrants in case any of the persons were known. I answered I could not say who they were.

The next day being Thursday the 14th, Mr William Savage before-.

mentioned having committed to paper what he knew respecting the riot was desirous of making oath to the same. I went with him and called Enoch Freeman Esq., a Justice of the Peace, and after sending for Mr Benjamin Titcomb and reading it to him, I desired he might be admitted to his oath, which he declined doing. I then called another of the justices who was of opinion it had better be laid before the said court. Soon after I went to the Collector and the Sheriff of the County and desired they would go with me to the said court, where they went and the beforementioned William Savage offered his deposition and desired he might be admitted to his oath, which after a debate of an hour or more was refused by the justices of the said court. And not afterwards expecting the least support and being in danger of having my life taken away, I have repaired to this town and humbly hope your honours' protection. *Copy*, certified by John Cotton, deputy Secretary. [C.O.5/761, fo. 9]

CXVIII

Clergy of Connecticut to Earl of Hillsborough

25 November, Connecticut

May it please your Lordship, the clergy of the Church of England in His Majesty's English colony of Connecticut in New England beg your lordship's favour as President of the Board of Trade and Plantations to solicit that honourable board to use their interest and influence in behalf of the Church of England in America, the support and encouragement of which is apprehended would be most conducive to the interest of true religion and the best security of loyalty.

The grievances we labour under are chiefly of a religious nature: in order for a happy removal of these the clergy of this colony have with all humility presumed to forward a petition to His Grace the Archbishop of Canterbury, to be presented by him to our most Gracious Sovereign who is ever attentive to the best good of his people, for the appointment of a resident bishop or bishops for America in such manner and method and with such powers as His Majesty in his great wisdom shall think proper, not aiming nor requesting any encroachment upon the civil or religious privileges of any of the Dissenters here but only that we may enjoy like indulgence and all the privileges of our happy constitution.

The inconveniences and troubles we labour under by being destitute of resident bishops are too obvious to escape the notice of your honourable board; and we have that confidence in your goodness and concern for the national religion that we suppose we may with propriety address your board to second our application preferred to the Throne that we may be blessed with such an officer residing with us as Christ placed over his Church at first.

May it please your lordship, we esteem the present time the most favourable of any that has been for the introduction of a bishop into this colony. And our reason for it is this: the whole body of Dissenting ministers in all the provinces of America had laid a scheme to bring the civil powers of this colony to pass some spirited resolves against a bishop's being sent here, and for this end put in a petition to the General Assembly signed The Multitude, which was read in the House but the principal gentlemen of the House of the Dissenting side warmly opposed the motion of passing any resolves against a bishop, and openly declared it was their opinion that the Church in this colony ought to have a bishop. The whole strength of those Dissenters who would oppose a bishop has been exerted, and it appears too inconsiderable to be taken notice of. Now is the time to introduce a bishop into this colony without any opposition, and it is a pity so favourable an opportunity should be neglected.

How far these things will merit the notice of your lordship, or properly deserve your attention, we who are so unacquainted with state affairs cannot tell. If our application to you as a body be judged improper we beg the forgiveness of your lordship as we have no sinister views but only a hearty desire and concern for the interest of true religion, especially of that Church of which we have the honour to be ministers.

Not doubting the zeal of your lordship for the prosperity of the best of Churches and your desire that we may enjoy the blessings of it in these remote provinces, has caused us to forward this address.

With the greatest respect, reverence and esteem, we are, may it please your lordship, your lordship's most obedient humble servants, the clergy of Connecticut. *Signed,* Jeremiah Leaming, secretary. Signed by order. [C.O.5/1284, fo. 114]

CXIX

Seizures in Port of New York[1]

29 November, Custom-house, New York
Account of seizures made by ships of war in the port of New York vizt.

A small schooner without name from Connecticut with twelve casks of sugar on board, seized by Captain Talbot of His Majesty's ship *Lively,* now depending in the Court of Vice-Admiralty of this province.

Also a small schooner called the *Nancy* from Virginia and fifteen casks of tobacco, also seized by Capt. Talbot and depending in the said court.

Also the pilot boat called the *Harliquin* belonging to this port with nineteen chests of tea and two small cases containing medicines, painted feathers and beads, seized by Mr Tinsley, Lieut. of His Majesty's ship *Deal Castle,* commanded by Capt. Maxamilian Jacobs, not yet libelled but is to be prosecuted in the said court.

Account of seizures made by officers of the Customs in the port of New York vizt.

One tierce, one box and a small paper package of tea, seized by Alexander Colden, Surveyor and Searcher of this port, prosecuted and condemned in the Mayor's Court of this city, to be sold at the Custom-house on Wednesday the 4th December next.

1   Enclosed in Tryon's letter of 4 December to Hillsborough, Vol. I, No. 1658.

Also eighteen casks of sugars seized by James Cogeshall, land-waiter of this port, out of the schooner *Two Friends*, Thomas Simpson master, prosecuted by the Collector and Comptroller of this port in the Mayor's Court of this city and now depending. (Signed) Andrew Elliot, Collector, Lambert Moore, Comptroller. *Copy*. [C.O.5/1103, fo. 8]

CXX

Earl of Hillsborough to Governor Earl of Dunmore (No. 4, Separate)

2 December, Whitehall

My Lord, Mr Norton, a Virginia merchant, came to me this morning to lay before me some directions which he has received from the Treasurer of the colony of Virginia concerning a copper coinage to circulate in that dominion. I take the liberty to refer your lordship to certain letters which have passed between the late Lord Botetourt and me, and Mr President Nelson and me, on that subject. These will inform your lordship of the state of this matter and you will find that the directions now sent to Mr Norton are in consequence of an information received by Mr President Nelson from me of the manner in which the kingdom of Ireland is supplied with copper coin. But the Treasurer explains the ideas of the gentlemen who seem to approve of and to adopt that mode in such a manner as makes it necessary for me to trouble your lordship with some farther explanation concerning it and observations upon it.

Mr Norton and I considered the Treasurer's letter with all the attention we could give to it, and we both thought that there is some ambiguity in his expressions which gave us room to suppose that the proposition might be taken in two ways: the first, that 52 halfpence being coined out of copper equal to the value of two English shillings, each halfpenny should still pass at 25 per cent more than an English halfpenny does in England although only 48 English halfpence are coined out of the same quantity of copper. But we could scarcely suppose this to be the intention as it would be a manifest fraud. The other proposition is not attended with any fraud, and as we apprehend is this: that the change of two English shillings shall be 52 halfpence instead of 48. This might certainly be done but it appears to me that the gentlemen had hastily adopted the idea of the Irish copper coinage without considering the just and useful proportion which it bears to the nominal value of the English shilling and other English silver coins current in that country, for, as the English shilling there is denominated 13 pence, 26 halfpence divide it into equal parts and make the change most easy and convenient, and therefore they have chose to coin the avoirdupoise pound of copper into 52 halfpence equal to two English shillings. Now this may be with great facility adapted to the case of Virginia, for the two English shillings passing for 30 pence Virginia currency, the useful division in the coinage of copper would be to make 60 halfpence out of the avoirdupoise pound of copper equal to two English shillings; and if this plan should be agreeable to His Majesty's subjects in that colony there is no objection to it that immediately occurs to my mind, and I am of opinion that it would be of very essential service especially to the poor. I shall however take no other step in this matter than to obtain all the information that I can with regard to a measure of this sort from those departments of government to whom it more particularly belongs; and in case no objections arise from them, and your lordship finds what I now mention is agreeable to the gentlemen on your side of the water, I shall be ready to do my part in carrying the measure into execution.

I take the liberty further to observe to your lordship that in the plans hitherto proposed the colony has intended to lay out £2,500 in copper coinage, and I submit to your lordship's consideration whether this be not too large a sum for the first experiment and whether it might not be more prudent to make the trial upon £1,000, which you will observe from the account I sent over of the Irish coinage will amount to five tons of copper. It will be necessary if the colony adopt this measure to employ Mr Norton or some other agent to execute their commands in this matter, and the person they employ shall have all the assistance I can give him. I ought in justice to Mr Norton to inform your lordship that I thought I observed great disinterestedness in his conversation upon this subject.

I have troubled your lordship with a very long letter but the matter I conceive is of real importance to the colony, and it will give me the greatest satisfaction if I can be the promoter of any measure that may conduce so essentially to its interest and advantage as I really think this will do. PS. There may be such a proportion of farthings coined as the colony shall think proper. *Draft.* [C.O.5/1349, fo. 175]

CXXI

Governor William Tryon to Earl of Hillsborough (No. 10)

3 December, New York

My Lord, I was in great expectation I should have been able to have transmitted to your lordship by this time the complete survey of the partition line between this government and the province of Canada, but by the omission of Mr Bentzell to attend that duty in September last and his appointing Mr Smith who had the fever and ague on him when he set out on that service, as the deputy of Bentzell in conjunction with Mr Collins appointed on the part of Canada, these two gentlemen ran only twenty-two miles of the course, when Mr Smith was too ill to proceed on the service. Enclosed is a copy of their survey [Vol. I, No. 1637i]. I have proposed to Lieut.-Governor Cramahé the first of next March for the commissioners to proceed on the survey and have not the least apprehension but it will be carried to the main branch of Connecticut River, which I am informed rises to the northward of the 46th degree of north latitude, and by the reports of the Indians who attended the above survey the line of 45 degrees on a due east course will strike the river about forty-five miles from the place where the commissioners stopped. The Council have advised me to appoint some gentleman who will give his personal attendance in the room of Mr Bentzell who preferred a trip to Canada to his duty on this important and necessary service, especially when the intrusions of the New

Hampshire people so much alarm the peace of this government. *Signed.*
[C.O.5/1103, fo. 3]

CXXII

Earl of Hillsborough to Lieut.-General Thomas Gage (No. 49)

4 December, Whitehall

Sir, I have not failed since my return to London to give the fullest
consideration to the dispatches received from you during my absence.

The only letters which appear to require any particular or immediate
instructions are those which regard the military works now carrying
on, proposed to be undertaken in West Florida, the state of the interior
country as well in respect to the repairs wanting at all the posts as to
the hostile disposition of some of the Indians of the Western confederacy, and the great disorders and abuses in the Illinois district.

I observe from the estimates [Vol. I, 1349i–viii] enclosed in your
dispatch No. 62 that the expense of the works in West Florida will be
very large, but the security of the harbour of Pensacola and the preservation of the health of the King's troops, stated to be exposed to great
distress for want of barracks, are objects of so much importance as
to leave no room to doubt that Parliament will cheerfully make provision
for those services, and therefore the King having the fullest confidence
that the utmost economy will be observed in every service where
expense is incurred has commanded me to signify to you His Majesty's
pleasure that the batteries should be completed and that such barracks
as are necessary for the reception of the troops should be built as soon
as may be.

The state of the interior country and more especially of the establishments in the district of the Illinois affords a very large field of discussion,
and the King's servants have given the fullest attention and consideration to so important a subject and have weighed with great deliberation
the different opinions and propositions that have been stated on the
one hand and the other respecting those establishments.

I have already in my former dispatches so fully explained to you
my sentiments on this subject that it is unnecessary for me to repeat
the many difficulties that occur to any plan that either has been or can
be suggested for that country. The King's servants, however, unanimously concur in opinion that considering the many disadvantages
which have been represented to attend the situation of Fort Chartres
in every respect and the little chance there is of preventing its destruction by the ravages of the Mississippi, it ought to be abandoned
and therefore I am commanded by the King to signify to you His
Majesty's pleasure that you should give the necessary orders for that
purpose and for a reduction of all the establishments incident to that
post at such time as you shall think it can be effected with the greatest
facility and convenience.

In your letter No. 63 [Vol. I, No. 1441] you speak of a plan suggested
by Col. Wilkins for forming an establishment at Kaskaskies, and you
seem in some measure to adopt it upon an idea that it might be formed
upon a much narrower scale of the expense than his calculation amounts

to; if therefore you are of opinion that after the abandonment of Fort Chartres the state of that country will absolutely require that some temporary establishment should be effected either at Kaskaskies or any other part of the district, it is the King's pleasure that you do in that case carry into execution whatever plan you shall judge most effectual to answer that object until some resolution shall be taken with regard to the arrangements that may be finally necessary for that country.

It is very much to be wished not only from considerations of economy but also of the discipline of the King's troops that all that are now stationed in the Illinois district might be withdrawn in consequence of the abandonment of Fort Chartres or at least that the number to be retained there with a view to the temporary establishment before suggested, if any should be necessary, might be as small as possible; but as this is a matter which depends upon the nature of that establishment and the state of the district in many other particulars it must be left entirely to your discretion.

I have always thought and am still of opinion that the thing most to be wished for in regard to the Illinois district would be the removal of the inhabitants to situations within the limits of Quebec or of some other established colony; but I fear there are but too many obstacles to such a measure, and therefore it will be the more necessary to consider whether any permanent plan ought to be adopted. And the King's servants having submitted to His Majesty their wishes to receive from you your thoughts at large upon that subject, it is His Majesty's pleasure that you do give it the fullest consideration, and if you shall think that a permanent establishment is necessary, that you do report your opinion what that establishment should be and how it may be carried into execution and supported upon the lowest plan of expense. In the meantime it is very much to be wished that the garrison of Fort Pitt may in consequence of the abandonment of Fort Chartres be also withdrawn and the fort demolished; and it is His Majesty's pleasure that this service be accordingly effected unless you shall be of the opinion that it is absolutely necessary to be kept up with a view either to the temporary establishment above proposed or to any permanent plan that you may recommend.

From what I have already said you will observe that His Majesty's attention and that of his servants have been confined chiefly to the case of the Illinois district and Fort Pitt which has never been stated as otherways useful than as an entrepot between the established colonies and that district. With regard to the other posts on the Lakes and the establishment necessary for preserving a communication along those Lakes, it is agreed on all hands that they ought to be kept up and supported at least for the present, and therefore it is His Majesty's pleasure that the necessary repairs should be carried into execution.

I am not sufficiently informed of the state of those nations of the Western confederacy which you say have commenced hostilities to form any judgement how far it may be either necessary on the one hand or dangerous on the other to engage in a war with them; it is a matter that must be left to your own discretion, and all I could do upon this occasion has been to instruct Sir William Johnson to give every assistance in his power to the measures you may think fit to pursue. But as it is evident that the settlement forming at the post of St Vincent is in every respect of the most dangerous tendency and must have the effect to keep us entangled in perpetual dispute and quarrel with the Indians, it is His Majesty's pleasure that you give notice to the inhabitants of that place forthwith to return from it, and in case of their refusal that you do immediately acquaint me therewith, reporting to me at the same time your opinion of the measures it may be advisable to pursue for compelling them to relinquish that country.

The account which you have seen in the public prints of an insult offered to one of His Majesty's armed schooners off the coast of Carthagena in America is so circumstantial and so much nearer the truth than such accounts generally are, that it is not necessary to state that business more particularly; and I have only to add that there is good reason to hope from the manner in which the Governor and Admiral of Carthagena have stated this affair in their letters to Captain Hay of His Majesty's ship *Carysfort* (an account of which has been received within these few days) that the answer of the Governor to Sir George Rodney's letter to him on the subject will be satisfactory.

I am persuaded that all His Majesty's faithful servants and subjects will most heartily rejoice in the intelligence which has been received of His Royal Highness the Duke of Gloucester's recovery from the violent and dangerous disorder with which he was attacked at Leghorn, and I do on my part most cordially congratulate you on that happy event. *Draft.* [C.O.5/89, fo. 180]

CXXIII

Earl of Hillsborough to Governor Thomas Hutchinson (No. 11)

4 December, Whitehall

Sir, Mr Pownall has already acquainted you that your letters numbered from 5 to 10 [Vol. I, Nos. 1269, 1310, 1334, 1380, 1399, 1455] had been received, and since my return to London I have received your dispatches numbered 11, 12, 13 and 14 [Vol. I, Nos. 1508, 1546, 1569, 1580] and have laid them before the King.

The proceeding of the House of Representatives with regard to the 27th article of your instructions and Mr Richardson's detention in gaol from the doubts of the judges in respect to the effect of the King's pardon in the shape in which it has been notified to you, seem to be the only points that require any immediate instruction; for although the representations which have been made of the state of the country eastward of Sagadahoc contain matter of very great importance to the kingdom yet that business is certainly not yet ripe for consideration, nor can it be I conceive proceeded upon till the surveyor sent out by the Treasury shall have made his report of the state of that district.

The doctrines and principles held forth in the address of the House of Representatives in answer to your message on the subject of the 27th article of your instructions are of so dangerous a tendency and strike so deep at the just dependence of the colonies upon the Crown and Parliament that His Majesty is unwilling to believe that they can possibly be avowed by any real friends to the constitution or that the sentiments and opinions of his faithful subjects in the Massachussetts Bay do in any degree correspond therewith.

If the unwarrantable proceeding of the House of Representatives could be viewed in any other light, or if it could be supposed that there was any settled resolution in that House to deny the King's right to instruct his governor in the exercise of his negative on their Acts, His Majesty's resolution to support the constitution with firmness would undoubtedly have induced His Majesty to have laid this proceeding before his Parliament; but the King is graciously disposed to consider what passed on that occasion as the result of a rash intemperate moment, and doubts not that when heat and passion shall have subsided the justice and propriety of the instruction will stand fully evinced and that the Assembly will not hesitate to put into their Supply Bills such clauses of exception as may prevent their operation in the cases to which that instruction refers. For I trust it will appear to every reasonable person that (without applying the case to any particular description of office) a tax imposed in the government of Massachussetts Bay upon the income of any transient officer of the Crown, which income does not arise from a salary payable out of monies granted to His Majesty in that colony, is as unjust in its principle as it must necessarily be arbitrary in the assessment. It was not therefore from any attention to the case of the Commissioners of the Customs in particular that the instruction was given, but from a consideration that the assessors of the provincial tax possibly might and probably would consider themselves as bound by the general words of the Act to assess not only those Commissioners but every other officer of the Crown both civil and military that might chance to come into the colony.

I am sensible, sir, that this argument might be more forcibly stated but it is unnecessary to enlarge upon it further seeing that it is not the instruction itself but the King's right to give it that is questioned by the Representatives. Whenever they think fit to desist from arguments that cannot be admitted without violating the constitution, they will be treated with the most favourable attention. In the meantime it is the King's pleasure that you do firmly adhere to the instruction you have already received and refuse your assent to any Supply Bills that may have the effect to subject any servants of the Crown whose offices have no immediate relation to the colony to be taxed for their incomes arising from salaries not payable out of monies granted to His Majesty by the legislature thereof.

His Majesty approves of the coolness and temper with which you received the very extraordinary and indecent answer to your message, and at the same time that His Majesty is pleased to command you to adhere with firmness to the instruction I am to recommend to you to endeavour to bring back the Assembly from these excesses by argument and persuasion, not forgetting to state to them that it will be to their unjustifiable conduct that the inconveniences which the colony may suffer from the rejection of the Tax Bill must and will be entirely imputed.

With regard to the case of Mr Richardson, his unmerited sufferings excite my compassion and I feel a real concern for the obstacles which have prevented his being released from his confinement. Had the manner in which the King's warrant for his pardon was notified to you been without precedent there might have been some ground for the objections taken by the judges; but I have already acquainted you that the same form has been followed in all cases of the like nature that have occurred in the colonies for more than fifty years past, in every one of which the transmission of a copy of the King's warrant to the Recorder of London by one of His Majesty's Principal Secretaries of State has been admitted as a sufficient authority for the release of the prisoner. Amongst these cases several of them have occurred since I have been in office, nor has there been any one instance at any time in which that authority has been questioned, and therefore I hope that when these circumstances are duly considered the difficulties of the judges will be removed and that they will admit the copy of the King's warrant transmitted to you in my dispatch No. 5 to be a sufficient ground for releasing the prisoner upon his giving bail to plead the King's pardon when called upon, which I find upon enquiry is the invariable practice of the judges in this kingdom who in the case of the pardon of a convict require no other authority for his release than a like warrant from the King to the Recorder of London to insert his name in the next General Newgate Pardon.

I have not failed, however, to submit the difficulties which have occurred on this occasion to the consideration of the rest of the King's servants, together with your proposition for removing them by a warrant from the King for passing a pardon under the seal of the colony, and I am to acquaint you that it is their unanimous opinion in which His Majesty concurs that there is not sufficient ground in the objection stated by the judges for making an alteration in the form of proceeding in cases of this nature, which is warranted by so many precedents and supported by the invariable usage and practice both in this kingdom and the colonies for such a length of time. As it appears, however, upon enquiry made in consequence of your letter to Mr Pownall that a General Newgate Pardon has not been taken out for some years, I have reason to believe that the consideration of this case will induce the necessary orders for passing such General Pardon under the Great Seal, and so soon as it is completed I will send you an authenticated copy of it to be kept upon record in the colony; but as this may take some time I hope the poor man will not be kept in confinement till this pardon can be transmitted. *Draft.* [C.O.5/760, fo. 308]

CXXIV

Earl of Hillsborough to Governor William Tryon (No. 6)

4 December, Whitehall

Sir, I take the first opportunity after my return to London to congratulate you upon your arrival at New York and to acquaint you that it hath given His Majesty much satisfaction to find that you have met with so favourable and affectionate a reception from all ranks of His Majesty's subjects in that colony.

I have long lamented the disorders which have prevailed on the lands heretofore considered as part of the province of New Hampshire but which were annexed to the government of New York by His Majesty's Order in Council of the 20th July 1764.

By this order, however, all contests between the two governments in respect to territorial jurisdiction were finally decided, and therefore if acts of violence have been committed with impunity and the authority of government insulted it is not to be attributed to any want of decision of government here.

It is true indeed that His Majesty hath thought fit to suspend any final determination with regard to the different claims of property in those lands until the state of each claim could be fully examined, and it might reasonably have been expected that in a case where so many different rights and interests were in question the servants of the Crown in the several departments would not proceed without due caution and circumspection and would avoid hastily deciding upon a matter of so much difficulty and importance. I have the satisfaction, however, to acquaint you that the Board of Trade did some time since make a full report [Vol. III, No. LXIII] to the Privy Council upon this subject, and I doubt not but that I shall soon be enabled to send you the necessary instructions in consequence thereof.

The King approves of your conduct in having demanded reparation of the governor of St Domingo for the losses which Captain Frisby of the *Hawke* sustained by the seizure of the vessel and the unjustifiable treatment he met with from the Spaniards in that government, but the King's servants are inclined to think that you went rather farther than belonged to your situation in demanding the punishment of the officers who made the seizure.

It was very natural in a matter of that consequence for you to think of taking the advice of your Council. I believe, however, upon reconsideration of the subject you will be of opinion that it is not proper to lay before a provincial Council for their consideration any matters of a general public nature which have no immediate relation to the affairs of that colony, and I am to signify to you His Majesty's pleasure that you do for the future avoid taking that step in any instance of a like nature.

I have read with attention the report of the committee of Council upon the extract of my letter No. 2 which you thought fit to communicate to them, on which I have only to observe that as the minutes of the Council to which they refer for their justification were not received at the Plantation Office till more than a month after my letter was wrote, I had nothing to form my opinion upon but Lord Dunmore's representation of the case in which he neither states the ground for drawing into question the right of the patentees of 1706 nor makes any mention of other persons being associated with Col. Bradstreet.

As the mode, however, of granting lands in New York and the Council's proceedings thereupon are matters of very great importance as well in respect to the interests of the Crown as to the rights of the subject, and will most probably be the subject of serious consideration at a proper opportunity, I must desire you will as soon as may be report to me for His Majesty's information a full state of the method of proceeding upon application for grants of lands in order that His Majesty may be informed whether such method does or does not correspond with the letter and spirit of the royal instructions given for that purpose; for if it should turn out that grants are made to persons by name who never personally appear at the Council board or are examined as to their ability to cultivate and improve the land they petition for, and that the insertion of names in a patent under pretence of their being associates or co-partners is only a colour for giving to any one person more than he is allowed by the King's instructions, it is an abuse of so gross and fraudulent a nature as deserves the severest reprehension, and it is highly necessary both for the interest of the Crown and for the dignity of His Majesty's government that some effectual measure should be taken to put a stop to it.

As the report of the committee of the Council will I trust lead to a discussion that has become so highly necessary, I am not on this account sorry that my letter to you which produced that report was communicated to the Council; but as it contained no directions from the King that it should be made that use of, His Majesty observes that you have not attended to his order signified in my circular letter of the 2nd of September 1768, of which lest it should be mislaid I enclose you a copy.

I am happy to be able to confirm to you the recovery of His Royal Highness the Duke of Gloucester from the disorder that put his life in so much danger at Leghorn, an event that I am persuaded will give general satisfaction and joy to all His Majesty's faithful subjects. *Draft.* [C.O.5/1102, fo. 311]

CXXV

Earl of Hillsborough to Governor Josiah Martin (No. 4)

4 December, Whitehall

Sir, I have not failed to lay before the King your dispatch No. 1 [Vol. I, No. 1461] which was received at my office a few days before my return to London, and I beg leave to congratulate you on your safe arrival in your government and to express to you my sincere wishes that your administration may be happy and prosperous.

The advice and opinion of Governor Tryon would have been alone sufficient to have justified your declining upon your arrival to convene a new Assembly, but the inconveniences which you state would have attended a general election in the month of August and the other reasons you assign are additional arguments against it, and your conduct on that occasion is approved by the King.

The tranquillity which you say now reigns in that country, which has of late exhibited scenes of so disagreeable a nature, is most pleasing to the King; and it is His Majesty's command that you should pursue every lenient measure that may conduce to quiet people's minds, to extinguish the remembrance of such unfortunate events, and to obviate all just ground of future uneasiness and discontent.

The heavy burthen brought upon the whole colony by the measures which the madness of a few desperate men compelled the late governor to pursue is not one of the least of the evils flowing from the late disorders; and though, as I have repeatedly observed to Mr Tryon, the King cannot concur in any Act for creating a paper currency upon conditions inconsistent with the law of England, yet His Majesty commands me to say that any plan 'for that purpose which shall not contradict the provisions of the Act of Parliament for restraining paper bills of credit in the colonies will be considered in the most favourable light, and every facility given to it that His Majesty's faithful subjects in North Carolina can wish. But I am more particularly called upon on this occasion to direct your attention to the Act of Parliament as some other colonies have, by framing their Acts for establishing a paper credit in such a manner as to make those bills a legal tender at the Treasury of the colony, laid the Privy Council under the necessity of advising the King to disallow them.

I observe, sir, that in one part of your letter you seem to apprehend that the creating a paper credit for defraying the expense of the late measures will meet with difficulties that cannot be removed without instructions from His Majesty; but as you do not explain yourself as to what those difficulties are likely to be, it is impossible for me to foresee them and consequently to propose any instructions on that head.

In the last letter I received from Mr Tryon relative to the affairs of North Carolina, and which is dated from New York, he expresses a wish that the plantation and estate of Benjamin Merril, a captain of the militia and who was one of the six rebels executed on the 19th of June, may be granted to a wife and eight children he left behind him, and I have it in command from the King to signify to you His Majesty's pleasure that you do accordingly take the proper measures that whatever property belonging to that unhappy person became forfeited to the Crown by his conviction should be regranted to his widow and children. *Draft.* [C.O.5/314, fo. 280]

CXXVI

Earl of Hillsborough to President James Habersham (No. 39)

4 December, Whitehall

Sir, I have received and laid before the King your letter to me of the 3rd of August [Vol. I, No. 1436] and am commanded to signify to you His Majesty's approbation of your conduct in not convening a new Assembly until His Majesty's pleasure was signified to you for that purpose.

As the violence of the late Assembly and the unwarrantable and unconstitutional doctrines and principles held forth in their resolutions with regard to the governor's right of negativing the Speaker do not correspond with those sentiments of loyalty and duty so repeatedly expressed by His Majesty's faithful subjects in Georgia, His Majesty is graciously disposed to believe that such doctrines are not the sense of the people in general but that they have been either rashly taken up in a moment of inconsiderate heat or from the suggestions and mis-leadings of ill-disposed and designing men, and therefore His Majesty has the fullest confidence that they will be discountenanced by every honest man who is a real friend to the constitution and zealous for the true interests and happiness of the colony.

It is however the King's command that when a new Assembly meets, which it is His Majesty's pleasure should be convened at such time as will best suit with the convenience of the inhabitants, you do in your speech signify to them His Majesty's disapprobation of the conduct and proceedings of the late Assembly and His Majesty's resolution to resist with firmness every attempt to violate the constitu-tion, and that you do so soon as any person whom they shall elect for Speaker shall have been presented to you for approbation put your negative upon such election; and in case the Assembly shall thereupon by any proceeding or resolution of what nature soever deny or draw into question the right of such negative, it is His Majesty's pleasure that you do forthwith dissolve the Assembly and transmit to me an account of your proceedings in order to be laid before His Majesty. *Draft.* [C.O.5/661, fo. 73]

CXXVII

Earl of Hillsborough to Sir William Johnson (No. 17)

4 December, Whitehall
Sir, I have received and laid before the King your dispatch No. 16 [Vol. III, No. LXXXVII].

The detection of the author of the false reports spread amongst the Indians upon the Ohio with a view to engage them in a general plan of hostility is a very happy event and leaves no room to doubt of the propriety of the measure which led to so important a discovery.

I am satisfied from what passed at the congress at Johnson Hall that the fidelity of the Six Nations is not to be doubted, and whilst they continue firm we have little to fear from the machinations of the Senecas at Chenussio who seem for private purposes of their own to have separated themselves from the rest of their tribe and whose intrigues appear to be founded in views inconsistent with the interests of and disapproved by the confederacy in general. Their motions however ought to be watched and there seems nothing wanting to defeat their designs but their knowing we are not ignorant of them.

I am happy to find that my sentiments with regard to the advan-tages to be gained from the jealousies subsisting between one tribe of the Indians and another correspond with your own ideas upon that subject. I agree with you however that the operation of those jealousies to defeat any dangerous plan that may be proposed is not always to be relied on, and I am now satisfied, as well from what you state respecting the congress at Scioto as from what appeared at the congress at Johnson Hall, that our intervention in the business to be proposed at the first of those meetings was necessary and that the sending deputies thither from the Six Nations was a proper step.

The plan for Indian affairs, which was referred to your consideration when I was formerly in office, renders it almost unnecessary for me to say how much I lament that your authority does not extend to redress those grievances which are most material; and I am persuaded that could it have been foreseen that the colonies would have been so backward and negligent in meeting those gracious intentions of the King which induced His Majesty to leave the regulation of the commerce to them, their representations on the subject would not have so far prevailed as to have occasioned such a deviation from the plan at first proposed as has almost entirely defeated every useful object it had in view. But as the matter now stands, nothing further can I apprehend be done until the King's servants are apprised of the measures which the commissioners, who I find were to meet at New York on the 1st of this month, shall have thought fit to recommend.

As you do not mention the defection of the Kickapous and Pouteatamis, two nations of the Western confederacy, I presume you had not received any certain advices of their hostilities nor had been apprised of the opinion General Gage has stated to me of the necessity of chastizing them. Gen. Gage has not however proposed to me any plan for this purpose or explained the steps he intends to pursue, and therefore I am unable to give you any particular instruction with regard to your conduct on this event. But it is His Majesty's pleasure that you should co-operate as far as belongs to your Department in every measure which General Gage shall think necessary for the King's service on this occasion.

You will have observed from the public prints the danger in which His Royal Highness the Duke of Gloucester has been from the attacks of a very violent disorder at Leghorn and his happy recovery from it. It is with very particular satisfaction I am able to confirm to you the latter part of that intelligence and to congratulate you upon an event that cannot fail to give the greatest pleasure to all His Majesty's faithful subjects. *Draft*. [C.O.5/72, fo. 317]

CXXVIII

Lieut.-General Thomas Gage to Earl of Hillsborough (No. 67)

4 December, New York
My Lord, since my last to your lordship Sir William Johnson is returned from the Indian country greatly satisfied with his negotiations. The Six Nations deputed a number of their chiefs at his desire to go immediately and take away the bad belts that had been sent to the Western nations in their names and without their knowledge; and another deputation was to be sent to Scioto, the deputy before sent to inform those nations of the real sentiments of the Confederacy having died on his return home, and none of his party being returned his proceedings were not fully known. The Six Nations seem resolved to manifest their fidelity to the English and to pursue such measures as will bring the Western nations to good order or otherwise to show themselves able

to preserve their ascendancy over them and compel them to due submission.

The intelligence sent from the Ohio is not so favourable. I am informed from thence that eleven villages of the Ouabache, Miamies and Lake Mitchigan Indians have determined to attack the Ilinois country next spring, and that a party from each of those villages were hunting about the falls of the Ohio to be ready to intercept any boats going down the river. The Ohio tribes are also discontented on account of the great number of people who have crossed the Allegany Mountains and settled between the west side of said mountains and the Ohio, so near to the Indians as to occasion frequent quarrels. Mr Croghan, deputy Indian agent, declares if the grievance is not soon removed, which at the same time he explains the impossibility of doing, that a war must be the consequence. The tribes have sent a speech on the subject of their complaint to the governors of Pennsylvania, Maryland and Virginia, and delivered it to the officer commanding at Fort Pitt to be sent also to me; and I have the honour to transmit a copy of it to your lordship [Vol. III, No. CXXIX]. I imagine the latter part of it means only to show that they want presents, for before that Indian affairs were put under the management of His Majesty's agents it was customary for the provinces to hold councils with the Indian nations and at such times to make them considerable presents.

Mr Croghan, who is settled on lands near to Fort Pitt, complains that the expenses unavoidable at that place, which from its situation must exceed all other posts, are not allowed him. He says from what I have wrote to him he does not expect payment from me, nor can he expect it from Sir William Johnson out of the sum allowed him for his department, which he well knows is not sufficient to gratify the Six Nations only. Upon that account he acquaints me he has given up his employment and desired Sir William Johnson to consider him no longer as his deputy.

The engineer employed at Castle William reports that he had collected a large quantity of materials, good and cheap, and was prosecuting the repairs of the platforms and gun-carriages with all dispatch, that he had put a stop to the mason's work for the present, and proposed closing all the works on the 23rd ultimo and to repair to this place to give an account of his proceedings. I apprehend from his report of the little that has been done this year in the repairs of the above fortress that they will not be completed before the middle of next summer. The estimate of the repairs wanted was very considerable. *Signed.* [C.O.5/90, fo. 3]

CXXIX

Delawares, Munsies and Mohicans to Governors of Pennsylvania, Maryland and Virginia[1]

[4 December]
Brethren, in former times our forefathers and yours lived in great

1 Enclosed in Gage's letter of 4 December to Hillsborough, Vol. III, No. CXXVIII.

friendship together and often met to strengthen the chain of their friendship. As your people grew numerous we made room for them and came over the Great Mountains to Ohio. And some time ago when you were at war with the French your soldiers came into this country, drove the French away and built forts. Soon after a number of your people came over the Great Mountains and settled on our lands. We complained of their encroachments into our country, and, brethren, you either could not or would not remove them. As we did not choose to have any disputes with our brethren, the English, we agreed to make a line and the Six Nations at Fort Stanwix three years ago sold the King all the lands on the east side of the Ohio down to the Cherokee River, which lands were the property of our confederacy, and gave a deed to Sir William Johnson as he desired. Since that time great numbers more of your people have come over the Great Mountains and settled throughout this country. And we are sorry to tell you that several quarrels have happened between your people and ours, in which people have been killed on both sides, and that we now see the nations round us and your people ready to embroil in a quarrel, which gives our nation great concern, as we on our parts want to live in friendship with you, as you have always told us you have laws to govern your people by (but we do not see that you have). Therefore, brethren, unless you can fall upon some method of governing your people who live between the Great Mountains and the Ohio River and who are now very numerous, it will be out of the Indians' power to govern their young men, for we assure you the black clouds begin to gather fast in this country. And if something is not soon done those clouds will deprive us of seeing the sun. We desire you to give the greatest attention to what we now tell you as it comes from our hearts and a desire we have to live in peace and friendship with our brethren the English. And therefore it grieves us to see some of the nations about us and your people ready to strike each other. We find your people are very fond of our rich land. We see them quarrelling every day about land and burning one another's houses. So that we do not know how soon they may come over the River Ohio and drive us from our villages, nor do we see you brethren take any care to stop them. It's now several years since we have met together in council, which all nations are surprised and concerned at. What is the reason you kindled a fire at Ohio for us to meet you (which we did and talked friendly together) that you have let your fire go out for some years past? This makes all nations jealous about us as we also frequently hear of our brethren the English meeting with Cherokees and with the Six Nations to strengthen their friendship, which gives us cause to think you are forming some bad designs against us who lives between the Ohio and Lakes. I have now told you everything that is in my heart and desire you will write what I have said and send it to the Great King. A belt. Killbuck, speaker. *Copy*. [C.O.5/90, fo. 5]

CXXX

John Wentworth to Earl of Hillsborough

4 December, Portsmouth N.H.

May it please your Lordship, I have had the honour to receive youɪ lordship's most obliging letter of the 3rd July last [Vol. I, No. 1376]. The approbation of the Lords Commissioners for Trade and Plantations of my conduct and zeal in His Majesty's service and their lordships' generous intentions to give testimony thereof to His Majesty cannot fail of yielding me a happiness to which nothing could add but your lordship's great kindness in the communication thereof, a singular instance of favour for which I now beg leave to return your lordship my dutiful and most grateful acknowledgements. As my aim is particularly directed to give satisfaction to my superiors, their favourable opinion must consequently animate my constant endeavours to promote His Majesty's service in all its branches under my superintendence and management.

The reports of Mr Jackson on the questions stated to him on the Acts of Parliament for the preservation of pine timber, which your lordship was pleased to enclose and refer me to [Vol. III, Nos. LII, LXII], have proved very useful to me in that service. These reports confirmed me in the persuasion that all the pine timber on the tract of land lying on both sides Kennebec River and now held under grants from the Council of Plymouth, belongs to His Majesty, and I have therefore continued to assert and maintain the right of the Crown to be exclusive, and shall persist so to do until I receive His Majesty's final determination on the subject.

The proprietors of the land notwithstanding still hold up their claim to the pine timber. I offered them to bring it to a legal trial at any time, acquainting them that the sooner the point was determined upon the better. This they declined, but solicited me to make them a compensation for the timber cut on those lands by licence for masting the Royal Navy, which solicitation they urged with very numerous arguments. I acquainted them that nothing of the kind rested with me, my office being only executive. Thereupon they came to a resolution to lay a petition before the Right Honourable the Lords Commissioners of the Admiralty with a state of their claim annexed thereto. At their request I transmit the said petition to their lordships, a duplicate whereof I beg leave to enclose, whence your lordship will instantly see the circumstances whereupon they rely to support their claim. As to their proposal of getting a compensation for every tree cut on the soil, it perhaps may be a measure deserving of consideration to grant some stated allowance for every good mast according to its dimensions when cut and hauled for the King's service, not as a matter that they were by right entitled to but as a gratuity for the timber being found well-preserved upon their land.

With regard to the several allegations set forth by them to maintain their title as private property under the purchase from the late Colony of Plymouth, they are matters that will be more clearly understood by your lordship when taken under consideration than anything I can presume to offer on the subject. But I think it necessary to observe in regard to the material points asserted in this state that I am not myself acquainted with the authenticity of the facts, not having seen the original vouchers from whence they are taken, yet entertain no doubt but the petitioners can support what they advance.

I shall now beg leave to report to your lordship what appears to me principally to give ground to what is complained of in the following paragraph of the petition vizt.

"That the persons employed by the said agents having no interest on the soil and its growth are wholly regardless of the damage they do to either, and through ignorance or to make advantage by it cut down many trees unfit for masts for the Navy, which they afterward convert into lumber, thereby making great destruction of the timber to the great detriment of your petitioners".

The loss and waste of timber here complained of is in some measure true and almost in an equal degree unavoidable. In cutting trees for masts the grearest care is taken to select the best and fairest timber, yet many, very many trees prove rotten or are sprung in falling. In trees of the largest size, fit to make 34 to 38-inch masts, 48 out of 50 may happen to be defective, although while standing they appear to be perfectly sound. Such large trees must of course be very old and thence subject to decay in the heart of the wood. This season the mast-cutters for His Majesty's contract found in one district a fine growth of large and uncommonly fair trees. But upon cutting them 102 out of 106 proved rotten in the heart and not worth a shilling, upon which a protest was made to save the penalty of the contract which by this defect the contractor was unable to fulfil. These are difficulties beyond the reach of human knowledge until experience fixes the tract. Some very good trees are broke in falling, nor is it possible to prevent it. Trees of 45 or 50 yards long and from 4 to 6 feet in diameter are of such immense weight that it is almost beyond the power of man to use any secure management in lowering them. Much is done by bedding with bushes and small trees to help to secure them, but notwithstanding there still remains a great risk. The mast workmen hired to do this work are paid by contract for the number of good trees they haul for which they get but small prices, so that they will not be prevailed upon to bestow much time on the necessary preparations for securing the trees in falling; and the Surveyor-General has no power to compel them to observe any particular mode in performing this service. By this deficiency some valuable timber is wasted and perishes on the ground, for none is permitted to be hauled away but those that are intended for masts and are delivered to the agent of the mast-contract, if upon hewing they prove agreeable to the Navy schedule and no defect is yet discovered, to which they are so liable that after all the care in this country (which being rooted in mercantile interest cannot be thought deficient) many trees are rejected when offered in His Majesty's Navy Yards in England. The licence granted for cutting masts is for so many masts to be delivered to the agent of the mast-contract; but such as are discovered before shipping to be imperfect and rejected by him, of course not being licenced, have been suffered to be used in making and securing the mast-docks here, hoping by such means to make the people more careful, and this in some degree has a good effect. In other instances much of the defective and rejected timber remains on the ground until it totally decays. By this your lordship will see that the waste and loss of timber here complained of arises from a variety of causes without my having any power to prevent it. But it may not be improper here to examine with what degree of propriety such a complaint comes from the petitioners. If the exclusive right to the pine timber is vested in the Crown as is apprehended to be the case, the proprierors of the soil it is presumed can suffer no detriment by its waste as they cannot under severe penalties meddle with it themselves or convert it to their own private use. It is however a pity that the timber should perish and should be utterly lost, and it were much to be wished that the evil could be remedied. With respect to the loss of trees sprung in falling, was that work to be performed by labourers hired by the day under the inspection of the Surveyor-General and his deputies, it would in all probability prove a remedy against all damage that way. And with regard to the waste of timber by reason of trees found defective and unfit for masts after they are cut, though perhaps useful for other occasions, it seems to be unavoidable unless it may be thought expedient to import such trees for timber, plank, balks, and other purposes for the use of the Royal Navy yards, whereby a very great saving of pine timber may be made. But even here it is suggested whether the Crown has a right to such timber, the laws for preservation of the woods being intended for masting only.

There are at present some prosecutions instituted for trespasses on the King's Woods of which I shall be able speedily to give a particular account to your lordship. In the meantime I shall take the liberty to observe that in my report of the 22nd October 1770 I gave your lordship an account of sundry prosecutions I caused to be set on foot against trespassers on the King's Woods in New York and the difficulties I met with in carrying on the same to effect owing to the combination of many persons (of whom I then considered Judge Wells of the province of New York a principal leader and supporter, and am still of the same opinion) interested in defeating the said prosecutions and radically frustrating the operation of the Acts of Parliament for preserving timber, that they may with impunity and without interruption cut trees in the King's Woods at their discretion and deter and disenable the Surveyor-General from prosecuting them by throwing the costs upon him. In the prosecutions now mentioned they have but too well succeeded, the whole of which amounting to £162 19s. 4¾d. fall upon the Crown by the unworthy interposition of Judge Wells in taking a fictitious conveyance of the goods and chattels of the convicted tres-passers, which was fully proved by the depositions already transmitted to your lordship and is still manifested by their being immediately reinstated and now remaining in the possession of their goods and chattels, which but for this collusion must have paid those costs. Copies of the bills of costs are enclosed [Vol. I, No. 1660v]. I have forwarded a memorial with the original bills of costs to the Right Honourable the Lords Commissioners of the Treasury praying to be reimbursed this sum, and beg leave to request your lordship's interposition on my behalf for obtaining an order for payment of this sum, so necessarily expended and directly essential in the support of this important service.

I would further beg leave to remind your lordship of the measures I suggested in my letter of the 22nd October 1770 [Vol. II, No. CX], the necessity of which every day's experience makes more striking in instances at present too numerous to incumber your lordship with a repetition of, although in fact of great consequence to His Majesty's service in this department.

Mr Ruggles and Mr Scammel have applied to me and produced their commissions and instructions as Surveyors and Inspectors of the Woods in certain districts. Captain Benzel has also informed me of his appointment by letter. I shall use all means in my power to put them in a proper course of being beneficial to the service of which I shall not fail to give your lordship information. *Signed.* [C.O.5/73, fo. 109]

CXXXI

Governor William Tryon to Earl of Hillsborough (No. 13)

10 December, New York

My Lord, in consequence of my proclamation in August last requiring all persons who had claims under French titles to any of the lands on Lake Champlain to make known their pretensions to this government, Mr Chartier Lolbiniere came from Canada and on the second of this month presented his memorial and papers to the Council board; by which it appeared he claimed the seigniories of De Hokart and D'Allainville, and desired to be put into the possession of them. Upon examination it was discovered that almost the whole of the seigniory of De Hokart on the east of the lake above Crown Point was granted away under the seal of this province, but that the greatest part of the seigniory of D'Allainville on the west side of the waters (that lead from Lake George to Lake Champlain, and to the southward of Crown Point) remained yet ungranted by this province. It was therefore advised in Council that he should have the preference to take up all the vacant lands in the said seigniories not granted by this government, all which proceedings will more particularly appear by the petition of Mr Lolbiniere and the report of the Council thereon, copies of which are herewith transmitted [Vol. I, No. 1665i-ii]

It is my duty to acquaint your lordship that the Council did not esteem Mr Lolbiniere's title to the seigniory southward of Crown Point to be founded on any colour of right and even that to the northward of Crown Point only on an equitable claim.

In consideration to the peculiarity of his pretensions I proposed to give him up my fees of office, but his not being of ability to discharge the fees that would become due on taking out the patents to the other officers of government, he could not benefit by my offer; therefore not meeting with the satisfaction he expected and desired from the government, he has taken the resolution of repairing to England and of imploring His Majesty's gracious attention to the singular circumstances of his case.

Last week I received a letter from Lieut.-Governor Cramahé informing me he had forwarded me several papers under the seal of his province respecting the French claims to lands on Lake Champlain. As soon as they come to hand they shall be laid before the Council, reported upon, and transmitted to your lordship; after which some principle I hope may be established by His Majesty that will finally settle the disputes between the two governments to the lands bordering on Lake Champlain. *Signed*. [C.O.5/1103, fo. 18]

CXXXII

Governor Josiah Martin to Earl of Hillsborough (No. 7)

12 December, Newbern

My lord, I have the honour to transmit to your lordship herewith a copy of my speech at the opening of the session of the General Assembly on the 19th of last month with the addresses of the two Houses and my answers [Vol. I, No. 1668i-v].

As far as I am able to discern at present the most difficult business of this session will be to make provision for the service of the militia forces employed to suppress the late insurrection, which appears to me to be indispensable to the present peace and the future security of this country; for, my lord, if any delay occurs on this head many poor people who forsook their homes and left their crops to perish in order to support government in that time of defection, depending on its faith for recompense, must starve, a circumstance such as must necessarily abate the forward loyalty that has so lately triumphed over rebellion here, and for want of which the colony at a future day may become a prey to sedition and violence, a consideration that involves an endless train of consequences to His Majesty's American empire. The representations made by Governor Tryon of the state of the finances of this country and your lordship's knowledge of the expedient that was resorted to in a less pressing emergency in the year 1768 of issuing debenture notes induced me to hope that I should have been delivered from all embarrassment on this subject, and the rather as I solicited it in the first letter I had the honour to write to your lordship from hence. It was in this expectation partly that I prorogued the General Assembly beyond the period to which it stood prorogued at my arrival. It is most certain, my lord, that the present exigence can only be supplied by extraordinary means: what they may be I cannot precisely tell but I will endeavour that they be such as shall be the least injurious and exceptionable. If I am obliged to countenance the same expedient that served a former necessity, your lordship may be assured it will only be upon the clearest evidence that it is the last shift, and then with true repugnance, not only on account of the difficulty with which I see the Lords Commissioners for Trade and Plantations before get over it, but as it is inducive of a fraudulent medium of circulation which I am clearly of opinion it is contrary to good policy to augment. That I may not here appear inconsistent I must inform your lordship that my opinion of the expediency of a new emission of paper bills of great amount, offered to your lordship's consideration in my first letter, was formed upon the judgement of Governor Tryon, with which mine upon closer examination of this subject does not correspond; but although such is my fixed principle, my lord, I cannot think this province under its present circumstances, considering the great deficiency of specie, can dispense with the want of such a medium of circulation altogether. The legal tender bills of credit now current amounting to £42,800 ought before this time to have been sunk, but the funds established for that purpose have proved deficient, which is in part owing to erroneous destruction of other late emissions of paper in their stead and to the insolvency of the collectors of taxes, but chiefly from neglect to replace sums that have been at sundry times drawn from it and from the withdrawing prematurely in the year 1768 a poll tax of three shillings appropriated to that fund. By an accurate state of the public accounts made in consequence of a vote of the Assembly at the last session, it appears that there is due to the public on the several funds upwards of sixty-six thousand pounds which is in the hands of the tax-collectors of various denominations. Of this sum only twelve thousand pounds arises from the sinking fund. Its deficiency must therefore be made up from the surplusages of the other funds when the outstanding debts are collected, and it cannot be doubted that a future Assembly will readily make such an application as the only means of sinking this money for which the public faith is pledged. I shall think it my duty to press the Assembly to effectual measures for calling in the public debts, which being taken will bring into the Treasury it may be presumed at least fifty thousand pounds that will there lie dead and be ready I hope at the next session for application to the sinking fund as far as may be necessary to the extinction of the legal tender paper. Under these circumstances, my lord, I apprehend if I am compelled to give in to the expedient of issuing debenture notes to satisfy the clamours of the people who lately stood forth here in support of government, this country may admit of such an augmentation of the paper medium without depreciation below its present standard with respect to the sterling exchange, which is at this time lower here than at New York.

I now transmit to your lordship a copy of a message from the Assembly desiring me to grant a pardon to the insurgents with certain exceptions, and my answer thereto [Vol. I, No. 1668vi-vii], which I hope will meet with His Majesty's and your lordship's approbation.

Having received a petition in behalf of certain persons (of whose names I now send your lordship a list) [Vol. I, No. 1668viii] excepted in one of Governor Tryon's proclamations under the description of persons concerned in destroying General Waddell's ammunition, I laid it before His Majesty's Council, and it appearing that the young people guilty of this heinous offence had been ever well-affected to government, of good character and seduced by misrepresentation to this violence, the Board unanimously joined in request to me to recommend them for His Majesty's most gracious pardon which I thought it out of my own power to extend to them [until] after I had referred the matter to the consideration of my royal master.

I am of opinion, as I had the honour to tell your lordship in a former letter, that a pardon of as great extent as His Majesty shall see fit may be now a healing measure well-applied, and I therefore most humbly recommend it to the royal consideration.

Benjamin Merrill, one of the six criminals executed soon after the action with the insurgents, has left an innocent and miserable family, consisting of his widow and seven young children who must starve unless His Majesty should be graciously pleased to continue to them possession of the lands of the delinquent. I am therefore, my lord, engaged by the feelings of humanity to implore His Majesty's favour to this wretched and fatherless family.

Your lordship will receive herewith a copy of a message from the Assembly relative to the detention of a vessel, the property of one of His Majesty's subjects in this colony, and her crew at La Vera Cruz, with copies of papers therein referred to authenticated under the province seal [Vol. I, No. 1668ix-xii]. I propose as a means of obtaining the speediest release of His Majesty's subjects and reparation for this injury to make application to the commander-in-chief of His Majesty's squadron at Jamaica. In the meantime, I thought it my duty to transmit to your lordship the best evidence on this matter for His Majesty's information, and lest satisfaction should not be had through the intervention of that officer.

I received last month a visit from King Pow of the Catawba nation who came with three of his chiefs under the usual pretext of respect and amity to furnish themselves with conveniences and luxuries, which they beg with no very scrupulous delicacy. I learned from them that their whole tribe does not amount to six hundred and that having made peace with all their enemies they are resolved quietly to devote themselves to the culture of their lands and to the attainment of knowledge in religion and the arts that tend to civilize crude nature. *Signed.* [C.O.5/315, fo. 19]

CXXXIII

John Thomas to John Stuart[1]

12 December, Fort Bute

Sir, I have been attentive in making strict enquiry whether a Choctaw congress is to be held at New Orleans. I cannot at present give you a certain information if such a dangerous attempt is intended, but the earliest intelligence that can be procured shall be sent you with all the expedition that can be expected from one of His Majesty's [?officers] in my remote situation. I have placed some confidence in a few people that will give me all the intelligence that may be procured of utility. I am now informed that several Choctaw chiefs and warriors are expected at New Orleans the latter end of this month. You may be assured that the French commanding officers in the Spanish service do everything in their power to gain over the English Indians in the Spanish interest; otherwise I should not have been under the absolute necessity of writing to the Spanish governor and one of his commanding officers

---

1 Enclosed in John Stuart's letter of 12 June 1772 to Hillsborough, Vol. V, No. XLIX.

as expressed in the copies of the letters sent for your perusal and approbation. You will be pleased to observe that I am very particular and cautious in giving the least offence to Spanish punctilios and that I do not neglect the interest of the King my master in the least disobedience of your orders. If the Spanish governor's answer to my letter should not be so satisfactory as it might be (I have much more influence among the savages than any of the Spanish subjects), in such case I flatter myself that no time will be lost in gaining over the Arkansas, and favour me with a few more medals and presents to be sent immediately as you will naturally consider the trifling quantity I had to distribute among such numbers and different nations of Indians is not sufficient, they being more numerous than Governor Durnford imagines fron his short acquaintance and misinformation. You must know the difficulty of dividing such small quantity of presents among so many tribes; had all their warriors been under two or three chiefs the proportion would have answered much better and more satisfactory.

I am now to proceed with my particular remarks on my voyages up the Mississippi, vizt. on the 25th of October I went on shore at the Tonica village and met with a tolerable reception. The next morning I embarked in company with Lattannash and his head-warrior Mingo Tiallio. We landed on the eastern banks of the river opposite the village of Boloxies, Pascaogolas, Choctaws and Mobiliens. All the chiefs and headmen (except the Boloxies) came over and dined with me. I perceived that they were not so well pleased as I expected. I asked them the reason of the Boloxies' absence; the chiefs answered me that they were all settled in one village on the Spanish side of the river, they having been neglected for the space of several years past, and that the English were a very bad people from various reports, having a black intention to enslave them according to information of John Terrasco, as appears by the enclosed affidavit. I immediately recollected my situation (without troops for my defence) and was successful in my arguments to persuade them that the bad talk that had been given was false and infamous, as they are a generous and brave nation that opposed the united powers of France and Spain and most of the Northern savages in the late war and carried their conquering arms to the conclusion of the peace, they having conquered all North America to the east of Mississippi except the little island of New Orleans. Notwithstanding the Tonicas and other Indians have killed the King's subjects on the Mississippi since the peace, you Tonicas and other chiefs now see me come along you as a single warrior authorized to tell you that the past insults are forgiven; but in case any savages should presume to disturb the peace of His Majesty's subjects for the future that it was determined to cut such savages from the face of the earth, root and branch. As to all those that behave themselves well, [they] should have English traders and justice done them in trade with such annual presents that may be ordered for them. Some of the Boloxies were present and immediately carried my talk to their village. In the meantime all the chiefs and warriors present promised peace and friendship to the English and embarked for the other side of the river with a promise to pay me a visit at Fort Bute on my return from the

Natchezs. As my batteau was pushing from the shore the Boloxi and a few chiefs arrived and desired a talk with me. I informed them that they had the same opportunity to talk as their neighbours had done from the same village; therefore if either of them had anything to say to me that they must follow at the distance of a league where I should halt till next morning. They came into my batteau and joined the place of my appointment. My talk to [MS: and] the Boloxies was as already mentioned much to the satisfaction of the Boloxi chief Mathaah Cush Cush, who said he was very much governed by the advice of the other [Sic: Ofo?] chief Peraque (a fellow that talks French and a foreign enemy to the English in his heart) a man of no consequence in my opinion, he having but seven warriors to oppose a just English resentment which ought to take place with the man of honour that is authorized to do his duty and from his conscience as a good man to oppose the least insults and oppression at the hazard of his life. I gave the Boloxi some gunpowder and ball and informed him that if he was to be governed by the insulting and treacherous Peraque I would never hear his talk nor think him worthy the notice of the English. He immediately determined to follow the example of the Pascogolas, Choctoes and Mobilians who have agreed to come over to the English side of the Mississippi, and they seem very desirous to return to their old settlements on the Lakes provided a firm peace can be procured with the Tallapuss's; otherwise they will make a settlement on the eastern banks of the river. The Boloxi chief desired me to excuse him from coming to Fort Bute till after the hunting season. All the chiefs at first were much inclined to speak in favour of the French, but the moment the French were mentioned I told them I would not hear the name of a Frenchman as a subject of the French King as all the Frenchmen in North America have been conquered by the English except the few French on the Mississippi who are now Spanish subjects. On my arrival at the Natchezs I got a list of one hundred and four men, women and children that came there in expectation of vacant land. Great complaints were made of the extensive tracts of land that had been granted and reserved by government, which prevented them from settling within the space of several miles, as the vacant lands on its banks was swamps or high broken [land], and the want of water in the interior parts of the country prevented them from settling. Some families talked of returning to the country they came from, others said they would follow the example of many English families and go over to the Spaniards, being like them disappointed on their arrival on the Mississippi. However, I have prevailed on these people to search for a spot of land and settle near each other as possible. I have sent them to find a large river said to be about thirty miles back into the country according to the Indians' information which I believe to be a true one as I have discovered a strong stream of waters that falls into the Mississippi (not marked in the suryeor's plan of the river). I halted at this place and walked about three miles on the banks of this stream and perceived that the further up I went the wider it was and the quantity of water increased in abundance; but it lessened much as it approached the Mississippi by sinking into the oozy banks of the river. I really think this is the river so much talked of by the savages who say it is a fair stream of fine water forty yards wide and that they are obliged to swim their horses in crossing. The country is both rich and pleasant, not inferior to the deserted paradise of the Natchezs. Hearing that great number of Choctaws was at the Grand Gulf and that a common practice was made of trading with rum, I proceeded for that place (about twenty leagues up the river) and met there a few savages and two Indian traders without licence, Mr Barber and Mr Thomas James, who were in hopes of my being able to grant them licence which would save them from the trouble and expense of going to Pensacola on a voyage that would require the space of three months to pass and repass. I believe them to be men of honest intention in the Indian trade and I would have granted them licence had it been in my power, having good reason to think they had only rum sufficient for themselves and their servants. On my return to the Natchezs I met about thirty Choctaws almost naked. Their headman Buffalo Head (a true friend to the English) begged me to take notice of their miserable situation and send traders among them. I did not neglect to mention that the Choctaws had nobody to blame but themselves as they had burnt the fort and pillaged Mr Bradley, likewise drove off all the traders from the Natchezs. He was sensible of the charge of pillage and desired that it might be forgiven, but the Choctaws absolutely deny having any hand in burning the fort and declare that it was done by the white men for the nails and that they also burnt the carriages of the cannon for the ironwork which was of no service to the savages, but the barracks when standing was of great use to them.

My conduct among the savages has at all times been agreeable with your directions, with a firm resolution and good intentions to support the tranquillity of the savages on the English and Spanish frontiers. Notwithstanding, nothing can be more agreeable to the Spaniards and Spanish French than my recall, they being truly sensible of my influence among the savages and their esteem and regard for me. My recall or being ordered to leave this country would likewise give great pleasure and satisfaction to vagrants of all nations on the Mississippi, (per example) the 18th of November one John Clark arrived here from Pensacola and gave me information that his partner in trade, Mr Woodhouse Gooding was lost in the woods about eight miles distance. The said John Clark having no papers to entitle him to a valuable quantity of goods which he said he purchased of Mr Cummins at Pensacola entirely to his own risk, on various suspicions a regular protest was made to prevent Clark from proceeding up the Mississippi with the goods till advice was received from Mr Cummins or the man lost. Notwithstanding, John Clark embarked with the goods by night in a clandestine manner. Early in the morning I received intelligence of his illegal departure; having no troops or a sufficient number of English subjects to strengthen the hand of justice, I sent an immediate express to order fourteen Allebamon and Tensa warriors to join me under arms without loss of time, which orders they obeyed with the alertness of veteran soldiers. Mr Harrison joined me as a volunteer in pursuing Clark. On our arrival at a point about ten leagues distance, four men there informed me that John Clark and seven of his men had passed by that same morning and declared that they expected to be pursued and further said they had rifle-barrel guns, well-loaded, and would perish to a man in preference of returning with the goods. I immediately appointed a constable, and Mr Harrison had the command of four men well-armed in the first boat in order that the law might be put in execution by English subjects. I commanded the savages and soon came up with those daring villains who were upon the banks of the river. Mr Harrison and the constable did their duty and seized Clark. Some of the rifle-barrel men was then in the canoes about twenty foot distance with fixed places for taking aim. I gave orders if a villain fired to return it from whence the smoke came and the savages to scour the thickest, which order being heard had all the desired effect as the fellows immediately came from the canoes and were instantly disarmed. It is probable I may be found fault with for commanding savages by those accustomed to disapprove of well-intended proceedings, but it ought to be considered that the savages under my command were only as a reserve guard or body of men appointed to assist the civil power in case of any violent resistance by killing or wounding any person or persons empowered by me (as a civil magistrate) to execute the well-known laws of the British constitution, so just and equitable even to surprise foreigners' ideas and foreign conceptions to the honour of the English nation. I returned here with Clark and seven of his men, but having no provisions, troops or a fund for bringing such fellows to justice, I was not displeased at their escape. A great number of those Carolina Regulators or late rebels are expected on this river, therefore I leave you and my superiors to judge how far a military power would be absolutely necessary for the protection of His Majesty's subjects that are now and coming to settle on the banks of the Mississippi. Mr Woodhouse Gooding has been found by the Huma savages after being lost seventeen days and almost perished by fatigue and hunger; he has confirmed me in opinion of Clark's bad conduct by returning me thanks and assuring me that Mr Cumins will always be much obliged for my proceedings.

The Tonica chief and his warriors have been here and gave me a dance, the eagle's tail, and calumet of peace, likewise the Pascoagolas, Choctaws, Allebamons, Pacianas and Tansas. The Spanish Indians, Humas, have presented me with the eagle's tail and soon determined to settle on the hunting ground near the Amite River without the least encouragement. The Chittemashaws (settled on the western banks of the Mississippi on the conclusion of the peace) have given me the eagle's tail and great professions of friendship for the English: Champaign their chief had forty-two of his warriors with him. I remarked at the time of their dancing the calumet that every man held a large knife in his hand pointed upwards and that it was the third day's council that determined the calumet in favour of the English. The chief asked for an English medal which I refused him, at same time I gave the Alebaman and Tansa chiefs medals; my reasons for so doing were that the Chitemashaws are Spanish Indians. The chief and the voice of his warriors declared that they would settle on the English land in preference of being treated with less respect either from the firing of cannon or receiving a proportionable quantity of presents. In answer I informed him that I received him and the Humas as visiting friendly Indians till some matters were settled between me and the Spanish governor. The following is a list of warriors that have given me the eagle's tail, except the Boloxies and Mobilians who are to give me one each in the spring: Pascaogolas, Boloxies, Choctoes, Mobilians, united, 90 warriors; Tonicas, 28 warriors; Allebamous and Paccanas, united, 64 warriors; Tansas, 12 warriors; Chittemashaws, 58 warriors; Humas, 46 warriors. Total, 298.

The Offon chief Peraque, an enemy to the English, has seven warriors. I do not know the number of the Little Taccassas and Apulasas but from the best information I believe they are about one hundred and sixty warriors who have promised to pay me a friendly visit from the Spanish side of the river. The Indians that claim the land on the Mississippi, the River Ibberville and the Lakes Maurepas and Ponchartrain are the Tonicas, Pascaogolas, Boloxies, Choctoes, Mobileans, and the Humas have hunting ground on the Ibberville and River Amite. If a peace takes place with these small nations and the Tallapussi or Creeks I shall be able to settle all the Indian affairs to the satisfaction of my superiors by the end of May, that the rugged savage path may be made smooth for the English. After such pains and hazard of life I am certain that no son of humanity will prevent me from keeping the path clear, more especially as my successor, though a good man he may make it more rugged than the first. I am not only in friendship with the savages but, give me the word, I can command them on any occasion. The land belonging to the above Indians I believe is not less than eighty square miles which I believe I could purchase with goods to the amount of three hundred pounds sterling in the humour they are in at present.

The peltry trade on the Mississippi is worth the attention of the English government. I remember when the French were in possession of New Orleans the English made a common practice of selling their peltry there. At present the Spanish French traders sell their peltry to the English and purchase their manufactures such as powder and ball, blankets, strouds, etc. The English are chiefly supplied with goods from Pensacola and Mobille. The goods purchased for the Indians at New Orleans are manufactured in England, I have not seen a French white or blue blanket since my arrival in the country. A piece of blue stroud is sold at New Orleans from 25 to 30 dollars per piece, other goods for the Indians in proportion. The Allebamous, Paccanas and Tansas are determined to settle on the banks of the Mississippi but you will perceive, sir, that the good land is either granted or reserved for the King from the River Ibberville at a considerable distance above the Red River except the small spot of land the Tonica village stands on. All the Indians for various reasons insist and declare that the white people must settle at least at the distance of one league from the villages. The savages cannot be prevailed on to settle on any spot disagreeable to themselves, notwithstanding they have a place of residence on the banks of the River Mississippi, and if a peace is not immediately to take place with the Creeks and little nations, the Pascaogolas, Boloxies, Choctoes and Mobilleans will settle in the spring on the banks of the river opposite their village. I am informed that a man has a grant for some Indian cleared land on the Lakes and Mr Canty likewise intends to petition for some Indian old fields in that neighbourhood. I desired he would not as the Indians intended to return and settle there if a peace could be procured for them. He said if he could obtain such a grant, he would take and keep possession and live on the Indians sooner than part with a valuable tract of land. I beg some speedy method may be taken to prevent such proceedings in granting land belonging to the Indians. If Canty's talk and assuming title was to take place in firing on the Indians, it would probably be the means of an Indian war. It is true the nations of Indians are but small. It ought to be considered that such rash proceedings would alarum the great Choctaw nation as those little tribes are in great friendship with them. The most convenient and central place for me to do my duty as a deputy Superintendant of Indian affairs is at three leagues from Fort Bute where I have fixed on a spot for that purpose. The Spanish French are thrown into great consternation on my arrival on the Mississippi, not from the consequence of my proceedings with the savages but from their guilty conscience, some of them having been villains enough to tell them that the English were a most infamous and cowardly people and when insulted they are not capable of showing a proper resentment. The 22nd Regiment retreat from the attack of the Tonicas and the pillage of the post of Ibberville in the year 1765 are given as proofs of such an infamous and ungenerous assertion. The French say with truth that the Kickepore Indians kill the English on the Ohio and the circumjacent country. As the barbarous tale was reported to be [? me] with a smiling countenance, I thought it prudent to reply that the English were truly sensible of the affair and not ignorant of some Frenchmen's activity amongst them, which consequence would come under a speedy and severe consideration. The Spaniards have been pleased to make it appear that there is a practicability of marching cannon from Mexico to the Fort Adize from which place there is an easy communication to New Orleans. I have received intelligence that three hundred and fifty Spanish soldiers are now on their march from Mexico for the said fort with seven hundred mules and horses. As to further particulars I am not informed and leave you to judge whether it would not be immediately prudent to inform his Excellency General Gage and General Haldimand with my report from information which I believe to be founded on truth.

The town of New Orleans was not fortified when delivered up to Spaniards. They have since thrown up a fascine battery for six pieces of cannon, four to fire on the river, the other two to scour the road that leads to the uppermost part of the town. Two field six-pounders can be marched to silence the battery in the space of six minutes if properly conducted. From the knowledge of the adjacent country from my former knowledge of New Orleans, and the present, it appears to me that at least one half of the inhabitants have left the town. A plantation that would sell for 10,000 dollars about four years ago may be purchased at present for 1000. An order is arrived from the Court of Spain not to suffer or permit the French to depart from Louisana. The troops to guard and defend them are about three hundred regulars and three or four hundred militia, the latter body of men I really believe would never fire a shot on the English as an enemy; if the Spanish governor had the reason to think as I do he would disarm them to a man.

The licence traders on the Mississippi are Mr Fitzpatrick, Mr Harrison and Mr McIntosh, the number of inhabitants on the Mississippi is 208 men and women and children. Their place of residence is mentioned on the enclosed plan of the river. I shall forward the Spanish governor's answer by the first opportunity if he should think proper to favour me with a line. I am informed that I am to be discharged from the Indian department in a very short time; the attempt without a proof of my misconduct would be so very ungenerous that I cannot believe it, but if I am to be recalled my successor will be better liked among the Indians, and you will do me the justice of paying my passage to England. I think every particular circumstance of my proceedings is now mentioned. If not, my being daily surrounded by savages, vagrants etc. in a small hut will in some measure plead my excuse. As I have not time to write to the General or the Governor you will be so good as to make my apology as you will have it in your power to furnish them with every material circumstance you may think proper. PS. The annual presents should arrive here in August or September and [be] given to the Indians before their hunting season comes on. *Copy.* [C.O.5/73, fo. 196]

CXXXIV

Memorial of Governor James Wright to Earl of Hillsborough

[12 December]

Humbly sheweth, that whereas His Majesty's very flourishing province of Georgia from the present small number of inhabitants who from the nature of their settlements and improvements are and must be scattered over a great face of country, and which from its vicinity to the several Indian countries and settlements lies greatly exposed to the invasions of the said Indians who often rob and plunder His Majesty's subjects of their property and sometimes murder them. And whereas although by the several treaties now subsisting between His Majesty and the said Indians and particularly by that entered into at Augusta the 10th of November 1763, they did in the most solemn manner engage for themselves and their several nations and tribes "that they would in all cases and upon all occasions do full and ample justice to the English and use their utmost endeavours to prevent any of their people from giving any disturbance or doing any damage to them in the settlements or elsewhere either by stealing their horses, killing their cattle or otherwise, or by doing them any personal hurt or injury, and that if any damage should be done as aforesaid satisfaction should be made to the party injured and that if any Indian or Indians whatever should thereafter murder or kill a white man the offender or offenders should without any delay, excuse or pretence whatever, be immediately put to death in a public manner in the presence of at least two of the English who may be in the neighbourhood where the offence is committed".

That notwithstanding the said treaties and solemn engagements entered into as aforesaid, yet the Creek Indians have frequently stolen great numbers of horses and cattle from many of His Majesty's subjects and have also committed several murders since that time, the last of which was in August 1770 when some of the said Indians in cool blood and without any cause or reason whatever barbarously murdered Thomas Jackson and George Beeck, two of the inhabitants of Wrightsborough Township, and that notwithstanding a complaint was made and satisfaction regularly demanded by your memorialist agreeable to the treaty aforesaid, yet no satisfaction has been given by the said Indians, and although not positively denied yet the same is evaded by them and none intended to be made or given on account of the said murders.

That crimes of this nature having been so often committed and suffered to pass with impunity, on the one hand gives great encouragement to the ill-disposed part of the Indians to commit robberies and murders, and on the other hand is cruelly distressing to His Majesty's good subjects who live in constant fear, and has and must continue very much to impede the further peopling and settling of the province when they see that from its weak and defenceless state they cannot be protected even in their lives but are liable at all times to be robbed and murdered by the Indians.

That at present it is out of the power of the province by force of arms to enforce the treaties by compelling the Indians to make satisfaction, which if they could once do would entirely prevent anything further of that kind in future as they would be very careful not to offend when they knew satisfaction must be made. But as they well know that there is not a single soldier in His Majesty's pay in the province, nor has been since April 1767, that the inhabitants of Georgia are not in a condition to take satisfaction, and that the trade with them is on such a general and very improper footing that neither the province of Georgia nor any other can have any influence over them in that respect; so that as things are now circumstanced there is no kind of power or control whatever over the said Indians, all which they are too sensible of, also that they are powerful enough and can whenever they please greatly distress if not totally ruin that most flourishing province.

And your memorialist further shows that from the present mode of carrying on the trade with the Indians they have arrived at the height of mischievous wantonness and insolence, and from the frauds and abuses committed by those who go amongst them and their natural propensity and thirst after blood your memorialist conceives 'tis highly probable that a rupture with the Creek Indians would have happened ere now had they not been engaged in a war with the Choctaw Indians; and that your memorialist has had great difficulty in restraining the injured parties from taking their own satisfaction which he conceives would at once have plunged the province into an Indian war.

And from this true and undisguised state of the situation of affairs with the Creek Indians in particular your memorialist apprehends it will appear to be absolutely necessary that some steps be speedily taken in order to support His Majesty's honour and authority with them, to compel them to do justice and observe the treaties, and to protect the lives and properties of His Majesty's subjects and promote the peopling of so valuable a province.

To do this, my lord, by force of arms, though probably the most honourable way, yet for many obvious reasons it may be wished to avoid. Your memorialist therefore begs leave to point out other means of reducing the Indians to reason, keeping them within bounds, and of obtaining justice and security to His Majesty's subjects. And first a regulation of the trade with them, that is by dividing the several nations or tribes of Indians into districts and allotting to each province contiguous to them a particular district and leaving it in the power of that province to settle the mode of regulating the trade and limiting the number of traders who shall go there; and by an instruction restraining the different governors from granting licences to trade out of their own district or interfering with each other. By this means it is conceived many abuses, grievances and inconveniences may be prevented and avoided, and which in a great measure depends on the number and conduct of the persons licenced to trade amongst them. And if power is lodged in the hands of those who from their situation and knowledge of people and things there must be the most competent judges, care may be taken that none are concerned or suffered to go amongst them but men of property and character who can be confided in, and that the Indians are supplied with goods sparingly or otherwise according to their conduct and behaviour. For it is well known, my lord, to those conversant in Indian affairs that an over-supply of goods makes them wanton, insolent and ripe for every kind of mischief, and that a moderate supply keeps them within decent bounds and makes them observe a submissive, proper behaviour, and that as they have no supply or can have any of any consequence but from the English they may be reduced at any time to comply with all reasonable demands and do full justice by a stoppage of the trade or even by a stoppage of arms and ammunition as occasion may require. But, my lord, upon the footing the trade is now carried on, agreeable to His Majesty's proclamation of October 1763, it is impossible to effect any good purpose for His Majesty's service or the safety and welfare of his subjects. On the contrary the trade has been and still is productive of every bad consequence for such an unlimited vast number of people now go amongst them that they are over-supplied with goods, got greatly indebted, and grown wanton and insolent. And as the traders are rather of the worst sort of people and commit every kind of fraud and abuse towards the Indians, so it disposes them to resent it by robbing and murdering His Majesty's innocent subjects. All which grievances and distresses it is humbly conceived might be in a great measure prevented and avoided by a proper regulation of the trade and an instruction to the several governors to unite and co-operate in a partial or total stoppage of the whole trade as the conduct and behaviour of the Indians in any particular province may require.

Your lordship will see the necessity of such an instruction, as a stoppage by one or two provinces can answer no effectual purpose whilst the Indians can get a supply from any other province or colony or from Indians trading with any province or colony. And it is hardly to be supposed that the governors of four or five different provinces will concur in a measure of that kind without an instruction from His Majesty so to do.

Your memorialist well knows and is aware of the objection against making a kind of monopoly of the Indian trade but, my lord, if it were really so yet if the necessity of the case or times require it, it seems better that an inconvenience of that sort should be submitted to for a few years than that great numbers of His Majesty's subjects should be cruelly murdered and a flourishing province reduced to the greatest distress and ruin. And, my lord, such a regulation is what the most sensible and discreet among the Indians themselves wish for and have often applied to me to settle for them, and in which case it is conceived that the trade would be carried on by a fair settled tariff and the Indians relieved from the frauds and abuses they now suffer and which cannot possibly be prevented whilst the trade remains on the footing it now is.

And now, my lord, give me leave to propose a matter which I have long had in view as a thing I conceive greatly for His Majesty's interest and of the utmost consequence to his province of Georgia.

There is, my lord, a very considerable body of land which lies between our present boundary line with the Indians and a river called Broad River to the north-west, which empties itself into Savannah River about forty miles above Little River as it is supposed or computed, and another river called the Oconee River to the westward and south-ward and which empties itself into the Alatamaha River about 50 or 55 miles above where our present boundary crosses that river as it is supposed or computed. The branches at the heads or sources of Broad River and the Oconee River nearly meet or interlock and if this tract of land could be obtained from the Indians it would undoubtedly in a few years make Georgia as considerable if not the most considerable province on the whole continent of North America as I hope I shall clearly show.

Great part of this land, my lord, is of the richest and best quality and very fit for tobacco, indigo, hemp, flax, wheat and every kind of grain. The whole tract of land, my lord, that lies between our present line and the aforesaid two rivers is supposed to contain at least five millions of acres, and that part of this land which lies on Savannah River to the amount of between two and three millions of acres is claimed by the Cherokee Indians and who in order to pay the debts they owe to the Indian traders have voluntarily offered to cede the same to His Majesty for the payment of their debts, as your lordship will see by the several applications made by the Indians to your memorialist herewith presented. But your memorialist must not omit to observe that the Creek Indians also claim these lands as well as the Cherokees; the claim of each he conceives to be much the same vizt. by right of conquest at different times. But the Cherokees are determined to assert and support their right as your lordship will see by their talks and messages on the subject.

And now, my lord, I shall beg leave to state this matter in the light it strikes me with such observations and propositions thereon as have occured which are humbly submitted to your lordship's superior wisdom and judgement.

Suppose then that the tract of land which the Cherokee Indians desire to cede to His Majesty contains 2,500,000 acres, as this part of it is all exceeding rich fine land I would propose that it should not be granted as His Majesty's other lands are granted but that it should be sold in small tracts at the most not exceeding 1,000 acres to one person or family and who should bring into the province and forthwith settle the same either with whites or blacks at the rate of one person for every 50 acres of land, and at the same time to pay suppose only at the rate of 6d. per acre, the purchase-money would amount to £62,500 sterling and likewise subject to the quitrents and taxes as usual. The debts due from the Cherokee Indians to their traders are supposed to amount to from £40 to £50,000 sterling, say 45,000. And if the land is sold only at 6d. per acre it will be say £62,500 sterling; the Cherokee debts say 45,000; remains 17,500. And your memorialist would humbly propose that a troop of rangers should be raised consisting of a captain, two lieutenants, a quarter-master, surgeon, four corporals, two drummers and one hundred private men, or rather two troops of fifty men each, the expense of which it is supposed would amount to about £3,100 sterling per annum to be paid out of the above sum and the residue to be applied to the building of such stockade-forts as may be thought necessary, and churches, school-houses and gaols and for the support of clergymen and schoolmasters etc. or otherwise as His Majesty may be graciously pleased to order and direct.

Your memorialist will proceed to mention some of the many advantages which he apprehends would result to the Crown and province in case the scheme now proposed shall be approved of and take effect.

And first the quitrents arising upon 2,500,000 acres of land at 2s. per 100 acres will amount to £2,500 per annum, and the provincial taxes is generally the same, £2,500 per annum, besides the taxes arising on the number of negroes that may be brought into the province by the settlers; suppose only one negro to every family, will be 10,000 negroes at 2s., say £1,000 per annum. And it is hoped there will not be more negroes as it is conceived that the settling these lands with industrious white people, say farmers and planters, will be much more for the good of the province. 2,500,000 acres of land at 50 acres per head will accommodate 10,000 families of 5 in each family, and if there is only one effective man in each family that will be an addition of 10,000 to the militia, but it is rather supposed the number of effective men, say from 16 to 60, in 10,000 families will amount to 15,000 on the militia muster-rolls, and, my lord, what a vast additional strength would that be to the province, sufficient it is conceived to give it entire security against the Indians without having recourse to arms or putting Great Britain to any expense on that account. Whereas at present should there be a rupture with the Indians the province of Georgia would certainly be ruined without the immediate aid and assistance of some of His Majesty's troops.

And, my lord, as it is proposed that no persons should have any of these lands but those who purchase, they will or course be something better than the common sort of back-country people, and having purchased their property they will naturally be more industrious and better disposed to protect it. But as there is always some scattering parties of runagate Indians lurking about all new settlements, and who it is well known rob, plunder and murder etc. it will certainly be necessary that there be two troops of 100 men, say 50 each, as before mentioned kept on foot for at least two or three years or for such a time as it may appear to be necessary for the protection and support of the inhabitants and to be so posted and ordered as may best answer the end proposed.

And, my lord, it may fairly be presumed that each family after being two or three years settled will send to market produce to the amount of £10 sterling per annum, an increase of produce after three years of £100,000 sterling per annum and which will undoubtedly increase greatly every year and soon become very considerable and of great importance to the mother country as well as the province.

And your memorialist begs leave further to observe that these lands are in general so rich and good that there is no doubt of people coming in to purchase and settle; and your memorialist is well-informed that great numbers of very well-disposed and industrious white people are now ready to remove from Virginia and the rest of the Northern Colonies and only wait till it be known whether His Majesty shall be graciously pleased to approve of and direct this matter to be carried into execution. And if so, there will soon be a considerable number of tobacco plantations settled as this plant has been already tried and found to come to the greatest degree of perfection on some of those lands.

The above calculation is on a supposition that only the lands proposed to be ceded by the Cherokee Indians is obtained and sell at 6d. per acre, but if it should be thought proper to grant them free of quitrents for 10 years and to send an instruction for passing a law to exempt them also from taxes for five or seven years and to exempt the settlers there from attending at Savannah on juries and all other duties except in the militia and such as their local circumstances and security may require, in such case instead of 6d. per acre the purchasers may very well afford and I am certain will cheerfully pay at the rate of 10d. per acre, and then the purchase-money will amount to £104,166 sterling. And if the Creek Indians can be prevailed upon not only to join with the Cherokees but also to cede the residue of the lands cross to the Oconee River and down that to the Alatamaha River in satisfaction of their debts, in that case the advantages resulting therefrom in a few years would probably far, very far exceed what is above mentioned. And your memorialist has no doubt but if the above exemptions take place the lands will sell at 10d. or 12d. per acre as they have the great advantage and convenience of three fine rivers to carry their produce to market, vizt. Savannah River, Ogechee River and down the Oconee and Alatamaha Rivers to the proposed new town of Brunswick.

And if His Majesty shall be graciously pleased to approve of the matters herein mentioned, your memorialist would humbly propose that an instruction should be sent to Mr Stuart, the Superintendant, to call a meeting or congress of the Creek and Cherokee Indians at Augusta or some other convenient place, to be held by the Governor of Georgia and the Superintendant with the said Indians in order to settle and agree upon everything that may be necessary on this occasion and to receive a formal surrender and cession of the same to His Majesty, his heirs and successors.

And your memorialist apprehends that it would be very proper that all persons who have any demands on any of the said Indians should liquidate and prove the reality of their debts and demands before the Governor in Council and in such manner as may be required and appear altogether satisfactory to them; and the same to be paid in proportion or dividends as money may be received, first deducting thereout what may be sufficient for the pay and support of the troops of rangers aforesaid which is absolutely necessary for the reasons above mentioned and without which men would be afraid to bring in their families and trust their wives and children there.

And for the more easy and better conducting and managing this matter it might be useful to have certain commissioners appointed who should give security for the faithful discharge of their duty and be paid a reasonable sum for their time and trouble out of the monies arising by the sale of the said lands, and who in order to make it easy and less expensive to the people should reside at Augusta or in Wrightsborough and receive applications for lands and swear them to the amount of their number in family etc., all which to be certified by such commissioners and transmitted by them to the Governor in Council that grants may be ordered for the land.

And your memorialist further proposes that if any of the lands ceded shall remain unsold or disposed of in the manner aforesaid for the space of three years, that then at the end of three years the same be immediately put up at public sale and the whole matter brought to a final settlement.

All which matters and things herein beforementioned and proposed are most humbly submitted to your lordship's consideration[1]. *Signed,* J. Wright. [C.O.5/651, fo. 90]

CXXXV

Thomas and John Penn to Earl of Hillsborough

24 December, London

My Lord, in answer to your letter of the 19th of July last [Vol. III, No. LXXX] relative to the violences committed in the city of Philadelphia in April and October 1769 on occasion of certain seizures made by the officers of His Majesty's Customs, we beg leave to assure your lordship that we are sincerely sorry that any complaints of this nature should have been made against a colony which we can venture to say is amongst the first in loyalty and duty to His Majesty; and we further assure your lordship that from the tenor of your letter we are satisfied these matters have been very unfairly represented to the Lords Commissioners of His Majesty's Treasury.

1 For enclosures to this document, see Vol. I, No. 1669i–ix.

We are certain that the officers of the Customs have ever met with all the assistance that could be afforded them both from the governor of the province and the magistrates of the city. Your lordship must be sensible of the impracticability of preventing the sudden and unexpected outrages of a numerous and ungovernable mob, and the difficulty of bringing anyone concerned in it to justice from the backwardness most people have to become informers, more especially in cases of this kind.

In the affair of April the officers of the Customs had not the least reason to complain of wanting support from the governor or magistrates (indeed at that time they expressed themselves in very different language), for after a short time by the interposition of some of the principal people of the town who were magistrates the seizure was delivered up to the Collector and disposed of in the usual manner. The affair of October was of a very short duration (we are informed it lasted little more than half an hour) so that it would have been impossible for the magistrates to have assembled, and indeed had it been in their power they could have done nothing against the violence of the mob nor have prevented the mischief that was done. When it was over they took every step in their power to detect the persons concerned but there was nobody to be found who would give them the least information. The corporation had frequent meetings upon this business alone and were very desirous of bringing the offenders to justice. It appears to us that all the legal methods as well as the most effectual measures (at least such as were judged so) were taken on both occasions.

We have at all times enjoined the governors of Pennsylvania to support the officers of the Customs in the execution of their duty in the most effectual manner and never had reason to suppose them negligent in their duty before; nor can we imagine it would appear so to your lordship were the matters abovementioned truly and impartially represented to you.

We can speak with the more confidence as the second of us was deputy governor of the province of Pennsylvania during the year 1769 and will at all times be ready to answer any charges made against him by the Commissioners of the Customs in America for any part of his conduct during that or any other period of his administration.

We beg your lordship will believe that we are solicitous in the highest degree to prevent the least cause of complaint against the province of Pennsylvania, and nothing on our part has been as we conceive or shall be wanting to enforce a due submission to the laws of this kingdom within that government. *Signed.* [C.O.5/1284, fo. 25]

CXXXVI

Governor Josiah Martin to Earl of Hillsborough (No. 8)

26 December, Newbern

My Lord, I have the honour to inform your lordship that at the conclusion of the business of the session of the General Assembly of this province on the 23rd instant, I dissolved the Assembly, a measure taken, my lord, not only in conformity to His Majesty's instructions but as expedient in my opinion towards conciliating the minds of the people very intent upon a new representation, which I am assured cannot be selected so bad as the last. It was, however, indispensably necessary to keep that to provide for the present exigencies since it is universally agreed that a future Assembly would not have been found to do it.

A great part of the time of this session, my lord, was consumed in the most visionary speculations such as I am informed are constantly the offspring of a necessity to raise money in this country. A majority from the southern district, in which the people are almost universally necessitous and in debt and whose policy it seems it has ever been to overflow the province with paper money, would have availed themselves of this exigence and made it a pander to that pernicious design; the minority from the northern districts as warmly opposed this system. The first plan was again and again retrenched of extravagances; long contention at length began to create ill humour on both sides; and I entertained apprehensions that no measures would be taken to satisfy the poor people who, relying upon the public faith, had so notably stood forth in support of government and were actually starving for want of their promised stipend. I was therefore, my lord, glad at last to close with the only expedient they would adopt that could serve the present emergency, and I have given my assent to an Act for raising the sum of sixty thousand pounds proclamation money, the vast amount of the expense of suppressing the late insurrection, for which stamped debenture notes are to be issued forthwith. I have likewise, my lord, given my assent to an Act to indemnify the people who acted in behalf of government on that occasion, who would otherwise have been torn to pieces by malicious and vexatious prosecutions in this country, where a spirit of litigation prevails beyond example. For both these steps, my lord, out of the ordinary course of things and over the limits to which I wish to confine myself, I must build my hopes of justification on the sole ground of necessity, to which I thought my duty to His Majesty called upon me to yield in these instances to prevent the certain confusion that a suspense of such measures would have occasioned by alienating the affections of the very people who had been so recently the bulwark of His Majesty's government in this province, and who now looked up to that government for justice from their country.

The assurances given me by the Assembly that they had taken effectual measures to call in the public debts afford me hopes that this emission of paper, considerable as it is, will not depreciate especially when I consider it will be near four months before it can be uttered, in which time by a proper exertion of the Treasurers I apprehend a sum nearly equal will be taken out of the hands of the public debtors which will thenceforth lie dead until another session when the public faith will call upon the next Assembly to make up the deficiency of the fund established for sinking the legal tender paper; that can only be done by the application of as much of this excess of the other funds as shall be necessary to its aid, and this I shall bend all my strength to accomplish as essential to the preservation of the public credit.

The Acts and Journals of the late session of the General Assembly I will transmit to your lordship as soon as I can obtain fair copies of them.

I received a few days ago under your lordship's cover, through the hands of Lord Charles Montagu, His Majesty's royal instruction directing me to appoint commissioners to act jointly with commissioners to be appointed by the governor of South Carolina in running a boundary line between the two provinces. Accordingly, my lord, I communicated without loss of time His Majesty's commands to the Assembly and desired they would enable me to defray the charge of the service prescribed, which was refused upon the reasons which will appear to your lordship in their message in answer to me herewith transmitted [Vol. I, No. 1690i]. I am now at a loss, my lord, how to proceed in this business and shall be more so if Lord Charles Montagu does not according to my proposition engage the province under his government to bear the whole expense.

The embarrassments of the last session have been such as to leave me no opening to procure the amendments in the laws as prescribed by the Lords Commissioners for Trade and Plantations by their lordships' letter of the 12th of last December to Governor Tryon. At the next session I hope I shall be able to accomplish that business to their lordships' satisfaction. It is indeed, my lord, matter of wonder to me that under my circumstances of ill-health I have been able to endure the weight of business with which I have been oppressed; nothing I think can have supported me but my earnest desire of doing right. If I shall be so happy as to find my conduct approved by my royal master, such a recompense, my lord, will alleviate all my sufferings and animate me to encounter with cheerfulness every difficulty that can present itself.

The loyal struggle lately made here and the distressed state of this country's finances I am hopeful, my lord, will recommend it to His Majesty's royal consideration and induce a Parliamentary relief.

By the returns made to me it appears that after the action with the insurgents six thousand four hundred and nine men came into the several detachments of the army and took the oaths to government in consequence of Governor Tryon's proclamations, and that between seven and eight hundred stand of arms were collected from them, which are for the most part unserviceable. *Signed.* [C.O.5/315, fo. 46]

CXXXVII

Governor James Wright to Commissioners for Trade and Plantations

27 December, Berners-street, London
My Lords, I lately took the liberty to communicate my sentiments to your lordships against granting large tracts or bodies of land to individuals or to a man and his associates within or bordering upon the settlements in the province of Georgia, and had the honour to offer some reasons in support of my opinion which I flatter myself will have due weight with your lordships and hope may prevent any grants or orders for grants to persons here or indeed to any persons whatever of large tracts for land in that province.

And now, my lords, I beg your patience a moment while I consider this matter in a more extensive point of view and go a little further in declaring my sentiments and opinion with respect to the granting of large bodies of land in the back-parts of the province of Georgia or in any other of His Majesty's Northern Colonies at a distance from the sea coast or from such ports of any province as is already settled and inhabited.

And this matter, my lords, appears to me in a very serious and alarming light, and I humbly conceive may be attended with the greatest and worst of consequences. Now [MS: nor], my lords, if a vast territory be granted to any set of gentlemen who really mean to people it and actually do so, it must draw and carry out a great number of people from Great Britain, and I apprehend they will soon become a kind of separate and independent people and who will set up for themselves, that they will soon have manufacturers of their own, that they will neither take supplies from the mother country or from the provinces at the back of which they are settled, that being at a distance from the seat of government, courts, magistrates etc. they will be out of the reach and control of law and government, that it will become a receptacle and kind of asylum for offenders who will fly from justice to such new country or colony, and therefore crimes and offences will be committed not only by the inhabitants of such new settlement but elsewhere and pass with impunity, and that in process of time (and perhaps at no great distance) they will become formidable enough to oppose His Majesty's authority, disturb government and even give law to the other or first-settled part of the country and throw everything into confusion.

My lords, I hope I shall not be thought impertinent when I give my opinion freely on a matter of so great consequence as I conceive this to be. And, my lords, I apprehend that in all the American colonies great care should be taken that the lands on the sea coast should be thick-settled with inhabitants and well cultivated and improved, and that the settlements should be gradually extended back into the province and as much connected as possible to keep the people together in as narrow a compass as the nature of the lands and state of things will admit of, and by which means there would probably become only one general view and interest amongst them and the power of government and law would of course naturally and easily go with them and matters thereby properly regulated and kept in due order and obedience, and they would have no idea of resisting or transgressing either without being amenable to justice and subject to punishment for any offences they may commit.

But, my lords, to suffer a kind of *province within a province* and one that may, indeed must, in process of time become superior and too big for the head or original settlement or seat of government, to me conveys with it many ideas of consequences of such a nature as I apprehend are extremely dangerous and improper, and it would be the policy of government to avoid and prevent whilst in their power to do so.

My ideas, my lords, are not chimerical, I know something of the situation and state of things in America, and from some little occurrences or instances that have already *really* happened I can very easily figure to myself what may and in short what will certainly happen if not prevented in time.

And from your lordships' great knowledge in American affairs and superior penetration and judgement, I doubt not but my imperfect attempts will suggest to your lordships many more cogent reasons than have occurred to me. *Signed.* [C.O.5/651, fo. 153]

CXXXVIII

Governor Peter Chester to Earl of Hillsborough [No. 39]

28 December, Mobile

My Lord, since my last dispatches to your lordship we had the pleasure of meeting most of the chiefs of the Upper Creek nation at Pensacola and I now embrace this first opportunity which has offered since the meeting of communicating to you the result of our conferences.

They met the Superintendant and myself with assurances of their friendship and good disposition towards us and seemed pleased to find that the encroachments which they complained had been made upon their lands by our settlers proceeded through mistake, and I hope their jealousy upon that head is entirely removed.

As it was uncertain when we should have another meeting with this nation in presence of the Superintendant, and their good humour concurring, we thought it a favourable opportunity to ask a small cession of lands on the banks of the River Escambia which would not interfere with their hunting grounds. This tract had been previously explored, and upon which by the surveyor's report there are lands very proper for cultivation. A request of this kind we thought could not tend to excite the least jealousy as we explained to them that the lands which they had formerly ceded to us were nothing but a bed of sand and the extent not so great as they had formerly suffered the Spaniards to possess. They evaded our request by saying the property of their lands was vested in common among them and belonged equally to every man and child in their nation, and that they were not authorized to make any grant without consulting their whole nation, but at the same time proposed to increase our boundary four miles up the River Escambia. The lands contained within this proposed increase of boundary we knew to be barren and not worth the acceptance. We therefore thought it best to decline their offer and give them time to consider and consult among themselves of our request. The result was that they could not deviate from their former answer, and we thought it highly improper to press the matter but rather to commend their firmness, thank them for the offer they had made, and leave them to consult the whole nation upon this requisition.

We also recommended to them that the old boundary line between us should now be finally settled and marked in order to prevent all misunderstandings on that head for the future, and agreed with them upon the course where the line between us is to run, the marking of which they would not attend at present, although so strongly recommended to them, alleging that it would interfere with their hunting season; but their chief promised that he would himself attend the marking of it in the month of May next.

We heard all their complaints with great attention and made them every promise to redress their grievances that will be in our power to perform. On the other hand, we did not omit to tell them of their faults and misconduct, which they seemed sensible of but attributed these proceedings to their young men who had acted contrary to the advice and opinion of the chiefs of the nation.

The Superintendant gave them considerable presents upon parting and they all appeared to go off well-satisfied and contented.

Mr Stuart tells me that he has great reason to believe our requisition for the lands on the River Escambia will be granted by the whole nation without tending to create jealousies in any of their minds, and he is in daily expectation of a messenger from them with a favourable answer.

As I have not yet been furnished with a copy of this congress I must refer your lordship for a particular account of our proceedings to the copy of the minutes thereof forwarded by the Superintendant to your lordship in this packet [Vol. III, No. CXII].

My attendance at Mobile being necessary to assist Mr Stuart at the ensuing congress with the Chickesaw and Choctaw nations, I accordingly set out from Pensacola on the 27th of last month on this business, and have been detained here a long time waiting the arrival of the Indians who have been exceeding slow in their movements. There are now between fifteen and sixteen hundred arrived and more are expected. The arrangements necessary to be done before the opening of the congress are now gone through with, and we propose to begin our talks in a few days. I shall not fail when the business is completed to transmit to your lordship an account of our proceedings.

I am now to acknowledge the receipt of your lordship's dispatch No. 4 [Vol. III, No. LXXIV], together with its enclosures, which arrived in the last packet, as also a letter from Mr Pownall dated the 4th of September last [Vol. I, No. 1503] acknowledging the receipt of several of my dispatches. I shall take care to publish His Majesty's Order in Council of the 7th of June last [Vol. I, No. 1295] disallowing three Acts passed in this province in 1767 and 1769.

I must beg your lordship will excuse my not transmitting duplicates of my last dispatches by this packet and attribute the reason to my being absent from Pensacola. *Signed.* [C.O.5/589, p. 13]

NOTE ON INDEX

References are to pages, *not* to document numbers.

The Introduction has not been indexed.

Opinions of correspondents on certain topics have been indexed, e.g. Wright, James, opinion of, on western settlement. The letters contain so many expressions of opinion that it has been possible to bring within the scope of this index only those on the most striking and important topics.

As in Volumes I and II, Indians have been indexed (a) under national names, e.g. Cherokees, (b) under colonies, e.g. West Florida, Indians, and (c) generally under Indians.

INDEX

Abekas (Abikas, Abuccas), Upper Creeks, 118, 213, 218.
Abekoutchies, Creek country, 224.
Acadie, settlers from, in La., 58.
Adams, [Samuel], 90.
Adize, Spanish fort, 268.
Admiralty, concerned with E. Mass. timber, 74, 256.
Africa, West, cruelty in, a reason for stopping slave-trade to Mass., 91.
Alabama (Alibama, Allebamon, Allabamont) Indians, 213: on Lower Miss. R., 198, 265, 266, 267.
Alabama (Alibamon) River, W. Fla., Creek lands on, wanted, 174, 177–178; white encroachment on, 225–226.
Alamance, N.C., battle of, described, 98–99, 116–117; letters dated at, 97, 98.
Albany, N.Y., gaol, 158; proceedings of Circuit Court at, 47, 51.
Albany Co., N.Y., Sheriff (Ten Eyck, H.), and deputy, resisted by armed men, 47, 51–52.
Alexander, [Moses], col. in N.C. militia, 68.
Allainville, see D'Allainville.
Alleghany (Allegany) Mts., white encroachments across, 254, 255.
Almy, Job, in Mass., 140.
Altamaha (Alatamaha) River, 272, 274.
America, North, coast of, should be settled before interior, 279.
Amherst, Sir Jeffrey, 22, 75, 76, 237.
Amite (Amit) River, W. Fla., 267: Indians on, 124, 125; map of, mentioned, 195, 199.
Anderson, Robert, cattle driver on Creek lands, 224.
Annundoswesauwack (Sioux) Indians, 146, 147.
Anson Co., N.C., militia, 151.
Apalachicola (App-) Indians, Creeks, Governor Chester made member of, 213.
Appalusas (Aupulasas), Indians on Lower Miss. R., 198, 267.
Arkansas Indians, chief, at New Orleans, 207; could be won to British interest, 263.
Army, British, in N. America (see also principally under forts; Gage, T.; regiments; and under most colonies), grants of land to reduced officers and soldiers of, 63, 77, 110–115, 162–163; labour furnished by, for works at St John's, N.F.L., 232; recruiting of, in

N. America, 22, 76.
Ashcahoula, Creek chief, treaty signed by, 230.
Atkinson, Theodore [jnr.], Secretary of N.H., 164.
Attorney-General, of England, letter to, 135; reports of (1726 and 1752), cited, 99, 160.
Auchmuty, Rev. Samuel, D.D., of New York, letter signed by, 210.
Augusta, Ga., 275,
   congresses at, 119, 134, 215,
   Indian traders of: break agreement with Indians, 221; cession of land to, in payment of debts, 72–73, and see under Cherokees,
   Indian murdered at, 216,
   letter dated at, 118,
   treaty of, 269.
Avery, Waightstill, of N.C., 84, affidavit of, 59.
Axkin River, N.C., see Yadkin.

Baillie, Richard, cattle driver on Creek lands, 224.
Bainard, Edward, Indian trader, petition of, 127.
Balize, at mouth of Miss. R., 195.
Banyar, Goldsbrow, deputy Secretary of N.Y., 176, 185.
Barber (Barbar), trader on Lower Miss. R., 207, 208, 265.
Barclay, student at King's College, New York, 170.
Bardin, Charles, J.P. of R.I., 145.
Barnes, Henry, sufferer through non-importation in Mass., 172.
Barnstead, N.H., Act for road at, 188.
Barrington, N.H., Act for road at, 188.
Baton (Batton) Rouge, 197.
Beale, Richard, proposed as deputy Collector of Customs, R.I., 82.
Beaver Tooth King, Upper Creek chief, 213.
Beeck, George, murdered by Creeks, 270.
Bennington, (N.Y.), riot by people of, 50–51.
Benzel (Bentzell), [Adolphus, Inspector of Lands and Surveyor of White Pines], 243–244, 259.
Berger, captain of militia, Salisbury, N.C., 68.
Berkeley, Norborne, Viscount Botetourt, former Governor of Va., 36, 37, 175, 242.
Bernard, Sir Francis, former Governor of Mass., 38, 89, 155, 172.